Philosophical perspectives on accounting

Philosophical Perspectives on Accounting commemorates the life and work of Professor Edward Stamp, founding director of the International Centre for Research in Accounting at Lancaster University, a pioneer in the development of theories for corporate financial reporting.

Many people see accounting as a very practical activity, based upon a mass of complex, practical rules, but lacking any coherent theoretical explanation. In modern societies, accounting has a pervasive role in reporting the activities of organizations, including large business enterprises with many thousands of employees and stake-holders. Careful analysis reveals logical patterns underlying the mass of rules, some laid down by law, some less formal, which determine reporting processes. Accounting theory is concerned to make sense of these patterns.

The authors in this volume, mostly qualified accountants, share interests in the philosophical dimensions of accounting. Some are heavily involved in framing accounting standards, while others study the processes of standard setting and the challenges of the 1990s for justifying standards. All are concerned with the nature and development of accounting theory, sometimes taking a broader perspective of theory and underlying theories of knowledge.

The book offers a lively and varied review of modern accounting theory, with special reference to external corporate reporting. The contributors address such issues as the need for a 'conceptual framework' for setting standards, accounting as a science, ways to assess reporting and the many relationships between theory and practice.

It will interest accountants, regulators, business economists and lawyers as well as social scientists concerned with methodology, and it will stimulate debate on the complex and intriguing nature of accounting.

Philosophical perspectives on accounting

Essays in honour of Edward Stamp

Edited by
M.J. Mumford and K.V. Peasnell

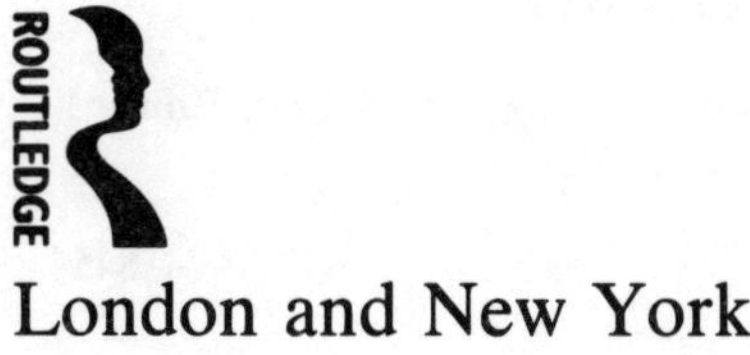

London and New York

First published 1993
by Routledge
11 New Fetter Lane, London, EC4P 4EE

Simultaneously published in the USA and Canada
by Routledge
a division of Routledge, Chapman and Hall, Inc.
29 West 35th Street, New York, NY 10001

Typeset in Times by J&L Composition Ltd, Filey, North Yorkshire
Printed and bound in Great Britain by
Mackays of Chatham PLC, Chatham, Kent

British Library Cataloguing in Publication Data
A catalogue record for this book is available from the British Library.

Library of Congress Cataloging in Publication Data

Philosophical perspectives on accounting: essays in honour of Edward Stamp / edited by M.J. Mumford and K.V. Peasnell.
p. cm.
Includes bibliographical references and index.
ISBN 0-415-08093-2
1. Accounting. 2. Corporations—Accounting. I. Stamp, Edward. II. Mumford, Michael J. III. Peasnell, K.V.
HF5625.P57 1993
657—dc20 92-18454
CIP

Contents

Figures and tables

FIGURES

TABLES

Contributors

David Tweedie: Chairman of the Accounting Standards Board; formerly a partner in KPMG Peat Marwick Mclintock, he is currently Visiting Professor at the University of Bristol (and formerly at Lancaster). A member of the Institute of Chartered Accountants of Scotland, he also holds a doctorate in industrial relations.

Ken Peasnell: Director of the International Centre for Research in Accounting (ICRA) and Professor of Accounting at Lancaster University. A chartered accountant, he took his Ph.D at Lancaster under the supervision of Professor Edward Stamp.

Michael J. Mumford: Senior Research Fellow at ICRA and a former head of the Department of Accounting and Finance at Lancaster, he is a Council member of the Chartered Association of Certified Accountants.

Alister K. Mason: a Fellow of the Institutes of Chartered Accountants of England and Wales and of Ontario, he is a partner in the Toronto office of Deloitte & Touche, and former Research Studies Director of the Canadian Institute of Chartered Accountants. He took his Ph.D at Lancaster under the supervision of Professor Edward Stamp.

Michael K. Power: having read philosophy and taken his doctorate in the subject, he then qualified as a chartered accountant and now teaches in the Department of Accounting and Finance at the London School of Economics.

Simon Archer: read politics, philosophy and economics at Oxford before qualifying as a chartered accountant and working in consultancy in London and Paris. He later taught at London Business School and Lancaster University, before taking up a chair first at the University of Wales at Bangor and latterly at the University of Surrey.

Robert R. Sterling: holds the unusual distinction of having had his doctoral thesis published as a book which won international renown. He is a certified public accountant and has pursued his distinguished teaching career at a number of major universities in the USA and Canada, including appointment as Kendall D. Garff Professor of Business Enterprise at the University of Utah.

Colin Lyas: the only professional philosopher amongst the contributors, he teaches at Lancaster University, where his advice and guidance was much sought after by Edward Stamp during his studies in philosophy and jurisprudence.

Richard Mattessich: Arthur Andersen Alumni Professor emeritus of the University of British Columbia, he is an elected member of two national academies (Austria and Italy), a Ford Foundation Fellow (USA), a Distinguished Erskine Fellow (New Zealand), and a Senior Killam Fellow (Canada). He has been awarded the Gold Medal and the AICPA/AAA 'Award for Notable Contribution to Accounting Thought' as well as the CAAA's 'Haim Falk Award for Distinguished Contribution to Accounting Thought'.

R. Murray Lindsay: met Edward Stamp while studying at the University of Saskatchewan (where Stamp, a naturalized Canadian citizen, was awarded an honorary doctorate in 1985). He took his Ph.D at Lancaster under the supervision of Professor David Otley, qualified as a certified management accountant, and now teaches at the University of Saskatchewan.

Philip Stamp: Edward Stamp's son, and a professional physicist, with degrees from Sussex and Lancaster. He currently holds a professional research fellowship at the University of British Columbia.

Preface

The accountant: a tradesman or a professional?

David Tweedie[1]

I first heard the name of Eddie Stamp one Saturday morning. It was some twenty years ago when I was a chartered accountant apprentice sitting in the auditing class at the Scottish Institute and listening with increasing incredulity and respect to extracts from his 1969 article in *The Times* attacking the UK profession's deficiencies in regulating accounting practice (Stamp 1969a). Stamp was a wordsmith. His article, as usual, was not only trenchant but beautifully crafted. For me, a trainee accountant, his style and the message coming through in his writings were ideal models for a young professional. The accountant had to be independent, rely on sound judgement and above all had to base his thinking on logical foundations.

> Medical practice is based on judgement but it is also based on principles with a sound theoretical foundation. This is not so in the case of accounting, and most of the accountant's so-called principles are merely descriptions of current or, even worse, past, practice; rules which in many cases were drawn up on an *ad hoc* basis to deal with the expediencies of a passing moment.
>
> The fact that these rules have in many cases been codified by the Institutes of Chartered Accountants should not delude us into thinking that they were drawn up inside any theoretical framework. Indeed, it has been calculated by one authority that the profession has authorised so many different ways of doing the same thing that the rules for valuing the assets on a balance sheet can be combined together in over a million different ways to produce over a million different 'true and fair views' of the same facts.
>
> This situation will persist so long as the profession regards principles merely as an attempt to describe what is being done in the best firms. This approach may be satisfactory in prescribing

> the 'principles' of plumbing, or of wallpapering, or of carpentry. It is surely not good enough for a profession which believes itself to be the intellectual equal of the legal and medical professions.
> (Stamp 1969a)

As is well known, Eddie's article in *The Times* and the resulting exchange with the then President of the English Institute, Ronnie Leach (Leach 1969), led to the formation of what became the Accounting Standards Committee. Regulation in financial reporting practices was about to take a new turn in the United Kingdom.

I began to follow Eddie's writings especially after publication of his paper to the 1971 Scottish Institute Summer School on income and value determination (Stamp 1971). That paper introduced many Scottish accountants to the notions of current cost and 'real' terms accounting.

The advocacy of accounting in 'real' terms, not unnaturally, led Eddie into conflict with the ASC's first current cost proposal, ED18, in 1976. The Scottish Institute organized a conference to discuss the new Exposure Draft and I shared the platform with Eddie – our first meeting. Eddie assailed the Exposure Draft from all sides – theoretical compromise was unacceptable to him. There was an absence of logical thought in determining profit, the valuation proposals were too subjective, the capital maintenance concept was not clear, the ASC would have to think again (Stamp 1977a).

Two years after our first meeting Eddie asked me to apply for a vacant chair at the University of Lancaster to which he had moved in 1971 to set up the International Centre for Research in Accounting (ICRA). At the same time, however, the Scottish Institute had approached me to become their Technical Director, a position to which I was appointed in early 1978. A few months later came the offer from Lancaster University to take up a visiting chair in accounting in the International Centre for Research in Accounting – the Centre of course being directed by Eddie Stamp. We met frequently in Edinburgh, Lancaster and London and discussed the problems of the profession and the standard setting process in particular. We exchanged drafts of papers, discussed ideas for research, encouraged the other – in particular Eddie enabled Geoff Whittington and me to lay the foundations for our book on inflation accounting during a joint sabbatical at ICRA (Tweedie and Whittington 1984).

The final work Eddie and I shared began in 1984 and was completed just before Eddie's death. The then National Coal Board (NCB) in the midst of its year-long miners' strike had been attacked by five academics in the pages of *Accountancy* (Berry *et al.* 1985). Their article claimed that the pit whose closure on the grounds of being uneconomic had precipitated the strike (Cortonwood, in Yorkshire) was, in fact, economically viable. The article led to questions being asked in Parliament about the industry's accounting practices and thoroughly embarrassed the NCB. The Board therefore decided to put together a team to investigate the academics' claims and asked whether I could suggest an academic whose independence would be unimpeachable. It was very easy to think of Eddie Stamp. Eddie therefore joined a team which, apart from the two of us, consisted of Paddy Custis, former finance director of GKN, and Sir Douglas Morpeth of Touche Ross and former Vice-Chairman of the Accounting Standards Committee (and, incidentally, Chairman of the Inflation Accounting Steering Group whose Exposure Draft, ED18, Eddie had so vigorously attacked at the Scottish Institute conference!). We considered the article that had been written by the academics, heard the counter-arguments of the NCB and then began to assemble our evidence.

Eddie loved the assignment. He was at his best in the midst of controversy dealing with disputed facts and methods of accounting and above all in a situation which of necessity required complete independence. Our research brought us into contact with national and regional officers of the NCB and culminated, on one field visit, in the never to be forgotten sight of a blackened-faced Professor Edward Stamp half a mile underground, clad in miner's protective clothing and helmet, hugely enjoying himself as we sought to assess what exactly causes a pit to become uneconomic. A few months later the project was completed (Custis *et al.* 1985) and shortly afterwards Eddie passed on.

THE CONCEPTUAL FRAMEWORK AND THE PROBLEMS OF THE PROFESSION

Eddie's death left unfinished what would have been the culmination of his years of professional and academic experience. For several years he had been researching what would have been his major work, a book on the conceptual framework. He had seen the problems faced by the profession as it tried to meet the challenge of a rapidly evolving financial system with the somewhat outdated accounting methods of the past. Accounting standards had been developed to deal with particular problems and inevitably were not based on any overall set of principles. The working parties that developed each standard began their tasks from differing viewpoints.

Eddie was concerned that the inconsistencies left loopholes which would be exploited by those seeking to present their results and financial position not simply in the best light but in one which did not fairly reflect the economic reality of a company's performance and state of affairs. In his office at Lancaster University Eddie had a framed cartoon in a prominent position in which two middle-aged businessmen were discussing a set of accounts. One was saying to the other 'My accounts are prepared in accordance with Generally Accepted Accounting Principles – if you know what I mean'. On the cartoon someone had inscribed: 'Do you know what he means Eddie?'. Eddie knew well enough and was determined to ensure that the rules, to the best of his ability, would not be exploited in the future.

Eddie had always been interested in an overall plan for financial reporting. He (and his successor as director at ICRA, Ken Peasnell) were major contributors to *The Corporate Report*, a consultative document which discussed the objectives of financial reporting issued by the UK's standard setting body (the Accounting Standards Committee) in 1975. Unfortunately, one month after publication this document was swamped by the report of the Sandilands Committee on Inflation Accounting (HMSO 1975) which diverted the profession's attention from the scope and aims of the reporting process. In the late 1970s, undeterred, Eddie accepted an invitation from the Canadian Institute of Chartered Accountants to write a research study dealing with the need for a conceptual framework. The study was eventually published in the Autumn of 1980 under the title *Corporate Reporting: Its Future Evolution* (Stamp 1980). Thereafter Eddie's thinking was directed towards solving the problems he recognized when writing the Canadian booklet.

Eddie regarded the approach of the Financial Accounting Standards Board (FASB) in the USA to a conceptual framework as being too complex. He believed that the FASB's attempt to define the various elements of accounting would simply shift the debate about accounting standardization from quarrels about the standards themselves to arguments about the definitional changes desired by various interest groups to produce standards advantageous to them. He gave as an example the definition of assets used by the FASB: 'assets are probable future economic benefits obtained or controlled by a particular entity as a result of past transactions or events' (Stamp 1982). While, he argued, the definition seemed eminently reasonable it was nonetheless arbitrary. It failed to deal with the crucial question of whether the item must be severable from an enterprise in order to be treated as an asset. Nor did it specify the level of aggregation of separate items that are to be considered as assets. The significance of his criticism could be seen when it was realized that goodwill and a major portion of research and development expenditure might be covered by the definition of an asset if severability from the enterprise was not required. On the other hand, he stated, if severability were to be included in the definition then all of the difficulties of asset valuation relating to uncertainty about the future benefits that might be derived from such 'assets' as goodwill and research and development would be eliminated, as the items would not be classified as assets under the definition.

Similarly, by ignoring the level of aggregation he argued that the FASB's definition failed to provide a basis for distinguishing between 'full cost' and 'successful efforts' methods for accounting for oil and gas drilling costs. (Eddie's two objections, however, could be deemed not to relate to the definition of an asset but to recognition criteria determining whether the asset would be shown in the accounts.)

Instead Stamp argued that the essential components for a conceptual framework consisted of three elements:

1 General agreement on the overall objectives of financial reporting;
2 General agreement as to the nature and needs of the various groups of users of financial reports;
3 Identification of a set of (ideally, mutually exclusive and collectively exhaustive) criteria to be used in choosing between alternative solutions to standard-setting problems – and in assessing the quality and utility of financial reports.

With the agreement of the Accounting Standards Committee Eddie undertook empirical testing of the third element. He polled the members of the Committee and discovered that there was wide agreement among the nineteen members who responded to his questionnaire that conservatism was the least important criterion in making decisions on accounting standards. He also discovered that there was unanimity within the Committee that the most important criterion was relevance. Further questioning established that as a whole the ASC preferred replacement cost to any other accounting measurement base. Encouraged by his initial work Eddie began to read widely in the fields of philosophy, law, science and history in his attempt to deepen his understanding of the most appropriate method of portraying economic reality. At the time of his death, however, he had still not begun to assemble his proposed book and sadly the project died with him.

FINANCIAL REPORTING PROBLEMS FACING THE PROFESSION TODAY

The major problems facing the profession today have changed little from those prevalent when Eddie first made an impact on the UK accounting scene. There is now greater statutory control over accounting following the implementation of the European Community's Second, Fourth and Seventh Directives. Disclosure levels are higher, standards regulate practice in many aspects of the professional's work, but nevertheless some of the central problems of UK reporting are still to be resolved. In particular, UK accounting is still affected by loopholes in the law, some longstanding, others introduced from European practice as a result of the EC Directives. These anomalies give those who wish to take them 'escape routes' from what would be considered by many practitioners and theoreticians to be good practice. Some of the problems arising as a result of the collision of the law and accounting theory will be mentioned below as we consider the major problems facing British accounting today. In essence the three main interrelated problems affecting financial reporting are:

1 The valuation system;
2 The function of the balance sheet; and
3 The concept of profit.

The valuation system

It is common practice for British accountants to pour scorn on their American counterparts for their failure to revalue assets and therefore, according to many British accountants, their failure to reflect reality in the balance sheet. However, British practice is far from ideal. It is not simply a case of comparing historical cost America with current value Britain. British balance sheets only show certain assets at current value (usually properties, although occasionally stock is shown at market value) and they are a confusing mixture of current revaluations, revaluations of many years ago (there is no requirement to revalue regularly) and of historical costs. The valuation of liabilities, too, varies. Most liabilities of an entity are shown at the amounts ultimately due. However, the premium potentially due on a convertible, redeemable debenture is not generally accrued. Some liabilities (finance leasing obligations) are shown at net present values, none are shown at their market value (for example, where debentures are publicly traded). There is consequently today no logical basis underlying the financial position statement of many British companies. In part this is due to a dispute over the function of the balance sheet.

The function of the balance sheet

Valuation of assets (and liabilities) is but one aspect of the problems afflicting the balance sheet. The other major part of the problem is asset recognition, particularly the recognition of intangible assets.

The problem became acute with the publication of the Statement of Standard Accounting Practice (SSAP) No. 22, *Accounting for Goodwill*, in 1985. This standard gave preparers of accounts a choice in the accounting treatment of goodwill. The preferred method was to write off the asset to reserves. The alternative was to amortize goodwill over its useful economic life. The latter policy was not popular as it reduced earnings per share, one of the key financial indicators in the eyes of management and analysts. The former policy, too, began to lose popularity as acquisitive companies began to use up their reserves and their gearing ratios rose, thereby affecting yet another key financial indicator. Many companies would have liked to have returned to the pre-standard position where the goodwill was carried in the balance sheet until it could be shown to have lost value. The European directives, however, required that goodwill be written off over its useful life and, as interpreted by the British government, without residual values being brought into the calculation.

Practice suddenly began to change. Goodwill had been defined in SSAP22 as being the difference between the fair value of a consideration paid for a company less the fair value of the identifiable tangible and intangible assets which could be disposed of by being separable from the business as a whole. Companies now began to look very closely at their intangible assets and a debate developed over the definitions of 'separability' and 'the business as a whole'. Could, for example, a business holding a portfolio of interests be deemed to be able to dispose of one of those interests without selling the business as a whole, or was it selling the whole of that particular interest?

The debate was driven by four factors affecting companies:

1 The need to restore gearing ratios damaged by the write-off of goodwill to reserves (this was given special force by the fact that many of the acquisitions were deemed by shareholders and management alike to have been bargains yet, especially in the service industries where few tangible assets existed, the effect on net worth of the predator company seemed to indicate that losses were being written off);
2 The takeover of Rowntree where 'goodwill' comprised a major proportion of the purchase consideration and gave an indication of the worth of brands unrecognized in the balance sheet. Some companies may have believed that they could ward off predators by showing valuable intangibles on the face of the financial position statement;
3 Many companies' borrowing requirements were linked to a multiple of net worth. The instant write-off of goodwill was therefore reducing the amount of borrowing which would be available to a company;
4 The Stock Exchange rules required companies to issue expensive and time-consuming circulars to their shareholders when the effect of an acquisition would increase their net assets by a certain percentage. For predator companies which had acquired expensive service companies which possessed few tangible assets such circulars would be used far more often than the predator ever envisaged, as the goodwill write-off reduced the company's reserves.

The current argument over the showing of intangibles on the balance sheet calls into question the whole purpose of a balance sheet:

- Is it a list of balances resulting from previous transactions (as it used to be) or is it a value statement?
- Should it show intangible as well as tangible assets?
- Should it only show assets acquired as a result of a transaction or should self-created assets also be included?
- Should a balance sheet attempt to value the overall worth of the enterprise as opposed to the value of its assets?
- Should estimates of the value of difficult-to-measure intangible assets be shown in the notes rather than on the face of the position statement?

At present the UK balance sheet is a mixture of many of these concepts, resulting in a statement which causes embarrassment to any British accountant who is forced to attempt to justify its present form. Until accountants in the United Kingdom resolve some of the above issues our balance sheets will continue to be of little real use to readers of the financial statements.

Some assets and liabilities were, however, deliberately not recognized. In the mid-1980s off-balance sheet schemes began to be marketed heavily by many of the financial institutions. Off-balance sheet finance is, of course, by no means a new phenomenon; for example, leasing and factoring are long-established off-balance sheet techniques. What was new, and of very great concern to many people, was that many of the schemes now being promoted relied upon a narrow and literal interpretation of the law and arrangements made for the purposes of the schemes. The result was that assets and borrowings could be removed from balance sheets while it was clear that there was little change in the true financial position of the companies entering into such schemes. The potential to mislead was very great.

The problem was exacerbated in group accounts. Parent companies hid the assets and liabilities of a subsidiary by taking advantage of the Companies Act rules (since revised in the 1989 Companies Act) which meant that a subsidiary only existed if over 50 per cent of the equity capital was held or if the composition of the board was controlled. Companies could have *de facto* control over another but by ensuring that the two criteria above did not apply they were not obliged to show consolidated accounts. Instead they simply showed a '*de facto* subsidiary' as an investment or as an associated company thereby concealing a great deal of information from the reader, especially when the subsidiary company had high levels of debt which were now hidden from prying eyes. Even recourse to the 'true and fair view' concept did not seem to be of assistance. The accountant's attempt to appeal to substance rather than form by invoking the concept of truth and fairness was promptly rebuffed by the Law Society (see the articles by Tweedie and Kellas 1987, 1988 and Aldwinckle 1987).

At one time it appeared that so many assets and liabilities were disappearing off-balance sheet that, as one technical partner cynically remarked, the balance sheet was really becoming an optional extra. It seemed hardly worthwhile producing it to show what little was still visible!

A great deal of attention was, however, given to this issue; an exceedingly good paper was produced at ICRA by Ken Peasnell with Anaab Yaansah (1988). The gradual pressure from academics, practising accountants and the financial press firstly led to the profession's own attempts to amend the situation in the form of ED42 'Special

Purpose Transactions' which for the first time in ASC's twenty-year life employed conceptual constructs to recognize assets and liabilities. (The definition of assets as 'probable future economic benefits controlled by and accruing to a particular enterprise' and of liabilities as 'present obligations entailing probable future sacrifices of economic benefits' have been taken from the FASB's Conceptual Statement No 6 *Elements of Financial Statements*.) The Companies Act of 1989 also attempts to eliminate the practice of off-balance sheet accounting by redefining subsidiaries in terms of control by a parent company and by threatening further definitional amendments if loopholes are shown to exist in the proposed criteria defining a subsidiary company.

It is probably true to say that the ASC would have preferred not to have started out with a few elements for a conceptual framework introduced of necessity in response to a particular problem. However, the fact remains that the UK did not have a conceptual framework and that elements of it were needed for the purpose of controlling off-balance sheet financing schemes. While Eddie Stamp would not have agreed with the ASC's proposals (indeed, as noted earlier, he had already attacked the FASB's definition of an asset) he would certainly have applauded the use of concepts rather than a series of detailed rules to deal with the matter in hand.

The concept of profit

The conceptual basis of the current UK income statement cannot be corrected by the accounting profession alone. Statutory accounting principles and anomalies in the law restrict the standard setter's freedom of action.

While the UK balance sheet and income statement are articulated, as we have discussed earlier, not all changes in balance sheet values flow through the income statement. Current practice breaks with a 'pure' articulation by allowing or requiring 'capital' items not to appear in the UK's profit and loss account. Thus changes in the valuation of assets are reflected in a revaluation reserve. Similarly, the premium over nominal value arising on the issue of shares and the discount on the issue of debentures are taken to a reserve, the share premium account (although the discount on debentures does not have to be so treated).

Some of the problems of the profit and loss account arise from our earlier discussion of the valuation system and the function of the balance sheet. Revaluation, while having the advantage of strengthening the balance sheet, also has the disadvantage that it confuses the capital maintenance concept, can affect gains on disposals and most certainly will affect the level of depreciation charged. Since the EC Fourth Directive demands that only realized profits can be shown in the income statement, British accounting practice appears not to question the practice of taking the surplus on the revaluation of assets to reserve. Depreciation charged to the profit and loss account is based on the revalued amount. Confusion now reigns. Are UK accounts based on an attempt to maintain the historical cost of the asset or are we trying to maintain its operating capability, i.e. current cost? There is no answer in British practice today. Gains on disposal are frequently measured in terms of the historical cost gain. In other words, the amounts credited to the revaluation reserve are often, but not inevitably, brought back into profit. Some companies, however, base their gains on revalued book value. If, of course, gains are to be based on book value (which is part of the ASC's latest thinking) then there is a reduced incentive for companies to revalue assets as the profit and loss account will 'suffer' from increased depreciation charges and reduced gains on disposal in the profit and loss account. The overall effect is always to show the down side – the growth in the company's wealth due to the rise in value of its assets is not reflected as part of income.

Prudence, as MacNeal rightly concluded, can be a barrier to the truth (MacNeal 1939). A profit and loss account which is based on realized profits fails to reflect the gradual growth in wealth of an enterprise and thereby is seriously deficient. The present Companies Act is not even-handed in its treatment of unrealized changes in the value of assets. The Act demands that assets that fall in value on a permanent basis have to be written down and the amount of the loss (below historical cost) charged to the profit and loss account. This can cause a major anomaly when, for example, a portfolio of hotels is owned. If 95 per cent of the hotels rise in value the law demands that the loss from the declining 5 per cent should be taken through the profit and loss account while the gain on the appreciating 95 per cent would not appear in income but would be taken straight to revaluation reserve. (The company would then, of course, be forced to depreciate the increased values.) Not surprisingly this does not make sense to many hotel owners and makes little sense to me. We are simply failing to reflect a major change in a company's financial position and increase in wealth by a result of rather outdated European rules based on distribution measurement (i.e. a prudent measure of realized profit) rather than on profit determination.

British accounts are, of course, centred on the income statement.

Companies are obsessive about the measurement of earnings per share and will cheerfully adopt policies which can result in adverse balance sheet effects (until, as we discussed above, the gearing ratio is seriously affected) but which enhance profit. Professor Solomons' proposals (1989) for a conceptual framework for the UK are balance sheet based. He, like Eddie, believes in the measurement of the change in wealth rather than merely the consideration of all losses but only realized profits. Professor Solomons, however, still clings to the notion of charging the current cost of an asset against income over the asset's lifetime. A recent Scottish Institute study, *Making Corporate Reports Valuable* (ICAS 1988), which is also balance sheet based has, on the other hand, accepted Thomas' notion of the arbitrariness of depreciation and proposes that diminution in value should be the sole criterion for writing down assets against income. To be implemented this proposal would, however, require both a change in accounting practices of a lifetime and an amendment to an EC Directive.

The absence of a recognition of the change in value of assets is only one aspect of the failure to adopt an all inclusive concept of income. To assess a company's overall income it is not sufficient to look at the profit and loss account alone – the interested reader of UK accounts has, in addition, to study reserve movements very carefully indeed. We have already discussed problems in reflecting diminutions in value. Further, in Britain today we are witnessing complex capital issues which are designed simply to ensure that a company's reserves rather than its profit and loss account bear the brunt of interest charges, i.e. the absence of full articulation between balance sheet and income statement enables changes in wealth to bypass the profit and loss account.

As a result of an anomaly in the law, discounts on loan stock can be charged to the share premium reserve. When the law was first enacted such discounts would be of a nominal level. Nowadays, however, the discount may be a material proportion of the loan stock's value rather than a mere 2 or 3 per cent. The annual interest payable to the loan stock holders may, depending on the discount, be at a low level or even zero. In essence, as the loans are redeemed at their full nominal value, the full interest payment is simply deferred. It would seem that the correct accounting policy would be to charge the true interest rate to income over the life of the loan stock, thereby building up a provision to meet its redemption. Many companies, however, make no provision and, when it falls due, could simply charge the additional amount direct to share premium account. A similar problem arises when loans stocks are redeemed at a premium. The premium on redemption may also be charged to the share premium account and once more no accrual of interest through the profit and loss account need be made over the loan stocks' life. The profit and loss account, therefore, does not reflect the full interest charge paid. Reserve accounting is alive and well in the United Kingdom today.

In his plenary address to the American Accounting Association (AAA) annual meeting in Portland, Oregon, 23 August 1977, Eddie, in his role as AAA Visiting Lecturer, stated:

> Let me conclude with two or three lessons which I think can be learned by Americans from the British experience.
>
> First there is the need to give top priority to solving the conceptual problems. For example: what is profit? How shall we treat holding gains? How should we take account of changes in the value of the monetary unit in measuring income?
>
> Second, I suspect we will have to accept that many of our questions have more than one answer. If this is so it would be futile to continue insisting that the essentially complex ideas of value and of income can be enshrined in single columns of figures, as Sandilands insisted. I believe we will eventually be driven to accepting the notion of multi-column reporting. And I also believe that an adequate system of financial reporting will have to take account of *both* specific *and* general price changes . . .
>
> (Stamp 1977b)

Geoff Whittington and I have written extensively on the British experience of inflation accounting elsewhere (Tweedie and Whittington 1984) and I shall not do so here. At present inflation in the United Kingdom is at a relatively low level and while its effects on financial statements are insidious there is no current demand for inflation accounting. If, however, inflation rises once more to the levels of the mid-1970s and early 1980s the inflation accounting debate will surface once again – consensus will I suspect still be as far away as ever.

THE ROLE OF THE AUDITOR

Eddie's academic interest did not simply revolve around income determination and value measurement. He always had a sympathy for the plight of the auditor. He was an early advocate for harmonized international auditing standards. As the UK representative on the International Auditing Practices Committee from 1983 to 1988 I noted with interest how often the book Eddie wrote with Maurice Moonitz (Stamp and Moonitz 1979) was mentioned – on one occasion the Committee debated whether or not it was living up to the ideal set for it in that seminal work.

Eddie was well aware of the problems of an auditor. In the autobiographical introduction to his *Selected Papers on Accounting, Auditing and Professional Problems* (Stamp 1984) he indicated that he resigned as a partner in a professional accounting firm because he felt his independence was being compromised. He believed that the auditor was faced with very difficult tasks and conflicts but should be single-minded in his pursuit of what he deemed professionally to be right. In other words he believed wholeheartedly in the concept of auditor independence. He was aware of the increasing pressures on auditors. His view of the Accounting Court (see, for example, Stamp 1969b) was one way of preventing what is every auditor's nightmare – what he may deem to be the false precedent set by a competitor, in other words a treatment which the auditor personally finds unacceptable but which, if unchallenged, forms part of the corpus of accepted practices. Such a treatment, if advantageous in terms of favourable profit measurement or appropriate gearing ratios, will lead to a surge of support from preparers who find themselves at a competitive disadvantage in comparison to their rivals who have succeeded in persuading their auditors that the precedent is worth following.

In this respect I expect that Eddie would have welcomed the proposals of the Dearing Committee (CCAB 1988). The ASC with its extremely limited resources did a magnificent job but due process of consultation took a long time and standards were inevitably still being developed two or three years after the problem they were designed to solve had emerged. The Emerging Issues Task Force in America (and proposed in the UK by the Dearing Committee) may well help the auditor deal with the unacceptable precedent. The auditor does not wish his own clients to be at a commercial disadvantage if a practice has become accepted by other preparers and auditors. Truth and fairness on which the auditor must opine is, as Hoffman and Arden have written, based on accepted practice.

> The expectations of the readers will have been moulded by the practices of accountants because by and large they will expect to get what they ordinarily get and that in turn will depend upon the normal practices of accountants.
>
> (Hoffman and Arden 1983)

Consequently an unchallenged precedent slips into the corpus of accepted practices and it is extremely difficult for an auditor to claim that all his peers are out of step when the practice is widely accepted – a more theoretically robust proposal may carry little weight if it does not produce an answer so 'favourable' to the preparers of accounts concerned with earnings per share and appropriate balance sheet ratios – a problem recognized in the Dearing Committee report.

> Once an interpretation has been adopted, and especially if it is perceived to give an advantage in commercial terms, there is pressure on others to follow suit.
>
> (CCAB 1988)

To that extent bad accounting can drive out good.

The standard setters are thus faced with a dilemma. Should they produce a rule book and try to outlaw unacceptable practices as they appear or should they instead rely on broad principles, the spirit of which should be instinctively obeyed by the auditor (see Tweedie 1988)? While most auditors, being professionals, would instinctively opt for the latter, there is no doubt that the rule book by removing a large degree of judgement makes life easier for some of them. To that extent auditors are divided – for some while rule books might be too rigid they stop arguments!

I know where Eddie would have stood. He was a true and fair man, not a rule book man. He would have wished the corpus of accepted practices to have been based on solid theoretical foundations. That was the driving force behind Eddie's major work. There is still much to be achieved.

NOTE

1 This Preface was written before the author became Chairman of the Accounting Standards Board.

REFERENCES

Aldwinckle, R. (1987) 'Off-balance sheet finance – the legal view', *Accountancy*, June.

Berry, A., Capps, T., Cooper, D., Hopper, T. and Lowe. A. (1985) 'NCB accounts – a mine of mis-information' *Accountancy*, January.

CCAB (Consultative Committee of Accountancy Bodies) (1988) *The Making of Accounting Standards*, report of the review committee, Chairman, Sir Ron Dearing, London: Institute of Chartered Accountants in England and Wales.

Custis, P.J., Morpeth, D., Stamp, E. and Tweedie, D.P. (1985) *Report of an Independent Committee of Enquiry on Certain Accounting Matters Relating to the Affairs of the National Coal Board*, London: National Coal Board.

HMSO (1975) 'Inflation accounting', report of the Inflation Accounting Committee, Chairman, F.E.P. Sandilands, Cmnd 6225, London: HMSO.

Hoffman, L. and Arden, M.H. (1983) 'Legal opinion on "true and fair"', *Accountancy* November.

ICAS (Institute of Chartered Accountants in Scotland) (1988) *Making Corporate Reports Valuable*, London: Kogan Page.

Leach R.G. (1969) 'Accountants and the public interest', *The Times*, 22 September.

MacNeal, K. (1939) *Truth in Accounting*, Houston: Scholars Book Co.

Peasnell, K.V. and Yaansah, R.A. (1988) 'Off-balance sheet financing', paper issued by Chartered Association of Certified Accountants.

Solomons, D. (1989) *Guidelines for Financial Reporting Standards*, booklet, Institute of Chartered Accountants in England and Wales.

Stamp, E. (1969a) 'Auditing the auditors', *The Times*, 11 September.

—— E. (1969b) 'The public accountant and the public interest', *Journal of Business Finance*, April.

—— E. (1971) 'Income and value determination and changing price-levels: an essay towards a theory', *Accountant's Magazine*, June.

—— E. (1977a) 'ED18 and current cost accounting: a review article', *Accounting and Business Research*, Spring.

—— E. (1977b) 'Toward current value accounting in the UK', plenary address to AAA annual meeting, Portland, Oregon, 23 August.

—— E. (1980) *Corporate Reporting: Its Future Evolution*, Toronto: Canadian Institute of Chartered Accountants.

—— (1982) 'First steps towards a British conceptual framework', *Accountancy*, March.

—— (1984) *Selected Papers on Accounting, Auditing and Professional Problems*, New York and London: Garland.

Stamp, E. and Moonitz, M. (1979) *International Auditing Standards*, Englewood Cliffs, New Jersey: Prentice-Hall.

Tweedie, D.P. (1988) 'True and fair v the rule book: which is the answer to creative accounting?', *Pacific Accounting Review*, December.

Tweedie, D.P. and Kellas J.H. (1987) 'Off-balance sheet financing', *Accountancy*, April.

—— (1988) 'Setting the accountants' record straight', *Accountancy*, January.

Tweedie, D.P. and Whittington, G. (1984) *The Debate on Inflation Accounting*, Cambridge: Cambridge University Press.

1 Introduction

Ken Peasnell

Accounting is widely regarded, by lay people and accountants alike, as a practical subject largely devoid of intellectual challenge. This collection is intended to dispel such illusions of certainty (for illusions they are), showing how accounting generates issues of a fundamental character concerning the nature of knowledge and how philosophical developments elsewhere might be of interest and relevance to accountants.

The book is dedicated to the memory of the late Professor Edward Stamp, who will long be remembered for his pioneering work in the field of accounting and the vital role he played in the creation of the Accounting Standards Committee, the predecessor to the Accounting Standards Board (ASB), the professional accounting body responsible for promulgating corporate financial reporting guidelines in the UK. Professor Stamp devoted himself to the development of a conceptual framework for the accounting standard-setting process akin to that which jurisprudence provides for the law. Driven to the conclusion that many accounting problems were essentially philosophical in character and therefore similar to those which have dogged other fields, he turned his mind to questions of scientific method, epistemology and aspects of legal theory, and he sought out scholars in these areas. Tragically, Stamp's premature death never allowed him to bring his own work to fruition. However, his work engaged the professional interest of people in a number of different fields, resulting in the publication of what were probably the first articles on accounting ever to appear in a leading philosophical journal.

The Preface to the book is contributed by Professor David Tweedie, for some years an academic colleague of Stamp, and later a practising accountant of eminence. David Tweedie was a partner in KPMG Peat Marwick McLintock at the time of writing his contribution and he has since been appointed chairman of the ASB. He shares Stamp's view that corporate financial reporting has to be based on a conceptual framework setting out the overall objectives of financial reporting, the nature and needs of various groups of users and the criteria to be used in choosing between alternative solutions to particular reporting problems.

The philosophical dimensions of accounting can best be appreciated by considering some of the fundamental problems and questions which arise in accounting and accountability relationships:

1 The central task of the accountant is to portray in a financial report (balance sheet, cash flow and income statement) a 'true and fair' view of a company's economic position and progress. The facts are often complicated, the portrayal necessarily incomplete, and the reports are required at low cost and without undue delay. 'True and fair' are, at best, ill-defined terms in this kind of setting. Is it therefore meaningful to postulate the existence of an 'economic reality' which accountants can represent in a 'scientific' manner? Does the fact that the economic values of many infrequently traded assets are contingent upon uncertain future events mean that accountants cannot evaluate them? What lessons are there to be learned from other fields about the most promising ways of tackling such measurement problems?
2 What is or should be the basis on which companies disclose details of their financial affairs to the outside world? Are fundamental 'rights to know' involved? Should 'user needs' be the paramount considerations underlying the preparation of financial statements? If so, which users and which needs should be considered? Alternatively, is the most promising approach to leave disclosure decisions to the best judgements of the company's directors and owners? Do accountants and auditors have moral responsibilities (as well as legal duties) and, if so, to whom and for what?
3 Auditing and accounting standards exist in order to reduce and 'manage' the conflicts of interest which can arise between the preparers (corporate managers) and users (investors, creditors and others) of financial statements. If the attempt to found accounting on objective principles or discoverable facts is abandoned, how are these conflicts of interest to be managed? – by codification, on German and French lines, in detailed disclosure requirements set out in statutes? – or by the quasi-judicial, 'case-law' type of standard-setting process favoured by Edward Stamp? – or by leaving it to market forces? What qualities should be required

of the members of the accounting profession who have to carry out these tasks?

The issues addressed by accountants and auditors concern the nature of (and access to) knowledge, power, authority and justice, all in relation to economic entities, often of enormous size, to be found in modern society.

One of the themes which consistently emerges in this volume is the need for the accountant to exercise judgement and make choices. Accordingly, a far greater burden is placed on accountants than is commonly supposed; independence of circumstance and caste of mind is at a premium. Alister Mason, a partner in Deloitte & Touche, Canada, highlights some of the areas where an auditor has to exercise professional judgement and the form those judgements take. The problems facing auditors are not narrowly culture-specific, but evidently recur in different societies.

Stamp's contributions to accounting thought, particularly its methodological and philosophical bases, are addressed by Michael Mumford. Stamp started life as a scientist, obtaining a first-class honours degree in natural sciences from Cambridge before becoming an accountant, and he retained his interest in science thereafter. It was therefore not surprising that Robert Sterling's 1979 book *Toward a Science of Accounting* should attract his attention. Stamp (1980, 1981) formed the contrary opinion that accounting was fundamentally different from sciences like physics, and its problems could not be solved by applying the methods of science. A conceptual framework was needed which would serve a function akin to that of jurisprudence in the law, recognizing the social nature and context of accounting.

In his contribution to the volume, Robert Sterling (Kendall D. Garff Professor of Business Enterprise at the University of Utah) takes a very different tack, arguing that the major conceptual problems of accounting have their roots in accountants being unwilling to 'measure', as the term is commonly understood in the empirical sciences. Accounting practice is a calculational activity and the results of those calculations have no empirical referents. Sterling provides a demonstration of how scientists find it virtually impossible to believe the mind-set of accountants, while the great majority of accountants are unable to accept that there could be an alternative way to think about accounting. Moreover, he suggests that little is being done by the academic accounting community to ameliorate this state of affairs: contemporary research has largely abandoned the search for improved methods of accounting in favour of studying the behaviour of preparers and users of financial reports. Sterling takes the position that it is confusing to refer to this kind of work as 'accounting research' – it would be just as confusing to describe the study of biologists as 'biological research' – and suggests there are reasons to query whether such studies can ever bear fruit.

Colin Lyas (Senior Lecturer in Philosophy, Lancaster University) provides a philosophical perspective on how accountants use terms and how these are used by those outside the discipline. The concepts of accounting are internal to accounting and can only be understood by studying the operations of accounting; to evaluate the concepts of accounting we have to consider the aims of accounting. Philosophical problems abound. As Lyas puts it, 'the very statement of the aims of accounting, namely, to give a true and fair account of some reality, is loaded to the gunwales with a philosophical cargo of millenia of discussions about truth, reality, justice and fairness'.

Michael Power (Lecturer in Accounting, London School of Economics) analyses the concept of a conceptual framework for financial reporting from a philosophical perspective. One of the recurrent doubts expressed about the American conceptual framework concerns its operational credibility: whether it actually helps the standard-setting process. Power suggests that discussion of this issue has been hindered by an absence of meta-theoretical considerations. His contribution is to appropriate the methodological structure of John Rawls (1972) and to outline its possibilities for enhancing our understanding of the idea of a conceptual framework for financial reporting.

Simon Archer (Midland Bank Professor of Financial Sector Accounting, University of Wales, Bangor) tackles a related theme, the way the American conceptual framework for financial reporting was constructed, identifying a number of methodological issues (institutional power, intellectual authority, purpose and meaning) which have been problematical for the project. He considers how methodological jurisprudence could form the basis for a different and more fruitful approach to these issues, and draws attention to the affinities between this methodology and others developed by systems analysts for the handling of complex organizational and social problem-situations.

The next two chapters address the philosophical foundations of modern accounting research. Richard Mattessich (formerly Arthur Andersen & Co Alumni Professor of Accounting at the University of British Columbia) examines whether such ideas as Lakatos' research programmes, Balzer's and Stegmüller's theory-nets, and Bunge's family of research fields, can meaningfully be applied to modern accounting theory and agency-information analysis. He identifies two or three research traditions or theory-nets, and suggests avenues for a more formal treatment which could more clearly reveal accounting's logical structure as well as its empirical claims.

University research in accounting has changed enormously in the last two decades, in many ways mirroring developments which have taken place in social sciences like economics (particularly) and social psychology. Much effort is being devoted to the development and testing of hypotheses about the kinds of accounting systems and reporting methods employed by different businesses and the uses to which they are put. Statistical investigations are now commonplace. Murray Lindsay (Associate Professor of Accounting, University of Saskatchewan) expresses concern that there is no sign of accounting researchers conducting their studies within the context or meta-methodology of the critical attitude which is the essence of the scientific method. After reviewing developments in the philosophy of science, he concludes that there is no reason why the social sciences should not be scientific in much the same sense as the physical sciences; but we must mend our ways. He stresses the importance of repetition and replication as required features of empirical research in accounting which are currently lacking.

In the final chapter Philip Stamp (the son of Edward Stamp and a theoretical physicist by profession) adopts a different tack. He argues that many academic accountants (and philosophers of science, too) have outdated conceptions of what constitutes 'reality' and 'fact' in physics. In particular, modern developments in quantum theory and meteorology pose considerable challenges to the common-sense views of nature inherited from the nineteenth century. This chapter is designed to address, in a relatively accessible form, the myth, popular amongst some academic accountants, that physics represents an ideal scientific paradigm to which accounting theoreticians might aspire.

Taken together, the contributions to this collection serve to illustrate the growing interest of scholars in the philosophical and methodological dimensions of accounting. It is to be hoped that the links being forged will be of mutual benefit to both communities. Accounting scholars can benefit from the study of philosophy and the help of philosophers, because many of the problems they confront are ones which are essentially philosophical in nature. It is to be hoped, too, that philosophers will find some of the concerns of accountants less mundane than they had previously imagined, and thereby uncover some interesting problems to grapple with.

The practical importance of these issues is considerable. Accountants and auditors face difficult tasks in trying to portray the often complex financial affairs of business enterprises in ways which conform to legal requirements, fit into the accounting framework and are understandable to a wide variety of users of financial statements. Disagreements abound. The activities of BCCI and Robert Maxwell and other notable financial causes célèbres only serve to remind us that the already difficult job of the accountant is often made much more difficult when the enterprises are under the control of unscrupulous managers determined to conceal what is going on. The task would be a little easier if the foundations were agreed to be secure. Accounting standard setters are responding in a variety of ways, including the development of conceptual frameworks which will serve as guidelines for financial reporting. The difficulties are considerable. Our hope is that the papers in this volume will be of some assistance in this process.

REFERENCES

Rawls, J. (1972) *A Theory of Justice* Oxford: Oxford University Press.

Stamp, E. (1980) *Corporate Reporting: Its Future Evolution*, Toronto: Canadian Institute of Chartered Accountants.

—— (1981) 'Why can accounting not become a science like physics?', *Abacus*, 17 (1): 13–27.

2 Users, characteristics and standards

Michael J. Mumford

INTRODUCTION

This chapter has three objectives. The first is to trace the development of accounting theory up to the mid-1970s, when the American Accounting Association (AAA) published its *Statement on Accounting Theory and Theory Acceptance* (AAA 1977).

The second is to place in context the methodological developments identified with the 'decision relevance' school about this time, and to consider specifically the work of Edward Stamp. Stamp is notable as one of the few people who can be identified as the (sole) author of a major paper on the principles of corporate reporting (Stamp 1980), and he also wrote at length on accounting methodology. For reasons shown, he regarded jurisprudence as the model to follow.

The third purpose of the chapter is to reconsider the place of accounting theory in the light of Gaa's 1988 paper (Gaa 1988), which questions whether it makes sense to look for any single, complete theoretical framework to use in setting standards. Such a 'post-modernist' view admits as valuable a much wider range of evidence, including material more specifically addressed to identifiable user needs. Seen from such a perspective, Stamp's contribution still appears promising; but it is not the only way of making progress.

THE SEARCH FOR A THEORY OF CORPORATE FINANCIAL ACCOUNTING

Textbooks on bookkeeping, particularly double entry bookkeeping, have been published for six centuries, but accounting theory can only be said to have appeared around the start of the present century, with the writings of American academics such as C.E. Sprague, H.R. Hatfield and W.A. Paton, and British writers like F.W. Pixley and L.R. Dicksee.

It is significant that the expression 'accounting theory' has come to be used almost exclusively in relation to the problems of financial reporting by corporate entities to external parties. It is not, for example, used to describe the statistical properties of accounting numbers (a field of study which has come to be known as 'financial statement analysis'), or the study of interactions between reporting systems and the power relations from which they develop (which falls within 'contingency theory' and perhaps overlaps with 'agency theory' and 'corporate governance').

This no doubt reflects the major preoccupations which have confronted accountants in practice. The problems of corporate financial reporting to external parties first became acute in America from about 1890, and rather later in Britain, as the ownership of managerially controlled corporations became widely dispersed, giving rise to a 'divorce between ownership and control' (Berle and Means 1932).

Indeed, to a large extent the term accounting theory has come over the past fifty years to refer to just a single aspect of corporate reporting, namely the choice between different valuation bases for recording assets and income. This, too, is understandable. There are three aspects to corporate financial reporting for external parties: recognition, valuation and disclosure.

Valuation is the only one of these that has been discussed at length by accountants. Recognition rules consist of a set of practical conventions which have long grown out of familiar usage. They possess little theoretical purity, and they are difficult to justify except in terms of practical convenience (see for example Sprouse and Moonitz 1962, and Johnson and Storey 1982). They tend often to be taken for granted. Disclosure has usually been regarded by accountants as falling outside their discretion.

Since their earliest days, companies in Britain have always been faced with regulations addressing the publication of accounts, specifying general headings of disclosure but saying little about the detailed conventions which determine recognition and valuation (Littleton 1981). It was largely left to accountants to determine these detailed rules of recognition and valuation. Until 1970 individual accountants in Britain had to make such decisions for themselves, although the Institute of Chartered Accountants in England and Wales published a series of non-binding *Recommendations on Accounting Principles* from 1942 (Zeff 1972). In 1970 a new standard-setting body was established, the Accounting Standards Steering Committee (ASSC), later renamed the Accounting Standards

Committee (ASC). In 1990 this was replaced by an Accounting Standards Board. None of these bodies had direct statutory authority to lay down or enforce accounting standards, but they acquired a rather imprecise authority of their own to augment existing law.

In America, companies are set up according to state law, rather than federal law, and states formerly had considerable latitude in drawing up corporate regulations. However, the 1934 Securities Exchange Act set up the Securities and Exchange Commission (SEC), with powers to determine accounting disclosure rules in detail for all listed companies, including rules for recognition and valuation as well as disclosure. In practice, the SEC has since 1934 always delegated much of this function to the accounting profession (Zeff 1972), but there has been pressure upon the profession to demonstrate that it is exercising this function responsibly and capably. There is no doubt that the SEC has strong formal powers, augmented by enforcement rules relating to the filing of accounts by listed companies. These powers are exercised only occasionally to overrule decisions of the Financial Accounting Standards Board (FASB), and the common law tradition thrives alongside the written constitution.

The nature and authority of accounting theory in relation to standards has been problematic throughout. Neither in Britain nor in America have standard setters so far adopted a 'conceptual framework', that is to say a complete formal statement of the assumptions which underlie their detailed rules. The absence of such a conceptual framework may be surprising after some fifty years of standard setting.

The American Accounting Association (AAA) publishes views on the current state of accounting theory from time to time over the years, and these views reflect the state of current opinion. Thus in 1940 the AAA published Paton and Littleton's statement of the established conventions of historical cost accounting (Paton and Littleton 1940). Then, after several statements on general price level adjusted accounts during the 1940s and 1950s, the Association published in 1966 a study which set out a much more radical set of proposals for multi-column accounting disclosures, using different valuation bases and designed to serve the supposed information needs of several different classes of users (AAA 1966). This study, *A Statement of Basic Accounting Theory*, acknowledged not merely the possibility of distinguishing between the information needs of users, but argued that this was the most fruitful place to begin the process of setting standards.

By 1977, however, the AAA Committee on Concepts and Standards for External Financial Reports presented a markedly different review of theory. Rather than urging a new set of accounting practices, this study viewed the prospects for accounting theory with some signs of alarm. *A Statement of Accounting Theory and Theory Acceptance* (SOATATA) (AAA 1977) examined in particular the possibility of securing consensus among accountants over a theoretical basis to use in choosing between alternative accounting models for corporate reporting. The authors were not optimistic: there was unlikely to be 'theory closure', even though the committee clearly hoped to be able to find 'a sufficient and compelling basis for specifying the content of external financial reports' (AAA 1977: 39). This issue will be considered further below.

However pessimistic its conclusions appear to be, the study performs a number of valuable functions. For example it reviews the literature then available on accounting theory and distinguishes three distinct theoretical approaches, broadly grouped into: 'classical' models; decision usefulness approaches; and information economics.

'Classical' models

The first group includes both 'true income' expositions (that accounting may be defined from some basic precepts which will be true by definition), and 'inductive' explanations (which identify an underlying rationale which is present in observable practice).

Decision usefulness approaches

Decision usefulness theorists concentrate either upon the characteristics of decision models that are supposed to be in general use, or upon the characteristics of decision makers (individually or collectively). It is acknowledged that value judgements must be made in deciding priorities, and these are often impounded in lists of characteristics supposed to make accounts 'useful'. This tendency to concentrate upon lists of abstract qualitative characteristics will also be considered more fully below.

Information economics

The third approach recognized by SOATATA is that of the 'information economics' school. Here accounting information is treated as a commodity in its own right. Considerable debate has arisen among theorists over the question whether market forces alone, unconstrained by regulation, could be sufficient to ensure the provision of accounting information which would be 'optimal' in some economic sense. It is generally taken for granted in this context that competitive economic market equilibrium, if attainable, would entail optimal conditions for information disclosure, but there is disagreement as to how far institutional forces in the market would allow this to happen in practice. Without such a state of equilibrium, it is argued, it may be necessary for regulators to 'intervene' in order to correct the effects of market failure. There are obvious problems with such analysis. For example, while the theory of general market equilibrium has been well analysed over the past century, there are many problems still unresolved over the analysis of market dynamics, and in particular the dynamics of forces towards, or away from, equilibrium (see, for example, Hicks 1966).

The three approaches are presented in SOATATA in the order above, reflecting their chronological development in the literature. However, all three tend to persist alongside one another. One implication of the lack of theory closure is that no one approach dominates the others in terms of general acceptance, either as a positive explanation for accounting practice or as a normative basis for a policy prescription.

DECISION USEFULNESS THEORIES RECONSIDERED

Over the past twenty-five years in particular, studies of the nature and role of financial accounts, in America, Britain and elsewhere, have repeatedly emphasized decision relevance as the central requirement of published financial information. Although SOATATA refers to a number of writers before the 1950s who make use of this claim, SOATATA credits the 1973 Trueblood Report as the first major statement of decision usefulness in accounting.

The Trueblood Report (the report of the American Institute of Certified Public Accountants study group, *Objectives of Financial Statements*, AICPA 1973) can be seen as the first step in the extensive conceptual framework project undertaken by the FASB since its inception, all of which is thus infused with decision usefulness as a goal. However, the authors of the FASB statements are not alone. User needs have been claimed by many of those in the Anglo-American tradition as the primary justification for financial reporting, not only in the six FASB *Statements of Financial Accounting Concepts* (FASB 1978, 1980a,b,c, 1984 and 1985), but also in *A*

Statement of Basic Accounting Theory (AAA 1966), *The Corporate Report* (ASSC 1975), the 1980 Canadian study *Corporate Reporting: its Future Evolution* (Stamp 1980), the 1981 Macve Report, the 1989 Solomons Report, the Scottish Institute's report *Making Corporate Reports Valuable* (McMonnies 1988), and most recently the 1989 IASC *Framework for the Preparation and Presentation of Financial Statements* (IASC 1989).

One feature that is striking about this apparent support for decision usefulness is the fact that the studies themselves do not generally cite any empirical evidence either about decisions or about users. One might expect them to adduce research on the identities of users, their numbers, the value of transactions depending upon accounting information, and the types of decision model actually employed, backed up by estimates of the costs and the benefits of producing information and of using it. There has been research published on user groups and their needs, and on decision models; moreover, some at least of the authors of the studies listed above have been well aware of this work (see, for example, Stamp 1978, reviewing Lee and Tweedie's 1977 study of UK shareholders). The linkage between evidence on user needs and the normative propositions in these studies is largely missing.

Most of the studies cited above refer to the problem of potential conflict between user interests – they point out how disclosing information to one class of user may disadvantage another group. Practical solutions to this problem may be difficult, but they often have to be found in society. Making such comparisons often involves a range of further questions on which empirical as well as ethical research can throw light; it is highly probable that a survey of actual cases (or alleged cases) of conflicts of interest will enable a judgement to be made that will be widely approved and supported.

Again, no such evidence tends to be produced at present by standard setters. It is as though the debate was concluded in the literature at the stage when tentative hypotheses were put forward, with no need for relevant facts to be established. Granted, it may be difficult to obtain convincing evidence to support accounting hypotheses; however, the same can be said about other areas of knowledge (such as the sociology of law, or the study of corporate governance, or educational research, or much of economics).

STAMP'S PROPOSALS FOR A JURISPRUDENTIAL APPROACH

In the late 1960s Professor Stamp criticized the British profession robustly for the poverty of its conceptual thinking on financial reports. This criticism was central to the campaign which led to the foundation of the Accounting Standards Steering Committee in 1970 (Leach 1981). Stamp is a particularly interesting member of the 'decision usefulness' school, partly because of his personal input into two major conceptual studies (the 1975 ASSC study and the 1980 Canadian study (Stamp 1980)) and partly because he analysed in some detail his views on methodology and the role of research in the accounting profession (Stamp 1985).

Stamp was the principal author of *The Corporate Report* (ASSC 1975), which sought to establish a broad consensus in Britain over reporting obligations, and he was the author of the 1980 study for the Canadian Institute of Chartered Accountants' *Corporate Reporting: its Future Evolution* (Stamp 1980). He regarded the 1980 study as the basis for a workable conceptual framework to support detailed accounting standards, and in later articles (Stamp 1981b, 1982, 1983) he showed how he intended to implement these ideas in practice.

Early in the 1980 study, Stamp mapped out the possible range of research methods available to him.

> Many of the uncertainties of accounting measurements . . . result from ambiguities in what aspect of value it is we are trying to measure. Others result from uncertainties that are inherent in our inability to predict the future. Still others, (as will be explained in Chapter 2), depend upon more subtle problems of measurement. Because of all this, many people have concluded that accounting is an 'art', an attitude that bewilders people who are impressed – however wrongly – by the apparent precision and certainty of a public company's Balance Sheet.
>
> Others who have thought about the nature of accounting regard it as a social science, similar in many ways to law, and see the authority of accounting standards depending upon a consensus.
>
> Still others see accounting as a subject whose problems could be solved if they were tackled in the same fashion as in the natural sciences, where hypotheses are propounded in an attempt to explain observed facts, and the hypotheses are then either supported or rejected by using them to make predictions which are tested against further empirical evidence.
>
> Still others argue that accounting standard setters should adopt the approach used in such branches of mathematics as geometry, where axioms are established (through intuition or through observation) and from which an internally consistent set of standards is developed through a process of logical analysis.

> Perhaps the most obvious way of looking at accounting is to regard it as a language, a vehicle whereby information is conveyed from the preparer to the user of financial statements. Yet although his view presents a vivid description of the nature of accounting it is not very fruitful, since it provides little guidance as to how to go about developing the language in such a way as to maximize its utility and its acceptability to its users.
>
> (Stamp 1980, chapt. 1, paras 27–31)

Stamp concludes that legal methods, and specifically those of jurisprudence, are in fact the appropriate models for his own research. In a 1981 review of Sterling's book *Toward a Science of Accounting* (1979) Stamp writes:

> Accounting, like the law but unlike natural science, deals with a system created by people, hence its fundamental characteristics *are* constantly changing and evolving. . . . Accounting deals with a system which is a human creation, designed to satisfy human need, and which must therefore, above all, be useful. The accounting environment is prone to many influences of a non-deterministic nature, influences related not only to long-term legal, cultural and political traditions, but also to short-term movements of mass psychology . . . Sterling is troubled because accounting employs so much legal methodology. But accountants *must* adopt legal approaches to the solutions of their problems because accountancy, like the law, deals with problems involving equity and balance and the resolution of conflict between different groups of human beings with widely varying interests and objectives.
>
> (Stamp 1981a: 21, emphasis in the original)

This still leaves it unclear what forms of evidence might be used to formulate and justify accounting policies. The fact that the 'fundamental characteristics' of accounting are constantly changing and evolving is not enough to rule out scientific processes of analysis. Science often has to deal with fast-changing matter, like nuclear particles. Neither does the social significance of the subject make it unscientific. However, the central part played in accounting policy decisions by 'equity and balance and the resolution of conflict' makes for an ethical component that is bound to impinge. Empirical data can never be enough. It is this, evidently, which leads him to think of accounting as akin to jurisprudence.

It is clear from his views in the Canadian study that Stamp had by 1980 come to regard the FASB's conceptual framework project, initiated in 1973, as ill-founded. The FASB had proceeded by attempting precise definitions of terms based upon a framework of axioms. This Stamp considered to be too rigid and prescriptive, and he referred to it dismissively as a 'rule book approach'.

> The ultimate goal of the rule book approach is to define the answer to every problem in advance. This is impossible in accounting, as has been stressed throughout this Study, because, strange as it might appear at first sight to a layman, accountants do not deal with problems where quantitative factors can invariably be substituted for value judgements.
>
> (Stamp 1980, chapt. 10, para. 20)

> As rules develop auditors are faced with a situation where their use of judgement is circumscribed or curtailed. This runs counter to our notions of professionalism, yet auditors often feel they need the protection that is afforded by such rules. What is clearly needed is a system which provides precedents (which can give protection in the exercise of judgement) without the construction of a straightjacket of rules and definitions that diminishes flexibility and inhibits progress.
>
> (ibid., para. 22)

Unfortunately, there is too much missing from Stamp's writing to be able to understand precisely how he interpreted the meaning of jurisprudence, but some idea is conveyed in the passages quoted below. Here some evidence is presented of the way in which he argued the need for accounting institutions to develop along lines analogous to legal institutions. He evidently regarded with profound misgivings any attempt to lay down the basic rules of accounting in an inflexible code. Corporate reporting must be responsive to the changing demands of users.

> The evolution of standards is not merely a technical matter. It is also dependent upon ethical values and economic, cultural, social, historical and political factors in the environment. Standards are an aid in the resolution of potential conflicts of interest between management and users (and occasionally between one user group and another) and this is not simply a technical matter.
>
> (ibid., para. 24)

> The approach now being developed by the FASB has many of the earmarks of that used by lawyers in civil law jurisdictions. Yet it might be argued that the FASB, which of course operates in a

common law country, is in fact doing no more than developing definitions and rules such as are commonly thought to exist in the laws of property, contract and tort in common law jurisdictions.

In fact, however, there is no such codification of the common law relating to property, contract, tort, etc. throughout most of the common law countries of the world. There have been moves towards codification of parts of the common law in all of the common law jurisdictions, but except with respect to the criminal law such moves have not progressed very far because of fears of the ossification that could result.

How, one might well ask, are judicial decisions made in common law countries, in the absence of explicit definitions and rules? The general procedure is that the judge, from many years of knowledge and experience, discerns broad principles, and then uses his judgement and his intuition in interpreting legislation and precedents in reaching his judgement, and these pronouncements, often in the form of *obiter dicta*, will be used as guides by other judges in future cases. The task of defining the essential features of, for example, a contract is left to academics and other textbook writers, although their work is obviously of enormous importance in the education of future lawyers – and judges.

(ibid., paras 32–4)

Stamp's use of the term 'codification' here is puzzling. He evidently does not mean the systematic description of present practice (or 'summary rules', Gaa 1988: 98), but, rather, incorporation into statute law as opposed to the more malleable forms of common law. Yet he apparently sees accounting standards as having the authority of statute law, or something close to it (as they already had in Canada, despite its common law tradition):

The relevance of all of this to the problem of accounting standard setting seems clear. The sources of authority in accounting consist of the law itself (in the form of statutes such as the Corporations Act, and Case Law), professional accounting standards (which have the force of law in Canada), and business custom.

If in developing accounting standards we follow the example of our own legal system, we can see that accounting standards and other laws correspond to statute law, whilst the daily decisions made by management and auditors throughout the country in interpreting standards are the equivalent of case law.

The accounting system, however, lacks two features that are of

> enormous importance and which are taken for granted in the legal system, namely,
> (a) the precedents that are established in everyday accounting and auditing practice are scattered among a wide variety of auditing firms and their clients, they are not published since they are confidential, and there is no systematic way of ensuring consistency throughout the country in the interpretation of accounting standards;
> (b) no procedure exists in accounting for appeal. . . .
>
> It is an integral part of the philosophy of this Study that the development of accounting standards should be evolutionary, and that it is not right to adopt a deterministic, authoritarian, or normative approach. The parallel with a common law legal system has been drawn above, and is clear enough. It is also apparent that if an evolutionary system is to work in accounting, as it has in the law, it will be necessary to ensure that precedents as they are established are consistent, and to provide some means of appeal.
>
> (ibid., paras 35–8)

Rather than a system of courts, accounting principles were to be developed, and revised whenever necessary, by a body of accountants acting in the capacity of standard setters. The authority for their standards was not to be drawn from any survey of user groups or user needs, although Stamp listed fifteen classes of users and thirteen categories of user need. Instead, standards would be evaluated using a set of agreed criteria based on the ideal qualitative characteristics of published accounts. It would be possible for other forms of evidence to be used too; for example, Stamp clearly thought that a standard could succeed or fail in practice even though it met the test prescribed for it at the time it was promulgated. It is not the final part of the standard setting process – far from it. As Stamp comments:

> The development of such a framework into an effective instrument to secure 'truth and fairness' in financial reporting will be no easier than the development of a system of laws and legal administration that secures justice for all.
>
> (Stamp 1982: 124)

Before examining in greater detail his proposal for using qualitative characteristics, the next section returns to the issue of whether a single accounting theory can be expected to produce 'theory closure'. So far in this chapter it has been taken for granted that this debate between theorists over the nature of accounting theory addresses a real issue, of some significance. As mentioned earlier, this view was taken in SOATATA, even though the authors were pessimistic about the outcome. However, there is reason to doubt whether there is any point in looking for a single statement of theory that would be complete and sufficient as a basis for standard setting.

THE ARRIVAL OF 'POST-MODERNISM'?

In 1988 the American Accounting Association published a research paper by James Gaa entitled *Methodological Foundations of Standardsetting for Corporate Financial Reporting* (Gaa 1988). Gaa argues with some vigour that a single theoretical viewpoint is neither necessary nor sufficient as a basis for standard setting. The method used in his study 'has been variously called rational reconstruction, explication, codification, and a search for reflective equilibrium' (Gaa 1988, Preface: xxi). The debate over whether accounting needs a scientific approach or a jurisprudential approach is not particularly helpful he says; both can be advanced by the use of 'codification', in which the processes of deliberation, justification and explanation all have a role to play in creating a state of reflective equilibrium. He argues that:

> It is perfectly possible for reasonable persons rationally to disagree over which financial reporting standard is best. Unanimity regarding the desirability of a set of financial reporting standards, or 'theory closure' (AAA, 1977), is neither required nor even expected. At the same time, the existence of a logic of standard-setting denies that the inevitable result is 'subjectivity'.
>
> In addition, the affinities of this approach to naturalism mean that it can take account of the obvious relevance of contingent facts about the world (concerning the expected consequences of alternative rules) in choosing standards.
>
> (Gaa 1988: 122)

Gaa distinguishes between those existing branches of accounting theory that he categorizes as 'naturalistic' (i.e. attempts to base standards on scientific, inductive or 'foundationalistic' statements) (p. 94), and those that he describes as 'aggregational' (p. 71). Neither branch on its own is adequate as a basis for justifying standard setting; but both may have some role to play in a broader analytical framework. Gaa's categories are similar to those in SOATATA: his 'naturalistic' group conform to what SOATATA refers to as 'true income' theories; and his 'aggregational' group would include SOATATA's decision-useful and information economic theories.

While Gaa's paper is challenging, indeed exciting, readers need to be warned that it suffers from a lack of clarity at some points. For example, chapter 5 is concerned with aggregational theories – mainly those which seek to use welfare economics as a starting point for analysis. The first six pages (pp. 71–6) seek to make distinctions between collective choice processes based upon 'social preference ordering' and other methods of 'social choice'. These pages are very difficult to follow (even to a reader with some knowledge of welfare economics). This is partly because the material is difficult, but partly also because the writing is unhelpful. The terminology, in particular, becomes formidable at this point. Evidently the term 'collective choice rule' is important (defined on page 74), and it seems clear that such rules can be divided into 'social welfare functions' and 'social decision functions' according to whether or not the rules for social ordering are 'reflexive, complete and transitive'. However, it is left unclear how to define 'consistent social choices' and 'collective choice decisions' and 'choice functions' (all on p. 75), and even less clear for which of these a social welfare function or a social decision rule is either sufficient or necessary.

The point is not trivial. It is clear that Gaa will accept the value of evidence of different forms, and that even the partial aggregation (of preferences or of utilities) can provide useful justification. He accepts, apparently quite happily, that user groups need to be identified (indeed, more than one such group will be recognized under the 'Extended Primacy Model', p. 62). Yet he later maintains that their interests can be fully taken into account by standard setters on the basis of one 'representative user' (p. 160) – how representative? – of what characteristics? – how many user groups will be needed, and what sort of evidence is to be sought of their needs? Given that interpersonal comparisons of utility are accepted as feasible, aided if necessary by 'creative empathy' (p. 89), Gaa needs to elaborate on his model.

It is clear that various types of evidence have a role to play in Gaa's view of methodology. He rejects the plausibility of a single method dominating all others (i.e. the 'modernist' contention); but it is left unclear by Gaa what roles there are to be played, and even if there are ways to address the question. It is interesting to compare Gaa's evaluation of jurisprudence with Stamp's. Gaa accepts the value of Rawls' distinction between 'summary rules' and 'practice rules' (pp. 98–101). He also accepts Rawls' concepts of the 'narrow' and 'wide reflective equilibrium' (p. 126). No doubt Stamp would also have found the concepts useful. Where there could be a difference between them is in the weight each would attach to the processes of deliberation, justification and explanation. Stamp doubts if processes alone are sufficient.

> Although . . . judgement is of considerable and inescapable importance in making accounting decisions, one has to recognise that it is often very difficult to assess its quality. Thus, although it is frequently possible to recognise bad judgement before all its consequences become evident, it is almost invariably impossible to assess in advance the quality of what appears to be good judgement.
>
> (Stamp 1980: 54)

By contrast, Gaa places greater emphasis on the conditions under which the decision was made.

> Debates about whether a specific standard is in the public interest are moot. It is more important to look at the process of deliberation and justification which yielded the standard.
>
> (Gaa 1988: 204)

If one accepts that there are different forms of evidence that contribute, in whatever ways, to justification, deliberation and explanation, this still involves analysis of the logic of any single type of contribution (however 'relativistic' that may be). The use of qualitative characteristics is a case in point.

QUALITATIVE CRITERIA AS A BASIS FOR STANDARD SETTING

The American Accounting Association made an attempt to apply decision usefulness criteria in its 1966 study *A Statement of Basic Accounting Theory* 'ASOBAT' (AAA 1966). ASOBAT used four criteria: relevance, verifiability, freedom from bias, and measurability as the basis for the 'basic theory'. The authors argued that any data which met these criteria should be reported, and any that did not should be excluded. Chatfield (1977: 296) reports that critics of the study objected to the way the criteria were used:

> The four postulates were loosely defined and coordinated, their relation to lower level criteria was not specified, nor did the committee show how to implement these standards in judging

> accounting practice. The scope of the theory was not clearly indicated. And in general it seemed that principles extracted from the accounting environment by a kind of authoritarian intuition, so useful in codifying practice during the preceding two decades, had by the mid-1960s taken the profession as far as they could.
>
> (Chatfield 1977: 296)

Nevertheless, it was one of Stamp's major ambitions to develop an approach of the kind set out in ASOBAT, remedying its weaknesses, and turning it into an operational system. He wanted to identify certain key characteristics of useful reports, next to establish the strength of preferences of a group of experts for particular characteristics, and finally to use the weighted list of characteristics to discriminate among (a limited set of) alternative accounting models. He believed that the theoretical linkages missing from ASOBAT could be supplied, and he attempted to do this in his 1980 Canadian study.

Although studies in the 'decision usefulness' school often list groups of plausible users, the decision models employed are usually left implicit. Even when specified, they are only rudimentary. Little evidence is presented to support the claims that the specified characteristics actually matter to any of the user groups listed. In principle it would be plausible to ask, say, bankers if they found 'relevance' more or less important in using their clients' accounts than 'verifiability', 'freedom from bias', or 'measurability'. It may perhaps be claimed that bankers do not know their own self-interests sufficiently clearly to make a rational choice in the matter, but even so it is feasible to investigate the question further by studying their decision processes. Yet weight has evidently been placed upon unsubstantiated lists of characteristics by several writers of the 'decision usefulness' school over the past fifty years, from Sanders *et al.* (1938, cited in SOATATA (AAA 1977) p. 11) up to the present day (Solomons 1989, chapt. 4).

Stamp saw the difficulties which come from attempting to set out an array of all possible user needs, and then trying to measure the degree of relevance, verifiability, freedom from bias, measurability and so on needed for each purpose. He believed there was a need to short-cut such a laborious and controversial process, and the set of criteria offers a way to evaluate policy alternatives for company financial reports.

> It is essential that the information so provided shall be credible, and this depends in part upon its meeting criteria that are defined

> later in Chapter 7. These criteria have been developed not only to provide a means of assessing the quality of the accounting by a public company to various groups of outsiders; the criteria are also required in order to assist in the development of accounting standards (by providing a means by which the quality of proposed or existent standards can be judged, and a means by which a choice between alternative possible standards on any particular issue can be made).
>
> (Stamp 1980, chapt. 4, para. 15)

The fundamental criteria which Stamp says should be used as a basis for standard setting are, he admits, qualitative in nature, diverse, and overlapping. Moreover, he says, accountants are all too likely to identify the term 'fundamental criteria' with certain technical terms of an instrumental nature. He has much broader characteristics in mind when he discusses the issue in chapter 7:

> The fundamental criteria analysed and explained in this chapter do not include such concepts as the matching concept, or the realisation concept, or the proprietorship or entity concepts. Important though such concepts may be, they are only devices, means to an end. The criteria developed in this chapter provide the yardsticks whereby standard setters, as well as preparers and users of financial statements, can decide whether the end has been achieved, namely whether published financial statements are indeed meeting the needs of users and the objectives of financial reporting explained in Chapter 4.
>
> (Stamp 1980, chapt 7, para. 4)

> In using the criteria developed below, the Accounting Research Committee should follow the practice in future of deciding (and announcing in the published standard) which user groups the standard is intending to cover, and it should then use the following criteria in order to satisfy itself that the standard is in fact compatible with the various users' needs and is optimal in the way in which it steers a path between the often opposing requirements of the various criteria.
>
> (ibid., para. 7)

These criteria are set out in Table 2.1 (drawn from Table 3, p. 55, of the study (Stamp 1980). The repeated occurrence of these terms (or synonyms) in previous pronouncements is remarkable. Whether the conceptual study comes from America, Canada or Britain, from the 1960s, 1970s or 1980s, the same words appear repeatedly as

Table 2.1 Criteria for assessment of standards and of accountability

Criteria that may be in conflict with those in the other column, or require 'trade-offs'		*Criteria that are compatible with those in both of the first two columns*	*Constraints that may apply against any of the criteria in the first three columns*
Relevance (to users' needs)	Objectivity (i.e. not subjective)	Isomorphism	Substance over form
Comparability	Verifiability	Freedom from bias	Materiality
Timeliness	Precision	Rationality	Cost/benefit effectiveness
Clarity		Non-arbitrariness	Flexibility
Completeness, or full disclosure		Uniformity	Data availability
			Consistency
			Conservatism (a very minor constraint)

Source: Stamp 1980

embodying the key features of financial reporting. The output of the process would constitute what Gaa (1988: 183–5) refers to as an 'information quality map' (a form of evidence that he specifically recommends, on page 210).

The study later emphasizes the public role to be played by these qualitative criteria:

> The approach that is advocated is an evolutionary one, and the conceptual basis upon which it is founded has been defined in Chapters 3 to 8 inclusive. The objectives of financial reporting are overriding, the primary consideration being to ensure that the contents of published financial reports meet all the reasonable needs of the legitimate users of such reports. Criteria for doing this have been spelled out in Chapter 7. All these concepts should be regarded as the guiding principles to be used in defining and implementing accounting standards. Finally, in order to win general acceptance for the standards that are developed it is necessary that there be public justification of the standards and a public examination as to how the standards are seen as meeting the criteria and the objectives of good financial reporting.
>
> (Stamp 1980, chapt. 10, para. 10)

In Gaa's terms, Stamp is clearly concerned with the justification and explanation of the standard-setting process.

AN EVALUATION OF STAMP'S SURVEY OF CHARACTERISTICS

Stamp used the term jurisprudence to describe the academic tradition that most closely resembles his approach. There are clearly some links between his work and jurisprudence. For example, he acknowledges the importance of conflict resolution, the value-laden nature of the concepts employed, and the special role of experienced and learned practitioners in judging the way in which stated principles have been and should be applied to particular circumstances.

The distinctive feature of his project was his sustained attempt to refine what carefully selected groups of expert accountants meant by the twenty key words that embodied the essential characteristics of financial reports. But how did his programme of opinion surveys (designed to produce consensus) fit into established patterns of social scientific research?

His survey resembles the study in America by Joyce *et al.* (1982) in which the authors carried out a similar survey among twenty-six former members of the Accounting Principles Board and the Financial Accounting Standards Board. They stated their intention to test the assumption 'that identifying and defining the appropriate attributes (qualitative characteristics) of accounting information will help standard setters in selecting financial accounting methods' (ibid., p. 654). They tested eleven terms, taken from the FASB's *Statement of Financial Accounting Concepts No. 2: Qualitative Characteristics of Accounting Information* (FASB 1980a): relevance, reliability, understandability, representational faithfulness, comparability, neutrality, verifiability, predictive value, timeliness, feedback value, and cost ('ten qualities listed in figure 1 of the Statement plus the cost portion of the benefits-cost passive constraint' (Joyce *et al.* 1982: 660, footnote 4)).

Joyce *et al.* concluded that, by their standards, their test failed.

> Two of the characteristics – verifiability and cost – are operational as defined in the statement, but not the others. In addition, while the qualitative characteristics appear to constitute a comprehensive set of attributes for accounting policy choices, the set is not parsimonious.
>
> (ibid., p. 655)

On the other hand, as this was their first trial of a comparatively new form of test, the results might well be improved. Evidently the FASB itself was interested in trying a similar approach (ibid., p. 670).

At a Clarkson Gordon Foundation Research Symposium in Toronto in 1981 (Basu and Milburn 1982), it was reported that a survey by John H. Waterhouse of standard-setting issues had been carried out in collaboration with the Canadian Institute of Chartered Accountants, and this clearly resembled the approach used in the Study in concept and application.

In terms of research design there is nothing very remarkable about Stamp's questionnaires. The key words are ranked in order of their importance, as well as being given a numerical weighting. Next the ranked criteria are each applied to four alternative measurement bases. In a later development, a comparison is made (by way of a Spearman rank correlation) of the views of three different groups of accountants, one of which comprises the complete membership of the British Accounting Standards Committee. Statistically there is little here that would not figure in a typical university student feedback appraisal questionnaire.

The layout of Stamp's 'Table 3' (Table 2.1) draws attention to the possibility of conflict between criteria, and at two different levels. There may be incompatibility between items in the first two columns ('clarity' and 'verifiability' for instance), or between any in the first two columns and those in the fourth column (such as 'materiality' or 'flexibility'). Stamp recognizes that the list is tentative and possibly unsatisfactory. Indeed, by the time of his 1981 Scottish Institute paper he had decided that 'Completeness, or Full Disclosure' belonged in the second column rather than the first. On the other hand, the twenty items persisted into the later, empirical, developments of the research, in which standard setters, user group representatives and others were to compare and rank them in order of importance.

Another difficult problem is likely to arise from the development of a false consensus, in which respondents interpret the same word in ways quite different from one another (maybe without realizing it). Furthermore, there is no way to prevent respondents from 'playing games' – by anticipating the ways in which the outcomes are going to be used, and giving responses that help their own preferred results. For example, it is plausible that someone who favours historical cost accounting over replacement cost will be inclined to rank 'objectivity' above 'relevance'. Moreover, these preferences may be representative of wider populations of accountants (and others), or they may alternatively represent merely the personal whims of those being surveyed. Stamp points out that the ASC membership represents a 100 per cent sample of that particular set, but this population changes quite frequently; moreover, once the rules of the game are known, representation on the ASC might be manipulated in a manner inconsistent with the welfare of one or more user groups, maybe even major ones.

The major problem with the procedure is not so much its feasibility, despite the lack of success claimed by Joyce *et al*. The difficulty is in the lack of any theoretical connection between the views of a sample of accountants, even senior ones, who are members of a standard-setting board, and any demonstrable set of user needs. The only reason for being interested in relevance, clarity, precision and so on is that these make financial reports more useful to actual users.

The research findings would be supported if it were found that the decisions of actual groups of users were affected by the clarity and precision of the information they received. This means studying user groups. It may well be impossible, both in theory and practice, for standard setters to determine a complete, transitive and persistent weighted list of users before drafting standards; such evidence is directly related to the ostensible purposes of published accounts. With the more open-minded attitudes towards methodology typified by Gaa, there would be hope for new advances in standard setting, and the ways in which evidence is used. Stamp's research programme, while it might well need modification, could still play a valuable role.

CONCLUSION

This chapter has traced the development of accounting theory up to the mid-1970s, when the American Accounting Association was still seeking to find a single dominant paradigm to use in establishing 'theory closure' for a theoretical basis to use in setting standards for corporate financial reporting. It noted three groups of theories before 1977, the 'true income', 'decision usefulness' and 'information economics' schools.

The school of thought to which Edward Stamp belonged was the 'decision usefulness' school, and he was particularly interested in extending the use of abstract qualitative characteristics. Stamp was unusual as a writer in this school because of his commitment to empiricism as a source of relevant evidence. There were other empiricists too, such as Lee and Tweedie (cited in Stamp 1978), but Stamp's own contribution was to develop the idea of using these qualitative characteristics as a means of testing the strength of priorities among standard setters in order to infer preferences for particular policy choices.

Decision usefulness still remains much in favour among those writing on accounting standards and conceptual frameworks. However, the impetus seems to have been lost for the particular line of enquiry that Stamp was pursuing.

Stamp believed it was necessary to establish a single, dominant, theoretical paradigm to use in setting standards. He was understandably a scholar of his generation in this respect. He looked to jurisprudence for guidance, for reasons set out at length above. Since Gaa 1988, it has become less clear that a single paradigm is either necessary or sufficient to justify standard setting. While Stamp might well have disputed Gaa's suggestion that due process is probably the strongest test of good standards, he would no doubt have enjoyed contesting this challenge with the robust energy he displayed in his many other campaigns. Meanwhile, there is little doubt that his research programme would have provided new and interesting evidence for establishing standards.

REFERENCES

AAA (American Accounting Association) (1966) *A Statement of Basic Accounting Theory*, Committee to Prepare a Statement of Basic Accounting Theory, Evanston, Illinois: AAA.

—— (1977) *A Statement on Accounting Theory and Theory Acceptance*, Committee on Concepts and Standards for External Financial Reports Sarasota, Florida: AAA.

AICPA (American Institute of Certified Public Accountants) (1973) *Ojectives of Financial Statements*, report of the Study Group, Chairman, Robert Trueblood, New York: AICPA.

ASSC (Accounting Standards [Steering] Committee) (1975) *The Corporate Report*, London: Accounting Standards [Steering] Committee.

Basu, S. and Milburn, J.A. (1982) *Research to Support Standard Setting in Financial Accounting: a Canadian Perspective*, Toronto: Clarkson Gordon Foundation.

Berle, A.A. and Means, G.C. (1932) *The Modern Corporation and Private Property* New York: Macmillan.

Chatfield, M. (1977) *A History of Accounting Thought* (revised edition) Huntington, New York: Krieger.

FASB (Financial Accounting Standards Board) (1978) *Statement of Financial Accounting Concepts No. 1: Objectives of Financial Reporting by Business Enterprises*, Stamford, Connecticut: FASB.

—— (1980a) *Statement of Financial Accounting Concepts No. 2: Qualitative Characteristics of Accounting Information*, Stamford, Connecticut: FASB.

—— (1980b) *Statement of Financial Accounting Concepts No. 3: Elements of Financial Statements of Business Enterprises*, Stamford, Connecticut: FASB.

—— (1980c) *Statement of Financial Accounting Concepts No. 4: Objectives of Financial Statements of Business Enterprises*, Stamford, Connecticut: FASB.

—— (1984) *Statement of Financial Accounting Concepts No. 5: Recognition and Measurement in Financial Statements of Business Enterprises*, Stamford, Connecticut: FASB.

—— (1985) *Statement of Financial Accounting Concepts No. 6: Elements of Financial Statements*, (A Replacement of FASB Concepts Statement No. 3, incorporating an amendment of FASB Concepts Statement No. 2.) Stamford, Connecticut: FASB.

Gaa, J.C. (1988) *Methodological Foundations of Standardsetting for Corporate Financial Reporting*, Studies in Accounting Research No. 28, Sarasota, Florida: American Accounting Association.

Hicks, J.R. (1966) *Capital and Growth*, Cambridge: Cambridge University Press.

IASC (International Accounting Standards Committee) (1989) *Framework for the Preparation and Presentation of Financial Statements*, London: IASC.

Johnson, L.T. and Storey R.K. (1982) *Recognition in Financial Statements: Underlying Concepts and Practical Conventions*, Stamford, Connecticut: Financial Accounting Standards Board.

Joyce, E.J., Libby, R. and Sunder, S. (1982) 'Using the FASB's qualitative characteristics in accounting policy choices', *Journal of Accounting Research*, 20: 654–75.

Leach, R. (1981) 'The birth of accounting standards', in R. Leach and E. Stamp (eds) *British Accounting Standards: the First Ten Years*, Cambridge: Woodhead-Faulkner.

Littleton, A.C. (1981) *Accounting Evolution to 1900* (originally published in 1933 by American Institute Publishing Company, New York) Alabama: University of Alabama Press.

McMonnies, P. (ed.) (1988) *Making Corporate Reports Valuable*, London: Kogan Page (for Institute of Chartered Accountants of Scotland).

Macve, R. (1981) *A Conceptual Framework for Financial Accounting and Reporting: the Possibilities for an Agreed Structure*, London: Accounting Standards Committee, Consultative Committee of Accounting Bodies.

Paton, W.A. and Littleton, A.C. (1940) *An Introduction to Corporate Accounting Standards*, Monograph No. 3, Columbus, Ohio: American Accounting Association.

Sanders, T.H., Hatfield, H.R. and Moore, U. (1938) *A Statement of Accounting Principles*, New York: American Institute of [Certified Public] Accountants.

Solomons, D. (1989) *Guidelines for Financial Reporting Standards* (a paper prepared for the ICAEW Research Board and addressed to the Consultative Committee of Accountancy Bodies), London: Institute of Chartered Accountants in England and Wales.

Sprouse, R.T. and Moonitz, M. (1962) *A Tentative Set of Broad Accounting Principles for Business Enterprises*, Accounting Research Study No. 3, New York: American Institute of Certified Public Accountants.

Stamp, E. (1978) 'Review of T.A. Lee and D.P. Tweedie *The Private Shareholder and the Corporate Report* (ICAEW 1977)' *Accounting and Business Research*, Autumn: 285–8.

—— (1980) *Corporate Reporting: its Future Evolution*, Toronto: Canadian Institute of Chartered Accountants.

—— (1981a) 'Why can accounting not become a science like physics?', *Abacus* 17 (1): 13–27.

—— (1981b) 'Accounting standards and the conceptual framework: a plan for their evolution', *Accountant's Magazine*, July: 216–22.

—— (1982) 'First steps towards a British conceptual framework', *Accountancy*, March: 123–30.

— (1983) 'Financial accounting standard setting criteria: some comparisons', in M. Bromwich and A.G. Hopwood (eds) *Accounting Standard Setting: an International Perspective*, London: Pitman, pp. 90–7.

—— (1985) 'The politics of professional accounting research: some personal reflections', *Accounting, Organisations and Society*, 10 (1): 111–23.

Sterling, R.R. (1979) *Toward a Science of Accounting*, Houston, Scholars Book Co.

Zeff, S.A. (1972) *Forging Accounting Principles in Five Countries*, Champaign, Illinois: Stipes Publishing Co.

3 Professional judgement and professional standards

Alister K. Mason

> Uniformity for its own sake is inconsistent with professionalism. If all that accountants are expected to do is to follow the prescriptions contained in a book of rules, they are not acting as professionals. They are merely practising a trade like a plumber or an electrician. It is of the essence of a profession that a high degree of judgement is required in its practice. This is as true of doctors and lawyers as it is of accountants. One of the main purposes of standards, in any profession, is to increase the probability that the expert judgement of a series of different practitioners will result in similar decisions on how to deal with a particular accounting problem.
>
> (Stamp 1980: 62)

This brief excerpt from a research study Eddie Stamp wrote for The Canadian Institute of Chartered Accountants (CICA) in 1980 encapsulates some of his opinions about two matters of fundamental importance to the accounting profession: judgement and standards.

The present writer's views were shaped by close contact with Stamp while his PhD student in Lancaster in the mid-1970s, and in the course of many subsequent discussions – in person and by correspondence – of papers and studies Stamp was working on. Some of these views no doubt influenced the recent research study *Professional Judgment in Financial Reporting* which the CICA commissioned from Professor Michael Gibbins, the late Howard Lyons and the present writer (Gibbins and Mason 1988); its focus is on the judgements on accounting issues which are made by preparers and auditors of financial statements.[1] This chapter discusses certain key recommendations made in that study (referred to henceforth as the 'PJFR study').

ACCOUNTING JUDGEMENTS

In preparing all but the very simplest set of financial statements, several judgements must be made. Many arise from the use of the accrual basis of accounting: if the only transactions recorded were those reflecting the receipt or payment of cash, there would be no need, for example, to make judgements about the allowance to provide for doubtful accounts receivable, or about the amount to accrue in respect of legal services rendered but not yet billed.

Other judgements arise from the requirement to prepare periodic financial statements (rather than just one financial statement at the end of the enterprise's life). This gives rise to allocations, and each allocation requires one or more judgements.

Further judgements are made with regard to financial statement presentation. Should a liability be offset against a related asset? Should an unusual expense be classified as an 'extraordinary item'? What is the best way of disclosing a subsequent event – if indeed it should be disclosed at all?

Each of these judgements may be poor: it may reflect the personal preference or selfish interests of the statement preparer, or of the owner of the enterprise; it may ignore legal requirements, relevant standards and current practices; or it may even be aimed at misleading the statement users. Moving to the other end of the spectrum, each judgement may be 'professional', as described in the next section.

Regardless of the quality of judgements, a very large number are needed under our present accounting model. Standards reduce the number of judgements to be made, and detailed standards may necessitate fewer judgements than those worded more broadly, but even the most detailed standards would require judgement as to their applicability to a certain transaction. (The PJFR study sets out six reasons why standards would not work without judgement; these are summarized under 'Relationship between judgement and standards' later in this chapter, p. 35.)

WHAT IS 'PROFESSIONAL JUDGEMENT'?

In the PJFR study, we identified seven aspects of professional judgement in chapter 1 (Gibbins and Mason 1988: 5); we used these in formulating a working definition. Eleven additional points about its nature which emerged in the following chapters were listed in chapter 12, where a summary was made of circumstances which are likely to exist and the attributes of professionalism which should be present.[2]

We then arrived at the following definition:

> The process of reaching a decision on a financial reporting issue can be described as 'professional judgment' when it is analytical, based on experience and knowledge (including knowledge of one's own limitations and of relevant standards), objective, prudent and carried out with integrity and recognition of responsibility to those affected by its consequences. Such professional judgment is likely to be most valuable in complex, ill-defined or dynamic situations, especially where standards are incomplete, and should normally involve consultation with other knowledgeable people, identification of potential consequences and documentation of the analytical processes leading to the decision.
>
> (Gibbins and Mason 1988: 132–3)

For clarity, three points about this definition of professional judgement should be stressed:

1 There must be a meaningful choice. Without this, the judgement decision will be trivial.
2 'Professional judgement' describes the quality of the judgement, rather than who makes it. Thus, professional judgements on financial reporting matters may be made by persons who are not professionally qualified accountants – provided they have appropriate knowledge and experience, and the required personal characteristics.
3 If one does not have expertise in an area, one cannot make professional judgements concerning it. For example, an accountant might have views about the appropriate strength and size of the steel girders to be used in building a bridge, but, without appropriate experience and knowledge (including knowledge of relevant standards), he would not be qualified to express a professional judgement regarding them. Similarly, a couple approaching retirement might have to make decisions about where to invest their capital: while they may have clear ideas about the security and return they are seeking, they may need advice about investment opportunities. An experienced investment counsellor may assist them in making professional judgements on this matter.

With regard to this last point, it is interesting to recall Stamp's comments on the Sandilands Report – the report issued in 1975 by the UK Government-appointed committee to study inflation accounting. In a review article, he wrote:

> What really bothers me is the fact that proposals for a half-thought-out system of current value accounting are being foisted upon the accounting profession by a committee composed largely of amateurs. If you are as proud of your membership in our profession as I am then I hope you will do all you can to ensure that this never happens again. The Government is presently in the throes of a conflict with the medical profession, but the conflict is over pay and administrative arrangements, not over the determination and enforcement of the standards and principles of medical and surgical practice. That remains the responsibility of the medical profession . . .
>
> Accounting standards are complex technical matters, and it is because they are complex technical matters that the accounting profession exists. They cannot be left to amateurs, enthusiastic or otherwise. If the contractors who constructed a fine hotel had entrusted the installation of its electrical system to a gang of twelve people composed of three electricians, six company directors, an economist, a lady, and the ex-Secretary General of the TUC, it would not surprise me if the management received a shock when they turned the lights on.
>
> (Stamp 1975: 411)

Stamp abhored the idea of the government setting accounting standards. He frequently lauded the Canadian situation, where corporations and securities Acts have, since the mid-1970s, specified that the accounting standards to be used in reporting under the acts are those established by the CICA.[3] He recognized that a change to such a position would give rise to a constitutional problem: it 'would give a professional committee the right to determine environmental constraints beyond which non-members of the profession in the form of management are now free to move (subject to actions against them in the courts)' (Stamp 1979a: 108), but he noted that many non-professionals, e.g. air traffic controllers, are given powers that can mean the difference between life and death to members of the public who enter their jurisdiction.

ENVIRONMENT IN WHICH PROFESSIONAL JUDGEMENTS ARE MADE

The PJFR study sets out three findings with regard to the environment within which professional judgements are made in financial reporting (Gibbins and Mason 1988: 147–8):

1 There may be a lack of respect for professional judgement and accounting standards: non-accountants may not think it important to adhere to standards, or they may view professional judgement as a convenient justification for departing from the spirit or letter of the standards. The financial vice-president or auditor of a company may therefore have difficulty in explaining to the non-accountant president why the accounting policy which gives the most favourable results should not be followed.
2 A closely-related point is the support the financial vice-president and the auditor will receive from their senior colleagues. Will the president recognize that the financial vice-president has a professional and/or (in some jurisdictions) legal responsibility to exercise professional judgement? Will the senior partner of the accounting firm support the audit partner's professional judgement decisions, even at the risk of losing an important client?
3 Colleagues can provide advice and help. No-one knows everything, and discussion with a colleague can help in two ways:
   (a) The colleague may have more knowledge about the particular area, or may have had greater experience in reasoning from fundamental accounting principles.
   (b) The process of explaining the facts and circumstances to the colleague may help to clarify the issues.

These findings led to the following four recommendations in the PJFR study, based on the understanding that truly professional judgements are easier to make, and are doubtless more often made, in a supportive environment:

> The necessity for professional judgment in financial reporting and the need for a supportive environment for it should be officially recognized by professional accounting bodies in their activities, particularly in submissions to and meetings with regulators, legislators, industry groups, educators and other such interested parties.
>
> Public accounting firms, business and government organizations and other employers of people involved in financial reporting should ensure that a supportive environment is provided for professional judgment in financial reporting.
>
> Audit committees should enquire, at least annually, of their companies' senior officers, and of their auditors, whether they have been put under any duress or otherwise had their capacity to exercise judgment in a professional manner constrained.

> Individual professionals should themselves impress upon their superiors and colleagues the necessity for professional judgment in financial reporting and the need for a supportive environment for it.
>
> (Gibbins and Mason 1988: 148–9)

A further recommendation addressed the need for consultation:

> The person exercising professional judgment should consult with others whenever a better decision, or a better judgment process, may be expected to result. Consultation should ordinarily happen after the person responsible for the judgment has obtained the information and analyzed the alternatives, but before any final conclusion has been reached or any implementation has begun.
>
> (Gibbins and Mason 1988: 154)

This recommendation should *not* be interpreted to mean that consultation is considered necessary for virtually every judgement. Where a judgement to be made is, in substance, very similar to one made previously and nothing has happened since then which would indicate the earlier judgement to have been inappropriate, consultation may not be needed. Experienced preparers and auditors should therefore not have to consult as often as those who have made fewer judgements, but some of the really tough judgements will always benefit from consultation – perhaps with more than one person. (A Canadian example would be one of the rare business combinations which appears to meet the criterion in Canadian standards for using pooling-of-interests accounting, i.e. a dominant acquirer cannot be identified.)

RELATIONSHIP BETWEEN JUDGEMENT AND STANDARDS

The PJFR study has a good deal to say about the relationship between professional judgement and professional standards. For example:

> The relationship between professional judgment and professional standards is important but not straightforward. It is important because both judgment and standards are central to professionalism and therefore both involve expertise, professional integrity and other such elements. Standards are not written for neophytes: understanding and applying them require extended study and experience. . . . The relationship is not straightforward because, while it might be true that professional judgment is particularly

> needed when standards are absent, standards make specific demands on judgment at the same time as they provide support for judgment.
>
> (Gibbins and Mason 1988: 29)

The study identifies seven reasons for having standards, three of which pertain to the accounting profession alone, and four apply to other professions too (Gibbins and Mason 1988: 30–1).

The PJFR study then proceeds to give reasons why accounting standards would not work without the exercise of judgement. These may be summarized as follows (Gibbins and Mason 1988: 31–2):

1 Judgement is needed in relating relevant standards to the particular circumstances; it would be impracticable for standards to cover every possible circumstance or type of enterprise.
2 Standard setters use words like 'significant' or 'predominantly' in conveying their own judgements.
3 Judgements have to be made about materiality.
4 Some standards cannot be implemented without judgement, e.g. those requiring estimates or allocations.
5 Because transactions can be structured to fit – or avoid – the form of a standard, judgement must be exercised to ensure that it conforms to the standard's substance.
6 Changes in the accounting environment may result in standards which, while having worked well at one point, are no longer as effective; judgement will be needed until the standard can be changed.

Ways in which standards may increase the need for professional judgement are also considered in the study (Gibbins and Mason 1988: 33). One of these is where financial statements have to comply with more than one set of standards, and judgement would have to be exercised in selecting and applying accounting policies, to keep conflicts to a minimum. An example would be a Canadian company whose shares are listed on the New York Stock Exchange, and thus has to provide a reconciliation from the Canadian net income figure to that computed under US generally accepted accounting principles (GAAP). Probable differences would be in such areas as development expenses, gains on foreign currency translation, joint ventures, accounting changes, and capitalization of interest costs. (A likely future difference will be income taxes, unless the proposed Canadian re-examination of its standard leads to a change from the deferral to the liability method of income tax allocation – a change the FASB made in its Statements Nos 96 and 105.)

This example reminds us anew of the need for international standardization. Stamp's insightful paper, 'Uniformity in international accounting standards – a myth or a possibility?', delivered at the Jerusalem World Congress on Accounting in 1971 (Stamp, 1971), was one of the earlier writings in this area. Later, when his prime international standardization interests moved from accounting to auditing, the book he wrote in 1978 with Professor Maurice Moonitz, *International Auditing Standards* (Stamp and Moonitz, 1978), was – and still is – the only book on this subject.

He was particularly critical of the major UK company Imperial Chemical Industries (ICI), whose securities are traded in the United States:

> the Accounting Standards Committee has become a paper tiger, and this is well illustrated by the behaviour of ICI in its 1975 accounts.
>
> This major British company disagreed with the accounting standard requiring benefits from government grants to be amortized, and so they credited the full amount of the benefit (which was only £11m) to income in the year in which it was obtained. Despite the relatively tiny sum involved they were willing to flout the standard and have their auditors qualify their report.
>
> However, it was a different matter when ICI filed its 20-K document with the Securities and Exchange Commission (SEC) in the United States. The SEC refuses to accept filings containing auditors' qualifications of this kind, so in its SEC filing ICI conformed to the requirements of the accounting standard, and thereby avoided the auditors' qualification.
>
> It is indeed a sad commentary on the authority of the Accounting Standards Committee when we find a British company flouting British standards in Britain in the face of a qualification from British auditors, while at the same time acquiescing in the imposition of the same British standards in the United States because an American government agency requires that the British standard shall be used in that country in reporting to American investors.
>
> (Stamp 1977: 19)

Elsewhere, in writing about the need for improved disclosure in the UK, he said:

> Even today in the United Kingdom very few companies disclose their cost of sales or gross margin figures. Even ICI does this only in the 20-K return that it files with the SEC; its annual report issued to British shareholders provides no such information.
>
> (Stamp 1979b: 122)

EXPECTATIONS ABOUT JUDGEMENT IN APPLYING STANDARDS

The PJFR study notes that Canadian and UK accounting standards explicitly anticipate professional judgement being used in applying accounting standards. The 'Introduction to accounting recommendations' in the *CICA Handbook* (in which Canadian accounting and auditing standards are set out) includes the following paragraph (p. 9, revised December 1987):

> In issuing Recommendations, the Accounting Standards Committee recognizes that no rule of general application can be phrased to suit all circumstances or combination of circumstances that may arise, nor is there any substitute for the exercise of professional judgment in the determination of what constitutes fair presentation or good practice in a particular case.

The six accounting bodies in the UK which jointly issue Statements of Standard Accounting Practice (SSAPs) have published an 'Explanatory foreword' which applies to each standard. Paragraph 5 from this Foreword refers to 'informed judgement':

> In applying accounting standards, it will be important to have regard to the spirit of and reasoning behind them. They are not intended to be a comprehensive code of rigid rules. They do not supersede the exercise of an informed judgement in determining what constitutes a true and fair view in each circumstance. It would be impracticable to establish a code sufficiently elaborate to cater for all business situations and innovations and for every exceptional or marginal case. A justifiable reason may therefore exist why an accounting standard may not be applicable in a given situation, namely when application would conflict with the giving of a true and fair view. In such cases, modified or alternative treatments will require to be adopted.
>
> (*Members Handbook* 1986: section 2–100, p. 1)

The *CICA Handbook* neither defines nor explains what is meant by 'professional judgement'. Similarly, the UK 'Explanatory foreword' to SSAPs provides no guidance regarding 'informed judgement'.

Somewhat surprisingly, there is no such overriding proviso about the use of judgement in US accounting standards. Some may assume that, because US standards tend to be very detailed, the need for judgement is greatly reduced, but analyses conducted for the PJFR study indicated that a surprising number of judgements is required.[4] The Commission established by the AICPA to study auditors' responsibilities – known as the Cohen Commission, after its Chairman – reached a similar conclusion:

> Judgment pervades accounting and auditing. It is exercised in considering whether the substance of transactions differs from their form, in resolving questions of materiality and adequacy of disclosure, in deciding whether an estimate can be made of the effects of future events on current financial statements, and in allocating receipts and expenditures over time and among activities.
>
> (Commission on Auditors' Responsibilities 1978: 16)

Also, a comment by the Chief Accountant of the Enforcement Division of the Securities and Exchange Commission is pertinent to the judgement to be exercised by auditors:

> The essence of professionalism in accounting is the ability to exercise an independent judgment, even when that judgment runs counter to the client's wishes, and especially where the judgment cannot be supported by a clear statement in the literature.
>
> (Sack 1987:2)

US auditors are also governed by the requirements of the AICPA's Statement on Auditing Standards No. 5, 'The Meaning of "Present Fairly in Conformity With Generally Accepted Accounting Principles" in the Independent Auditor's Report', paragraph 4 of which requires that the auditor base his opinion as to fair presentation in conformity with GAAP on his judgement as to whether:

(a) the accounting principles selected and applied have general acceptance;
(b) the accounting principles are appropriate in the circumstances;
(c) the financial statements, including the related notes, are informative of matters that may affect their use, understanding, and interpretation;
(d) the information presented in the financial statements is classified and summarized in a reasonable manner, that is, neither too detailed nor too condensed; and
(e) the financial statements reflect the underlying events and transactions in a manner that presents the financial position, results of operations, and changes in financial position stated within a range of acceptable limits, that is, limits that are reasonable and practicable to attain in financial statements.

The PJFR study notes that, while there is no corresponding explicit requirement in US GAAP for preparers of financial statements to exercise judgement on these matters, it may be inferred that all are implicit.

Three recommendations about accounting standards made in the PJFR study are now considered briefly:

1 The first recommendation deals with the need to clarify what is meant by professional judgement:

> 'Professional judgment' should be defined in financial reporting standards, so as to be applicable to all measurement, presentation and disclosure standards.
>
> (Gibbins and Mason 1988: 139)

Such a definition would serve to emphasize the importance of professional judgement in applying standards.

2 The second recommendation is aimed at being helpful in determining the spirit of a standard, rather than just its literal meaning, and in deciding on the appropriateness of applying it to a new form of transaction:

> The background wording to each financial reporting standard should explain (a) the main objectives of the standard, and (b) the most common types of transaction to which it applies, if this is not self-evident.
>
> (Gibbins and Mason 1988: 140)

3 The third recommendation is intended to inform (or remind) financial statement users that, despite the apparent precision of the amounts, professional judgements have been made in preparing them:

> Standards requiring the presentation of a summary of significant accounting policies should require that reference be made in the summary to the fact that professional judgments have been made by management in preparing the financial statements.
>
> (Gibbins and Mason 1988: 145)

A point of interest here is that a Canadian study on the public's expectations of audits (published while the PJFR study was in press) reported on the findings of a public opinion survey it commissioned: one of these was that 45 per cent of the public hold the view that, because there are accounting standards, little judgement is required in the preparation and presentation of financial statements (Macdonald Commission Report 1988: 14).

There may be similar perceptions in the United States. In July 1988 the Securities and Exchange Commission issued for comment proposed rules requiring registrants to provide a report of management's responsibilities for financial statements and internal control. Under the proposal there would be a description or statement of management's responsibilities for the preparation of the financial statements, including the determination of the estimates and judgements used in them (Securities and Exchange Commission 1988: 7). Such a reference to management's judgements might help to educate statement users about how the application of accounting standards depends on the exercise of judgement.

THE PUBLIC INTEREST

This chapter started with a quote from Eddie Stamp's writings. Let it close with one too: one about the public interest, yet another matter about which he thought a great deal. This quote, while made with regard to British standards (SSAPs), applies to all accounting standards – and to judgement:

> I was asked recently what I thought was the most important accounting standard. My answer is not to be found in any SSAP, but it ought nevertheless to be engraved over the door of every senior partner in the profession: 'The public interest comes first'.
>
> Placing the public interest above self interest is the hallmark of a profession.
>
> (Stamp 1983)

NOTES

1 The PJFR study includes thirty-two recommendations, about the nature of professional judgement, about standards, and for those exercising professional judgement. These recommendations are based on analyses of prior judgement research and of the judgements required by Canadian, US, UK, and international accounting standards; also, responses by experienced preparers and auditors of financial statements provided numerous insights into the judgement process, as did a review of some complex professional judgement problems.

Subjects specifically excluded from the PJFR study's terms of reference were the auditor's judgements regarding the evaluation of internal control and the nature, extent, and timing of audit tests. (A CICA research study, *Extent of Audit Testing*, was published in 1980.) Judgements regarding materiality were not covered either; another CICA study, *Materiality – the Concept and its Application to Auditing*, by D. A. Leslie, was published in 1985.

2 The following is a summary of circumstances which are likely to exist and the attributes of professionalism which should be present:

(i) Circumstances likely to exist:
- complex, ill-defined, volatile, continuing and/or evolving issues;
- important but unclear choices;
- uncertain or risky consequences;
- sensitivity to precedents;
- practicalities such as time pressure, data limitations and cost/benefit trade-offs;
- presence (or absence) of relevant standards;
- issues flowing from the nature of accrual accounting and other aspects of modern financial reporting;
- several people involved;
- participants and interested parties differing substantially in ability, knowledge, experience and motivation (interests may well conflict);
- a sequence of events taking some time to conclude.

(ii) Attributes of professionalism which should be present:
- objectivity and balanced analysis (not just personal preference), in awareness of alternatives; and using the higher cognitive skills required to conduct analysis and design solutions in complex settings;
- integrity, prudence and acceptance of responsibility to those affected by the results;
- relevant knowledge and experience (applied with due care), including application and interpretation of any relevant standards to make the necessary estimates, allocations and disclosures;
- awareness of the threats to judgment quality that may arise from human perceptual and judgment limitations and such environmental forces as time pressure and stress;
- consultation, identification of potential consequences, documentation of the process and justification of the selected choice.

(Gibbins and Mason 1988: 131–2)

3 Stamp set out his views on this matter most completely in 'Accounting and auditing standards: present and future from an international perspective' (Stamp 1979a: 105–10). He noted then that he first advocated a position akin to the Canadian one in 1966.

4 See Gibbins and Mason (1988: 56), and compare the findings with those for similar analyses conducted in respect of Canadian, UK, and International standards set out on pages 44, 61 and 64, respectively, of that study.

REFERENCES

AICPA (American Institute of Certified Public Accountants) (1975) *Statement on Auditing Standards No. 5*, 'The Meaning of "Present Fairly in Conformity with Generally Accepted Accounting Principles" in the Independent Auditor's Report' New York: AICPA.

CICA Handbook (1987) 'Introduction to accounting recommendations'

Toronto, Canadian Institute of Chartered Accountants, pp. 9–10.

Commission on Auditors' Responsibilities (1978) *Report, Conclusions and Recommendations* New York: AICPA.

Gibbins, M. and Mason, A.K. (1988) *Professional Judgment in Financial Reporting*, Toronto: Canadian Institute of Chartered Accountants.

Leslie, D.A. (1985) *Materiality – the Concept and its Application to Auditing*, Toronto: Canadian Institute of Chartered Accountants.

Macdonald Commission Report (1988) *Report of the Commission to Study the Public's Expectations of Audits*, Toronto: Canadian Institute of Chartered Accountants.

Member's Handbook (1986) 'Explanatory foreword to statements of standard accounting practice' London, Institute of Chartered Accountants in England and Wales, pp. 1–2.

Sack, R.J. (1987) 'The anatomy of a fraud', *The Auditor's Report* (newsletter of the Auditing Section of the American Accounting Association) Winter: 1–4.

Securities and Exchange Commission, Proposed Rules 'Report of Management's Responsibilities', 14 July, 1988.

Stamp, E. (1971) 'Uniformity in international accounting standards – a myth or a possibility?', *Proceedings of the Jerusalem World Conference on Accountancy*. (Reprinted in *Canadian Chartered Accountant*, December 1971: 459–62, and (in part) in *Journal of Accountancy*, April 1972: 64–7).

—— (1975) 'Sandilands: some fundamental flaws', *Accountant's Magazine*, December: 408–11.

—— (1976) 'Sandilands and The Corporate Report: Where now?', paper delivered to the City of London Polytechnic, 23 January. (Reprinted in Stamp, E. (1984) *Selected Papers on Accounting, Auditing and Professional Problems*, New York: Garland.

—— (1977) 'Accounting standards: can the profession stir itself before the state steps in?', *The Times* 5 July, p. 19.

—— (1979a) 'Accounting and auditing standards: present and future from an international viewpoint', Australian Society of Accountants Endowed Lecture, University of Sydney, 17 September.

—— (1979b) 'International standards to serve the public interest', in W.J. Brennan (ed.), *The Internationalization of the Accountancy Profession*, Toronto: Canadian Institute of Chartered Accountants, pp. 116–25.

—— (1980) *Corporate Reporting: its Future Evolution*, Toronto: Canadian Institute of Chartered Accountants.

—— (1983) 'Only one accounting standard really counts', *Accountancy Age*, 24 February.

Stamp, E. and Moonitz, M. (1978) *International Auditing Standards*, Englewood Cliffs, New Jersey: Prentice-Hall.

4 On the idea of a conceptual framework for financial reporting

Michael K. Power

INTRODUCTION

This chapter analyses the concept of a conceptual framework (CF) for financial reporting. Its concerns emerge from a perception that, while massive financial resources have been expended by the Financial Accounting Standards Board (FASB) in developing a CF, little attention has been given to the *idea* of such a CF. While much has been written on the merits of the CF programme by professionals and academics alike, hardly anything has been said about what kind of thing a CF could be. Indeed little attention has been given to the role and status of what might be called 'conceptual considerations' in financial reporting. This relative neglect matters considerably.

One of the more acceptable legacies of the positivist tradition in philosophy is the idea that some deep form of agreement is a necessary precondition for rational and meaningful dispute. Thus if I say that there are two apples on the table and you say that there are none then, for this exchange to be meaningful, we must agree upon the concept of 'apple' and upon the conditions under which we would accept or reject its existence. Perhaps we are looking at different tables or perhaps they are peaches and I mistook them for apples. This would emerge from continued discussion. If it did not, then it is not clear that the dispute could be continued except by becoming explicitly philosophical. (I would enquire as to what could count as an apple for you.) If the case of apples is relatively straightforward, the form of agreement for rational debate about whether 'democracy' is a good thing is perhaps more contentious. Such moral and political concepts may be 'essentially contestable' and perhaps we could cripple substantive disputes of this nature with an unrealizable ideal of 'conceptual hygiene'. Nevertheless (although a defence of this claim is beyond the scope of this essay) it can be said that if we take ourselves seriously as engaged in rational dispute about anything, rather than engaged in a purely strategic exchange, then a commitment to conceptual agreement is at least a procedural ideal.[1]

If the discourse that has crystallized around the CF project (for example, see Macve 1981) is to be meaningful then there must be some general understanding about the concept or idea of such a CF. One party may assert that we need a CF for accounting and another may say we do not. But if this exchange means anything, they need to agree upon what a CF is. In other words we need a *meta-theory* of a CF for accounting. Elsewhere in this volume (p. 156) Colin Lyas claims that 'no discipline worth bothering about can seek to evade . . . conceptual enquiries'. In the context of the CF, this is very much a demand for a 'meta-theory' or what Kantian philosophers might call an examination of the conditions of possibility of a CF for accounting.

One of the recurrent concerns about FASB's CF project has been its operational credibility, i.e. whether it actually guides and helps the standard setting process. In this chapter it is suggested that the discussion of this issue has been hindered by an absence of meta-theoretical considerations and, particularly, the absence of a critical examination of the very idea of a CF being 'operational'. In the next section certain criticisms of FASB, particularly those raised by Dopuch and Sunder (1980), are themselves criticized with a view to exposing their implicit meta-theoretical commitments. In the third section the methodological structure of John Rawls' *A Theory of Justice* (1973) is appropriated and its possibilities for enhancing our understanding of the idea of a CF for financial reporting are traced in the fourth section. In the section 'Accounting and the scientific image' it is suggested that a form of 'scientism' at all levels of thinking about accounting has prevented a clearer understanding of the nature of a CF. In turning repeatedly to the model of the natural sciences accounting theorists may well be looking in the wrong place.

THE OPERATIONAL IDEAL

The development of a CF which could 'prescribe the nature, function and limits of financial accounting and financial statements' is forcefully criticized by Dopuch and Sunder (1980). They argue that FASB's claim that a CF would make the standard setting process 'easier' is simply unwarranted. Drawing upon a number of accounting policy issues, Dopuch and Sunder argue that the FASB definitions of assets and liabilities are too broad to aid decision making in these areas. Indeed, to the extent that these definitions are capable of supporting different views they are unlikely to be useful as a guide to standard setters.

The perceived operational shortcomings of the FASB CF prompt Dopuch and Sunder to consider the problems of establishing an agreed set of objectives for financial reporting. The heterogeneity of user interests presents difficulties enough, but they extend the terms of their critique to the claim that the 'extraordinary emphasis . . . on user primacy . . . ignores the behavioral position of the sender'. They thereby imply that the very coherence of the CF project is shattered by the recognition that financial accounting operates within a multi-person setting. Definitions will not resolve controversies since they cannot 'bear the burden of economic advantage between various interest groups'. So what does the CF represent? Dopuch and Sunder suggest it may be of utility to the profession by underwriting its external legitimacy but, in the context of shaping accounting policy, it is the power of various interested parties that will prevail.

The general structure of Dopuch and Sunder's critique could be represented by the following claims:

1 The FASB conceptual framework is not operational;
2 Because of this there must be some other explanation for its durability, for example its function as a legitimacy strategy;
3 From (1) and (2) it may be argued (although it does not necessarily follow) that financial accounting policy is essentially a question of competing interest groups. Therefore a CF is fundamentally misguided.

This argument structure (which may be slightly unfair to Dopuch and Sunder) is an example of what I shall call a 'reductive' critique of FASB's CF. Conceptual aspirations are reduced to, and reinterpreted as, interests in economic consequences (Zeff 1978).

Within the philosophy of science the term 'reduction' is used in the context of considering theories whose vocabularies and predictive power can be entirely subsumed without explanatory loss under another general theory. The former is thereby 'reducible' to the latter.[2] In general the reductivist strategy is to argue that one particular form of disclosure can be subsumed or reduced to another. The 'objects' of the latter are ontologically more primitive than the former which can be regarded as derived epiphenomena of them. Dopuch and Sunder's critique is reductivist in an analogous sense because their explanation of accounting policy is to be found at the level of economic and political analysis and not at the level of conceptual considerations. Because of this explanatory commitment (i.e. (3) above) anything like a CF is, on their own terms, both a theoretical and a policy mistake.

Elsewhere, 'political' analyses of the accounting standard-setting process have also been offered. For example Peasnell (1982) draws attention to the particular historical settings within which CF type projects have emerged. He argues that they have been essentially misguided since standard setting is appropriately conceived as a bargaining process, i.e. a dialogical process in which interests are formed and expressed, and not a monological appeal to some preordained set of concepts or rules. CFs emerge at times of 'legitimation crisis' (Habermas 1976) for the profession and this, it seems, undermines their authority. Hines (1989, 1991) has also argued that it is 'claims to knowledge' rather than knowledge itself which play a critical role in the maintenance of professional power. Or, as Hopwood (1988) argues, CFs represent a 'concern with the aspirations to knowledge rather than its technical specifics'.

The intention of the present argument is not to take issue directly with these and other analyses of the standard-setting process. Rather, it is to address the presuppositions of these critiques themselves. For example, an argument that situates a particular CF project within a context of crisis for the professional body concerned is one type of claim. However it does not follow from this that such a CF is thereby a mere contingent product of the context, nor that any form of conceptual thinking is necessarily to be understood in this way.

If we return to the structure of Dopuch and Sunder's critique outlined above, the argument of this chapter is not that the socio-political claims under (3) are false but that they have been insufficiently critical of the question posed in (1), i.e. 'is the FASB CF operational?'. In other words, a particular model of what it would be like for a CF to be operational has been implicitly assumed without any meta-theoretical enquiry into its validity. The particular model is so demanding that no CF could possibly be unequivocably operational in these terms. Thus, where the operational deficiency of the CF is perceived as its deepest flaw we could equally ask whether the idea of being operational in the required sense is appropriate. In short we could ask whether the *idea* of a CF for financial reporting is clear.

Dopuch and Sunder claim that the FASB CF is supposed to guide the selection of appropriate principles and rules of measurement and recognition. This is quite fair at one level since it is one of FASB's own claimed benefits for a CF. Yet the idea of such guidance is obscure. For Dopuch and Sunder the definition of liabilities is so general that it is impossible to 'predict' a position on deferred tax. It would seem to them that the 'guidance' of any CF must be to provide logically necessary and sufficient conditions for standard setting. In addition they argue that the CF supports *opposing* views in accounting for oil and gas exploration costs and cannot address the issue of a valuation basis for assets and liabilities. Thus, where we seem to need a CF most, in disputed contexts, it fails to deliver.

The whole question as to what it is reasonable to demand of a CF remains submerged in Dopuch and Sunder's text. They allude to critics of the Trueblood Report (AICPA 1973) such as Bedford (1974) who talks of the 'difficult task of logically deriving standards' and criticisms by Miller (1974) that the accept/reject criteria implicit in a CF are insufficiently precise. These texts in themselves demonstrate the underlying ideal for a CF. To borrow from the philosophical literature, it would seem that a CF is either 'deductive or defective'. In other words, to be operational in the required sense is to provide a set of axioms from which the standard setters can logically derive standards without appeal to processes of debate.

It is the contention of this chapter that the CF debate suffers from a significant meta-theoretical error about the role of concepts in financial accounting. CFs may emerge from specific concerns but are not necessarily context specific. For example, we are often forced to reflect upon the nature of our moral and political beliefs at a time of crisis. Such reflections are occasioned by specific circumstances but are not necessarily a mere residual effect of them. It may also be too conspiratorial to suggest that conceptual discourse in financial accounting is reducible to an external image consolidation strategy (as Watts and Zimmerman (1979) seem to do).

The suggested parallels with moral and political concept formation are worth pursuing. We might ask in what way a rule such as 'do not break promises' is operationalized. In practice it may be difficult to sustain for a number of reasons. First, there may be exceptions by which means one would wish to modify the imperative. Second, and crucially, one may simply break the rule. Not being 'operational' in this latter sense is not a defect of moral concepts themselves but is a product of the influence of other factors such as sanctions and personal interests. Without becoming embroiled in meta-ethical theory it is reasonable to suggest that a purely deductive model of the 'operational guidance' capability of moral concepts would be a mistake. Not only are moral agents somehow free (although this may be contested) but there remains the problem of deciding when an instance appropriately falls under the concept, since both the concept and our descriptions of the instance are to some extent fluid. There is, on such a view, a dynamic relation between moral concepts and actions which is inappropriately modelled as a unidirectional deductive relation. The failure of the CF in financial reporting to satisfy such a demanding ideal of operational guidance has aided 'reductive' accounts of its appearance.

In what follows we shall build upon the parallels between moral and political thinking and the conceptual dimension of financial accounting by developing the methodological structure of John Rawls' (1973) *A Theory of Justice*. (This methodological structure is our primary focus. Elsewhere Williams (1987) has drawn upon Rawls' work in a different way to challenge the principles of entitlement to financial information.) In many ways Rawls can be regarded as attempting to develop a CF for the moral and political domain yet, unlike FASB and its critics, with a realization of the need for a meta-theoretical clarification of the status of the CF. Borrowing from Rawls' work is not a piece of gratuitous theory raiding but can directly illuminate the idea of a conceptual framework for accounting. In addition it may suggest that Edward Stamp came close to a reasonable meta-theoretical idea of such a CF.

RAWLS AND THE MODEL OF REFLECTIVE EQUILIBRIUM

The use of the indefinite article in the title of Rawls' famous work is important. It signals a project which is not intended to offer an absolute, timeless account of justice but to construct *one* on the basis of our deepest moral convictions. Of course, the 'we' in question is ethnocentrically relative to European culture and our convictions shift over time. But Rawls is relatively uninterested in the classical philosophical preoccupation with universality as compared with the more modest task of rigorously thinking through the prevailing liberal ideas of a particular context.

A Theory of Justice can be regarded as an attempt to provide a determinate rational basis for the analysis and criticism of social arrangements which is not merely a rationalization of those institutions themselves (Rawls 1973: 21). Like many contractarian theorists before him, Rawls attempts to 'ground' principles of justice by interpreting them as the outcome of a social choice by agents. One of the meta-theoretical elements of this programme is the notion of 'reflective equilibrium'. Rawls confronts the problem of justifying a model of social choice under ideal hypothetical conditions and the general problem for such a model is clear. If the 'subjects' making the choice are themselves theoretical constructs, abstracted from the empirical heterogeneity of individual tastes, then a consensually grounded set of principles may emerge from the choice context but it is not clear what relation this bears to actual preferences. But when the subjects are conceived less abstractly, and as possessing a multiplicity of interests, then consensus is unlikely.

The concept of 'reflective equilibrium' is intended to address this dilemma. Its central idea is that our heterogeneous moral intuitions and preferences have no necessary epistemological priority over each other in evolving a theory of justice. They are themselves constructed. Thus the theoretical issue for Rawls' project is not simply a question of juxtaposing the interests of 'real' and 'constructed' social agents. Rather it is to recognize that the distinction between them is fluid and that the real interests or preferences of agents do not just exist objectively but are themselves constituted and are therefore negotiable.

The idea of 'reflective equilibrium' underlies what Rawls calls 'forward' and 'backward' argumentation. Clearly such terms are simply metaphors to interpret a dynamic process of argument and justification. This dynamic and the equilibrium upon which it settles can no longer, in the classical tradition, appeal to ultimate foundations in some ontologically primitive sense. Nevertheless, it articulates a structure in which certain features are more entrenched than others. We shall return to this idea shortly.

Rawls' forward argument begins with a specification of those principles that would be agreed upon in a hypothetically constructed arena of social choice (the 'original position') which embodies some basic procedural intuitions of justice as 'fairness'. The backward argument begins from an intuitive sketch of what he calls the 'well-ordered' society and works towards a reconstruction of the principles of justice that underly it. The idea of 'reflective equilibrium' is that the two argument structures – forward and backward – are in some sense iterative and should converge. According to Rawls, our intuitions about procedurally conceived principles of justice converge with a more formal theoretical account of their origin. There is of course no original position in a historical or other empirically determinate sense but it is one nodal point or construct within the whole edifice. Thus, for Rawls, there is a deep and mutually constitutive compromise between intuitions, practices and theoretical ideals. None of these has priority because no single element is simply 'given' independently of the other.

Rawls' appeal to 'reflective equilibrium' is consistent with Gadamer's (1975) idea of the 'hermeneutic circle' in which the parts and whole of any theoretical or practical level of understanding are mutually constitutive. According to Gadamer, we cannot ground our beliefs at any cognitive level in a transcendent or a historical point of reference. However, as his debate with Habermas (1977) shows, it is not certain what follows from this. Rawls is perhaps a little clearer on the matter:

> A conception of justice cannot be deduced from self-evident premises or conditions on principles; instead, its justification is a matter of the mutual support of many considerations, of everything fitting together into one coherent view.
>
> (Rawls 1973 :21)

While there are no ultimate foundations, certain elements of the whole can be regarded as more deeply embedded than others. This metaphor of relative depth allows us to locate an aspiring conceptual framework in a different relation to operational praxis than both FASB and their critics imagine.

Rawls' theory is far from being unproblematic. A great deal of critical commentary (see Daniels 1975) has concerned itself with the detailed specification of the 'original position' and the 'veil of ignorance' which it draws over its participants, thereby constructing them theoretically for the purpose of deriving principles of justice. Some critics regard this as a theoretical fix. Others are concerned with the 'validity' of the deduction of the particular principles. A detailed consideration of these difficulties can be legitimately placed beyond the scope of this essay since, if Rawls' theory is open to such specific substantive disputes, his meta-theory about the status of the project, and his claims for the notion of 'reflective equilibrium', can be left intact. It is this area of his work which can illuminate the idea of a CF for financial accounting.

Dworkin (1975) has claimed that Rawls' notion of 'reflective equilibrium' is a means by which we give structure to the moral intuitions that we have by supplying principles which both explain our feelings to some degree and provide a guide for action. But what sort of 'guide' for action? Should we require that particular presumptions should follow *deductively* from such principles? The problem is similar to that raised above in the context of Dopuch and Sunder's critique of FASB. The answer is that 'reflective equilibrium' de-emphasizes unidirectional logical relations, such as deduction. But if the relation of a CF to particular principles is not deductive then what can it be? We shall consider this important issue below.

It has also been asked of Rawls' theory why it is necessary to posit the 'original position' if the two principles of justice can converge via 'reflective equilibrium' with our intuitions and practices directly? Why is the backward argument not sufficient alone? We can represent Rawls' argument structure diagrammatically as shown in Figure 4.1. In terms of this structure it can be asked 'What would be lost if the forward argument were dispensed with?'

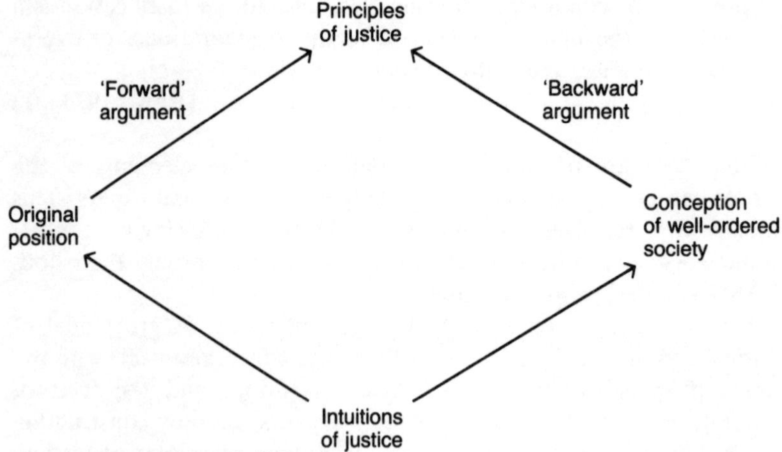

Figure 4.1 Rawls' model of 'reflective equilibrium'

Notwithstanding its problematic character, the place of the original position in the structure is critical. Rawls concedes that such a construct is expository and thereby mythical. Yet there is also a recognition that moral intuitions are ill-formed and that there is therefore a need for a coherence between them and some 'deeper' theory. The essential role of the original position is to interpret our moral intuitions as 'disassembled' parts of some construction. Such a construction is not objective in the sense of existing independently of real practices but is grounded in, and serves in turn to ground, them. For example, we may simply persist with our intuitions until 'rogue' principles either disappear or fall into shape. However Rawls requires a consistency within which our intuitions may themselves give way. It is this latter idea which lies at the heart of what Dworkin (1975) calls Rawls' 'constructive methodology'. According to Dworkin, Rawls' account depends upon a 'deep theory of rights' which both takes shape *within* reflective equilibrium and serves to shape our moral intuitions. In this sense the whole architectonic of Rawls' theory seems to depend upon some ultimate injection of value, i.e. a deep theory of rights. Critics regard this as arbitrary and unsupportable. But a more sympathetic reading interprets Rawls' theory as giving form to, i.e. (re)constructing, commonly held intuitions.

The function of a CF for financial accounting is loosely analogous to Rawls' 'original position' in the sense of articulating an underlying 'constructivist' approach to accounting policy. A CF is not an ultimate foundation in any classical sense but a point of reference in the network of accounting standards and practices that serves to 'organize' thinking about them. Rawls' theory may, as we have seen, depend upon the ultimate value input of a theory of rights. This does not undermine his claims but merely shows that different possible theories of justice may be possible. In the same way different possible CFs may be possible depending upon their deep point reference, e.g. user needs, true income, sustainable development, etc. These suggestions are considered at greater length below.

THE IDEA OF A CONCEPTUAL FRAMEWORK FOR FINANCIAL REPORTING

Stamp (1981, 1982) claims that the development of a CF to secure 'truth and fairness' in financial reporting will be 'no easier than the development of a system of laws and legal administration that secures justice for all'. Clearly there is an important meta-theoretical understanding of the idea of a CF here. Stamp is explicitly distancing his conception from that of FASB whose complexity, he argues, is unwarranted in the sense of misconceiving the fundamental nature of accounting. In effect FASB offer 'axioms disguised as definitions' which buy the advantages of consistency and comparability at the cost of arbitrariness.

From what Stamp says it is the axiomatic conception of the CF which is the deep meta-theoretical error. While the prospect of a logically rigorous CF which could be operational determinately within the standard-setting process is attractive, it flows from a dream of objectivity which is unattainable. A CF for accounting is more like a system of moral and political concepts than a geometric architectonic. Stamp's 'quasi-legal' conception of a CF for accounting flows from his own 'user needs' view, a view in which the standard-setting process is not entirely reducible to an arena for competition between economic interests. We could say that the development of the substantive contents of such a CF resembles the interaction between principle and instance at the heart of the common law process. Rawls' meta-theoretical model of the development of principles of justice is similar, and some general implications of his analysis for a CF for accounting can now be drawn.

First, the very process of explicating and interpreting the conceptual underpinnings of common accounting practices is not a purely descriptive exercise. It is not purely descriptive because there is an implicit procedural ideal for removing ambiguity and inconsistency. Common practice is not simply given and authoritative, and *A Theory of Justice* recognizes that our ordinary intuitive moral concepts are laden with assumptions. In making these assumptions explicit Rawls is aiming for a 'rational reconstruction' of them which, undoubtedly, has normative implications. Certainly, our point of epistemological access to such reconstructions is via our present practices but the latter do not possess any priority just as our manifest behaviour has none in the context of psychoanalysis.

Why does this matter to our idea of a CF for accounting? Solomons (1986) argues that an expensive CF project was unnecessary given the evolutionary philosophy espoused by the FASB. If current practice is actually dominant in shaping the nature of the particular concepts developed then a CF, far from being prescriptive and proactive in relation to that practice, is actually a mere residual product of it. In saying this Solomons is quite correct to bring out the tensions in FASB thinking and to show how conservative it is in relation to such issues as current cost accounting (CCA). However he is *meta-theoretically* mistaken to regard the FASB CF as merely evolutionary and descriptive as opposed to proactive and descriptive.

Another view of the issue emerges if we reconsider Rawls' forward and backward arguments. The difference between them corresponds roughly to that between normative-deductive and inductive-reconstructive based accounting theories. Rawls' model of 'reflective equilibrium' reminds us that the theorization process is constituted by *both* types. Deductive theories argue 'forward' from some given theoretical model, e.g. 'true' income, to various principles whereas inductive theories argue backwards to such principles from an interpretation of current practices. Crystallizing approaches as *either* normative *or* descriptive is effectively an abstraction from a more holistic theorization process. The problem for the idea of a CF is that it has been conceived by FASB and others as standing *outside* practices, i.e. as a fixed ahistorical construct from which accounting standards can be derived deductively.

The second and most important consequence of Rawls' model for accounting is for our understanding of how a CF could be 'operational'. Dopuch and Sunder assess the claimed benefits by FASB for a CF, one of which is that of providing 'bounds for judgment'. They claim that they do not understand this benefit nor how it could be observed or measured. However, this idea is at the very heart of a revaluation of the meta-theoretical status of the CF. Rawls' two general principles of justice are *not* intended to cater for every possible instance, such that the specific prescriptions follow logically. Rather, they are intended to provide boundaries or limits to the process by which particular judgements are made. In Rawls' case boundaries are delineated by a deep theory of individual rights, as Dworkin observes.

On such a view the relationship between general concept and particular rule is not that the latter follows deductively from the former but that the latter *presupposes* the former. Similarly the relationship between a CF and the standard-setting process is not the relation of scientific law or axiom to the instance that falls under it. It is more like the relation between a legal constitution and particular legal judgements. It is more like the relation between our deepest moral convictions and our many particular actions. In short, when thinking about the nature of a CF for accounting, theorists may have looked for models and analogies in the wrong places.

Much has been written about the logic of presupposition in philosophy. For the purposes of this chapter it is only necessary to distinguish it from *deductive* forms of entailment. A CF for accounting can only be operational in the sense of being *presupposed* in the standard-setting process. A CF on this view establishes general criteria that guide the process by giving a structure to the communicative processes involved. In just the same way, courts of law will be guided by general legal principles which may be interpreted in the face of particular instances.

The basis of the general guidance offered by a CF will depend upon deeply embedded views of what accounting is. It is important to recognize how such views *precede* the articulations of a CF. We can have different theories of the moral worth of human beings (e.g. bearers of rights, inputs into the labour process, pleasure seekers, etc.). Similarly we can have different 'deep' conceptions of accounting (serving investor needs, mapping economic reality, providing a basis for levying taxation) and for each of these a CF is possible. The

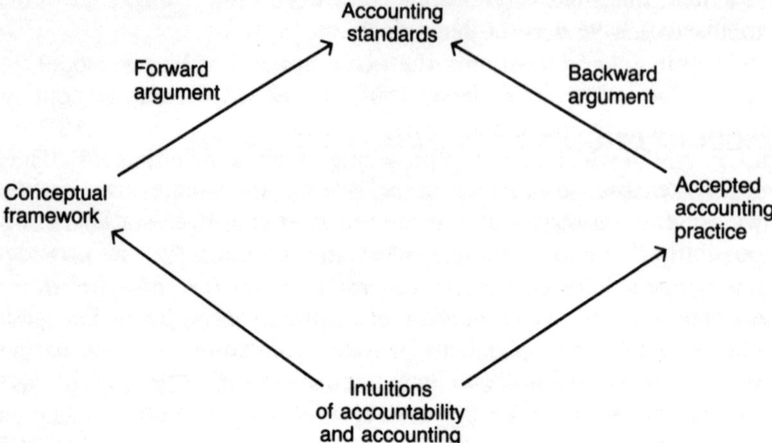

Figure 4.2 'Reflective equilibrium' for financial reporting

process of reflective equilibrium within which a CF for accounting is embedded could be represented as shown in Figure 4.2. The similarities with Figure 4.1 are not entirely artificial. The dual 'forward' and 'backward' argument structure (corresponding loosely to deductive and inductive type theories of accounting) can be seen to depend upon the intuitive grasp of what accounting is, i.e. which deep theory drives the whole process. A CF for accounting now emerges as an explication of those intuitions and thereby provides boundary conditions for the standard-setting process. Those who argue that we do not need a CF for accounting are similar to the critics of Rawls who claim he does not need the 'original position'. But the same defence is appropriate here. A CF is part of a 'constructive methodology', a reconstruction of the basic categories underlying a particular set of intuitions of what financial accounting is. A particular CF will naturally be 'relative' to those intuitions but is not therefore a mere epiphenomenon of them because it can in turn exert a normative influence within the reflective equilibrium process.

This is the briefest sketch of a meta-theory for a conceptual framework and more undoubtedly needs to be said about its components. Where do our intuitions about accounting come from? How would the 'economic consequences' view (Zeff 1978) fit into this picture? Answering these questions is a task for the future. For the present it is necessary to confront the two main difficulties about what has been said: what 'use' is a CF on this new model and what use is the fact that *many* CFs seem to be possible? These anxieties themselves have a meta-theoretical source and it is to this that we now turn.

ACCOUNTING AND THE SCIENTIFIC IMAGE

If this chapter is correct in suggesting that there has been a widespread misconception of the meta-theoretical status of any possible CF for accounting, it remains to be answered *why* this has happened. In a different context Peasnell (1978) discusses the attempt to evolve a meta-theory of accounting theories. He suggests that the philosophy of science, whether Kuhnian or otherwise, may well be the wrong place to look for such a meta-theory. The turn towards meta-theories of science for a rationalization of what one is doing implicitly assumes that it is sufficiently *like* science for such reflection to make sense. Yet this is highly questionable. Before the insights of Laudan, Feyerabend, Sellars and many other philosophers of the natural sciences can be appropriated to illuminate the theorization process in accounting, it must be asked whether it is sufficiently proto-scientific for this to make sense. The view that it is not cannot be defended here, but it is sufficient to note that the concern for peculiarly 'scientific' credentials (on whatever model of science one chooses) has led to the widespread neglect by many accounting theorists of areas such as jurisprudence, ethical theory and even the philosophy of the social sciences as a resource for thinking about accounting.

Why has this happened? At this point the claims of the 'reductivist' theories of accounting are important. The appeal to science and the construction of accounting and accounting theory in the 'scientific image' may be a function of the need for legitimation and credibility. Where a 'young' discipline like accounting is searching for settled foundations in times of crisis then it is natural that the scientific ideal and its inherent claims to objectivity and testability, independently of interest group pressures, should be an attractive intellectual resource. By contrast the jurisprudential image is unattractive by being too judgemental at its core.

An examination of the role of the scientific image or images in the self-understanding of accounting theory would require a more comprehensive study, but its impact upon the meta-theoretical idea of a CF is clearly visible. Both FASB *and* their critics are guided by a deep scientific conception of the CF. This in turn underpins their expectations of its operational capabilities in 'predicting' appropriate accounting policy. This 'scientific' meta-theoretical conception of a CF for accounting is so entrenched and so much a part of the 'unconscious' of accounting policy that the 'operational failure' of the CF raises questions among accountants about the CF in its concrete form but not about the *underlying* conception of it.

A further aspect of the underlying scientism of the idea of a CF is the apparent need for only *one* such CF. This creates tensions, particularly in reconciling a CF with approaches which recognize the plurality of user needs. FASB retain the coherence of the CF project by opting for the 'informed investor' perspective but this is weakly defended. Clearly the recognition of multiple CFs is unattractive because there seems to be something inherently self-contradictory about such an idea. This is understandable given that a CF is itself a metaphor; the very notion of a 'framework' suggests something durable, rigid and authoritative. But this is only a metaphor and we need to reflect upon its hold on our thinking. One such concern is that, if we recognize the possibility of multiple CFs, then this is the road to relativism and 'anything goes'. Elsewhere (Lyas 1984, Power 1986) it has been argued that the alternative to singular objectivistic understandings of accounting is not necessarily conceptual anarchy. Giving up the idea of one agreed CF does not necessarily lead to a multiplicity of CFs for each 'economic interest'. The model of 'reflective equilibrium' and its family resemblance to the ideas of hermeneutic philosophers is located beyond the either/or logic of objectivism and relativism (Bernstein 1983).

It remains a matter for speculation whether, had a modest and non-scientistic meta-theory of a CF for financial reporting been developed by FASB, financial resources would have been committed to the CF project as they have been. The scale of this generates an expectation of a recognizable pay-off ('better accounting standards'). Thus, it seems true to say that, in this instance, meta-theoretical *misconceptions* have been 'economic consequences'.

CONCLUSIONS

This chapter does not seek to argue for or against any *particular* manifestation of a CF for financial accounting whether that of FASB or any other agency for accounting policy. Accordingly it does not address any *particular* definitional or other issues concerned with elaborating a CF. Some readers will no doubt find this a source of irritation. But the intention is to raise a series of questions which are logically prior to any specific CF and are concerned with the idea of a CF for accounting as such. To address such questions one must have some prior model or image of accounting from which the appropriate, if any, form of CF can be conceptualized. It is argued that this meta-theoretical area of the CF has been largely neglected. This neglect can be traced within the texts of numerous critics of FASB – Dopuch and Sunder are selected here as one example. Borrowing from Rawls' *A Theory of Justice* and his notion of a 'reflective equilibrium' between our concepts and practices, a more appropriate model of the place of concepts, and hence anything qualifying for the title of CF, has been offered – one which offers a way of expanding upon some of Stamp's ideas on the quasi-legal character of the standard-setting process. It has also been suggested that the dominant, though partly unconscious, meta-theoretical conception of the CF flows from scientific dreams of objectivity in the face of which a modest hermeneutic understanding must appear relativisitic and therefore unacceptable.

The patient reader with an interest in accounting policy will now say that, while all this is very interesting, where does it now lead the CF project? The short answer is that it leads the standard-setting process in the same way a theory of human rights leads a court of law. This is not directly (or deductively) but as a background of tradition which is presupposed in the specific procedures and judgements. Of course this is a perilous relationship. Traditions may be eroded or changed abruptly. Other influences may dominate any particular context. On such a view it is worth remembering that 'morality is not a name for *whatever* influences choice . . . [but is] . . . one possibility for settling conflict' (Rorty 1982: 185). Similarly the articulation of a CF for financial reporting cannot influence all interested parties at once but represents certain conditions of possibility for the settling of conflicts. To say that the standard-setting process is merely an arena of conflict, politics and bargaining may be to give up on the possibility of a rational basis for that process, a basis expressed in the 'constructivist' aspirations of a CF within the context of a 'reflective equilibrium' between standards, practices and intuitions about accounting. This, I believe, lies at the heart of Stamp's claim that:

> A successful conceptual approach must be based upon a structure similar to that used by the law – in its concepts of jurisprudence, rather than by attempting to construct an axiomatic and deductive framework . . . the process of the development of a conceptual framework for accounting will be continuous and unending. It will

> never be possible for anyone to present to the profession a complete conceptual framework, and a great deal of misunderstanding will be avoided if this fact is recognised in the profession.
>
> (Stamp 1982)

NOTES

1 This theme is taken up by Habermas (1979) in his theory of communication. In brief, Habermas argues that in communication orientated towards genuine understanding we necessarily presuppose that we could come to a rational agreement.

2 There are, at least, two senses of reduction. One concerns the nature of scientific progress and the extent to which earlier theories can be 'explained' by successor theories. The other sense concerns the question of whether different sciences are reducible, e.g. whether biology is ultimately reducible to physics. The interpretation of a CF in economic and political terms is reductive in the latter sense.

REFERENCES

AICPA (American Institute of Certified Public Accountants) (1973) *Objectives of Financial Statements*, Report of the Study Group, Chairman, Robert Trueblood, New York: AICPA.

Bedford, N.M. (1974) 'Discussion of opportunities and implications of the report on objectives of financial statements', *Studies on Financial Accounting Objectives*, Supplement to *Journal of Accounting Research*, 12.

Bernstein, R.J. (1983) *Beyond Objectivism and Relativism*. Oxford: Basil Blackwell.

Daniels, N. (1975) *Reading Rawls: Critical Studies of A Theory of Justice*, Oxford: Basil Blackwell.

Dopuch, N. and Sunder, S. (1980) 'FASB's statement on objectives and elements of financial accounting: a review'. *Accounting Review*, 55(1): 1–21.

Dworkin, R. (1975) 'The original position', in N. Daniels (ed.) *Reading Rawls: Critical Studies of A Theory of Justice*, Oxford: Basil Blackwell, pp. 16–53.

Gadamer, H.-G. (1975) *Truth and Method* (translated by William Glen-Doepel) J. Cumming and G. Barden (eds), London: Sheed and Ward.

Habermas, J. (1976) *Legitimation Crisis*, (translated by T. McCarthy), London: Heinemann.

—— (1977) 'A review of Gadamer's "Truth and Method"' in F. Dallmayr and T. McCarthy (eds) *Understanding and Social Inquiry*, Notre Dame: University of Notre Dame Press, pp. 335–63.

—— (1979) 'What is universal pragmatics?', in *Communication and the Evolution of Society*, (translated by T. McCarthy), London: Heinemann, pp. 1–68.

Hines, R.D. (1989) 'Financial accounting knowledge, conceptual framework projects and the social construction of the accounting profession', *Accounting, Auditing and Accountability Journal*, 2(2): 72–92.

—— (1991) 'The FASB's conceptual framework, financial accounting and the maintenance of the social world', *Accounting Organizations and Society*, 16(4): 313–31.

Hopwood, A.G. (1988) 'Accounting research and accounting practice: the ambiguous relationship between the two', in A.G. Hopwood (ed.) *Accounting from the Outside*, New York: Garland Publishing, pp. 549–78.

Lyas, C. (1984) 'Philosophers and accountants', *Philosophy*, 59(227): 99–110.

Macve, R.H. (1981) *A Conceptual Framework for Financial Accounting and Reporting: The Possibilities for an Agreed Structure*, London: Institute of Chartered Accountants in England and Wales.

Miller, H.E. (1974) 'Discussion of opportunities and implications of the report on objectives of financial statements', *Studies on Financial Accounting Objectives*, Supplement to *Journal of Accounting Research*, 12.

Peasnell, K.V. (1978) 'Statement of accounting theory and theory acceptance: a review article', *Accounting and Business Research*, 8: 217–25.

—— (1982) 'The function of a conceptual framework for corporate financial reporting', *Accounting and Business Research*. 12: 243–56.

Power, M.K. (1986) 'Taking stock: philosophy and accountancy', *Philosophy*, 61(237): 387–94.

Rawls, J. (1973) *A Theory of Justice*, Oxford: Oxford University Press.

Rorty, R. (1982) *Consequences of Pragmatism (Essays: 1972–80)*, Brighton: Harvester Press.

Solomons, D. (1986) *Making Accounting Policy*, Oxford: Oxford University Press.

Stamp, E. (1981) 'Accounting standards and the conceptual framework: a plan for their evolution', *Accountant's Magazine*, July: 216–21.

—— E. (1982) 'First steps towards a British conceptual framework', *Accountancy*, March: 123–30.

Watts, R. and Zimmerman, J. (1979) 'The demand for and supply of accounting theories: the market for excuses', *Accounting Review*, 54: 273–305.

Williams P.F. (1987) 'The legitimate concern with fairness', *Accounting, Organizations and Society*, 12(2): 169–89.

Zeff, S.A. (1978) 'The rise of "economic consequences"', *Journal of Accountancy*, December: 56–63.

5 On the methodology of constructing a conceptual framework for financial accounting

Simon Archer

INTRODUCTION

A perceived need for some kind of theoretical basis or 'conceptual framework' for financial accounting has been felt in English-speaking countries for some decades. In the United States (where the perception of the need has been most intense) such a concern has been evident since the 1930s. Originally, the search was for a set of accounting principles which would form the basis of good practice; but more recently, the concern has been with establishing an intellectual basis for setting accounting standards, rather than with accounting principles *per se*. The difference is that the perceived need is now concerned explicitly with providing a basis for what is considered to be a crucial aspect of professional self-regulation, namely the setting of financial accounting standards, rather than with the establishment of accounting theory as a guide for practitioners in their individual decision-making capacity.

This shift in focus has manifested itself in two ways, particularly in the USA. One has been the change from academic studies of the issues, to studies carried out or commissioned by the self-regulatory body concerned with financial accounting practice. The second has been the replacement, in the USA, of an Accounting Principles Board by a Financial Accounting Standards Board to carry out the self-regulatory function.

Thus, historically, the first response to this demand was in the form of studies by academics: the study *A Tentative Statement of Accounting Principles Underlying Corporate Financial Statements* published by the American Accounting Association (AAA) under the leadership of Eric Kohler in 1936 (AAA 1936); the Sanders, Hatfield and Moore study published in 1938; the Paton and Littleton (1940) monograph; followed by the work of Moonitz (1961) and Sprouse and Moonitz (1962); and the multi-authored study published by the

AAA under the title *A Statement of Basic Accounting Theory* (AAA 1966). None of these studies, however, had any discernible practical impact. Subsequently, the AAA published another multi-authored study, the *Statement of Accounting Theory and Theory Acceptance* (AAA 1977), which presented an argument as to why the project of developing a coherent theory of financial accounting was not currently feasible.

Moreover, consistently with the disenchantment of the academic community with this type of theoretical endeavour, the more recent responses have come, not in the form of academic studies, but from the bodies concerned with accounting practice. The first of these was the US Accounting Principles Board's (APB) Statement No. 4, published in 1970 (APB 1970). This was followed by the UK and Irish Accounting Standards Committee's *Statement of Standard Accounting Practice No. 2* (ASC 1971), published in 1971 and showing the influence of the much longer APB Statement. However, APB Statement No. 4 was criticized in the US for failing to meet perceived needs, and in the Spring of 1971 the American Institute of Certified Public Accountants (AICPA) commissioned two study groups, one chaired by Francis B. Wheat to study the establishment of accounting principles, and the other chaired by Robert M. Trueblood to study the objectives of financial statements.

The first of these study groups produced its report (the 'Wheat Report') in March 1972. As a result of this report, the APB itself was replaced by the Financial Accounting Standards Board (FASB); and, whereas the APB was a committee of the AICPA, following the report's recommendations the FASB is part of a new self-regulatory structure headed by a Financial Accounting Foundation. The other study group published its report (the 'objectives study' or 'Trueblood Report') in October 1973.

It was thus in a somewhat febrile atmosphere of concern over the accounting profession, with regard to its role, organization and methods, that the FASB started work in 1973. The Board soon embarked on an ambitious and costly programme to develop a conceptual framework for financial accounting. The term 'conceptual framework' was now explicitly used to characterize the perceived need that was to be met (FASB, 1974: 1). This programme has resulted in a long series of publications, most of them substantial, starting with the FASB Discussion Memorandum *Conceptual Framework for Accounting and Reporting: Consideration of the Report of the Study Group on the Objectives of Financial Statements* (FASB 1974), and finishing with the *Statement of Financial Accounting*

Concepts No. 6 Elements of Financial Statements (FASB 1985a). The fruits of this massive endeavour have not, however, received a good press; for a bibliography as well as further criticism, see Aggrawal (1987). Some of these criticisms will be reviewed below.

Before doing so, however, let us note that no comparable pressure has been experienced in non-English-speaking countries, such as France and Germany. This can be explained by the subsumption in those countries of financial accounting standard setting (or rule making) under the more general rule-making processes of the law. An account of such processes in France can be read in Scheid and Standish (1988). Thus, in those countries the development and implementation of financial accounting standards is not seen as being primarily the responsibility of the accounting profession. Rather, the profession's role is to provide experts as members of statutory bodies or advisers to legislative committees, whose standard-setting work results in outputs with legal force. Examples of such outputs are the French General Accounting Plan (*Plan comptable général*) of 1982, and the German Accounting Directives Law (*Bilanzrichtliniengesetz*) of 1985.

The implications of this are that the pressure felt by bodies like the APB and the FASB is related to aspects of the socio-economic role of the accounting profession which differ as between the English-speaking countries (especially, it would seem, the USA) and other major developed Western countries. An argument might perhaps be advanced that there is also a difference in the level of theoretical development of financial accounting in the two groups of countries, and that this explains the much greater sensitivity in the English-speaking countries to theoretical issues, which have been more extensively discussed and analysed in the latter group of countries.

There is, perhaps, some substance in such an argument, yet the main thrust of theoretical work in financial accounting is no longer directed towards finding a conceptual basis for accounting conventions: rather, it is concerned with understanding the economic role and consequences of such conventions and of the institutions which develop and promulgate them. Such work is specifically concerned not to take for granted the assumptions regarding the economic importance of the rules governing the production of financial accounting information, which provided the intellectual motivation for the conceptual framework programme.

Thus, it is mainly the standard-setting bodies, particularly the FASB and latterly the Accounting Standards Authority of Canada and the International Accounting Standards Committee (IASC), that have been concerned in recent years with the development of a conceptual framework. Moreover, this has been on the basis of a set of assumptions that the academic research community considers to be in need of justification.

Dopuch and Sunder (1980) state four possible reasons why such bodies may 'search for a conceptual framework' (CF). The first is that there are good reasons, based on experience, for thinking that such a framework would be useful in resolving accounting issues and standard-setting problems. However, as Dopuch and Sunder (D&S) argue, experience would appear to indicate the opposite. The second is that the efforts to develop a conceptual framework have benefits for users of financial statements, in terms both of their increased confidence in and understanding of such statements, and of the enhanced comparability of the latter. Again, D&S argue that experience does not support this reason either.

It may be noted that while IASC cited both of these reasons when publishing its relatively brief *Framework for the Presentation and Preparation of Financial Statements* (IASC 1989), its Board acknowledged that there were limitations to the applicability of the first reason at least:

> The Board of the IASC recognises that in a limited number of cases there may be a conflict between the framework and an International Accounting Standard . . . [in which case] the requirements of the International Accounting Standard prevail over those of the framework.
>
> (IASC 1989, para. 3)

A third possible reason is that the language of conceptual frameworks, and particularly definitions, might provide a discourse similar to that of the law, whereby conflicting interests can be discussed and adjudicated according to agreed rules of discourse. D&S argue that this possible reason, too, fails:

> Definitions, no matter how carefully worded, cannot bear the burden of the struggle for economic advantage between various interest groups. Legal definitions survive in a similar environment only because their interpretations by the courts are backed by the power of the state to enforce them, a power not available to the FASB.

The final reason considered by D&S is related to the issue of the socio-economic role of the accounting profession which was evoked above. They suggest that a conceptual framework may be an ideological necessity for a self-regulating body such as the FASB:

> Being largely an offspring of the accounting profession, the FASB has (as did the APB) little defense against the criticism that it does not have legitimate authority to make decisions which affect wealth transfers among members of society . . . . The ability, intelligence, ethical character, and past services, etc., of the members of the FASB are not sufficient . . . . Rather, a conceptual framework is needed to provide the rationalization for its choices. If a more representative body were to take over the function of setting accounting standards, perhaps there would be less of a need for a conceptual framework.

This last argument is supported to some extent by the comparison made above between the English-speaking countries and the USA in particular, and other developed countries such as France and Germany. Moreover, it would appear that the FASB saw a conceptual framework as a means of enhancing its standard-setting powers and, perhaps, of reducing its dependence on the SEC (see p. 87). The argument of D&S implies that, were the SEC itself to take over the standard-setting role, it would not feel the same need as the FASB for a conceptual framework. Be that as it may, there do not seem to be any signs, in the English-speaking countries, of moves towards the replacement of self-regulatory mechanisms in financial accounting standard setting, by other mechanisms more directly identifiable with the democratic institutions of the State. To that extent, the perceived need for a conceptual framework is likely to persist. Arguably, also, the French General Accounting Plan is representative of a different (technocratic) type of conceptual framework, albeit one in the elaboration of which the accounting profession did not play a dominant role (Scheid and Standish 1988).

This being the case, the third possible reason mentioned by D&S for seeking a conceptual framework (the potential role of a CF as a conflict-resolving discourse), may merit some re-examination. As noted above, D&S themselves rejected that reason; but perhaps they did so rather too cursorily. After all, in a polity in which successive administrations and legislatures have seen fit to leave the greater part of the regulation of financial accounting in the hands of a self-regulatory body (the FASB) with a statutory body (the Securities and Exchange Commission – SEC) able to provide enforcement when necessary, it is not obvious that either dubious legitimacy or lack of enforcement powers are the roots of the problem, as D&S would have us believe. It is also worth noting that Rule 203 of the AICPA Code of Ethics provides institutional (but extra-legal) support for the standard-setting role of the FASB. Arguably, what is at issue is the potential role of a sort of 'jurisprudence of accounting'. The ineffectiveness of the efforts made to date may not be due simply to the institutional factors mentioned by D&S; there is also the question of how competently the efforts to establish such a 'jurisprudence' have been made.

One way in which this question can be pursued is to subject the various publications of the FASB on the conceptual framework to detailed critique, as was done by Aggrawal (1987). By its nature, however, such an approach cannot shed light on whether the inadequacies exposed by such a critique (incompleteness, inconsistency, ambiguity and tendentiousness) might in principle be avoided; or on what the consequences of avoiding them might be in terms of the effectiveness of the resultant conceptual framework. This chapter seeks to cast light on these issues.

In the first place, it does so by examining the FASB's efforts from the standpoint of jurisprudence as it relates to the law, and with particular reference to conceptual frameworks of law. This sheds light on two sets of questions which are relevant to the issue of how a conceptual framework might provide a source of authority for accounting standards.

First, what is the source of the authority of legal rules (laws), and of the ability of legal discourse to be effective for discussing and adjudicating disputed issues? Does it reside, as D&S allege, simply in the coercive power of the State to ensure enforcement of legal rules, or are more subtle institutional and other social factors at work? There is, for example, Wittgenstein's point, quoted by Lyas on p. 164 of this volume, that for a discourse (including legal discourse) to be effective, 'there must be agreement not only in definitions . . . but also in judgments'.

Second, to what extent do conceptual frameworks in jurisprudence provide a basis or rationale for specific legal rules? Are they essentially positivistic rational reconstructions of existing practice, and hence inherently static and unable to provide a basis for changing that practice other than marginally; or can they play a more dynamic role in facilitating change? Moreover, what may be learned from the methodology of jurisprudence in the establishment of conceptual frameworks? In particular, how successfully have jurists addressed the issue just mentioned, namely the handling, within a conceptual framework, of value judgements regarding desirable changes in the *status quo*?

One might have expected that, before deploying the very considerable resources at its disposal for its conceptual framework project, the FASB would have sought to investigate these issues. The affinities between rule making in financial accounting and the making of legal rules are fairly evident. The idea of looking to lawyers for guidance would not be new; Underhill Moore, the third member of the team which produced the Sanders, Hatfield and Moore study (Sanders *et al.* 1938), was an eminent jurist (though he was not a specialist in jurisprudence as such, nor did his membership of the team result in its work having a jurisprudential character). Moreover, there would seem to be little point in accountants trying to reinvent the methodological wheels developed by jurists in their grappling with similar issues.

Yet, as I shall argue below, the evidence from the way in which they went about the conceptual framework project is that the FASB made no such investigation. Elsewhere in this volume (p. 44), Michael Power remarks that 'little attention has been given to the *idea* of a CF . . . [to the issue of] what kind of thing a CF could be . . . [or] to the role and status of what might be called "conceptual considerations" in financial reporting'. The possibility needs to be examined that the FASB's approach, as criticized explicitly by D&S and Aggrawal and implicitly by Power, was substantially flawed by neglect on the part of FASB researchers of important issues concerning the epistemological nature and methodology of conceptual frameworks in general, and (as Power also suggests by his use of Rawls' *Theory of Justice* as a paradigm) particularly in jurisprudence. One task of this chapter is to present such a study, by examining what jurisprudence might have to offer, and comparing this to the FASB's approach.

Such an endeavour would, I believe, have appealed to Eddie Stamp. He was an advocate of the application of a jurisprudential approach to conceptual problems in financial accounting, and encouraged me considerably in my researches into this area. The helpful comments which he would have been able to make on this chapter are sorely missed.

In addition to the work of Stamp (1969, 1980), that of Moonitz (1961) has indicated the relevance of legal 'conceptual frameworks' for accounting theory. Nevertheless, the idea of looking to legal thinking for guidance on developing a conceptual framework for accounting may not be congenial to everyone; perhaps a distinction needs to be made between legal method in a technical professional sense, and jurisprudence in the sense of the philosophy of law and the methodology of legal theory (Lloyd 1979: 9).

For example, one of the contributors to this volume, Richard Mattessich, has criticized legal thinking in calling for 'a scientific–analytic, instead of a dogmatic–legalistic foundation' to be provided by accounting theory (Mattessich 1964: 17); but this should not be equated with a rejection of jurisprudence. In fact, the theoretical approach which Mattessich developed (Mattessich 1964, 1972), involved the characterization of accounting systems in terms of nineteen parameters (basic assumptions and assumption-schemata) in a manner comparable with certain analytical approaches in jurisprudence. In particular, Mattessich's inclusion of assumption-schema number nineteen (the need to articulate the required information purpose of an accounting system) has affinities with the insistence of Hans Kelsen (a leading figure in analytical jurisprudence) on the logical need for a 'basic norm' in any legal system from which the system's normative or purposive properties are ultimately derivable (Kelsen 1967).

Nevertheless, it might be questioned why accounting should look to jurisprudence for guidance in developing its conceptual framework, rather than to other disciplines such as economics or, as Robert Sterling has suggested, physics. I should not wish to deny, on any *a priori* grounds, that useful guidance might be sought from a number of disciplines. A particular claim of jurisprudence, however, is that the term 'conceptual framework' is commonly found in the literature of the discipline, and one may therefore obtain a good idea of what the term means in relation to jurisprudence, and thereby meet Michael Power's point. It is less clear what the term means in the context of either economics or physics. Perhaps Thomas Kuhn's idea of a 'disciplinary matrix' would fit the bill (Kuhn 1970: 272–3); but to seek to apply this concept to accounting would beg an important issue as to whether accounting was epistemologically ready for development through 'normal science' (see Kuhn 1970; and Masterman 1970: 69–74). The notion of conceptual framework as used in jurisprudence avoids begging this issue.

This chapter shows how a methodology for constructing a CF for financial accounting could draw on ideas from the field of analytical jurisprudence together with that of systems analysis (more specifically, the systems approach to policy analysis). These two fields may appear to be rather disparate, and the relationship of the latter to the construction of a CF for financial accounting may not be immediately evident. In the first place, however, both fields are concerned with the problems of practical (or, as Richard Mattessich has termed it, instrumental) reasoning (Mattessich 1978); and, as I shall indicate below, the problems raised by the endeavour to construct a CF for financial accounting are of the same nature. Secondly, analytical jurisprudence, in its concern to explicate the nature of legal systems, has been influenced by systems thinking; this will be evident from the work of the legal scholar Josef Raz which is considered below. Finally, certain developments in the application of systems thinking to policy analysis are particularly relevant to the problems of dealing with complex sets of policy issues such as those involved in constructing a CF for financial accounting.

The type of framework which would result from the approach set out in this chapter is of a fundamentally different nature from the CF which the FASB sought to develop. As I point out in the section 'The FASB's methodology of conceptual framework construction' below, it is not very clear exactly what the FASB was seeking, for it appeared to be pursuing two different goals: to develop a basis in accounting theory for standards of financial accounting and reporting; and to develop a kind of constitution which would provide political legitimacy for the FASB's standard-setting. The approach taken in this chapter would lead to the development of a framework for justifying financial accounting standards which is *methodological*; hence, the justification for a standard would lie neither in accounting theory (the inadequacy of which for the task is the essence of the problem) nor in appeals to institutional authority, but in the cogency of the reasoning used to establish its social desirability. This cogency would result from the use of a particular framework of analysis and evaluation, derived from the methods of analytical jurisprudence and systems analysis which are described below.

The following sections of this chapter are structured as follows. 'The FASB's methodology of conceptual framework construction' reviews the FASB's CF project from a methodological perspective, and identifies a number of methodological issues which have been problematic for the project. 'The methodologies of analytical jurisprudence and the problem of normativity' (p. 84) then examines how certain methods of analytical jurisprudence could form the basis for a different and more fruitful approach to these issues. In particular, work is considered which emphasizes the systemic properties of law, and which strives to move away from an inherently static type of legal positivism. In 'Soft systems methodology' (p. 99), attention is drawn to the affinities between such methodologies and others developed by systems analysts (the so-called 'soft systems' methodologies) for the handling of complex organizational and social problem situations. One particular approach, known as the 'gross balance' method, is singled out as offering a basis analogous to, but more powerful than, that offered by analytical jurisprudence alone. 'Conclusions' (p. 113) sets out some points that are relevant for any future endeavours in the construction of a CF for financial accounting, and for considering the kind of intellectual background that may be needed for leadership of the accounting profession.

It may be useful at this point to refer to another treatment of related issues by Gaa (1988). Gaa's work is concerned with the methodology of financial accounting standard setting, rather than with that of constructing a conceptual framework for such a purpose. However, a conceptual framework does play a role in the methodology developed by Gaa (ibid. chapter 8). Moreover, while Gaa's approach is based on the methodology of ethics rather than jurisprudence and systems methodology, there is some degree of convergence between the approaches. In particular, the notions of 'justification' and 'codification' expounded by Gaa (ibid. chapters 6–8) are jurisprudential as well as ethical concepts, and are not dissimilar to the concepts outlined on p. 95 in 'The "new analytical jurisprudence"'. In addition, Gaa's analysis of the problems of the methodology of social choice (ibid. chapters 4–6) is relevant in a number of respects to the implementation of the systems approach to policy analysis which is described on p. 99, in 'Soft systems methodology'. Finally, both Gaa's approach and the one proposed here are essentially non-positivist. There are also some points of apparent divergence, which it would be interesting to examine; but considerations of length preclude such an examination within the confines of this chapter.

THE FASB'S METHODOLOGY OF CONCEPTUAL FRAMEWORK CONSTRUCTION

Introduction

The FASB never made an explicit statement of its methodology of conceptual framework construction. We need, therefore, to delve into its various publications concerned with the CF project, going back as early as possible in order to identify any crucial methodological decisions taken initially (whether explicitly or implicitly). We must also examine later publications to see how the methodology was applied and how it evolved. The publications that seem to warrant particular attention are discussed below.

The first publication which expressly referred to the CF project was the FASB Discussion Memorandum, *Conceptual Framework for Accounting and Financial Reporting: Consideration of the Report of the Study Group on the Objectives of Financial Statements*, dated 6 June 1974 (FASB 1974). This Discussion Memorandum (subsequently referred to as DM1) was based primarily on a document published in October 1973 by the AICPA, Accounting Objectives Study Group, *Objectives of Financial Statements*, (the so-called Trueblood Report) (AICPA 1973a). Thus, so far as the objectives of financial statements were concerned, the Board took as its starting point the twelve 'objectives' and seven 'qualitative characteristics' set out in the Trueblood Report. It therefore also absorbed into its own methodology some important aspects of that which had been employed by the AICPA Study Group. The significance of this will be examined later.

On 2 December 1976, the Board published two important documents concerned with the CF project. One was entitled *Tentative Conclusions on Objectives of Financial Statements of Business Enterprises* (FASB 1976a), and was a sequel to the June 1974 DM mentioned above. The other was a new DM, *Conceptual Framework for Financial Accounting and Reporting: Elements of Financial Statements and Their Measurement* (subsequently referred to as DM2) (FASB 1976b). The latter was a very substantial publication, being 257 pages long plus appendices. On the same date, the Board also produced a twenty-four-page booklet, *Scope and Implications of the Conceptual Framework Project* (FASB 1976c), intended for a wider public, and containing an overview of the CF project, together with summaries of the two more substantial documents being published simultaneously. The *Scope and Implications* booklet was prefaced by 'An open letter to the business and financial community' signed by Marshall S. Armstrong, Chairman of the FASB. Although relatively brief, this booklet was important in that the overview which it provided of the project, its approach and its likely evolution, was not available from any other source. In fact, the Board bound the text of the *Scope and Implications* booklet into the front of the simultaneously published DM2.

Following the three publications in December 1976, the FASB proceeded to issue three interrelated series of publications as part of the CF project. One series was composed of further DMs. A second series comprised 'exposure drafts' (EDs) of planned 'statements of financial accounting concepts' (SFACs). The third series consisted of the six SFACs themselves, ending with SFAC 6 in December 1985. In general, for each subject area, there was first a DM, then an ED, then a SFAC, interspersed with 'Invitations to comment' on the two former. (In addition, the FASB published a number of research reports prepared for the Board by well-known academics on topics related to the CF project.)

A study of these and the earlier publications brings to light the crucial features of the methodology of the project. These can be summarized as follows:

1 A view of a CF as 'a constitution, a coherent system of interrelated objectives and fundamentals that can lead to consistent standards'. (*Scope and Implications* booklet, p. 2).
2 Adoption of the means–end schema, in the sense of an assumed hierarchical relationship between objectives (ends) and means, such that the former are logically prior to the latter, and the latter (i.e. standards and guidelines) can to some extent be derived from the former (DM1, Appendix A).
3 Incrementalism, that is, the notion of moving forward one step at a time, using the ideas expressed in the Trueblood Report as a starting point (DM1, p. 2).
4 Consensus-seeking, by means of a procedure of public consultation, based on Discussion Memoranda and Exposure Drafts, including public hearings as well as solicitation of written comments (Notice of Public Hearing included in DM1; Open Letter included in the *Scope and Objectives* booklet; DM2, p. 1; *Tentative Conclusions on Objectives*, p. 1; and numerous other examples).
5 Agenda-setting, that is, the concern to be in control of the questions to which answers were being sought (DM1, DM2, *Tentative Conclusions on Objectives*).

What do these five crucial features imply as regards the nature of the methodology of the CF project? This question is not altogether easy to answer, since there is (to say the least) an element of contradiction between the means–end schema and incrementalism, which will be examined below. However, one can make the general remark that the Board was seeking a constitution, not a theory as such. That is to say, the conceptual framework was not supposed to be a theory of financial accounting (for one hardly constructs a theory by public consultation); rather, some *underlying* theory of financial accounting was *presupposed*, in terms of which the methods used in the CF project could be seen to be appropriate. Yet this theory was never articulated; its nature and content are a matter of inference, not to say conjecture. This indeed raises the very question of whether the development of a conceptual framework (even in the sense of a constitution rather than a theory) can properly be undertaken by the body whose activities are to be governed, and whose authority is to be underpinned, by the framework in question.

In fact, it may be thought improper to consider the FASB as having a theory at all. The membership of the Board changed over time, and so did some of the views of its members on important issues (Gore 1989). In any event, let me make clear that by referring to a presupposed theory, I do not wish to suggest that the members of the FASB actually held a theory of financial accounting, even implicitly. Theories may be presupposed without being held.

Inferences regarding the theory presupposed by the FASB's approach

One source of inferences regarding this presupposed theory is Appendix A of DM1, which sets out certain ideas from the Trueblood Report. These ideas concern

> An interrelated and compatible system of objectives, standards or principles, and practices or procedures . . . . Objectives should identify the goals and purposes of accounting. Standards should follow logically from objectives, and should provide guidelines for the formation of accounting practices compatible with the desired goals.

This is the means–end schema to which reference was made above. It is set out in the Appendix to DM1 in the form of a diagram, reproduced here as Figure 5.1.

The Appendix states, however:

> It should be understood that this particular hierarchy is tentative and is itself subject to modification as a result of comments, experience, and further consideration. It is posed here primarily to provide an explicit context . . . an attempt to ensure that we are talking about the same thing . . . . The particular terminology utilized . . . tends to facilitate a direct linkage with the [Trueblood Report] and the *Rules of Procedure* of the FASB.

Another source of inferences is the *Scope and Implications* booklet. Here, the role of financial accounting is placed squarely within the framework of providing information for the functioning of capital markets. Thus, 'the principal role of financial reporting [is] to furnish the investor and lender with information useful to assess the prospective risks and returns associated with an investment' (p. 3). Furnishing useful information to those groups for that purpose is assumed

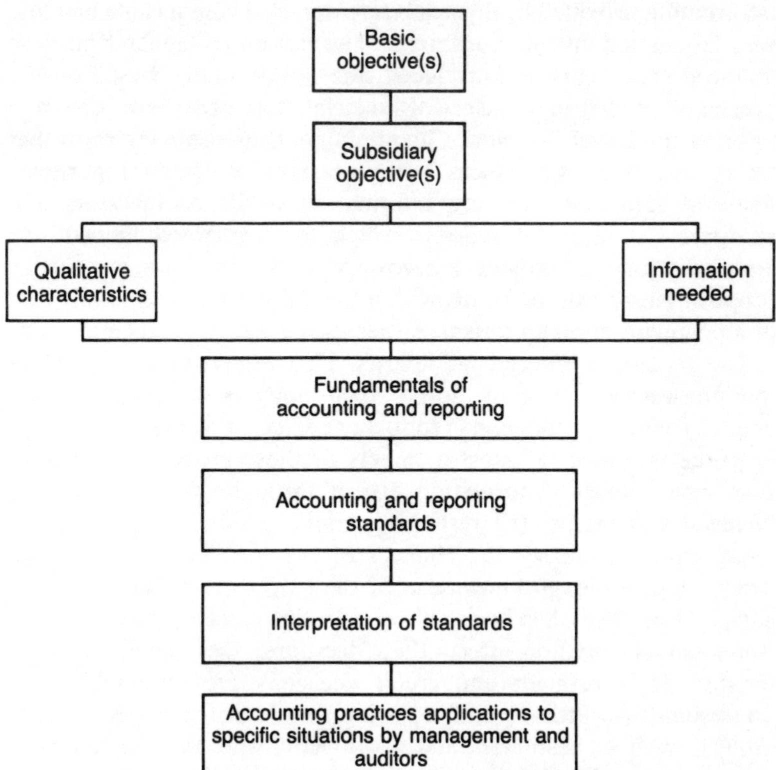

Figure 5.1 Hierarchy of elements in a conceptual framework for financial accounting and reporting

Source: FASB Discussion Memorandum No. 1, Appendix A (FASB 1974)

or postulated in the *Scope and Implications* booklet to be the primary or basic objective. The investor and lender groups relevant for the financial reporting of a particular entity presumably include potential investors in, and lenders to, that entity. In principle, this could mean virtually any individual or organization in society; but in practice, the set of likely members of investor and lender groups is arguably more restricted. However, this point is not discussed in the *Scope and Implications* booklet.

There is some discussion of the assumption in the longer companion document, *Tentative Conclusions on Objectives of Financial Statements of Business Enterprises*, paragraphs 8–22. Here, a number of other groups are mentioned as having 'a potential interest in the information provided by financial statements'. These include employees, labour unions and customers. The notion of 'general purpose financial statements' is introduced, the notion being 'based on the presumption that many users of financial statements have common information needs'. However, an argument is presented to show that 'there are reasons to focus the objectives of [general purpose] financial statements on the information needs of investors and creditors' (p. 3). For reasons which are explained below, this argument fails to provide a rigorous or cogent basis for such a proposition, so that its status within the CF remains essentially that of a postulate or an apriorism, rather than a well-argued conclusion.

The argument proceeds as follows. First, there is a statement of the presumption, already noted, that many users have common needs. Then, investors and creditors are selected as the focal groups on three grounds: (a) most members of these groups do not have access to financial information except through (general purpose) financial statements; (b) restricting consideration to the needs of these groups increases the chances of being able to satisfy those needs, and, although knowledge of their needs contains numerous gaps and no study has been able to identify precisely how financial statement information affects their decisions, the essential characteristics of investment and credit decisions are reasonably well understood; (c) little or nothing is known about the needs of other groups, such as customers and employees, who also do not have access to financial information except through (general purpose) financial statements.

A similar argument is deployed in the Statement of Financial Accounting Concepts (SFAC) No. 1, paras 24–31 (FASB 1978), albeit in more muted terms. The SFAC gives more emphasis to user groups other than investors and creditors, but reaches the same conclusions as those set out in the *Tentative Conclusions* document.

This argument for focusing the objectives of financial statements on the information needs of investors and creditors, with only cursory consideration of other groups, surely lacks the rigour and cogency required to support a fundamental decision in building a conceptual framework. The greater, albeit still deficient, knowledge of the relationship between financial statement information and the decisions of investors and creditors hardly seems an adequate reason for giving them this privileged status at so fundamental a level.

Moreover, the notion of 'general purpose financial statements' seems vague, and indeed there is a conceptual difficulty here, which has been remarked upon by Most (1982: 160–2). The notion of 'general purpose financial statements', he points out, is intrinsically problematic from an information perspective, since the distinction between information and mere data is that the former is intended to meet some known decision-making needs, while the latter are not; hence, strictly speaking, general purpose financial statements could serve only as data, not as information.

Consequently, it is questionable whether the CF project is in fact concerned with general purpose financial statements, rather than with statements specifically intended to meet the needs of investors and creditors, which would be expected to serve other user groups to a greater or lesser extent, without being designed to do so. Thus, SFAC 1 *Objectives of Financial Reporting by Business Enterprises* published in November 1978 (FASB 1978) likewise 'focus[es] the objectives of financial reporting primarily on investment, credit, and similar decisions. . . . [This does] not mean that the objectives apply only to investors and creditors and exclude everyone else' (para. 32). The *Tentative Conclusions* should therefore probably be interpreted as proposing that the CF project be concerned, not with general purpose financial statements as such, but with financial statements intended to meet the information needs of investors and creditors insofar as these needs are known (and relatively homogeneous), on the assumption that these will also serve other user groups whose needs are less well known. This, then, leads to the assumption or postulate put forward in the *Scope and Implications* booklet, as mentioned above.

Given the adoption of the means–end schema, the next step in building the CF is to move from the objectives to the means of achieving those objectives. This is done in chapter 3 of the *Tentative Conclusions*, and in paras 34–54 of SFAC 1. As already noted, the means–end schema is likely to prove problematic, given the incrementalism of the CF project, for reasons which will be examined below. An illustration of these difficulties is provided by the argument used by the FASB to derive the need for accrual accounting from the basic objectives.

The crux of this argument is that

> [Although] the fundamental concern of investors and creditors with an enterprise's cash flows might suggest that financial statements that report cash receipts and cash disbursements of an enterprise during a period would provide the most useful information . . . the cash receipts and disbursements of a short period, such as a year or a quarter of a year, are usually not related to

> each other in a way that makes them useful indicators of the enterprise's ability to bring in cash through its earning activities. . . . Therefore, financial statements for annual and interim periods are based on accrual accounting.
>
> (*Tentative Conclusions*, paras 147 and 158)

> Information about enterprise earnings and its components measured by accrual accounting generally provides a better indication of enterprise performance than information about current cash receipts and payments. . . . Accrual accounting is concerned with the process by which cash expended on resources and activities is returned as more (or perhaps less) cash to the enterprise, not just with the beginning and end of the process. . . . The goal of accrual and deferral of benefits and sacrifices is to relate the accomplishments and the efforts so that reported earnings measures an enterprise's performance during a period instead of merely listing its cash receipts and outlays.
>
> (SFAC 1, paras 44–5)

This argument is, in fact, no more than a statement of the standard rationale for accrual accounting as taught to first-year undergraduate students of the discipline. No research findings are cited in support of it. It is stated that 'investors, creditors and others often use reported earnings and information about the components of earnings in various ways and for various purposes in assessing their prospects for cash flows from investments in or loans to an enterprise' (SFAC 1, para. 47). But there is no mention of any research into what information such users might prefer to have, even though such research would have been perfectly feasible. Thus, on the basis of the standard rationale and their use of the type of information currently available, namely accrual accounting information, their preference for the latter was assumed. Such a lack of reference to research findings in order to support a crucial policy assumption was characteristic of the FASB's approach. In our discussion of the 'gross balance' method on p. 102, it will be seen that there are circumstances in which a decision to proceed with a policy decision without obtaining further relevant data may be justified; but here the relevance of research into user preferences seems to be so fundamental to the decision that the omission of any reference to it is striking.

In fact, by publishing DM2, *Elements of Financial Statements and Their Measurement*, simultaneously with the *Tentative Conclusions on Objectives*, the Board effectively pre-empted the basic issue regarding the role of accrual accounting. The reasoning employed in the *Tentative Conclusions* was reiterated in DM2, paras 1–9: and in DM2, the Board set out nine issues on which it sought responses from readers; these were all issues concerning the internal logical structure of accrual accounting. This illustrates what was called 'agenda-setting' (see p. 73).

While the answers seemingly had to be sought by a lengthy process of public consultation (which was followed by the publication of SFAC 3 in December 1980) (FASB 1980b) there was no analogous process of consultation prior to identifying the questions; the Board appeared very sure that it knew what these were. To a large extent, they are traceable to the Accounting Principle Board's *Statement No. 4, Basic Concepts and Accounting Principles Underlying Financial Statements of Business Enterprises*, published in 1970 (APB 1970). APB Statement No. 4 was an earlier and unsuccessful attempt to produce a conceptual framework. The failure of APB Statement No. 4 can be attributed to factors identified by APB member George R. Catlett in his scathing dissent from the Statement:

> [T]he concepts and principles set forth in this Statement are based upon ineffective foundations, along the lines of the following: (1) vague generalizations which are noncontroversial but serve no useful purpose; (2) circular reasoning, with undefined terms being defined by other undefined terms, such as the description of assets and liabilities as those items 'recognized and measured in conformity with generally accepted accounting principles'; and (3) reverse logic, by summarizing a wide variety of customs and practices, many of which need to be changed and improved, and then rationalizing back to principles that presumably support what now exists.
>
> (AICPA, 1973b: 9106)

Nevertheless, the view taken in APB Statement No. 4 of the issues that are crucial for financial accounting remained influential.

The FASB evidently considered that, by carefully structuring these issues and then seeking answers through a process of public consultation, it might succeed where the APB had failed. Its view of the CF as a constitution was thus accompanied by the idea that crucial aspects of that constitution needed to be based on a kind of referendum. A major characteristic of the FASB's 'presupposed theory' of financial accounting seems, therefore, to be the idea that there is a set of propositions analogous to a constitution which constitute its objectives and fundamentals and which, to an important degree, are dependent on the agreement of 'the leaders of the American business and financial community'.

Thus, just as constitutions in democratic societies are supposed to reflect the aspirations of the citizenry with regard to the political and legal framework of society, so a CF for financial accounting is supposed to reflect the aspirations of the 'business and financial community' (or at least of its leaders) regarding the framework of conventions and rules for the activities of financial accounting and reporting. The process whereby these aspirations become articulated is therefore seen as essentially a political process in which the FASB plays the role of political leadership (by structuring the issues, managing the process of public consultation and involving the leaders of the 'business and financial community'). According to this view, the search for a CF is not a process of scientific (or social scientific) enquiry, and it is the FASB's right and duty to use its role so as to lead opinion in particular directions on important value-issues such as the choice of objectives and fundamentals.

It would seem from studying the various FASB publications just mentioned that the objectives were carefully stated so as to provide a basis for asserting the fundamental role of accrual accounting and of information on earnings. This may in fact be a *post hoc* rationalization of a process in which such an assertion was not a foregone conclusion, the competing case for cash-flow accounting (and the corresponding threat to the status of accrual accounting) being taken seriously by some participants. In either event, the process exemplifies an important aspect of the incrementalism adopted by the Board; the strategy is to proceed gradually forward from the *status quo*, not to question it in any major way.

It is not my purpose here to criticize the Board for incrementalism as such, but to point out that it lacked a well-defined methodology for dealing with the type of questions which it was facing, namely a combination of difficult technical concepts and important social value-issues. This methodological inadequacy is revealed in its attempt to present the objectives as logically prior to the means within a means–end schema, when in fact the means were being articulated in parallel with the objectives, so that the articulation of the ends was conditioned by that of the means. Yet both the limitations of the means–end schema, and methodologies for dealing with problem-situations for which the means–end schema is inappropriate, had been discussed in publications by 1977, and the relevant methodological expertise could have been made available to the Board.

Limitations of the means–end schema

These limitations were the subject of an influential paper by Lindblom (1959), in which he made his often-quoted distinction between 'rational comprehensive' (or 'root') and 'incremental' (or 'branch') approaches to problem-handling. Checkland, in making the same distinction, uses the terms 'hard' and 'soft' systems methodologies. He describes the limitations of the hard (rational–comprehensive) approach as follows:

> Problems can be expressed as the search for an efficient means of reaching a defined objective or goal; once goals or objectives are defined, then systematic appraisal of alternatives, helped by various techniques, enables the problem (now one of selection) to be solved. . . . 'Hard' systems thinking is any structured problem solving which bases itself on this goal-seeking schema. . . . Well-structured problems . . . are capable of being expressed as a search for an end which is taken as given. . . . But what if ends are themselves problematical?
>
> (Checkland 1981)

Mattessich (1978: 37) similarly draws attention to the inappropriateness for instrumental reasoning of a methodology in which the value criteria regarding the desirability of objectives are 'externalized' from the theoretical system of a discipline. One could add the further observation that the 'hard systems' approach presupposes not merely that the objectives are given, but also that an adequate (even if probabilistic) knowledge exists of the cause and effect relationships relevant to the choice of means. Finally, and not least, means themselves are not value-free; in particular, their use is likely to entail an uneven distribution of benefits and costs over individuals, groups or generations, the acceptability of which depends on value judgements. Hence, the choice of objectives may be conditioned by judgements about what means would be acceptable. This, however, is impossible in a hard systems approach.

Lindblom's comparison of the 'root' and 'branch' approaches is given in Table 5.1 below.

Lindblom's ideas were introduced into the accounting literature by Gerboth (1972, 1973). However, Lindblom's 'science of muddling through' was far from being a developed methodology, and Gerboth was more concerned to present an apologia for the approach adopted by the APB than to pursue the question of alternative methodologies, to which we turn in the next section of this chapter.

Table 5.1 Comparison of the rational–comprehensive and successive limited comparison methods

	Rational–comprehensive (root)		*Successive limited comparisons (branch)*
1a	Clarification of values or objectives distinct from, and usually prerequisite to, empirical analysis of alternative policies.	1b	Selection of value goals and empirical analysis of the needed action are not distinct from one another but are closely intertwined.
2a	Policy formulation is therefore approached through means–end analysis: first the ends are isolated, then the means to achieve them are sought.	2b	Since means and ends are not distinct, means–end analysis is often inappropriate or limited.
3a	The test of a 'good' policy is that it can be shown to be the most appropriate means to desired ends.	3b	The test of a 'good' policy is typically that various analysts find themselves directly agreeing on a policy (without their agreeing that it is the most appropriate means to an agreed objective).
4a	Analysis is comprehensive; every important relevant factor is taken into account.	4b	Analysis is drastically limited: * Important possible outcomes neglected. * Important alternative potential policies are neglected. * Important affected values are neglected.
5a	Theory is often heavily relied upon.	5b	A succession of comparisons greatly reduces or eliminates reliance on theory.

Source: Lindblom 1959

Nevertheless, quite apart from the development of new methodologies in the mid-1970s to which reference was made above, enough was known in the early 1970s about the problems of the means–end schema for the FASB to have recognized that it was hardly more in a position to use the 'root' approach than the APB had been, and to have avoided using a language which ignored these problems. The FASB in fact acknowledged that means are not costless, and that the costs are unlikely to be borne in proportion to the expected benefits (SFAC 2, paras 133–44) (FASB 1980a); but it did not appear to draw the conclusion that objectives cannot be formulated, except in the most general of terms, without assumptions about means. Nor did the Board take any interest in the new approaches that were being developed in areas such as analytical jurisprudence and systems analysis applied to policy making. Instead, as we have seen, the Board remained trapped in the means–end schema; it attempted to establish the objectives in the expectation that the means would be seen to follow on from them, and in doing so was obliged to fudge the issue. In effect, the Board ended up using an incoherent combination of an epistemological approach characteristic of the 'branch' method and a rhetoric suggestive of the 'root' method.

The branch method ensures that no radical possibilities receive serious consideration; its essence is to permit no more than incremental departures from the *status quo*. Essentially, the branch method is intended to be used in domains in which the state of knowledge has not crossed what Foucault (1969: 243) termed 'the threshold of scientificity'. This refers to the step in the development of a field of knowledge which separates the beginnings of scientific knowledge from what may be described as 'clinical knowledge' (Archer 1988). These beginnings are characterized by the availability of definitions of elementary concepts, of variables related to these concepts, and of elementary methods of measurement leading to statements of the form '*x* varies from (or with) *y*' (Roethlisberger 1977: 393).

Knowledge of this kind permits policy analysts and others to evaluate the extent to which particular means are likely to be conducive to particular ends, a crucial component of the 'gross balance' method to be described on p. 102. Only when this is possible can the policy analyst begin to escape from the limitations of the branch method. It appears from the accounting research literature of the 1970s that financial accounting had crossed this threshold, thanks to the work of Ball and Brown (1968), Beaver (1968), and others. However, for reasons which will be briefly considered on pp. 202–5, but which lie largely outside the scope of this chapter and are addressed by Richard Mattessich on pp. 99–101, this development seems to find little or no echo in the conduct of the CF project by the FASB.

In 'Soft systems methodology' (p. 99), I hope to show that use of a 'soft systems' approach would have allowed the Board to grapple with the daunting issues facing it in a much more intellectually convincing way. First, however, it will be helpful to consider the FASB's problems from the standpoint of methodologies developed by legal scholars, concerned with analogous problems of authority and validity in relation to legal institutions and rules.

THE METHODOLOGIES OF ANALYTICAL JURISPRUDENCE AND THE PROBLEM OF NORMATIVITY

Introduction

Unless accounting standards are subsumed under the authority of the law, they need authority from some other source in order to possess generally accepted validity. This raises the issue of how the needed authority may be conferred upon an extra-legal, self-regulatory institution such as the FASB. Analytical jurisprudence offers a number of insights into this issue.

Analytical jurisprudence, as described by Raz (1979: 103), is concerned with three main problem areas. One relates to the special features of the judicial process and of judicial reasoning. A second deals with the idea of a legal system and the features which distinguish such systems from other normative systems. The third area involves the discussion of legal concepts, such as rights and duties, and of types of legal standards, such as rules, principles, duty-imposing standards and power-conferring standards. This third area, in particular, has a rather clear relevance to the conceptual problems of accounting standard setting, and it is the one to which most reference will be made here.

Historically, the first development in analytical jurisprudence was analytical positivism. The characteristic feature of positivism is that positivists insist on the dichotomy between fact and value, and eschew concern with value-issues except insofar as they can be considered as 'social facts'. Positivism has also been influential in accounting thought.

We therefore begin by considering analytical positivism, and will note the analogies between some major issues it raises and issues that have arisen in connection with certain past developments in accounting thought. This will draw attention to the difficulties that are encountered in addressing normative policy issues within a strict positivist framework. Certain methodological developments will be considered which have taken place in response to these difficulties. Finally, we examine what these latter developments could contribute to the methodology of constructing a CF for financial accounting.

Analytical positivism

Introduction

Analytical positivism in jurisprudence originated with the work of Jeremy Bentham and John Austin (not to be confused with the philosopher J.L. Austin) in the early to mid nineteenth century. In recent years, its best-known representatives have included Herbert Hart (e.g. Hart 1961) and Hans Kelsen (e.g. Kelsen 1967), while its leading opponent has been Ronald Dworkin (e.g. Dworkin 1977). An eminent scholar in the positivist tradition, who has continued the work of Kelsen and Hart, is Josef Raz (e.g. Raz 1975, 1979). The outline of analytical positivism in this paper owes much to the insights provided by Raz.

Rights (to financial information), duties (to make this information available), rules (power-conferring as well as duty-conferring), principles and standards (constitutive of generally accepted accounting principles), are among the main issues which have motivated the conceptual framework project. It is therefore of interest to see how analytical positivists have approached these concepts.

Rules and principles

Raz offers the following insights on the nature of rules:

> A valid law is a law, an invalid law is not. Similarly a valid rule is a rule and an invalid rule is not a rule at all. [One might] hold that an invalid rule is a rule which lacks the property of being valid. . . . This view is particularly appropriate if rules are identified with propositions or statements or some normative analogies of them, e.g. imperatives, prescriptions, or deontic propositions. . . . Endorsement of a deontic proposition (or . . . of imperatives) [that is, accepting the need to obey them] is conceived as being somehow analogous to belief with respect to ordinary propositions.
>
> [P]ersons . . . may have attitudes to deontic propositions or to imperatives which are analogous to belief if not identical with it. But all this has nothing to do with rules. Rules, but not propositions, are [*per se*] reasons for action. ('I believe that I ought to support my mother because of the rule (but not because of the deontic proposition) that children ought to respect their parents').
>
> These considerations of the role of rules as reasons may suggest that rules if not propositions or imperatives are *facts*, since facts are reasons for both action and for belief. . . . [W]e can rely on our linguistic intuitions which tell us that only to some deontic sentences can we fix 'it is a rule that' while preserving the truth value of the sentence. . . . Rules, therefore, are not statements nor prescriptions, not even justified or true prescriptions or

> statements. They are *things* the content of which is described by some normative statements and such statements are true if the rules exist, i.e. are valid. (Emphasis added)
>
> (Raz 1979: 146–50)

According to this view of rules, then, they are social facts; and such social facts may be considered as things. This reification of social facts is an ontological position characteristic both of legal positivists such as Raz and of structuralist sociologists such as Harré and Giddens (Burrell and Morgan 1979). The particular point made by Raz is that, in the case of rules, the social fact exists *only if the rule is valid*, for an invalid rule is no rule and therefore does not constitute a social fact.

The concept of validity is therefore crucial. As Raz points out, the view of the original legal positivists such as Austin was that the validity of a rule or norm lay not so much in its justification but rather in its being part of a system of rules that is *recognised as enforceable*. According to this view, the community, which incorporates the organs of enforcement, is considered as logically prior to the system of rules which regulates the behaviour of its members. More modern legal positivists such as Kelsen and Hart place greater emphasis on the way in which a system of rules or norms is itself constitutive of the community in which it prevails; and this is what they have in common with a number of sociological thinkers. Such an emphasis is consistent with the sociological insights of the writers already mentioned and also of Berger and Luckmann (1966). Rather than just coercion, it is the *normative force* and role of the system of rules, both in the constitution of individual thinking subjects and in the way in which the community reproduces itself over time, that are the basis of validity in a positivist sense.

We need to note that recognition in this positivist sense of the normative force and role of a system of rules does not entail moral approval of the system or of particular rules within it. From the perspective of a positivist jurisprudence, Raz argues that the normative force of a rule depends on considerations of *systemic validity*. According to this argument, the systemic validity of a rule is established by showing that it conforms to tests of validity laid down by some other rules of the system which can be called rules of recognition. These tests normally concern the way the rule was laid down by some recognized authority. The validity of rules of recognition is determined in a similar way, but to avoid an infinite regress the ultimate rules of recognition must be a matter of social fact, that is, a matter of their acceptance as binding in a given community (Raz

1979: 150–1). Thus, the ultimate rules of recognition for a country's legal system lie in that country's constitution and of the acceptance of the judgements of the country's highest court as binding (subject, in appropriate cases, to appeal to a superior court at a supranational level whose jurisdiction is constitutionally recognized, and whose judgement would be binding).

Raz's concept of systemic validity was developed in the context of an analytical positivist explication of the validity of rules within legal systems; its applicability to extra-legal systems of financial accounting rules cannot simply be taken for granted. Nevertheless, it seems perfectly reasonable to suggest that, from a positivist perspective, financial accounting rules either have validity in the sense that their normative force is, or exists by virtue of, a 'social fact', or else they are not rules at all (although they may be *proposed* rules). Let us use the terms 's-validity' and 's-valid' to indicate validity in this sense. If financial accounting standards are intended to be s-valid rules, then their normative force must be, or must exist by virtue of, a social fact. (This would not apply to the 'Statements of Recommended Practice' which the ASC and the ASB have issued, for these are not intended to be binding.) The following question is therefore crucial: what conditions must be satisfied in order for financial accounting standards to be s-valid, that is, for their obligatory character to be generally accepted 'as a social fact' within the community to which they apply?

Where financial accounting standards are promulgated as part of the law (as in Germany), they possess *ipso facto* the normative force of laws, and this is a sufficient condition for them to be s-valid rules. But where they are promulgated by a private sector body and do not receive legal backing, their s-validity cannot be subsumed under legal validity, and some other basis for s-validity must be sought.

It might be argued that insofar as SFASs possess s-validity in the USA, this is derived from the legal powers to regulate accounting vested by Congress in the SEC, and the latter's delegation of standard setting to the FASB under Accounting Series Release No. 150. This point is discussed further below. However, on the one hand, the FASB has followed the tradition in US accounting thought, which is to de-emphasize the role of the SEC in accounting standard setting, while seeking to ground the validity of financial accounting standards in 'general acceptance' within the American 'business and financial community' together with the observance of 'due process' in developing and promulgating new standards. On the other hand, such general acceptance is referred to as applying to *principles* rather that to rules, whence the familiar term 'generally accepted accounting principles' (GAAP).

This raises the question of whether there is any distinction between a (normative) principle and a rule. For example, Raz (1979: 214–18) lists a number of principles for the operation of a legal system which derive from the basic idea of the rule of law. These principles require that the law should conform to standards designed to enable it effectively to guide action, to ensure that the legal machinery of enforcement does not impair that ability to guide because of distorted enforcement, and to provide supervision of conformity to the law as well as effective remedies in cases of deviation from it. Such principles might be described as meta-rules, or rules that apply to the system as a whole. A more specific example might be the principle of *stare decisis* or legal precedent, whereby a court is normally considered as bound by the decisions of its predecessors on a point of law. However, the accounting literature has not introduced a clear distinction between accounting principles and accounting rules.

In the USA, 'promulgated GAAP' are considered to consist of:

1 The FASB's Statements of Financial Accounting Standards (SFASs) and Interpretations;
2 Unsuperseded Opinions and Accounting Research Bulletins issued by the APB and its predecessors the Committees on Accounting Procedure and on Terminology (APBOs and ARBs) (Miller, 1989: vii).

There is also reference to 'non-promulgated GAAP', that is, accounting principles which are generally accepted but have not been incorporated in ARBs, APBOs, SFASs or Interpretations (Miller 1989: vii). This might suggest a distinction between accounting standards (rules), which are promulgated by a standard-setting body, and accounting principles, which may or may not be incorporated into such promulgated rules; but such principles are not meta-rules. Their importance appears to lie in their being 'generally accepted' independently of being promulgated by a standard-setting body.

Thus, if s-validity derives from general acceptance being a social fact, then it would seem that, in the USA at least, there are two possible bases for the s-validity of accounting standards:

1 S-validity might be derived from the fact that accounting standards instantiate GAAP, when indeed they do so, for the latter are by definition generally accepted. This reasoning, which considers non-promulgated GAAP as analogous to common law principles, raises some difficulties which are discussed below.

2 Alternatively, s-validity might result from the accounting standards being backed up by the generally-accepted legal powers of the SEC, so that it would be lacking from a particular standard in the absence of the SEC's support.

On either of these views, it would not appear that the s-validity of accounting standards could result from their being promulgated by a recognized private sector standard-setting body such as the FASB; for that recognition does not extend to conferring on that body the power to create new rules that are *ipso facto* s-valid. However, an alternative thesis suggesting a stronger role for the FASB might be put foward as follows:

> As a matter of social fact in the USA, there is some generally-accepted but extra-legal *power-conferring rule*, by virtue of which the FASB is empowered to promulgate GAAP in the form of SFASs (and Interpretations) which are *ipso facto* s-valid (and perhaps similarly in the past for the APB and its Opinions and ARBs). This power-conferring rule, while extra-legal in itself, could be regarded as being s-valid by virtue of the delegation to the Board by the SEC of powers to set accounting standards which are legally vested in the latter body.

There are, however, two difficulties with this alternative. In the first place, it seems doubtful that this stronger role for the FASB can be asserted in the light of the SEC's power to oblige the Board to amend a standard, as happened in the case of SFAS No. 19. Secondly, it begs the question regarding the s-validity or otherwise of *non-promulgated GAAP*. If the latter are considered to be s-valid (on the analogy of common law principles), then it would be more logical to limit the alternative thesis to the following:

> One power conferred on the FASB is that to turn non-promulgated GAAP into promulgated GAAP – to codify GAAP, as it were.

The modified alternative thesis would be consistent with the notion that GAAP, or at least non-promulgated GAAP, are analogous to the principles and rules of the common law, which may be codified into statute law by the legislature if codification appears advantageous, for example, in order to remove ambiguities or lacunae. From the standpoint of Raz's analytical jurisprudence, however, this view of GAAP is problematic, since the principles and rules of the common law derive s-validity from their observance by the courts, whereas in the case of GAAP there is no institutional parallel (except possibly in the Netherlands, where this role is arguably played by the Enterprise Chamber, a division of the High Court of Justice). Hence, if non-promulgated GAAP possess s-validity in the USA, this must be by virtue of their observance by a duly empowered body in deciding which accounting practices are acceptable to it; and it would appear that this duly empowered body would be none other than the SEC (Bricker and Previts 1990). For example, it was the SEC that decreed that revaluations of property, plant and equipment were not a generally accepted accounting principle in the USA, whereas they previously had been generally accepted in the USA and have remained so in the UK.

Thus, it is hard to avoid the conclusion that the FASB's powers are limited to:

1 Codifying existing non-promulgated GAAP;
2 Creating new GAAP subject to the support of the SEC.

It is of interest at this point to enquire how the FASB appears to consider its own powers. Does it set out to create GAAP in at least some cases, or only to codify them? What does the Board suppose to be the role of a CF in relation to its powers? With regard to this latter question, the FASB's original idea seems to have been that the CF, as a *constitution*, would constitute the rules of recognition whereby the validity (s-validity?) of financial accounting standards could be established. The CF would thus, in effect, act in a power-conferring capacity so far as the Board was concerned. Armed with the CF, as it were, the FASB would have the power to create GAAP. But as Pelham Gore has pointed out, the Board's standard on pension fund accounting, SFAS No. 87, specifically states that the standard does not follow the CF, since to do so might be seen as too radical, that is, too great a departure from existing GAAP (Gore 1989: 6).

This behaviour on the part of the Board has two important implications: first, that it did not consider the CF to be an effective power-conferring device so far as SFAS No. 87 was concerned; and second, that it did not feel itself to be empowered to create substantially new GAAP in the area of pension fund accounting.

This stultifying outcome is hardly surprising in the light of the problems inherent in the FASB's basic approach to the CF, and in particular the element of contradiction between the means–end schema and incrementalism, to which reference was made on p. 81. Insofar as the CF was intended to confer powers of standard setting on the FASB *independent of those delegated to it by the SEC*, it was evidently unsuccessful.

Ideologically speaking, however, so far as self-regulation is concerned, appearance may be more important than reality. Thus, it may be acceptable for the FASB to be, in the final analysis, the SEC's catspaw, provided the final analysis is generally avoided. From this perspective, the CF might be seen as a partially effective effort to sustain a cherished myth of self-regulation; a myth which, for much of the time, is not in obvious contradiction to reality. This view would be consistent with the view of the CF as 'folk-science' to which reference is made on p. 112. If such a view were correct, then it would follow that in the final analysis the CF was intended to provide 'comfort and reassurance to some body of believers' (Ravetz 1971: 360), rather than effective intellectual guidance and authority for the development of accounting thought and practice.

The advantages and limitations of analytical positivism

The analysis provided above illustrates the ability of analytical positivism (as a methodology of jurisprudence) to cast light on the institutional problems of financial accounting, but it also shows one of its important limitations. It is a powerful tool for explicating the *status quo*, and helps to locate and characterize the problems of authority and validity facing the FASB. But in terms of guidance for change, it has little or nothing to offer. S-validity is explicated as the outcome of a social process, but this process is not itself analysed in any depth, nor are any means for influencing it suggested. For one thing, analytical positivists as legal scholars take sociology in general, and the sociology of law in particular, for granted. For another, positivists are typically uninterested in the normative problems of change. Yet the need being addressed in this chapter is for a methodology which avoids these limitations.

Therefore, while it would be possible at this point to continue by examining in some detail issues of rights and duties from the perspective of analytical positivism, for example those of 'accountors' and 'accountees' (Ijiri 1975, chapter 2), enough has already been said to illustrate both the insights to be gained from the application of this approach to the subject matter of this chapter, and also its limitations in that context. For a legal positivist, an accountee's right to financial accounting information is a matter of 'social fact', that is, of law or of established social norms that are s-valid, and not a matter of moral entitlement. One may have s-valid rights to do something that one is not morally entitled to do (e.g. to take advantage of loopholes in financial accounting standards in a way that is detrimental to the quality of the published financial information to which others have a moral entitlement); conversely, one may have a moral entitlement to something but no s-valid right to it (Raz 1979, chapter 14). Similar considerations apply to obligations or duties; an obligation conferred by a s-valid rule is not equivalent to a moral obligation, and vice versa.

It will be said that a major advantage of a positivist approach is that it focuses on issues of fact and can therefore avoid the issues of value which tend to be the subjects of so much controversy, such as the issue of whether employees (or some other group in society) ought to be included among accountees. The positivist is concerned with whether employees *have* that right, not with whether they *ought* to have it. The essence of positivism is insistence on the dichotomy between fact and value, which are seen as logically and epistemologically different categories, so that according to positivists one cannot infer normative propositions from only factual (positive) propositions or vice versa.

This led Kelsen, for example, to argue that the normativity of a system of rules, and in particular of a legal system, could not logically follow from a set of purely factual propositions, such as the proposition that the State brings sanctions to bear against transgressors. Rather, the normativity of the system presupposes at least one normative proposition, to which he referred as the fundamental or basic norm (*Grundnorm*). In this respect, Kelsen partially anticipated the later development of a formal 'deontic logic' (a logic of deontic 'must' or 'ought' propositions) by philosophers such as Georg Hendrik von Wright (von Wright 1961).

The approach taken by Raz is somewhat different, for he insists that a valid rule is not the same as a deontic proposition. In particular, such a rule constitutes a reason for action in a way in which a deontic proposition does not. Raz refers to such a reason for action as a 'protected reason' (Raz 1979, chapter 1); unlike a deontic proposition, it is 'protected' against being overridden by other reasons which, from a moral standpoint, may be equally or more weighty. It is relevant to our present concerns to consider to what extent the notion of s-validity, which reflects Raz's position, is a notion that is only compatible with a thoroughgoing positivism. In other words, can Raz's version of analytical positivism as a methodology of law be reconciled with a non-positivist epistemology, as Raz himself suggests might be possible? This is important, in that it would allow us to benefit from the insights of the analytical jurists while escaping from the constraints of thoroughgoing positivism.

I shall argue not merely that such a reconciliation can be made, but that Raz's sophisticated concept of normativity *needs* to be understood in the context of such an epistemology. In the following passage, Raz (1979: 158) envisages a 'cautious positivist', as follows:

> Even if the law is essentially moral – the cautious positivist would argue – it is clear that establishing the moral merit of a law is a different process relying on different considerations, from establishing its existence as a social fact'.

By being prepared to recognize that the law is essentially moral, the cautious legal positivist (and it would seem that Raz includes himself in this category) accepts that some social facts, namely laws, essentially have important moral implications; that is, they are essentially value-laden. Such positivists insist, however, that by rejecting the values inherent in some law (for example, its wealth-distributional intentions), one does not thereby deny its legal validity which depends on different considerations.

Raz distinguishes three theses which can be a basis for legal positivism: the social thesis, the moral thesis and the semantic thesis (1979: 37). The social thesis states that law is essentially a social institution, the existence of which is a matter of fact. The moral thesis asserts that conformity to moral values or ideals is in no way a condition for anything being a law or legally binding. The semantic thesis denies that terms like 'rights' and 'duties' can be used in the same meaning in legal and moral contexts. The cautious positivist accepts the social thesis but is uncommitted to either the moral or the semantic thesis. With regard to the moral thesis, the cautious positivist distinguishes between saying that rejection of the values inherent in some law does not entail rejecting its legal validity, and saying that there is no necessary connection between the law and any moral values or ideals. The first statement is accepted, while the second is rejected.

I shall argue below that the positivism of the cautious legal positivist is a limited methodological, and not a thoroughgoing epistemological, positivism. First, though, I want to review some objections to epistemological positivism, taking account of insights offered by sociologists of knowledge such as Thomas Berger and Peter Luckmann (Berger and Luckmann 1966).

Although epistemological positivism dominated mainstream philosophical and scientific thinking for over a century, and in accounting thinking has been particularly influential since the 1960s, it has recently been the object of searching criticism by both philosophers such as Hilary Putnam (Putnam 1981) and by systems theorists and practitioners such as Rowe (1977) and Checkland (1981). Putnam (1981: chapter 6) argues that 'every fact is value loaded and every one of our values loads some fact'. For a critique of positivism by the present writer, see Archer (1988).

In relation to our discussion of s-validity, it needs to be recognized that a positivist social science can hardly explain how certain propositions come to have, as rules and principles, the normative force in a human community described by Raz. To understand how normativity comes about, insight is obtained from considering the development of individuals as cognitive and moral subjects through intersubjective processes in their community, and how values and facts learned through these processes are intertwined in the development of the human subject *qua* subject through an intersubjective process (Berger and Luckmann 1966). Moreover, the identity of the human community over time depends upon the reproduction of its characteristics through intersubjective processes such as the communication of beliefs, and not least of values, taking place between its members. Giddens (1976) refers to this process as 'structuration'. If analytical jurisprudence could be made compatible with a non-positivist social science, then it would offer a more fruitful basis for methodological thinking with regard to financial accounting.

Raz (1979), as part of his exposition of legal positivism, frequently refers to legal rules as 'social facts'; and it should be clear that by the same token any s-valid rule is a social fact. Accepting that it is a separate issue whether the rule is morally commendable, one may nevertheless insist (as Raz allows) that the rule is *value-laden*. Thus, Raz's argument is hardly an argument for the rigid dichotomy of fact and value. The fact–value distinction may indeed be useful at a certain level of discourse (the methodology of determining 'what is the law'): but this does not imply that it is also appropriate at the more fundamental cognitive (logical and epistemological) levels. It follows that some forms of legal positivism may be compatible with a non-positivist social science.

My interpretation of the 'cautious positivism' described by Raz is that it is methodological rather than epistemological, and that his insights into the nature of the normative effectiveness of rules from the standpoint of systemic validity can be borrowed by accounting thinkers without entailing a commitment to epistemological positivism.

These considerations are relevant to our present concerns, for the thinking behind the FASB's CF project seems to be trapped in a typically positivistic impasse. This can be seen from their attempted espousal of the means–end schema, or (to use Checkland's term) of a 'hard systems' approach. Within such an approach, issues of value (goals, objectives, ends) are treated as logically and epistemologically different from matters of fact concerning cause and effect relationships which constitute the basis of means. As already noted, the approach requires the ends (normative propositions) to be stated first; it then becomes a factual matter (involving only positive propositions) as to which means are most efficiently conducive to those ends. Of course, the members of the FASB were aware that the problem situation they were facing was much more complex than that; but their attempt to structure it in a hard systems manner reveals the influence of positivism – an unhelpful influence, in this case.

Positivism was, indeed, embraced with pride by influential members of the academic accounting community in the USA during the 1970s. This was seen by writers such as Watts and Zimmerman (1979) as a necessary step in the emergence of accounting thought from dogmatism and tendentiousness, and in the development of the discipline as an applied social science. However, the distinction between methodological and epistemological positivism which was made above is relevant here. 'Positive accounting theory' in the epistemological sense, with its insistence on a strict fact–value dichotomy, offers no way out of the impasse of the means–end schema and the hard systems approach when considering a possible basis for a CF for financial accounting. If it is understood in the more limited methodological sense, its usefulness can be exemplified by the analysis of s-validity as applied to accounting rules which was given above.

The 'new analytical jurisprudence'

Earlier, we identified one of the main problems of analytical positivism as being its failure to provide normative guidance for change. Dissatisfaction with this state of affairs led Robert S. Summers in 1966 to propose an approach which he saw as more dynamic and forward-looking:

> If the analytical jurist is to provide the illumination and insight of which he is capable, he must commonly go beyond the conceptual status quo. He must go beyond analysing concepts within our conceptual scheme as it is, and devise improved ways of more adequately representing reality. The necessity for such creative

> and constructive effort stems from two sources. First, our existing conceptual framework does not always have things right initially. Second, things change, and our concepts lag behind, thus becoming outmoded.
>
> (Summers 1966)

Summers argued that analytical jurists should undertake three kinds of creative activity in addition to the analysis of the conceptual status quo:

1 conceptual revision, or the construction of new conceptual frameworks which take account of the changes in society;
2 rational justification, or analysis of the 'case' for, say, civil disobedience, or for punishment as such, or for the legal principle of *stare decisis* (legal precedent);
3 purposive implication, or tracing 'what the acceptance of social purposes, aims or values commits us to in terms of social arrangements and social ordering'.

The distinction between rational justification and purposive implication is that the latter is essentially a simulation exercise to consider the practical implications of particular value-positions, while the former consists of examining the arguments for and against such value-positions. The relationship between the two is that purposive implication may uncover new reasons which need to be considered by repeating part or all of the rational justification.

The analytical methodology proposed by Summers has affinities with the conceptual 'soft systems' modelling proposed by Checkland, and the 'gross balance' method proposed by Rowe, which are described on p. 102. These non-positivist methodologies exemplify the notion of an 'enquiring system', incorporating a dialectical concept of truth. As Rowe puts it, quoting Mitroff and Turoff (1973):

> The truth-content of a system of knowledge is the result of a plan and diametrically opposed counterplan. Their function is to engage each other in an unremitting debate over the 'true' nature of the whole system.
>
> (Rowe 1977: 195)

For illustrative purposes, I will briefly outline here an application of Summers' approach to two issues with which the CF project was concerned; the identity of those who have a right to be classed as 'accountees' and to receive corporate financial reports; and the type of information to which they thereby have a right.

A first step would be to use rational justification to analyse the case for and against classing various groups in society as accountees. One could then employ purposive implication to examine these cases in order to see which ones were consistent with various sets of social purposes, aims and values, such as concerns for wealth creation, for social equity or fairness, and for the environment. A final step would involve conceptual revision: how does the CF need to develop in order to underpin a system of corporate accountability whose appropriateness was indicated in the course of the two earlier stages?

The outline just given, however, begs a number of important questions. In particular, both rational justification and purposive implications involve requirements for information about cause and effect relationships regarding the extent to which particular means are likely to be conducive to particular ends. Such information may not be readily available, and the methodology needs to take this explicitly into account.

For example, in considering the matter of accounting for oil and gas reserves, not just conceptual but also empirical issues require careful attention. Important conceptual issues include the following: to what extent does the 'full cost' method, whereby the costs of dry wells are attached to those of productive wells, exemplify income smoothing (deliberate reduction of the fineness of the information) rather than 'fair presentation' in terms of accrual accounting? How can one locate the boundary between 'accruals' and 'smoothing'? Answering these questions is, however, not enough, for they raise equally if not more important empirical questions, such as: to what extent and in what circumstances are information users actually disadvantaged by income smoothing? Are they able to reconstitute the lost fineness of the information, and if so at what cost? Does this cause disadvantages to particular categories of user? Are smaller oil and gas producers actually disadvantaged compared to larger producers with regard to the capital markets as a consequence of using the 'successful efforts' method?

The point that rule making in accounting has to reflect the needs of accountors as well as those of accountees was made by Ijiri (1975: 45). Moreover, even if one accepts that, from the standpoint of public policy, 'users' needs are paramount', it is still necessary to ascertain what users' needs are and how they may be satisfied, rather than relying on the *idées reçues* and folk wisdom of accounting practitioners to provide answers to these questions. What would seem to be needed, therefore, in order to develop a CF for financial accounting is a combination of the conceptual rigour of the analytical jurist with the attention to empirical issues of the social scientist.

Thus, in the débâcle over SFAS No. 19, the FASB appears to have been equipped neither conceptually nor empirically to substantiate its case for the 'successful efforts' method, in the face of political pressure from the smaller producers. This pressure induced the SEC to withhold its support from that aspect of the Standard, and resulted in its revision by means of SFAS No. 25 – a somewhat ignominious defeat for the FASB.

In the section 'Soft systems methodology' (p. 99), I outline a methodology which has much in common with the 'new analytical jurisprudence' described by Summers, but which gives greater weight to the investigation of empirical issues and to coping with empirical uncertainty, as well as with possible lack of agreement over objectives.

Summary

Analytical jurisprudence has a number of insights to offer, relevant to the problems facing the FASB in its search for a conceptual framework. In the first place, we have been able to see how the existence of such a framework could, subject to certain conditions, provide a basis for the validity of accounting standards as a set of rules, and for the authority of the Board as the rule-making body. The possibilities of the FASB's idea of the CF as a constitution are thereby greatly clarified. So also is the nature of the severe limitations of the existing CF as developed by the Board. Perhaps these conditions for systemic validity could not be satisfied, in that no private sector body such as the FASB could expect to achieve a status and authority as a rule-making body analogous to those possessed by public institutions such as legislatures, even for a limited domain such as financial accounting. On the other hand, if the legislature permits the rule-making role in such a domain to be delegated by a governmental agency (the SEC) to a private sector body, this may have important implications for the status and authority of such a body within that domain. These are, indeed crucial issues which arise out of the consideration of the CF project from the standpoint of analytical jurisprudence; but they were not addressed as part of the CF project as it was conducted by the FASB.

Some of the intellectual limitations of the CF and of the methodology used to develop it were examined in 'The FASB's methodology' (p. 71). What emerges from the analysis presented in this section is the price paid by the FASB for the relative intellectual isolationism of the accounting thought exemplified in its work on the CF. Whereas a rich literature existed in jurisprudence which was directly relevant to several major issues involved in constructing a CF for financial accounting, the Board and its reseachers paid no attention to it. Nor indeed was attention paid to any other discipline, with the exception of some references at a general level to the economic theory of asset valuation.

Choi and Mueller (1984: 50) refer to a view of accounting as an 'independent discipline'; that is, presumably, one whose basic principles are not derived from any other disciplines. There is a sense in which the analytical positivist school of legal scholars regards the law as an independent or autonomous discipline, in that the law arguably has unique characteristics as a system of rules, a systemic validity *sui generis*, which is not derivable from sociology, economics, psychology or any combination of social sciences. At the very least, however, such legal scholars would admit, and even insist on, the crucial role of philosophy and logic in analytical jurisprudence. Accounting thinkers concerned with constructing a CF for financial accounting need to consider, among other things, just how 'independently' such a CF could be constructed.

Finally, we have been able to see one of the limitations of thoroughgoing or epistemological positivism, namely its focus upon explicating the *status quo* and the associated failure to provide normative guidance for change; and we have noted that this failure is also characteristic of the attempt, made by the FASB, to combine the means–end schema or 'hard systems' approach with incrementalism. It is time to examine 'soft systems' methodologies in order to see what assistance they may offer. One notable attribute of these methodologies is that, in contrast to the 'autonomous discipline' perspective, they emphasize the incorporation into the analytical framework of relevant theory and empirical enquiry.

SOFT SYSTEMS METHODOLOGY

Introduction

The term 'soft systems methodology' (SSM) appears to be due to Checkland (1981), who has played a leading role in developing one such approach. This, however, is essentially a micro- or organization-level approach which has been applied in numerous assignments of a management consultancy nature. In principle, what is needed in order to grapple with the problematic situation of financial accounting is a macro or societal level approach. Such an approach is described by Rowe, who states that what he terms the 'gross balance' method is 'particularly suited for decision making at the societal level' (Rowe 1977: 237). SSM should be distinguished from Lindblom's (1959) 'branch' method, which was, however, influential in its development.

The background for the development of this methodology lies in work carried out in the USA during the 1960s and 1970s in the sphere of public policy analysis and societal risk assessment (for example, by members of 'think tank' organizations such as the RAND Corporation and the MITRE Corporation). The experience gained from this work illustrated the shortcomings of the 'root' or hard systems approach, but the 'branch' approach as described by Lindblom was not felt to be an adequate alternative. Rowe makes the point as follows:

> [T]he need for societal risk assessment has become progressively more urgent as new and developing technologies thrust increasingly complex issues on a society [whose members are] more able to make individual choices than social choices. . . . Useful information [in making such choices] can be provided by both the root and branch approaches, but neither guarantees success or even help. In the root method the cost of dealing with many complex variables and the imprecise results may well outweigh the usefulness of identifying critical factors. Society seems to operate on the branch method, but . . . this is a major reason behind the increasing desperation of our plight.
>
> (Rowe 1977: 202)

Rowe's concerns were with issues such as the environmental impact of fast breeder reactors, and these are no doubt more momentous than the issues of accounting regulation; but the latter are no less complex for all that. How is accounting rule-making to deal in an intellectually rigorous manner with the combination of conflicting objectives, immature theories and inconclusive evidence which characterize its subject matter? This was the nature of the problematic facing the FASB with regard to the CF project. I shall argue that the 'gross balance' method described by Rowe illustrates a methodology, having affinities with the 'new analytical jurisprudence' described by Summers, which would have offered the FASB the means to develop a CF in an intellectually rigorous and systematic manner, avoiding the pitfalls of positivism and the means–end schema on the one hand, and the limitations of simply 'muddling through' on the other hand.

The crux of this argument is that the application of social science to issues in society, and in particular to the making of accounting rules, calls for the use of a soft systems framework such as that described by Rowe. This is because such a framework can offer two crucial advantages: both disagreements about the ends to be sought, and also uncertainties regarding the cause and effect relationships linking means to ends, may be handled in a systematic manner. Thus, instead of *ad hoc* expedients, there is a prospect of intellectually defensible and more durable solutions.

It is significant that the gross balance method had been developed by the mid-1970s, and would therefore have been available for use by the FASB had the Board's members or advisers been aware of it. This is not to claim that the method is above criticism, or that it may not have been superseded in some respects during the last fifteen years; but it is not hard to see that methodologically it was far ahead of the approach used by the FASB in the CF project.

At this point, however, some reference needs to be made to the proposition advanced by writers such as Watts and Zimmerman (1986: chapter 10), that the behaviour of the members of the FASB, as with other regulators, is best understood if one recognizes that while ostensibly concerned with maximizing social welfare (serving the public interest) in their regulatory domain, they are in fact seeking to maximize their own utility as regulators. If that is so, then it might be unrealistic to expect the FASB to adopt a public policy oriented methodology, for in effect the FASB is faced with the essentially private problem of how to thrive as a regulatory body in its domain. On this view, one might be drawn towards considering Checkland's methodology rather than Rowe's as a possible model for the FASB. Such an approach, however, would concern itself with modelling the relations between the FASB and the significant elements of its environment, and while it might result in much enlightenment as regards institutional issues of that kind, it would not necessarily lead to the consideration of questions relevant to the methodology of developing a conceptual framework for financial accounting. For this reason, Checkland's approach will not be considered further here. Instead, attention will be focused on the gross balance method described by Rowe (1977: chapter 12).

The gross balance method

Introduction

Rowe's exposition of what he terms the gross balance method forms part of his discussion of methodological problems and approaches in the quantification of risks, from a perspective of social choice. He concurs with Lindblom's critique (which was mentioned on p. 81) of the 'rational-comprehensive' or 'root' method of decision making in matters of social choice; but he argues that total rejection of the 'root' approach in favour of Lindblom's alternative 'branch' method (successive limited comparisons) is not justified.

> [While] the 'root' system does not by itself solve prolems . . . [or] answer overall policy questions, . . . it [can] provide focus on the important parameters and factors affecting such questions, . . . yield insight on the major issues . . . [and] allow decoupling of the problems . . . in the nearer term from the problems . . . in the long term. The point to be made is that useful information can be provided by both the root and branch approaches, but neither guarantees success or even help. . . . Since both approaches have some merit, hybrid approaches that use the best aspects of both and restrict their disadvantages should be considered. Such mixed approaches are based on the types and content of the information needed to obtain results, or conversely, [on] how uncertainty is reduced.
>
> (Rowe, 1977: 200–2)

With regard to the reduction of uncertainty, Rowe points out that two kinds of uncertainty need to be considered: descriptive uncertainty and measurement uncertainty. Analysis of what is involved points the way to the delineation of the gross balance method.

In the reduction of descriptive uncertainty under the root method, the process of definition entails many variables, each defined explicitly, with assurance that all variables are covered and properly defined. The problem is often so complex that purely semantic definition needs to be supplemented by graphic structures (hierarchies, tree structures, flow diagrams and the like). Mathematical techniques such as formal logic, set theory and matrix algebra can provide formal methods of definition and description; but only those trained in those methods can understand them. On the other hand, a large section of society can understand verbal or written definitions insofar as our language is able to provide the needed level of discrimination clearly and unambiguously; but our language is limited in its ability to do this.

By contrast, in the branch approach only the variables that incrementally affect the problem are considered, all other variables being excluded. This simplifies the problem, especially since both the definition of the variables and the definition of policies may be at the same level of detail, so that each set of definitions contributes to the other. There is, however, a danger of over-simplification.

In the reduction of measurement uncertainty, we are concerned with the values assigned to defined variables and the expression of functional relationships between them within a structure. In the root approach, the structure is established, then values are assigned to each independent variable within the structure. The values are entered into the structure (or model) for different policy alternatives and the values of the outcomes are compared. The outcome values are by definition measured on a scale of desirability in terms of achieving defined ends or goals.

Rowe comments that the shortcomings of the root approach in this context become apparent as the number of variables to be measured increases. In the first place, for outcome variables, while cardinal and ratio scales offer infinite precision, precision beyond a certain level may be irrelevant or even meaningless (as in 'I like ham sandwiches 1.95843106 times better than cheese sandwiches'); and in any case precision does not mean accuracy, since a measure may be precise but erroneous. Secondly, there is a limitation to the accuracy with which values may be assigned to variables, including the independent variables. This may be a particular problem when values of the latter are obtained empirically from direct observation, because of possible limitations of the measurement systems and the observers which may lead to statistical errors or bias. Rowe remarks that, although even larger inaccuracies may arise in the expression of value judgements, limited accuracy is expected and acknowledged in these cases, while 'the inaccuracies in empirical measures are sometimes masked by the elegance of the data acquisition methodology' (Rowe 1977: 204).

Here, the branch method has the advantage that the existence of imprecision and inaccuracy, both in assigning values and in stating policy alternatives, is accepted at the outset. Being incremental, the method compares values and policies on a relative basis, and precision and accuracy are needed only to the extent necessary to permit discrimination between alternatives at each successive limited comparison. The pragmatic character of this approach means that the information sought is limited to that necessary to make a decision, at least in principle; but one needs to be wary that significant factors may have been ignored or omitted.

Such an evaluation of the strengths and weaknesses of the root and branch approaches leads, therefore, to the development of hybrid approaches such as the gross balance method. According to Rowe, this method is essentially the process that evolved following the enactment of the US National Environmental Policy Act of 1969. He is thus not the inventor of the method, but has 'simply identified it, formalized it, and provided a stepwise structure for its implementation' (Rowe 1977: 207).

This structure consists of four steps, as follows:

Step 1 – structural modelling

This is the development of a theoretical, structural model that covers all significant possible considerations, the root method being used as a pre-screening technique to assure that all meaningful variables have been considered and described. Here, the model is supposed to provide insight into the problem under study, and to ensure that all critical variables and alternatives have been considered: there is no expectation of a direct contribution to a solution. The amount of resources committed to this step should be commensurate with the type of final decision to be made and the contribution made to the acceptability of that decision by the assurance of comprehensiveness in considering all relevant factors.

Step 2 – exercising the model

The objective of the model is realized when it is 'exercised', using gross estimates of initial values, to isolate the critical parameters. When data are not available, best guesses and value judgements may be used. Sensitivity analysis is then employed to determine which possibilities and variables are critical for policy choices, for example in determining the cost–benefit balance. This process tends to highlight the points at which particular features of the model, such as theoretical assumptions made and magnitudes used in particular estimates, are critical in arriving at a solution.

Step 3 – consideration of further data

The first points to be considered are whether further or better data are available on critical alternatives and variables or parameters, and if so whether the benefit of having them, in terms of securing credible policy agreement, would exceed the cost of obtention, including disbenefits resulting from delays in decision making. Note that the pragmatic objective is credible policy agreement, and if gross measures are sufficient for this, additional data acquisition may be desirable but not mandatory.

Step 4 – gross balance analysis

The critical parameters and the meaningful policy alternatives are available for analysis in this final step. The critical parameters are reviewed for completeness; personal and political parameters may be added. The analysis uses critical variables or parameters and policy alternatives together so as to reach an acceptable decision. Relative levels of importance may be assigned to different parameters, and policy alternatives are analysed to determine how well they achieve mitigation of conflicts between parameters. If no policy alternative clearly emerges as the most desirable, the analysis of interaction of alternative policies with each parameter is studied in an attempt to synthesize a new alternative which may be a compromise. Conversely, weights of parameters may be adjusted so as to 'force' a clear policy agreement. This does not imply coercion, says Rowe, but a studied re-evaluation of values and policies which may in itself help in reaching agreement. Thus, policies and values are successfully evaluated until a 'position' is reached, which may not be a solution but is the best that can be done in a given situation.

There is no straightforward mapping of these four steps into the three activities described by Summers as constituting the methodology of the new analytical jurisprudence (see p. 96). The first step has affinities with what Summers called 'conceptual revision', but without the idea that one would start off from some existing conceptual framework. Instead, structural modelling presupposes some theory on which the model would be based, and the 'revision' of that model is a possible outcome of 'exercising' it during the second step. This second step has some similarity to what Summers termed 'purposive implication', the latter being in effect a kind of exercising of the model in order to examine the social implications of particular normative or value assumptions. The fourth step, gross balance analysis, encompasses Summers' 'rational justification', or examining the case for various policy alternatives.

The crucial difference between the two methodologies lies in

Rowe's third step, with its commitment to empirical enquiry guided by the results of exercising the model. As already noted on p. 96, no such commitment is apparent in Summers' proposals. The tradition of analytical jurisprudence is one in which emphasis is placed upon the status of law as an autonomous discipline. Thus, there was no irony in the choice of the title of Hans Kelsen's famous treatise *The Pure Theory of Law* (Kelsen 1967). This view of law as autonomous seems, indeed, to be the common one; and, in practice, law has its own epistemology as reflected in its procedures and criteria for establishing the truth. This epistemological autonomy of law leads to the kinds of difficulties which are exemplified by the fact that the legal concept of insanity is quite distinct from the medical one. It is probably fair to say that, if law were obliged to adopt the epistemologies of the various sciences, it could no longer be administered by lawyers. Thus, the societal role of law and its institutions may be seen as imposing upon it a need for epistemological autonomy. Whether the same applies to financial accounting is an issue which we shall need to consider below.

The method's potential application to the CF project

The gross balance method seeks to be 'rational' while acknowledging that it cannot be 'comprehensive'. In other words, while policy decisions typically have to be made in the light of theories and evidence which are incomplete, this does not mean that we are stuck with nothing better than the very limited rationality of the branch method. It does mean, however, that rationality cannot be imposed in a rigid way by the policy analyst. Space must be left for different value-perspectives at certain stages of the decision process. In particular, this is done in step 4, termed 'gross balance analysis'.

The application of the gross balance method to the CF project would not result in anything like the FASB's CF. Instead, a methodological framework would be developed for reaching decisions about financial accounting standards. This framework is intended to structure the decision process in such a way as to provide what Summers termed 'rational justification' for the decision in the light of all the theory, evidence and value-perspectives that could practicably be incorporated into the analysis. By theory, one does not mean primarily accounting theory, but theory relevant to assessing the social desirability of whatever has been decided. Such a framework could be applied first to the decision to develop a standard or set of standards to cover one or more issues in financial accounting and reporting, and then to the individual standards proposed.

As noted above, the first step of the gross balance method consists of developing a structural model. The type of structural model most relevant to the CF project would be some kind of cost–benefit model of financial accounting and reporting (Daley and Tranter 1990). Such models are discussed in Rowe (1977: chapter 14). The relevant model would incorporate variables representing the costs, risks and benefits to various categories of user and preparer, to auditors, and to the wider public potentially affected by the costs of accounting regulation and the benefits (e.g. in terms of greater capital market efficiency) which might be associated with improved financial reporting.

Rowe distinguishes two kinds of cost which need to be considered in such a model. In his terminology, direct costs are costs in the classical economic sense, and comprise outlays to obtain specific benefits and to reduce indirect costs. The latter may be considered to consist of losses of an inherently probabilistic nature, that is to say, risks of both economic costs and other losses, involving probability of occurrence of consequences as opposed to relatively certain consequences. Benefits comprise gains, both direct and indirect.

If the same measurement scale could be used for benefits and indirect costs (risks), then an optimum position or balance could be found at which a marginal outlay (direct cost) to achieve a benefit would be no more efficient than a marginal outlay to reduce risk. But in practice this is seldom possible; two different scales are involved, and attempts to find weights to assign to them in order to equate them result in considerable uncertainty (Rowe 1977: 232–3). Finding an optimum balance thus involves a problem of aggregation.

It also involves difficulties resulting from uncertainty in measurement. Thus, even when the scales for benefits and indirect costs are, or have been made, equivalent, the uncertainties of measurement may be so large that meaningful analysis is not feasible. To estimate the level of meaningful precision of comparisons, it is necessary to examine all measurements, scale transformations and value judgements to determine their precision and levels of uncertainty, and to evaluate the feasibility of measuring the relevant parameters.

From the perspective of the gross balance method, therefore:

> Detailed cost–benefit analyses cannot provide precise answers to questions involving societal and political value judgements. . . . Cost–benefit analysis is thus a tool for gaining insight into decision-making parameters. It is not a means to make decisions.
>
> (Rowe, 1977: 242–3)

Various arguments might be deployed against the proposal to employ the gross balance method together with a cost–benefit model. One obvious set of objectors would be the ideological opponents of cost–benefit analysis, that is, those who believe that the market will always result in solutions which are socially preferable to those which are based at least in part on non-market considerations. Such objectors, however, are *ipso facto* opponents of accounting regulation. For such people, the entire role of the FASB is based on a misconception. Since such a view is hardly compatible with the kind of consideration of the FASB's problems with which we are concerned in this chapter, it can hardly be a reason for rejecting the proposal.

Another objection might be that such a proposal is inherently reductionist: that, in effect, it seeks to reduce financial accounting theory to welfare economics. As already noted, one of the characteristics of the US (and British) approach to financial accounting, according to Choi and Mueller (1984: 50), is that it is treated as an 'independent discipline' somewhat as law is so treated; the proposal would remove that independence or autonomy, if it exists. To this objection, a twofold reply may be given. In the first place, the societal and institutional reasons for the epistemological autonomy of law are not present in the case of financial accounting, except insofar as the latter is incorporated into the law; in which case, far from being autonomous, it becomes part of the domain of law. Secondly, the proposal does not entail the reduction of financial accounting to economics. It does not imply, for example, that accounting concepts such as capital and income should be the same as the economic concepts having the same names.

Insistence on intellectual autonomy for accounting would, however, be unrealistic and stultifying, as was recognized by Canning (1929) and others many years ago. One of the leading books on accounting theory of the 1960s (Edwards and Bell 1961) was firmly based on economics. More recently, much research into financial accounting has been, and continues to be, guided by theories from economics (information economics, agency theory, capital market theory). Finally, the proposal can be regarded as reductionist only if the status of accounting as an applied discipline is denied, which is hardly possible. Numerous accounting thinkers have recognized that the conceptual foundations of accounting are to be sought in economics, law, social psychology, socio-linguistics and other branches of the social sciences. Among others, Ijiri (1975) drew attention to this. For example, he referred to work in linguistics such as that of Whorf (1956) as being relevant to accounting, commenting:

> Accounting measurement which measures the economic performance of an entity is, therefore, not only a passive representation of real world phenomena, but is also an active agent affecting the real world through its influence on the decision maker.
>
> (Ijiri 1975: 188)

The issue, then, cannot be one of reductionism, but of what bodies of knowledge may be fruitfully applied to the domain of accounting. To be sure, so far as cost–benefit analysis is concerned, the methodological problems mentioned above must be borne in mind. With regard to the problems of welfare economics, such as defining social welfare functions and collective choice rules, Rowe comments on the understanding and use of revealed preferences as follows:

> Much of the improved power of these techniques has come from altering or abandoning assumptions that every citizen votes, that every citizen has a 'complete set' of policy references, and that policy references are unidimensionally transitive.
>
> (Rowe 1977: 193)

The gross balance approach, moreover, allows the implications of more than one collective choice rule to be studied. To explore such questions further, however, would require a separate chapter. A helpful discussion of them is provided by Gaa (1988, chapter 5). The applicability of a welfare economics approach to issues of accounting regulations has been addressed in formal terms by Bromwich (1980), and his conclusions are consistent with the feasibility of the approach outlined above.

'Exercising' a cost–benefit model of financial accounting would no doubt entail a substantial need for further information, for example on the comparative costs, risks and benefits of 'measurement' versus 'disclosure' standards to the various interested categories. Measurement standards imply the identification of one (or perhaps two) accounting methods that are at least as good as any alternatives from a cost–benefit standpoint. Such identification is often problematic, since it strictly requires information on costs and benefits that is not readily available. This typically results in decisions about measurement standards being arrived at in the absence of such information – a crude form of the 'branch' method. Disclosure standards are able to mitigate this problem by providing information so that users can to some extent choose the accounting method, rather than simply having it imposed upon them, albeit at the expense of incurring some data processing costs.

Requirements for greater disclosure may impose costs on reporting entities. Direct costs, except in cases such as the requirement for current cost accounting disclosure, will generally be modest. More significant from the standpoint of reporting entities, in the case of both measurements and disclosure requirements, are the indirect costs or risks potentially faced by them. Examples are provided by such requirements as that for a 'successful efforts' treatment of oil and gas exploration costs (SFAS 19), and that for segmental or line-of-business reporting (SFAS 14). The first was perceived as placing a major risk upon the smaller US extracting companies by making them appear less attractive to investors and lenders, and the requirement in SFAS 19 was later withdrawn by SFAS 25. The second is perceived as potentially imposing a risk of revealing commercially sensitive information to competitors, and SFAS 14 was so framed as to allow reporting entities considerable latitude in such reporting, which of course seriously detracts from the usefulness of the information to financial analysts and other bona fide users.

In neither of the cases just cited was the FASB able to deploy a robust decision-making model, and this left the Board completely vulnerable to political pressure against which the fruits of its CF project offered no protection. The gross balance method would call for such risks to reporting entities to be explicitly taken into account in the cost–benefit model, and for additional information on the magnitude of such risks to be sought if this were a key factor in the decision. Once taken, a decision regarding a financial accounting standard would consequently be much more robust. (In fact, with regard to the controversy over SFAS 19, the view that adoption of the 'successful efforts' method would penalize the smaller companies implies the existence of major informational inefficiencies in capital markets. Yet the Board did not consider that its standard needed to take into account research into this issue, even though such research was carried out – see Watts and Zimmerman (1986: 300n) for references.)

Thus, a gross balance analysis would mean that policy alternatives would be considered in the light of a considerable amount of evidence regarding cost–benefit issues, insofar as such information were shown to be crucial to the decision. No doubt, this evidence would be incomplete and often inconclusive; however, the process of exercising the model should ensure that it would be sufficient to permit the gross balance analysis to proceed. On this point, Rowe commented:

> In some instances it may not be possible to acquire better data, or to acquire it in a timely manner. . . . In many cases, even if data

> are available, the cost of obtaining the information may exceed its value in securing policy agreement; and if gross measures [or best guesses] are adequate to arrive at agreement, acquisition of additional data may be desirable but not mandatory.
>
> (Rowe 1977: 206)

By contrast, it might perhaps be said that the FASB was concerned to secure policy agreement on the basis of arguments which made relatively little use of empirical evidence, even in the form of gross measures, for or against testable hypotheses. The discussion memoranda, exposure drafts and SFACs issued in connection with the CF project are not characterized by the mode of reasoning that makes reference to evidence of that kind. Rather, insofar as cost–benefit issues were explicitly evoked, the mode of reasoning employed tended to rely upon unsupported or aprioristic assertions about alleged benefits to certain user categories. It is worth considering some reasons why this should have been so.

Cultural factors affecting the choice of methodology

The launching of the FASB's CF project in December 1976 preceded the publication of Rowe's book by no more than a few months. However, as noted on p. 72, the project had been in gestation since the publication of DM1 in June 1974. The unsuitability of the means–end schema in the context of accounting regulation had already been argued by Gerboth (1972, 1973), and it is apparent that, in spite of its use of the rhetoric of the means–end schema, the Board in fact adopted the incremental or branch method.

Following Lindblom (1959), Gerboth presented the branch method as 'the *science* of muddling through' (my emphasis). In contrast, for the new generation of soft systems methodologists represented by Rowe, 'society seems to operate on the branch method, but . . . this is a major reason behind the increasing desperation of our plight' (Rowe, 1977: 202).

In order for the FASB to have adopted the gross balance method, the Board would have needed to incorporate the discourse of the financial accounting research literature of the 1970s into the discourse employed in the CF project. By discourse, I do not mean vocabulary in a narrow sense, but the concerns and reasoning evinced in the research literature. Only by doing so could the Board have entered into the mode of reasoning required for 'structural modelling' and the subsequent steps described by Rowe. In fact, the discourse of the various CF publications is closer to that of the financial accounting research literature of the 1950s and 1960s, prior to the 'empirical turn' initiated by researchers such as Beaver (1968) and Ball and Brown (1968). Thus, it is assumed that investor and creditor decision models are sufficiently well known for inferences to be drawn as to the suitability of accrual accounting, as opposed, say, to cash flow accounting; but, as already noted on p. 78, the reasoning employed consists of no more than the conventional assertions which have been offered to successive generations of beginning students.

In the pre-empirical era, debate was conducted at a purely conceptual level; the endeavour was to establish first principles of an *a priori* nature from which accounting prescriptions could be derived. Examples are Edwards and Bell (1961) and Chambers (1966). Given the *a priori* character of the putative first principles, empirical testing of them or the prescriptions inferred from them was not part of the research programme. This is what changed as a result of the 'empirical turn'; research became predominantly concerned with the study of the practical uses of financial accounting data and with testing hypotheses regarding their practical effects. The gross balance method requires an empirical approach.

The FASB was fully informed about the empirical research programme in financial accounting, and several of the leading empirical researchers wrote reports for the Board. But this had relatively little effect upon the discourse of the CF project as evidenced in the discussion memoranda, exposure drafts and SFACs, which remained redolent of an earlier period. What the Board seems to have been interested in is the opinions of its constituents which (as noted on pp. 79–80) it sought both to guide and to test, rather than the specific results of empirical accounting research.

Ravetz characterizes what he terms 'folk-science' as follows:

> [A] body of accepted knowledge whose function is not to provide a basis for further advance, but to offer comfort and reassurance to some body of believers.
>
> (Ravetz 1971: 360)

It is hard to resist the conclusion that the FASB's approach to the CF project had something of 'folk-science' about it.

Although, in the better schools, final year undergraduate accounting students are now exposed to the issues, methods and reasoning of the empirical research literature, the leaders of the profession in the 1970s had had no such exposure, and the same may still be true of the majority of new entrants into the profession today. There have been complaints about the 'schism' between academics and practitioners, the latter finding much of the work of the former incomprehensible, irrelevant or both. These complaints were articulated in the Report on Conclusions of the Commission on Auditors' Responsibilities published in 1978, and similar concerns were repeated more recently in a survey report published by the AICPA in 1989 (Bricker and Previts 1990).

Such a state of affairs would doubtless have constituted a major impediment to the use of the gross balance method in the FASB's CF project. The issue was not simply to what extent the protagonists of the CF project could understand empirical research methods; it was also to what extent they were sympathetic to the way in which the empirical researchers of the 1970s specified the research issues. For although the CF project was launched in the mid-1970s, its *Weltanschauung* was firmly rooted in earlier decades.

CONCLUSIONS

In this section, I shall attempt to indicate some lessons deriving from the analysis offered above, with regard to any future endeavours to construct a CF for financial accounting. One might, of course, be sceptical as to whether any such future endeavours are likely. The FASB's attempt involved massive effort; but, in terms of conveying an increased degree of either intellectual or institutional authority upon the standard-setting process, the mountains evidently brought forth a mouse. Nevertheless, one may speculate that the need for 'folk-science' that led to the launching of the CF project is unlikely to go away in present conditions. The more recent publication by the IASC of a CF statement based closely upon the FASB's work is no doubt symptomatic of that need.

Perhaps the first lesson, which we may derive from the section on analytical jurisprudence, is that unless accounting standards are subsumed under the authority of the law, they need authority from some other source in order to possess generally accepted or systemic validity. The institutional issue, therefore, is how the needed authority may be conferred upon an extra-legal, self-regulatory institution so that it may set financial accounting standards that are generally accepted as valid.

This raises the crucial question of whether, outside the authority of law, institutional authority can be separated from intellectual authority. On the one hand, if people cannot be coerced, they must be persuaded. On the other hand, it is not just coercion that leads people to obey the law; it is their recognition of the validity of legal rules as special (or, to use Raz' sterm, 'protected') reasons for action. A possible objective of a CF project would be thus that the validity of financial accounting standards be recognized in a similar way.

Yet the issue of the FASB's authority has intellectual and moral as well as institutional dimensions. The methodology of the 'new' analytical jurisprudence described by Summers consists of a critical, enquiring, socially-aware approach analogous to the 'soft systems' approaches developed by systems analysts. As such, it offers a potentially powerful contribution to the establishment of intellectual and moral authority.

The second lesson, therefore, concerns intellectual, rather than institutional, authority. The literatures of law, economics and systems analysis contain a number of ideas that are highly relevant to such an endeavour. But these ideas need careful handling. One idea from law which has not served accounting well is the idea of the 'independent discipline'. As I have argued above, there may be reasons why law needs epistemological autonomy; but these do not apply to accounting, and the attempt to apply them would be stultifying.

Therefore, the third lesson is that accounting thinkers need to consider well what they mean by a CF for financial accounting. In what sense, and for what purpose, does an applied discipline such as accounting need a conceptual framework? If what is meant is a theoretical structure or a disciplinary matrix in Kuhn's sense, even supposing that an applied discipline requires one, it could hardly be produced to order by an essentially political, consensus-building process such as that employed by the FASB. The theoretical structure of a discipline develops through the efforts of the research community of that discipline, in a way that is not amenable to stage management by a regulatory body such as the FASB, though such a body may assist by providing funding and research data.

Moreover, if the objective of a CF project is to create a situation in which duly promulgated financial accounting standards are generally accepted as valid (as was suggested on p. 80), in what sense would a CF serve to create such a situation? To reiterate Wittgenstein's point which was quoted earlier: if the role of a CF is to provide a discourse within which conflicts over financial accounting issues may be resolved, 'there must be agreement not only in definitions . . . but also in judgements'. While it may certainly be said that the FASB attempted to bring about agreement in both definitions and judgements by means of a consensus-building process involving exposure drafts and public hearings, the nature and purpose of what the Board was attempting to develop was not made clear, and the analogy with a constitution stated in the *Scope and Implications* booklet was of limited help. If the purpose was to confer powers on the FASB enabling it to issue standards that would possess systemic validity, then the whole set of CF publications appears to be largely irrelevant.

In fact, as Dopuch and Sunder (1980) complained, the CF publications were not much more than APB Statement No. 4 'writ large'. Statement No. 4 (AICPA 1970) attempted to provide a comprehensive explication of accounting concepts and the interrelationships between them in terms of generally accepted accounting principles. The logical conclusion of this approach would be a set of postulates and axioms, as discussed by Ijiri (1975). It is essentially a 'closed system' approach, in that any practical consequences of its adoption need to be contained in the postulates; there are no systemic feedback loops from practice to these postulates. The CF project tried to 'open' the system by reference to user needs; but this opening was not well established, as the user needs were stated in stylized form and no feedback from actual use was envisaged.

Hence, I have argued that the FASB should have emulated Summers' 'new analytical jurists' by adopting an open-ended methodology in which 'rational justification' and 'purposive implication' are crucial elements. Further, I have suggested they should have given that methodology an empirical component, as with the gross balance method described by Rowe. This led to the proposal that the basis for the CF (Step 1 in the gross balance method) should be a structural model having the characteristics of a cost–benefit model.

Watts and Zimmerman (1986: 175–6) have cited what amounts to a paradox of regulation: the justification of regulatory actions must lie in social welfare, yet regulatory agencies are impelled to act so as to further their own welfare. This would suggest that the reason why the FASB did not adopt an explicit cost–benefit approach was because such an approach would not have been perceived by the Board as conducive to its welfare as a regulatory agency. However, cultural and educational factors surely played a dominant part in the Board's choice of approach.

There is also, to be sure, the fact that the Board saw as its constituency 'the financial and business community'. Yet this view of its constituency would not of itself preclude the use of a cost–benefit model; rather, it would tend to limit, to the members of that constituency, the set of those members of society whose welfare would be considered within the model.

These considerations lead to the fourth lesson to which I wish to draw attention: one concerning the importance of culture and education. Reference was made on p. 80 above to the apparent inability of the leaders of the US accounting profession in the 1970s to incorporate the developments in academic accounting thought during the late 1960s and early 1970s into their own thought processes with respect to the CF project. Indeed, the problem was of a more general nature, for the same leaders were apparently unaware of developments during the same period in the methodology of policy analysis (such as the gross balance method) or of jurisprudence, which were highly relevant to dealing with the types of issue with which they were grappling. It does not appear to have occurred to them to look outside the sphere of accounting and the issues regarding the profession and its methods raised by the reports of the Trueblood and Wheat Committees. This failure is indicative of a degree of intellectual narrowness which is problematic in the leadership of a prestigious but exposed profession, facing important and complex policy issues. Society is entitled to expect such leaders to be capable of addressing the issues facing the profession in the light of a wider awareness of relevant intellectual developments.

Hence, one needs to consider whether the predominantly technical character of the university studies undertaken by most future CPAs is suitable for those who will lead major firms and the profession. The requirement to learn the extensive corpus of 'promulgated GAAP' from a technical rather than an analytic and critical standpoint, that is imposed upon undergraduate students, serves little purpose in terms of intellectual development. Such learning constitutes one of the less intellectually rewarding elements of their professional training. It fails to promote analytical thinking or theoretical understanding. While it may be argued that these technical studies of financial accounting take place in the third and fourth years of their undergraduate studies, the first two years having a broader and more liberal character, it also needs to be borne in mind that in the USA entry into the legal and medical professions requires extensive study at postgraduate level. Moreover, in 1946, John Queenan, Chairman of the AICPA Committee on Education, declared:

> Tomorrow it is probable that the public accountant will obtain his education as a graduate student after having completed a general undergraduate college education . . . which will enable him to perform more intelligently his duties as an accountant and as a citizen.
> (Bricker and Previts 1990)

The fact that this prediction of postgraduate entry into the accounting profession was made, yet remained unfulfilled, tends to reinforce the impression that, relatively speaking, CPAs are being produced 'on the cheap' in terms of intellectual preparation. Robert S. Kaplan has drawn attention to a further problem, originally articulated by Herbert A. Simon, which relates to the education of accountants: even the more intellectually demanding educational programmes tend to overemphasize skills of analysis at the expense of those of synthesis or design (Kaplan 1987). Yet the development of 'soft systems' methodologies such as the gross balance method has been the work of people with a background in the engineering disciplines able to make the epistemological shift from 'hard' to 'soft' approaches, while still retaining the concern with 'how to make artifacts that have desired properties and how to design' (Simon 1981).

Such considerations are particularly relevant in the UK at a time when the Board of Accreditation of Educational Courses (BAEC) of the accounting profession has been considering the introduction of 'professional level accreditation' which would allow undergraduates to earn exemptions from a substantial part of the professional examinations. The effect of this would be to induce universities and other degree-awarding institutions to offer a mix of courses that is closer to the professional syllabus than would otherwise have been the case, and to induce students to opt for a mix of courses that offers the maximum number of exemptions. While preparation for the technical demands of a career in accounting is by no means an unworthy educational objective for undergraduate studies, its claim for a major place in the curriculum must be weighed against the need for an intellectual preparation that incorporates both breadth and rigour. Misgivings about the likely effects of the BAEC's initiative would therefore be justified, especially when one is told that the pressure for the initiative came from smaller professional firms desirous of reducing their training costs.

Writing over twenty-five years ago, Richard Mattessich began his well-known book *Accounting and Analytical Methods* strikingly, with these words:

> Modern accounting is a mode of thought, a manifestation of our chrematistic thinking and evaluating, a tool designed to help master our economic struggle. It unfolded its full breadth during the last hundred years and cannot be regarded as having exhausted its potential of technical as well as intellectual growth. Whether it is a trivial or a sophisticated means, whether it furthers the

> cognitive processes of science or . . . is a dogmatic body for pursuing the ritual of an industrial age, are [however] still controversial questions.
>
> (Mattessich 1964)

During the last quarter of a century, the character and potential for development of accounting as an applied social science have become more evident. The failure of the CF project indicates the magnitude of the need for further development in the understanding, not just of how financial accounting information may be related to the functioning of asset markets and to decision making at the micro level, but also of the broader societal and cost–benefit issues relevant to standard setting. The purpose of this chapter has been to indicate how methodologies from jurisprudence and systems analysis may be employed to assist in the latter aspect of this development.

The fifth and final lesson therefore concerns the future of accounting as an applied social and behavioural science. The notion of applied social science is problematic (Winch 1958). One does not need to refuse the status of science to the social and behavioural sciences in order to recognize their limitations from a strictly instrumental point of view. They cannot be applied to produce social technology in the sense in which physics, chemistry and biology can be applied to produce engineering, agricultural or medical technology.

Their application to issues in society in general, and to accounting rule-making in particular, calls for the use of a soft-systems framework, which can offer two crucial advantages: both disagreements about the ends to be sought, and also uncertainties regarding the cause and effect relationships linking means to ends, can be handled in a systematic manner. Accounting will avoid intellectual stultification as a 'folk-science', finding its basis for further advance, not in a search for its own 'conceptual framework', but in developing a framework which promotes its development as an applied social and behavioural science.

ACKNOWLEDGEMENT

The author wishes to thank Michael Mumford and Pelham Gore for their helpful comments on earlier drafts of this chapter.

REFERENCES

ASC (Accounting Standards [Steering] Committee) (1971) *Statement of Standard Accounting Practice No. 2: Disclosure of Accounting Policies* London: Institute of Chartered Accountants in England and Wales.

Aggrawal, S. (1987) 'On the conceptual framework of accounting', *Journal of Accounting Literature*, 6.

AAA (American Accounting Association) (1936) 'A tentative statement of accounting principles underlying corporate financial statements', *Accounting Review*, June.

—— (1966) *A Statement of Basic Accounting Theory*, Evanston, Illinois: AAA.

—— (1977) *Statement of Accounting Theory and Theory Acceptance*, Committee on Concepts and Standards for External Financial Reports, Sarasota, Florida: AAA.

AICPA (American Institute of Certified Public Accountants) (1970) *Accounting Principles Board Statement No. 4: Basic Concepts and Principles underlying Financial Statements of Business Enterprises*, New York: AICPA.

—— (1972) *Study on Establishment of Accounting Principles: Establishing Financial Accounting Standards*, New York: AICPA.

—— (1973a) *Objectives of Financial Statements*, Accounting Objectives Study Group, New York: AICPA.

—— (1973b) *APB Accounting Principles: Original Pronouncements as of 30 June 1973*, vol. 2, New York: AICPA.

APB (1970) Statement No. 4 'Basic Concepts and Accounting Principles Underlying Financial Statements of Business Enterprises', New York: AICPA.

Archer, S. (1988) '"Qualitative" research and the epistemological problems of the management disciplines', in A.M. Pettigrew (ed.) *Competitiveness and the Management Process*, Oxford: Basil Blackwell.

Ball, R. and Brown, P. (1968) 'An empirical evaluation of accounting income numbers', *Journal of Accounting Research*, Autumn.

Beaver, W.H. (1968) 'The information content of annual earnings announcements', *Empirical Research in Accounting: Selected Studies*, supplement to *Journal of Accounting Research*.

Berger, P. and Luckmann, T. (1966) *The Social Construction of Reality*, Garden City, New York: Doubleday.

Bricker, R.J. and Previts, G.J. (1990) 'The sociology of accountancy: a study of academic and practice community schisms', *Accounting Horizons*, March.

Bromwich, M. (1980) 'The possibility of partial accounting standards', *Accounting Review*, April.

Burrell, G. and Morgan, G. (1979) *Sociological Paradigms and Organisational Analysis*, London: Heinemann.

Canning, J.B. (1929) *The Economics of Accountancy*, New York: Ronald Press Co.

Chambers, R.J. (1966) *Accounting, Evaluation and Economic Behavior*, Englewood Cliffs, New Jersey: Prentice-Hall.

Checkland, P.B. (1981) *Systems Thinking, Systems Practice*, London: Wiley.

Choi, D.S. and Mueller, G. (1984) *International Accounting*, Englewood Cliffs, New Jersey: Prentice-Hall.

Commission on Auditors' Responsibilities (1978) *Report of Conclusions, Commission on Auditors' Responsibilities*, New York: AICPA.

Daley, L.A. and Tranter, T. (1990) 'Limitations on the value of the conceptual framework in evaluating extant accounting standards', *Accounting Horizons*, March.

Dopuch, N. and Sunder, S. (1980) 'FASB's statements on objectives and elements of financial accounting: a review', *Accounting Review*, January.

Dworkin, R.M. (1977) *Taking Rights Seriously*, London: Duckworth.

Edwards, E.O. and Bell, P.W. (1961) *The Theory and Measurement of Business Income*, Berkeley, California: University of California Press.

FASB (Financial Accounting Standards Board) (1974) *Conceptual Framework for Accounting and Reporting: Consideration of the Report of the Study Group on the Objectives of Financial Statements*, FASB Discussion Memorandum, Stamford, Connecticut: FASB.

—— (1976a) *Tentative Conclusions on Objectives of Financial Statements of Business Enterprises* Stamford, Connecticut: FASB.

—— (1976b) *Conceptual Framework for Financial Accounting and Reporting: Elements of Financial Statements and Their Measurement* FASB Discussion Memorandum, Stamford, Connecticut: FASB.

—— (1976c) *Scope and Implications of the Conceptual Framework Project*, Stamford, Connecticut: FASB.

—— (1976d) *Statement of Accounting Standards No. 14: Financial Reporting for Segments of a Business Enterprise*, Stamford, Connecticut, FASB.

—— (1977) *Statement of Accounting Standards No. 19: Financial Accounting and Reporting by Oil and Gas Producing Companies*, Stamford, Connecticut, FASB.

—— (1978) *Statement of Financial Accounting Concepts No. 1: Objectives of Financial Reporting by Business Enterprises* Stamford, Connecticut: FASB.

—— (1979) *Statement of Accounting Standards No. 25: Suspension of Certain Accounting Requirements for Oil and Gas Production Companies*, Stamford, Connecticut, FASB.

—— (1980a) *Statement of Financial Accounting Concepts No. 2: Qualitative Characteristics of Accounting Information* Stamford, Connecticut: FASB.

—— (1980b) *Statement of Financial Accounting Concepts No. 3: Elements of Financial Statements of Business Enterprises* Stamford, Connecticut: FASB.

—— (1985a) *Statement of Financial Accounting Concepts No. 6: Elements of Financial Statements* Stamford, Connecticut: FASB.

—— (1985b) *Statement of Accounting Standards No. 87: Employers' Accounting for Pensions*, Stamford, Connecticut, FASB.

Foucault, M. (1969) *L'Archéologie du Savoir*, Paris: Gallimard.

Gaa, J.C. (1988) *Methodological Foundations of Standardsetting for Corporate Financial Reporting*, Studies in Accounting Research No. 28, Sarasota, Florida: American Accounting Association.

Gerboth, D.L. (1972) '"Muddling through" with the APB', *Journal of Accountancy*, May.

—— (1973) 'Research, intuition and politics in accounting inquiry', *Accounting Review*, July.

Giddens, A. (1976) *New Rules of Sociological Method*, London: Hutchinson.

Gore, P. (1989) 'The formulation of a conceptual framework – lessons from the American experience', paper presented at the ICAEW Financial Accounting and Auditing Research Conference, London Business School, 17–18 July 1989.

Hart, H.A. (1961) *The Concept of Law*, Oxford: Clarendon Press.
Ijiri, Y. (1975) *Theory of Accounting Measurement*, Studies in Accounting Research No. 10, Sarasota, Florida: American Accounting Association.
IASC (International Accounting Standards Committee) (1989) *Framework for the Presentation and Preparation of Financial Statements*, London: IASC.
Kaplan, R.S. (1987) 'Research cultures in managerial accounting: empirical research', in B.E. Cushing (ed.) *Accounting and Culture*, plenary session papers and discussants comments from the 1986 Annual Meeting of the American Accounting Association, Sarasota, Florida: American Accounting Association.
Kelsen, H. (1967) *The Pure Theory of Law*, Berkeley, California: University of California Press, second edition.
Kuhn, T.S. (1970) 'Reflections on my critics', in I. Lakatos and A. Musgrave (eds) *Criticism and the Growth of Knowledge*, Cambridge: Cambridge University Press, pp. 231–78.
Lakatos, I. and Musgrave, A. (eds) (1970) *Criticism and the Growth of Knowledge*, Cambridge: Cambridge University Press.
Lindblom, C.E. (1959) 'The science of "muddling through"', *Public Administration Review*, XIX, No. 2. (Reprinted in H.J. Leavitt and L.R. Pondy (eds) *Readings in Managerial Psychology*, Chicago: University of Chicago Press.)
Lloyd, D. (1979) *Introduction to Jurisprudence*, London: Stevens, fourth edition.
Masterman, M. (1970) 'The nature of a paradigm', in I. Lakatos and A. Musgrave (eds) *Criticism and the Growth of Knowledge*, Cambridge: Cambridge University Press, pp. 59–89.
Mattessich, R.V. (1964) *Accounting and Analytical Methods*, Homewood, Illinois: Irwin.
—— (1972) 'Methodological preconditions and problems of a general theory of accounting', *Accounting Review*, July.
—— (1978) *Instrumental Reasoning and Systems Methodology*, Dordrecht, Netherlands: Reidel.
Miller, M.A. (1989) *Comprehensive GAAP Guide*, Orlando, Florida: Harcourt Brace Jovanovich.
Mitroff, I.I. and Turoff, M. (1973) 'The whys behind the hows', *IEEE Spectrum*, March.
Moonitz, M. (1961) *The Basic Postulates of Accounting, Accounting Research Study No. 1*, New York: American Institute of Certified Public Accountants.
Most, K.S. (1982) *Accounting Theory*, Columbus, Ohio: Grid Publishing, second edition.
Paton, W.A. and Littleton, A.C. (1940) *An Introduction to Corporate Accounting Standards*, Columbus, Ohio: American Accounting Association.
Putnam H. (1981) *Reason, Truth and History*, Cambridge: Cambridge University Press.
Ravetz, J. (1971) *Scientific Knowledge and its Social Problems*, Oxford: Oxford University Press.
Raz, J. (1975) *Practical Reason and Norms*, London: Hutchinson.

—— (1979) *The Authority of the Law*, Oxford: Clarendon Press.

Roethlisberger, F.J. (1977) *The Elusive Phenomena*, Cambridge, Massachusetts: Harvard University Press.

Rowe, W.D. (1977) *An Anatomy of Risk*, New York: Wiley.

Sanders, T.H., Hatfield, H.R. and Moore, U. (1938) *A Statement of Accounting Principles*, New York: American Institute of [Certified Public] Accountants. (Reprinted by the American Accounting Association, 1959.)

Scheid, J.C. and Standish, P.E.M. (1988) 'A case study of French and English-speaking perceptions of accounting standardisation', paper presented at the Annual Congress of the European Accounting Association, Nice, 26–30 April 1988.

Simon, H.A. (1981) 'The science of design: creating the artificial', in *The Sciences of the Artificial*, Cambridge, Massachusetts: MIT Press, second edition.

Sprouse, R.T. and Moonitz, M. (1962) *A Tentative Set of Broad Accounting Principles for Business Enterprises*, Accounting Research Study No. 3, New York: American Institute of Certified Public Accountants.

Stamp, E. (1969) 'Public accounting and the public interest', *Journal of Business Finance*, 1(1).

—— (1980) *Corporate Reporting: its Future Evolution*, Toronto: Canadian Institute of Chartered Accountants.

Sterling, R.R. (1979) *Toward a Science of Accounting*, Houston: Scholars Book Co.

Summers, R.S. (1966) 'The new analytical jurists', *New York Law Review*, reprinted in Lloyd, D., 1979 (q.v.)

Von Wright, G.H. (1961) *Norm and Action, a Logical Enquiry*, London: Routledge.

Watts, R.L. and Zimmerman, J.L. (1979) 'The demand for and supply of accounting theories: the market for excuses', *Accounting Review*, April.

—— (1986) *Positive Accounting Theory*, Englewood Cliffs, New Jersey: Prentice-Hall.

Whorf, B.L. (1956) *Language, Thought and Reality*, New York: Wiley.

Winch, P. (1958) *The Idea of a Social Science*, London: Routledge and Kegan Paul.

Wittgenstein, L. (1953) *Philosophical Investigations*, (translated by G.E.M. Anscombe), Oxford: Basil Blackwell.

6 The subject matters of accounting

Robert R. Sterling

A TRIBUTE TO EDDIE STAMP

> We are concerned here with some deep philosophical questions that I believe are of profound importance to accountants. . . . Practitioners as well as academics need to think carefully about these matters.
>
> (Stamp 1981)

This chapter was prepared to celebrate the life of Eddie Stamp rather than to mourn his death. More specifically, it was prepared to celebrate his professional life because the professional side of Eddie Stamp is the only side that I ever saw.

The Eddie Stamp that I knew was a consummate professional, totally dedicated to the improvement of accounting. His dedication was a major reason that I came to know only his professional side: all of our conversations, even on ostensible social occasions, focused exclusively on accounting or related topics, never on personal matters. He was a principled man, passionately committed to what he considered right and proper. His passion was a major reason that our exchanges are accurately characterized as zesty arguments, as opposed to bland discussions. His principles were a major reason that those exchanges are accurately characterized as arguments, as opposed to quarrels.

Since Eddie's many contributions to accounting will be recognized elsewhere in this volume, there is no need for me to repeat them here, but I must mention one contribution because it is likely to be overlooked by others and because it is one for which I am particularly grateful: he somehow managed to get a philosopher, Lyas, to write a paper about accounting (Lyas 1984). I have been privileged to have had many philosopher friends and acquaintances over the years but I have never been able to convince any of them that accounting is sufficiently interesting or important to warrant the effort of writing a paper. Indeed, I sometimes find it difficult to convince them that the subject is sufficiently interesting to warrant a ten-minute conversation. My failure in such attempts should explain why I am impressed enough to single out that particular, rather obscure, achievement when there are many other achievements that could be mentioned.

I have been informed that the audience for this volume will include scientists and philosophers, in additon to accountants. I will attempt to tailor[1] my remarks to make them more interesting and more easily understandable to the expanded audience in the hope that it will result in a further extension of Eddie's achievement. My fondest hope is that scientists' and philosophers' contributions to accounting will continue and multiply, eventually constituting a perpetual bequest to accounting from Eddie Stamp.

PURPOSE

> There is a method which might be described as 'the one method of philosophy'. But it is not characteristic of philosophy alone; it is, rather, the one method of all *rational discussion*, and therefore of the natural sciences as well as of philosophy. The method I have in mind is that of stating one's problem clearly and of examining its various proposed solutions *critically*.
>
> (Karl Popper)

The first purpose of this chapter is to stimulate (or provoke) scientists and philosophers to begin (and Lyas to continue) a critical examination of accounting. Toward that end I will attempt to describe the subject matter of accounting practice and accounting research clearly enough to permit interested scientists and philosophers to understand it and convincingly enough to permit them to believe it. My goal is to entice scientists and philosophers to make contributions to accounting thought by examining the fascinating problems that are the direct result of the unique subject matters of accounting.

The second purpose of this chapter is to stimulate (or provoke) other accountants to begin a critical examination of accounting. Toward that end I will attempt to explain how the subject matter of accounting differs crucially from the subject matter of scientific disciplines clearly enough to permit them to understand it and convincingly enough to permit them to believe it. My goal is to try to entice accountants to begin to critically examine accounting, and accounting research, rather than just doing it. I have no objection to doing accounting or doing accounting research but I do object to it being done mechanically, that is, without being clear about what one is doing and why one is doing it.

These two purposes present two formidable problems that seem to be completely separate but are in fact peculiarly related: scientists and philosophers find it difficult to believe that it is possible that accountants do what they in fact do and accountants find it difficult to believe that it is possible to do anything different.[2] Both are incredulous and the object of the incredulity of both is the subject matter of accounting. Thus, the heroic task of this chapter is to convince one sceptical audience that the subject matter *is* the way it is described and to convince another sceptical audience that the subject matter *could be different from* the way it is described.

THE SUBJECT MATTER OF ACCOUNTING PRACTICE

> If controversies were to arise, there would be no more need of disputation between two philosophers than between two accountants. For it would suffice to take their pencils in their hands, to sit down to their slates, and to say to each other (with a friend as witness, if they liked): let us calculate.
>
> (Gottfried Wilhelm von Leibniz)

Although differing in wording and in detail, statements of purpose or definitions of accounting practice invariably include something about the *recording* and *reporting* of economic resources (assets) and obligations (liabilities) and the changes in them. Briefly, it is the recording and reporting of *wealth* and wealth *changes*, including *profit*. A typical statement is provided by FASB:

> In accounting, the phenomena to be represented are economic resources and obligations and the transactions and events that change those resources and obligations.
>
> (FASB 1983: para. 63)

Although at the boundaries there are problems in deciding exactly which objects qualify as economic resources and obligations, it is quite clear that the subject matter of accounting practice includes such things as cash, claims to cash, stock-in-trade, machines, buildings, land, and the like. Unfortunately, that is the end of clarity: as soon as we move to a consideration of the *amount* of those things or events, we face a maze of murky ideas.

Reporting an amount paid

For reasons that are not pertinent here, accountants long ago decided to record and report the *historical costs* of assets (economic resources) and liabilities (obligations). Some academic accountants have proposed the recording and reporting of *current values* (current costs or exit values) instead of or in addition to historical costs. The discussion of the alternatives has been highly confused, in large part due to the multiple meanings of 'historical cost'.

In ordinary usage the 'historical cost of *x*' means the 'amount previously paid for *x*'. In accounting usage it sometimes means that, but it usually means 'a calculated amount based on the amount previously paid for *x*', and sometimes it just means 'a calculated amount assigned to *x*' without regard to what was paid for *x*. Thus, 'historical cost' is a term-of-art in accounting and non-accountants are often misled by interpreting it in its ordinary usage sense.

Surprisingly, accountants are also often misled by the term. They vacillate among the meanings which frequently results in the presentation of arguments that commit the informal fallacy of equivocation. For example:

> The criterion of, say, ease of determination should be used to decide what to report.
>
> Historical costs (amounts paid) are more easily determined than current values.
>
> Therefore, historical costs (calculated amounts) should be reported.

Lyas provides an illustration of both the multiple meanings of the term in accounting and how non-accountants usually interpret it. Since he is not an accountant, it is reasonable to assume that he relied on accountants' descriptions of alternative valuation proposals, and that such descriptions used the term-of-art 'historical costs' to describe current practice, when he wrote:

> Consider here, by way of elementary example, the problem of determining the present value for accounting purposes of a piece of machinery and the difference between making the value what was paid for it (in 'real' terms?) as opposed to (i) what one *might* get for it *if* one were to sell it and (ii) what it might cost to replace, *if* an exact replacement could be found.
>
> (Lyas 1984: 101)

Lyas' presentation of this typical accounting argument fails because he substituted 'what was paid' for 'historical cost' and thereby avoided the equivocation. Although there is no reason for a philosopher to know what accountants do, the fact is that accountants almost never report what was paid for anything. Thus, the implied conclusion that it is better to report 'what was paid' is irrelevant to those who are trying to assess the relative merits of 'historical costs' and 'current values'.

Philosophers' propensity to use clear, simple terms is a major reason that I welcome their examination of accounting. Lyas' statement of the argument is just one example of the benefit that would be derived from that propensity: using the clear 'what was paid' instead of the equivocal 'historical cost' is all that is needed to avoid a long-standing, pernicious error. More generally, philosophers' appreciation of the connection of clarity of language to clarity of thought (and communication) is the reason for welcoming them to accounting. Accountants seem to lack such appreciation and the result is the perpetuation of a number of errors and fallacies that can be traced directly to linguistic turbidity.

Reporting a calculated amount

Instead of reporting the amount paid, accountants usually report a calculated amount. One form of calculation, accurately described by Lyas (1984: 101) as 'ubiquitous in accounting', is the *allocation* (also called *apportionment*, *amortization*, and sometimes *accrual*) of the amount paid among various activities, products, time periods and the like. That is, the particular form of calculation called *averaging* or *dividing*[3] in ordinary language. Although subject to several unessential qualifications, the process is simply the calculation of an average unit cost (u) by dividing the amount paid for, or cost (C) of, an item by some observed, estimated or forecasted quantity (q) of that item.

$$u = C/q$$

Then the 'historical cost' is said to 'expire' as q declines (is used or sold or otherwise disappears) and the 'unexpired' amount of the 'historical cost' is the product of u and the amount of q remaining on hand. The 'expired' amount is an 'expense' to be deducted from revenues to get one's profit, and the 'unexpired' amount is an 'asset' to be added to other assets to get one's wealth.

A well-worn example in the economics literature is the apportionment of the amount paid for a steer between the carcass and the hide.

If the cost of the steer was £100, it weighed 500 pounds (and the accountant selected weight as the basis for apportionment), then the average unit cost per pound would be £0.20.

$$0.20 = \frac{100}{500}$$

Given that the carcass and hide weighed 450 and 50 pounds, respectively, the accountant would report the 'historical cost' of £90 and £10 for the carcass and hide, respectively.

A number of objections have been raised to this particular method of apportioning costs and a number of different methods have been proposed. A common objection is that the disparity of the 'value per pound' of the carcass and hide will result in reports that are 'unfair' or 'misleading' or some similar criticism. If, for example, the carcass were expected to sell for £135 and the hide for £5, then reporting the hide at £10 is thought to result in an 'overstatement' of the hide since its 'historical cost' is twice its expected selling price. Other objections are raised from considerations of reports of profits such as the following:

	Carcass	*Hide*	*Total*
Selling price	135	5	140
Cost (expired)	90	10	100
Profit	45	−5	40

One objection to such reports is that it is 'unfair' to report a loss for the hide department or activity since without the sale of the hide the total profit would be decreased by £5. Thus, the paradox of the elimination of an unprofitable activity causing profits to decrease. Another objection is that if the carcass were sold in different years, it would be 'misleading' to report a £45 profit in year 1 and £5 loss in year 2, or vice versa, when the profit over both years is expected to total £40.

The response to criticism of a given method of dividing costs has been to propose another method of division, for example, make it proportional to the forecasted total selling price rather than proportional to the weight. This selling price method has been subjected to similar criticism, which has resulted in proposals to employ other methods, which have been subjected to similar criticism, which. . . .

Perhaps as much as 90 per cent of the accounting literature in this century has, in one way or another, been concerned with discussing such cost allocations. Many accountants begin by explaining the reasons for allocating and almost all such explanations involve an argument to the effect that accountants *must* allocate because *the* alternative would result in reports that are, at best, indisputably inferior and, at worst, dangerously misleading. Thus, allocations are thought to be *unavoidable* or *indispensable*. Lyas (apparently echoing the accountants who have explained accounting to him) provides another example of this line of thinking when he writes (Lyas 1984: 101) 'The accountant sometimes has to allocate a value' which in the context seems to mean that he accepts the typical accountant's view that accountants *must* allocate, that allocations are unavoidable or indispensable.[4]

If the question were regarding the amount of the machinery to report in Lyas' comparison, for example, the argument would run to the effect that although the amount paid could be reported at the moment of purchase (when it is new), it would be 'unfair' or 'misleading' to report the amount paid at the end of years 1, 2, 3, and 4 (when it is used), and it would be 'unthinkable' to report the amount paid at the end of year 10 (when it is worn out or obsolete and ready to be discarded). Therefore, so the argument goes, we must use the familiar procedure of figuring an average (u) unit cost by dividing the amount paid for, or (C) cost of, an item by some observed, estimated or forecasted (q) quantity of that item ($u = C/q$). If the cost of the machinery was £100 and it was expected to provide 500 hours of operation (and the accountant selected machine-hours as the basis for division), then the average unit cost per machine-hour would be £0.20.

$$0.20 = \frac{100}{500}$$

At year end, when the machine has been used for, say, 50 hours the accountant will apportion £90 to unused machine hours, report it as the 'historical cost of the machine' and apportion £10 to the used machine-hours and, in the simplest case, report it as 'depreciation expense'. The interested reader will have noticed that this is exactly the same procedure as that used to apportion the cost of the steer to the carcass and the hide. It is also subject to the same sort of criticism and the same sort of proposals of different methods of dividing the costs.

The intriguing thing about such arguments is that they contrast the alternatives of reporting the amount paid to reporting a calculated amount. It should be apparent that this commits the fallacy of posing a false dilemma: the reporting alternatives under consideration have been restricted to the amount paid versus a calculated amount, overlooking all other alternatives including the proposal to report current values which was previously rejected in favour of reporting an amount paid.

An example of the combined arguments

The combination of the two arguments presented above is intended to replicate combinations found in the accounting literature. It is not the case that the two arguments are made by different authors or even by the same author in different works, but rather that both are usually found in the same work. The sequencing in the literature is also the same as above: (1) conclude (by equivocation) to report the amount paid and (2) conclude (by posing a false dilemma) to report a calculated amount.[5] Although I think these fallacies are sufficiently common to be easily found in the accounting literature after readers have had them brought to their attention, those who feel the need for a specific case to examine[6] could consult Butterworth *et al.* (1982).

The stated purpose of that work is to provide a theory of accounting choices, that is, a theory that explains why accountants elect to record and report one thing and not another. They are particularly concerned with *differences* between the choices of the *practitioner* and the *academic*, which they refer to as the 'paradox' of the 'extraordinary' 'consistency of practice' as contrasted to the 'disarray at the level of theory' (Butterworth *et al.* 1982: 3). It is the 'consistent application of specific reporting rules based almost exclusively on acquisition [historical] cost' that is of particular interest. Indeed, it seems that the major purpose of that work devolves to an explanation of why 'historical costs' have survived in the face of sustained attacks and suggested alternatives, as indicated by the 'major point' that 'all attempts to introduce changes in valuation methods that depart radically from historical costs have been resisted . . .' (Butterworth *et al.* 1982: 8) and eventually rejected. Thus, their purpose is not just to provide one more comparison of the merits of historical costs and current values but rather to provide a grand historical overview of those relative merits by explaining why accountants have continued to choose to report historical costs for 'six hundred years' (Butterworth *et al.* 1982: 3).

The cornerstone of their explanation is the *objectivity* of 'historical costs' which they equate to transactions or exchanges as, for example, when they explain that 'objectivity dictates the choice of transactions as the basis for accounting information' and that 'market exchanges that are not consummated cannot be verified, and therefore do not meet the objectivity criterion' (Butterworth *et al.* 1982: 25). In short, current values lack objectivity and verifiability because they are not based on transactions or consummated exchanges and therefore historical costs (amounts paid in consummated exchanges) have been and continue to be selected to be reported.

Later, however, they reject 'the exclusive use of cash exchanges [because it] does not satisfy the risk-constraint criterion' and they also reject 'the exchange value of all transactions of the period' because 'it is affected by the random (or deliberately chosen) occurrence of large transactions' (Butterworth *et al.* 1982: 27). Examples of 'large transactions' are the purchase of the steer and machine discussed above, and the problem with reporting those amounts is also the ancient one discussed above, although Butterworth *et al.* state it differently:

> So, faced with this dilemma, and insisting on reports that satisfy our six criteria, we are driven *inexorably* toward an aggregation method that eliminates the problem of moral hazard by *averaging* major expenditures over the periods that benefit from them.
>
> (Butterworth *et al.* 1982: 27–8, emphasis added)

The problem, of course, is that they posed the false dilemma of reporting the amount paid versus averaging or allocating, and they are driven inexorably toward averaging only because they overlooked other alternatives.

In summary, Butterworth *et al.* began by comparing amounts paid to current values and concluded that amounts paid are preferable because they are objective. Then they decided to report calculations because reporting the amounts paid did not yield satisfactory results. Thus, in essence, the argument is: one should report historical costs (amounts paid) because they are more objective than current values but reporting historical costs (amounts paid) yield unsatisfactory results so that one should report historical costs (calculated amounts).

The explanation for the survival of historical costs is similar: the primary reason that historical costs (calculated amounts) have been reported for six hundred years is that historical costs (amounts paid) are more objective than current values. In my view, a better explanation for the survival of historical costs is the survival of fallacious arguments that they are objective, not that they *are* objective.

Accounting numerology

Arguments similar in form and in conclusion to those discussed above have existed for many years. The outcome of the ancient arguments was that numerals became the subject matter of accounting practice. The outcome of the continuation of the arguments is the continuation of the subject matter of numerals.

The amounts reported by accountants, with few exceptions, are free-floating arithmetical constructs. Although characterized as 'objective' in the accounting literature, they are not objective in the sense of existing independently of a knowing subject; rather an accounting numeral is, within very broad bounds, nothing but an idiosyncratic product of a subject. They are not objective in the sense of conforming to fact without being influenced by personal feeling or prejudice; on the contrary, they are heavily influenced by personal feeling and there are no facts to which the reported amounts conform. They are not objective in the sense of depending on scientific test implications because there are no test implications that bear on them. In short, accounting numerals are not objective in any of the senses that are commonly found in the non-accounting literature.

None the less, accountants continue to characterize the numerals they report as 'objective' and they continue to reject suggested alternatives because they are 'subjective'. It seems that this characterization is due to a definition of 'objectivity' that is unique to accounting, a definition which has more to do with the certainty of the outcome of calculation than with referring to magnitudes of objects and events.[7]

In a few places accountants state quite clearly that their numerals do not and are not intended to refer to magnitudes of objects and events. The most lucid statement is the 'official' or 'authoritative' definition of 'depreciation' (the name for the particular allocation method applied to the machine discussed above) which is said to be a 'process of allocation' (calculation) in 'a rational and systematic manner' and 'is not intended to be a measurement' of the effect of such events as 'the physical deterioration . . . or of the decline in monetary value, or indeed, of anything that actual occurs during the year' (*Accounting Research and Terminology Bulletins* 1961: paras 56, 54).[8] Although there are many bits of evidence scattered throughout the accounting literature that would support the view that accountants embrace a radical rationalism, the above depreciation definition is one place where it is stated with such clarity that there can be no doubt of the position: depreciation is a rational and systematic calculation that is not intended to be a representation of any kind of phenomenon.[9]

In short, the subject matter of accounting practice is numerals, not magnitudes of wealth and profit. Although almost all accountants deny that, claiming that the numerals represent historical costs, the fact that historical costs are not in any sense observable or measurable[10] negates their argument. Indeed, accounting numerals do not yield any test implications whatsoever.[11] The questions that accountants ask are how to calculate, not how to represent or to test representations. Thus, Leibniz once again showed his perspicacity by selecting accountants to exemplify calculators.[12] Being one of the architects of rationalism, no one comes to mind who would be more appropriate as the intellectual patron of accounting and his 'let us calculate' would be an apposite motto.

THE SUBJECT MATTER OF ACCOUNTING RESEARCH

> Anthropology, the study of the origin of myth, legend and cult . . ., tells us how men have thought and what have been the purposes and consequences of different kinds of thinking. . . . Especially does the record of the growth of the various sciences afford instruction in those concrete ways of inquiry and testing which have led men astray and which have proved efficacious.
>
> (Dewey 1963)

That accounting is a social science is unquestioned by almost all accounting academics. For some time I was perplexed by accounting academics claiming that accounting *is not*[13] a science *and* that accounting *is* a social science. Originally I thought this was an ordinary, if obvious, howler but the persistent, earnest urging of the position caused me to begin to think that perhaps I was meant to conclude that a social science is not a science. The root of the problem is, once again, equivocation: the meaning of 'accounting' when it refers to accounting practice is quite different from when it refers to accounting research. Distinguishing the two allows the position to be stated without inconsistency: accounting research is (and ought to be) a science (social) whereas accounting practice is not (and cannot be) a science.[14]

The emphasis on *social* science provides the first clue as to the subject matter of accounting theory: it is the study of the behaviour of people, often people who are accountants or managers making accounting decisions.

Recording practitioner behaviour

The recommendation that we observe and codify practitioner behaviour is not new. Over twenty years ago I ventured (Sterling 1970: 449) that 'the most ancient and pervasive method of accounting theory construction is to observe accountants' actions and then rationalize those actions by subsuming them under generalized principles'. This method was so popular that the meaning of 'inductive' in accounting was narrowed to 'derived from observations of accountants' behavior'. The view seemed to be that there was no reason to retain the usual, broader meaning of 'derived from observations' because there was nothing to observe other than practitioner behaviour.[15]

At one time my claim that the dominant subject matter of accounting research is observations of practitioner behaviour was met with strong, concerted resistance. Non-inductivists did not believe that inductivists derived accounting theory from observing accountants and inductivists did not believe they could do anything else.[16] In more recent years the words have come closer to matching actions as neo-inductivists have become increasingly clear about what they are doing. Demski's description was selected to exemplify the neo-inductivists position because it is stated with admirable clarity.

According to Demski (1987: 89–90) 'an injection of the social science perspective' has resulted in a realization that the old questions about wealth and profit would not yield to attempts to 'sharpen our measurement instruments' so, except for vestiges in textbooks, we abandoned our search for how 'accounting ought to be done' and began to seek knowledge about the 'end user' but this 'remained an illusive goal' so we abandoned that search also. We have now entered the 'age of agnosticism wherein we [researchers] claim no ability to identify the best accounting system'. I wonder why he didn't call it the *golden* age of agnosticism because he concludes that 'this change is welcome, healthy and productive'.

I also wonder why he didn't call it the age of ignorance (absence of knowledge) rather than agnosticism (doubting the existence of knowledge) because he expresses the belief that the practitioner has knowledge. The agnosticism title comes from researchers' doubts about *their* ability to judge accounting or accounting systems.

> Note well that the agnostic's position is that the practitioner can, with error, identify the best accounting system but the researcher has no comparative advantage in this regard. Rather, the researcher assumes the role of *social recorder* of behavior. Here, with error, we observe, we document, we codify behavior. (Demski 1987: 90)

In this and other places Demski's argument appears to run along the lines that researcher ignorance and practitioner knowledge allows one to conclude that researchers should record the behaviour of practitioners in order to obtain knowledge.

Practitioners know best

It is admirably honest and becomingly modest for researchers to admit ignorance of what is best when they are in fact ignorant of what is best, but a moment's reflection reveals that such ignorance also prevents them from asserting that practitioners know what is best. It seems clear that if A identifies X as best and B identifies Y as best, then for C to claim that A knows best (or knows better than B), then C must know that X is best (or better than Y). It seems that Demski and other social-recorders[17] fall into that trap: when faced with practitioners who think that X is best and, say, non-social-recorders who think that Y is best, social-recorders apparently conclude that practitioners know best on the basis of the fact that social-recorders' are ignorant of which is best.[18]

It is difficult to know why Demski believes that practitioners know what is best because he presents neither argument nor evidence to that effect. One might think he is appealing to authority (*argumentum ad verecundiam*) were it not for the fact that he makes no attempt to qualify practitioners as authorities or experts. (Perhaps we need to invent a cynic's maxim to counter anticipated naive attempts at such qualification: experts are people who continue to repeat the same errors.) After looking carefully for argument or evidence and failing to find it, I am forced to conclude that 'practitioners know best' is an unsupported, tacit assumption. After coupling that to researchers' ignorance and supplying it as a premise, it appears that the argument is:

> Practitioners know what is best and researchers are ignorant of what is best.

> Therefore, researchers should record the behaviour of practitioners in order to discover what is best.

The argument is still enthymematic: we need to supply another premise to the effect that the best way to obtain knowledge is to record the actions of those who have knowledge. But that premise is also suspect: it is likely to be better (more efficient, more productive of knowledge, less productive of error, or some similar sense of better) to record the behaviour of the material rather than to record the behaviour of the people who record the behaviour of the material. Ornithologists, for example, who want to learn about the behaviour of birds find it better to record the behaviour of birds than to record the behaviour of ornithologists who are recording the behaviour of birds.[19]

In short, 'practitioners know best' is unsupported, indeed essentially unexamined, by those who apparently rely on it and there are several lines of criticism that render it lame if not dead. If 'practitioners know best' cannot be supported, there is no conspicuous reason to record practitioner behaviour save unadorned curiosity. Since the scientific community invariably requires a research programme to be supported by reasons beyond curiosity, the social-recorder-of-practitioner-behaviour programme would be rejected although, of course, such rejection would not prohibit individuals from researching whatever they want.

I suspect that the reason that 'practitioners know best' is unexamined is that it is not a fundamental tenet of those who are or want to be social-recorders. If one pays careful attention to what the social-recorders say, especially what they say about social science, and what they don't say, especially what they don't say about accounting, one is likely to come away with the view that the underlying reason is nothing more than a desire to be social scientists. My conjecture is that the desire is based on the feeling that being a social scientist is honorific and being an accountant-researcher is ignominious. To the Hatfield hounds!

Accounting anthropology

Arguments similar in form and in conclusion to those discussed above have existed for many years. The outcome of the ancient arguments was that the behaviour of accountants became the subject matter of accounting research. The outcome of the continuation of the arguments is the continuation of the subject matter of the behaviour of accountants.

The predominant subject matter currently being studied by accountant-researchers is the behaviour of accountant-practitioners, broadly conceived to include auditors and managers when they are making accounting decisions, and often called 'positive accounting theory' as well as 'social-recorder', both of which are offsprings of the old 'inductivist' theories. Although such studies and the associated theories are characterized as 'scientific' or 'social scientific' in the accounting literature, the study of the practitioners of one's own discipline is, to my knowledge, unique in the history of science. There are instances in the history of science where researchers *began* by observing skilled craftsmen but there are no instances to my knowledge where they *ended* with such observations.[20] The distinction is crucial: scientists take knowledge from wherever they can obtain it, including from skilled craftsmen, but then they try to extend, correct, and refine that knowledge by the research process, which improved knowledge they then pass back to the craftsmen for the purpose of improving the craft. They do not make the study of skilled craftsmen an end but rather a means to knowledge about what the craftsmen deal with. Nor do they prohibit trying to extend, correct and refine the knowledge of the craftsmen on some mistaken belief that accumulation of such knowledge is normative while accumulation of knowledge of the behaviour of the craftsmen is positive.

Of course, there are some scientists, notably anthropologists and sociologists, who make the study of people an end rather than a means. It was the striking similarity of 'inductivists' to anthropologists that caused me to describe their activities as the 'anthropological approach' to accounting theory construction. Assignment of that name was not for the purpose of prohibiting or discouraging such studies but rather an attempt to clearly distinguish the study of accountants from the study of wealth and profit. It was over twenty years ago (in 1970) when I naively thought that introducing the term 'anthropology' and drawing analogies to other disciplines would make the distinction abundantly clear:

> The theory of accounting ought to be concerned with accounting phenomena, not practicing accountants, in the same way that theories of physics are concerned with physical phenomena, not practicing physicists.
>
> (Sterling 1970: 450)

The distinction was repeated (in 1979) in response to efficient market researchers' belief that their subject matter (behaviour of capital market agents as exhibited by stock market responses) was the only appropriate subject to be studied, which belief they used as the basis for strong criticism of all other research that studied different subject matters:

> If a chemist rejected the research of a psychologist because the psychologist did not examine the atomic composition of chemical elements, we would easily recognize it to be inappropriate.
>
> (Sterling 1979: 53)

And made again in regard to 'positive theorists' by Christenson in 1983:

> Chemical theory consists of propositions about the behavior of chemical entities (molecules and atoms), not about the behavior of chemists.
>
> (Christenson 1983: 6)

And reinforced by Whittington (1987: 334) when he refers to it as 'the fundamental criticism' of Watts and Zimmerman (1986). Despite these repeated attempts to make this elementary distinction clear, most accountant-researchers continue to fail to make it, some from ignorance of the distinction and others from ignorance of the benefits of being clear about what one is talking about.

Failing to make the distinction between wealth and the behaviour of accountants is harmful because it perpetuates needless confusion and pointless strife. Prohibiting assessment of accountants' practices is fatal because it perpetuates ignorance. Had we prohibited scientific assessment of Greek medical practices, we would be ignorant of Galenian medicine as well as all subsequent work that built on it. Had we prohibited scientific assessment of Babylonian and Egyptian earth measurements, we would be ignorant of Euclidian geometry as well as all subsequent work that built on it. The perpetuation of such ignorance in accounting, paradoxically, is done in the name of science.

All of this was anticipated by John Dewey (1963) who characterized anthropology as telling us 'how men have thought' but goes on without pause to a consideration of 'the consequences of different kinds of thinking', noting that some kinds 'have led men astray' and other kinds 'have proved efficacious'. The possibility of being led astray was emphasized by mentioning that anthropology is the study of myth, legend and cult. The possibility of finding something efficacious was illustrated with a discussion of the development of empirical sciences and of mathematics and logic. Discovering what men think is relatively easy. Deciding whether what they think is myth or science is much more difficult but also infinitely more productive.[21]

SUMMARY AND CONCLUSION

> Eighteenth century [science] was a triumph of organized common sense. It had got rid of medieval phantasies. . . . It grounded itself upon what every plain man could see with his own eyes, or with a microscope of moderate power. It measured the obvious things to be measured, and it generalized the obvious things to be generalized. For example, it generalized the ordinary notions of weight and massiveness.
>
> (Whitehead 1967)

My summary in regard to accounting practice is that it is numerology. Although putatively a measurement of wealth and profit, accounting practice is in fact a calculational activity and the results of those calculations have no empirical referents. My conclusion is that such a state is a problem in need of correction. The most serious problem is that accounting practice numerals are *meaningless* in the logical positivist[22] sense of not being either analytic or verifiable, in the pragmatist sense of not being decision-useful, and in the operationist sense of not being operationally defined. Accounting practice numerals need to be made meaningful by making them empirically verifiable, demonstrating that they are decision-useful (not merely used), and defining them operationally.

My summary in regard to accounting research is that it is anthropology. Although ostensibly about accounting – that is, having something to do with the measurement and communication of wealth and profit – accounting research is in fact about accountants, broadly defined. My conclusion is that this state is also a problem that needs correction. The first problem is the confusion that has resulted. Just as referring to the study of biologists as 'biological research' would result in vast confusion, referring to the study of accountants as 'accounting research' has in fact resulted in vast confusion, even among accounting researchers. This problem is easily rectified by providing a descriptive title (such as 'accounting anthropology' or 'sociology of accountants') for such work. A second problem is that I don't see how studies of accountants can ever bear fruit, especially in view of the fact that proscribing the assessment of practitioner behaviour makes such study an end rather than a means. I think that courtship rituals of aborigines is a more interesting and potentially more fruitful topic than calculation rituals of accountants. Although I wouldn't want to deny anyone the right to study anything they want, including the rituals of accountants, I do want to title such studies descriptively, primarily to avoid confusion and secondarily in the hope that eventually they could be placed in anthropology or sociology journals where those with similar interests could more easily find them.

My summary in regard to the combination of accounting research and accounting practice is that they are divorced. My conclusion is that this state is also a problem that needs correction. I (and several others) have worried for some years about the growing estrangement of accounting practice and accounting research and have proposed various means of reconciliation. I failed. The divorce is now complete, as is evident when one compares the accepted purposes and consequent subject matters:[23] the customary, mutually beneficial ties between research and practice have been severed. In other professions or applied sciences, such as medicine or engineering, there is a fairly clear division of duties but also a fairly clear confluence of purposes. The purpose of medical practitioners is to provide good health and the purpose of medical researchers is to provide knowledge about health, including how to attain good or better health. In civil engineering the purpose of engineering practitioners is to provide good bridges and the purpose of physics and engineering researchers is to provide knowledge about bridges, including how to attain good or better bridges. In accounting the purposes do not join, which permits the subject matters to remain divergent. At the present time the stated purpose of accounting practice is to record and report wealth and profit whereas the stated purpose of accounting theory is to record and report the behaviour of accountants.

These summaries and conclusions can be restated as objectives. The first objective is to move accounting practice up to the eighteenth century state of science as described by Whitehead. This would require two steps: (1) getting rid of accounting fantasies, that is, those things that are said to be 'measured' but are in fact calculated because they cannot be observed or otherwise detected; and (2) measuring the obvious things to be measured[24] and (eventually) generalizing the obvious things to be generalized. In this way accounting practice would move toward a science.[25]

The second objective is to reconnect accounting practice and accounting research, to redirect accounting research to the study of the same subjects as that which is dealt with in practice. Then the purpose of accounting practice would be to provide good information and the purpose of accounting research would be to provide knowledge about information, including how to attain good or better information. When so redirected accounting research would soon discover that the prime characteristic of good information is that it should refer to something in the real world, that informative numerals have empirical referents.

ACKNOWLEDGEMENTS

David Bennett (Philosophy, University of Utah) provided many instructive and enjoyable general discussions and detailed discussions of commonly overlooked points regarding the analytic—synthetic and a priori—a posteriori distinctions, Carl G. Hempel (Philosophy, Princeton) provided discussion of logical positivism in general and the error of studying practitioner behaviour in particular, Clifton D. McIntosh (Philosophy, University of Utah) read and commented on arguments that had been challenged by others, K.V. Peasnell (Accounting, University of Lancaster) provided valuable editorial comment as well as thought-provoking argument, Michael Power (Accounting, London School of Economics) presented a general critique as well as specific criticism of an earlier title, C. Wade Savage (Philosophy, University of Minnesota) helped me to clarify several philosophical arguments especially some subtleties in the argument from design, and Ralph Walters (California Society of CPAs) was wickedly witty in response to several points. Kevin McBeth provided general research assistance as well as calling my attention to the Leibniz quotation. To all the above my warm thanks and the usual absolution.

NOTES

1 One tailoring device is to put much more material in 'Notes' than usual so that it can be easily ignored while still being available for those who desire it. Some of this material will be in the nature of background, sometimes background for scientists and philosophers about accounting, and sometimes vice versa.

2 It is my contention that accountants have been brainwashed in the sense used by Ziman (1978: 8) when he writes of the 'brainwashing implicit in the long process of becoming technically expert'. In psychology this brainwashing, called *einstellung* or habituation, has been experimentally demonstrated by Luchins (1942: 1) and described as follows: 'The successive, repetitious use of the same method mechanized many of the

subjects – blinded them to the possibility of a more direct and simpler procedure'.

I have experimentally demonstrated such habituation among accountants in the sense that they attempted to calculate where observation was obviously possible, and obviously appropriate. Specifically, they attempted to calculate the volume of liquids, which were expanding under conditions of increasing temperature, by the application LIFO–FIFO rather than by measuring (observing) the volume. The control group were scientists who insisted on measuring and rejected LIFO–FIFO calculations out-of-hand. The results of that experiment are reported in Sterling (1988).

It is this habituation that accounts for the difficulty in explaining the subject matter to both groups. Those who have been calculating all of their lives find it almost impossible to think about measuring – and vice versa.

3 It is the absence of an empirical referent for the result of the calculation, not the particular type of calculation, that leads to the problem. Many discussions of allocations of cost leave the impression that it is the division that causes problems, overlooking the fact that addition, multiplication, and subtraction cause problems of exactly the same kind. For example, 'the additivity problem' is that the sum does not have an empirical referent whereas 'the allocation problem' is that the quotient does not have an empirical referent.

4 In 1848 John Stuart Mill (1909: book 3, chapter 16) announced that a 'principle is wanting to apportion' joint costs. He did *not* announce that such apportionments are unavoidable or indispensable. On the contrary, his purpose was to advise others not to apportion because a principle was wanting. None the less, accountants continued to make such apportionments, continued to allege that they are indispensable, and continued to seek an acceptable or defensible method of making them. More than 150 years later, Arthur L. Thomas (1969) announced that 'all allocations are arbitrary'. He did *not* announce that such allocations are unavoidable or indispensable. On the contrary, he concluded that allocations produce nonsense and suggested that the least dangerous way to stop reporting nonsense is just to stop reporting nonsense (Thomas 1974: 114–15). None the less, to this day accountants continue to make such allocations, continue to allege that they are indispensable, and some continue to seek an acceptable or defensible method of making them.

Why have accountants continued to allocate in the face of the ancient, undisputed findings by Mill and the more recent, unrefuted findings of Thomas? Why do accountants say that they accept those findings, adopting 'all allocations are arbitrary' as a slogan, and then continue to argue that one allocation is 'better' than another? I agree with Butterworth *et al.* (1982) that such questions are interesting and important, but my answer is the exact opposite of theirs. Rather than accepting their explanation that it is the 'objectivity' of 'historical costs' that causes accountants to continue to report and defend them, my view is that it is the failure to recognize the reason for the arbitrariness of the allocations.

Compare the allocation of the weight of the steer to the allocation of its cost. If I were to suggest that the weight of the steer could be divided

80 per cent carcass and 20 per cent hide, my suggestion would be interpreted as a crude prediction. In the event where after slaughter the actual weights were discovered to be 450 and 50 pounds, I would be said to have been *wrong*. On the other hand, if I made the same suggestion about the cost, there is no way to discover whether I am *either* right or wrong, and it is the inability to discover rightness *or* wrongness that makes the allocation *arbitrary*. There is a world of difference between being wrong (or right) and being arbitrary. The major difference is that the weight of the carcass and hide can be measured but the cost can only be calculated. That is, the prediction of the relative weights refers to reality (can be empirically tested) whereas the calculation of the cost does not refer to anything.

Accountants have a tendency to reply to this by pointing out that weight and cost are different. I agree. It is the conclusion drawn from that difference where we disagree. My conclusion is that we abandon 'historical costs' because they don't refer to reality and find some other attribute that can be empirically tested. Their conclusion is that we continue to account for 'historical costs' and continue to lament the fact that they are arbitrary.

Compare the contrast of meaningless to true *or* false in Note 22 to the contrast of arbitrary to right *or* wrong in this Note.

5 One of the interesting characteristics of this line of reasoning is that the sequencing influences the ultimate conclusion. If the first argument were to chose to report a calculated amount and reject the amount paid, then the second argument would be forced into a comparison of a calculated amount and a current value, and current values usually satisfy the proposed criteria better than the calculated amount. Thus, the sequencing presented in the text is essential to the conclusion to report a calculated amount.

Lyas (1984: 101) is the only exception that I know of to this sequencing. He discusses the need for allocations prior to comparing the ease of determination of amounts paid to current values. The problem is that he seems to be unaware that allocations are calculations, usually divisions of amounts paid, as opposed to amounts paid. Again, there is no reason for a philosopher to know what accountants do but the fact is that an allocation is a calculation.

6 One of Stamp's major criticisms (Stamp 1981: 15) of my work was that 'when Sterling criticizes the work of others he frequently fails to give references to their writing. . . . Omissions of this kind make it very difficult (and in many cases impossible) for serious readers to refer back to the material that Sterling is criticizing or attempting to refute'. I thought I had provided sufficient justification for that omission by explaining that 'my purpose is to expose an error, not to expose those who have committed an error' and that I had avoided the problem of the serious reader by offering to 'supply the citations upon request' (Sterling 1979: 48, note). I still believe that my offer avoids the immediate problem but Stamp's criticism caused me to think that there might be a long-run problem – the slim chance that a future historian or student would want to examine a typical source – and therefore I decided to supply a citation in this paper. I selected Butterworth *et al.* for consideration and citation

because they make an argument, rather than an allegation, as well as because I was the assigned discussant (Sterling 1982) when it was first presented and therefore my more lengthy assessment of both its strengths and weaknesses is already on record.

7 Some years ago I became so puzzled by accountants' reversal of the meanings of 'objective' and 'subjective' that I began to entertain far-fetched speculations, such as a connection between Scotland being the birthplace of modern accounting and also of Duns Scotus. Perhaps ancient Scottish accountants had been influenced by Duns Scotus' usage of 'objective' as an idea in the mind without independent existence. (It was that Scotistic usage that previously caused me to suggest that accountants abandon the term because I thought it would be easier to replace the term than to change inherited, ingrained usage.)

Less far-fetched is that accountants have confused objectivity with certainty. Their abhorrence of uncertainty is long-standing and apparently universal, evidently because it makes them vulnerable to criticism and, more recently, to lawsuits. In the accounting literature certainty is thought to be achieved by consensus and, thus, consensus is equated with objectivity. For example, obtaining consensus that a particular cost allocation (calculation) is acceptable results in the numeral from that calculation being characterized as 'objective' without regard to questions about representation.

Eventually it occurred to me that accountants had substituted the certainty of calculation for the uncertainty of objectively representing reality. I don't recall whether that occurred to me before or after reading Einstein's remark that 'as far as the propositions of mathematics refer to reality, they are not certain; and as far as they are certain, they do not refer to reality' (Einstein 1954: 233), but his clear, succinct distinction cemented the thought if it didn't originate it.

The thought was reinforced by my experience at FASB where Board members seemed to be of the view that *the* solution to accounting problems is to achieve consensus among Board members about what accountants are required to calculate. It didn't seem to be of concern whether the numeral from the calculation 'faithfully represented' the 'phenomena it purports to represent' (as required by FASB Concepts Statement 2 (1983, para 63)) but it did seem to be of overwhelming concern that the Board reach agreement about the method of calculation. The Staff's adopted objective was to 'get some paper on the street' which expressed the Board's consensus, not to get the numeral to represent some phenomena.

I am indebted to Professor Tom Lee for discussions regarding the apparent universal interpretation of auditing as providing assurance that a numeral is calculated in conformance with the appropriate regulations (GAAP), without regard to whether the numeral corresponds to anything. I am indebted to Professor Bart Ward for a spirited defence of that (to me, indefensible) interpretation, and for pointing out its extension to the auditor's concept of 'materiality' so that an 'immaterial amount' (that is, a negligible amount or an amount within acceptable tolerance limits) is judged by how far the accountant has deviated from a strict application of the regulations rather than how far the numeral deviates from a faithful representation.

8 Staubus (1987: 11–12), in reviewing the harmful miscues in accounting history, says of the depreciation definition: 'No one seems to be able to say anything good about it, but no authoritative body has been willing to change it'. Staubus rhetorically asks why '*numbers representing no economic phenomena* should be of interest to users' which raises the question why accountants continue to report numerals that are of no interest to users and why authoritative bodies refuse to change the definition despite sustained attack. That is, it rephrases the question posed by Butterworth *et al.* in such a way that it demands an answer different from the objectivity of the numerals.

9 Perhaps this definition and my opposition to it will allow me to make my position clear enough for it to be understood by non-accountants. Lyas (1984: 103) interprets my position as 'the flight from judgement to calculation' whereas the fact is that my position is the flight from calculation to measurement. I am not trying to *eliminate* judgements and decisions made by people but rather trying to *redirect* them toward measurements and away from calculations. I have no disagreement with those who seek 'standards which, while not circumscribing judgement by some inflexible book of rules, none the less allow the quality of accounting judgements to be assessed' but I do disagree with those who want to make judgements about the way to calculate and then assess those types of judgements. I want to assess the judgements made about observations, including measurements, not about calculations. The distinction is between 'the kind of judgement that does not lend itself to verification by measurement' (Lyas 1984; 104) and the kind that does, not between judgement and no judgement.

Thus, Lyas (1984: 105) is correct when he says that 'Sterling's hypothesis . . . does not do away with the need for judgement' but is incorrect when he adds 'in the way that Sterling hopes'. In the discussion (Sterling 1979: 77) I made it explicit that such a hypothesis would 'increase the use of his professional judgment . . . not reduce it' and contrasted it to the current state where judgement is not required because it is a calculation and there is nothing 'to do but check the accuracy of the arithmetic'. I regret that my views were not sufficiently clear to permit Lyas to focus on where we disagree rather than using his valuable time and effort criticizing me for taking positions which I explicitly denied.

10 Previous experience convinces me that this sentence will be misunderstood by accountant readers because they have been taught to use 'measure' as a synonym for 'calculate', as is evidenced by the following 'official' or 'authoritative' pronouncement by FASB (1984, No. 5, para. 67, emphasis added):

> Items currently reported in financial statements are *measured* by different attributes. . . . Property, plant, and equipment and most inventories are reported at their historical cost, which is the amount of cash, or its equivalent, paid to acquire an asset, commonly adjusted after acquisition for amortization or other allocations.

That is, one 'measures' by making a calculation (allocation) based on the amount paid. Then this calculation is called 'historical cost'.

Textbooks imitate the 'authoritative' literature. Even the best texts are not immune to substituting logic for empirics – the logical operation of calculating for the empirical operation of measuring:

> Ending inventory is *measured* by first determining the quantity on hand, then *multiplying* this quantity times the unit acquisition cost [which was obtained by *dividing*]. A choice must be arbitrarily made on the assumed unit cost, and this depends on the flow assumptions made. The attribute being *measured* is historical cost in all methods.
> Wolk *et al.* 1984: 268, emphasis added)

Students learn two lessons from such texts: (1) how to obtain amounts by calculation, and (2) to think that they have 'measured' something by those calculations. From this comes the inability to distinguish and the misunderstanding of the sentence in the text.

11 For some years I have been trying to convince colleagues that the fact that calculations start with empirical inputs does not have any bearing on whether the output has an empirical referent. Borrowing from Kline's description (1972: 19) of an ancient error in geometry, I posed the case of area, A, being calculated as:

$$A = \frac{(a + b)}{2} \times \frac{(c + d)}{2}$$

where a, b, c, d are the length of the adjacent sides of a rectangle. Since the right formula for area is the product of length and width (i.e. a×b or c×d) this formula yields a false area (except for squares and accidents) despite the accuracy of the length of the sides. None the less, accountants have continued to insist that if they checked the accuracy of the inputs of the various cost allocations (such as for the steer and machine discussed previously), and they ensured that the calculation was arithmetically correct, then they would be faithfully representing historical cost. The fact that another method of allocation was equally as acceptable, and indeed used by other firms with identical assets, did not alter their belief that both represented the historical cost. In accounting, it is not considered a contradiction or an inconsistency to say that the 'historical cost of x is £y and it is £z' where y is significantly different from z.

To illustrate the point I have tried to find cases so extreme as to be manifestly absurd. For example, I have asked if 'hage' (the product of a person's height and age as described by Hempel (1967: 46) does represent some kind of reality. This absurdity hasn't worked. Instead of 'hage' and other such calculations causing accountants to rethink the numerals they calculate, they have embraced hage and defended it. The argument seems to be as follows:

> Numerals derived from accounting calculations represent the phenomena that they purport to represent.
>
> The numerals derived from calculating 'hage' are identical in relevant respects to the numerals derived from accounting calculations.
>
> Therefore, 'hage' represents the phenomena that it purports to represent.
>
> Of course this begs the question but more importantly it illustrates

accountants' confidence in accounting and their self-imposed isolation. If one listens carefully, one can almost hear: if science differs from accounting, then so much the worse for science, or as Boulding (1958: 95) put it: 'Accounting for the most part, remains a legalistic and traditional practice, almost immune to self-criticism by scientific methods'.

I am indebted to Professor James Loebbecke for reaffirmation of the (to me, wrong) view that both 'historical cost' and 'hage' represent some kind of phenomena.

12 When Japan imported western accounting they translated 'accounting' as *kaikei* which means 'calculate' and thus indicates that they fully understood what they were importing. I am indebted to Professor Gisuke Murase for informing me of this interesting titbit.

13 And, in rebuttal to my arguments, that it is impossible to convert it to a science, that it is inherently unscientific. Most of these rebuttals misunderstand my proposal, taking it to be that accounting should become a kind of physics. By contrast, Lyas (1984: 106) understood what I had tried to say:

> When Sterling argued that accounting could be a science, he did not wish to suggest that it should become a kind of physics but that scientific methodology has as much a place in the study by accountants of their material as it has in the study by physicists of their material.

It is the adoption of scientific methodology in accounting and the application of that methodology in the study by accountants of their *materials* that I have proposed, not the adoption of the materials of physics. I am grateful to Lyas for understanding that much misunderstood point and for stating it so clearly. I hasten to add, however, that the adoption of scientific methodology limits the kinds of materials to those that can in fact be studied as opposed to those that can only be calculated.

14 Perhaps this could be called the 'informal *non*-fallacy of equivocation' since it is the opposite of the informal fallacy of equivocation. That is, the compound sentence 'X is Y and X is not-Y' is true if the atomic sentences are both true and in this instance both are true because the meaning of X is different in each. When restated as 'X_1 is Y and X_2 is not-Y' it is obvious that it can be true.

15 The comments I made about accounting anthropology (Sterling 1970: 449) are reproduced beginning in the next paragraph in their entirety with only slight modifications and the elimination of footnotes. I think they are still appropriate. Indeed, the serious consideration of these remarks is probably more appropriate today since the current fad is 'positive accounting theory' whereas at the time I wrote the fad was 'efficient markets'. That is, the previous fad was the study of that collection of people known as capital market agents whereas it has now changed back to the 'inductivists' tradition of studying people who are accountants.

Probably the most ancient and pervasive method of accounting theory construction is to observe accountants' actions and then rationalize those actions by subsuming them under generalized principles. The result is not a theory about accounting or a theory about the things to be accounted for: instead it is a theory about accountants. The 'principles of accounting' then is a theory that says that under such and such conditions the accountant will act in such and such a way. The input is the condition and the output is the accountants' action.

This is quite similar to various anthropological theories which allow to predict that under certain conditions, primitive man will act in a certain way. The test of the theory is the observations of the actions of primitive man. In the same fashion, the test of an anthropological theory of accounting is the observations of the actions of accounting man. For example, if the accounting anthropologist has observed that accounting man normally records a 'conservative' figure and generalizes this as the 'principle of conservatism', then we can test this principle by observing whether or not accounting man does in fact record a conservative figure. If the accounting anthropologist sets forth the 'principle of diversity', then we can test this principle by observing whether or not accounting man does in fact record similar occurrences in different ways – and so forth.

There are several difficulties with this kind of theorizing. First, it is not necessarily true that accounting man acts in the manner in which he ought to act. It is an error to conclude that because *x is* the case, then *x ought* to be the case. There is no way to arrive at the way accounting man ought to act from observing and generalizing how he in fact does act. Thus, this kind of theorizing may provide us with an explanation of why accountants act in a certain way and it may provide us with the ability to predict their actions, but it does not yield a judgement about the goodness of their actions. To judge the goodness of their actions requires other criteria. Second, the process does not permit change. By requiring the present generation of accountants to act in accordance with generally accepted principles of accounting – which principles were derived by observing the actions of the previous generation of accountants – change has been prohibited. If the requirement were strictly enforced, each generation would act just like the previous generation and this could be traced back to the first generation. Of course, changes have been made in accounting theory, but these changes are not explained or provided for by the anthropological interpretation. Third, subsequent to the first generation, the process is circular. We observe accountants' actions to discover what to teach, then we teach them how to act, then we observe accountants actions to discover what to teach, etc. Fourth, and most importantly, is my judgement that the theory of accounting ought to be concerned with accounting phenomena, not practising accountants, in the same way that theories of physics are concerned with physical phenomena, not practising physicists. The anthropological investigations may provide useful information. It may turn out to be important for us to know how practising accountants act and why they act that way. Comprehension of those actions is aided if they can be generalized under a few 'principles' but to avoid confusion they should be called 'principles of the behaviour of accountants' rather than 'principles of accounting'. However, such knowledge of principles does not provide a basis for a theory of accounting, as opposed to a theory of accountants' actions, and it would be wholly beneficial to call them by descriptive names.

16 To illustrate the controversy consider the *brouhaha* that resulted from the issuance of Accounting Research Studies No. 1 and No. 3 and the

pacification from the issuance of Accounting Research Study No. 7. I commented at the time that the chief error of No. 1 (Moonitz 1961) and No. 3 (Sprouse and Moonitz 1962) was that they had strayed from anthropology and that the primary appeal of No. 7 (Grady 1965) was that it returned to anthropology. I was surprised that there was disagreement about that comment because the title of No. 7 – *Inventory of Generally Accepted Principles* – clearly revealed that its purpose was to record practitioner behaviour by recording an inventory of their practices in the same way one would record an inventory of stock-in-trade. None the less, a large number (perhaps a majority) of accountant practitioners denied that Grady was being an accounting anthropologist and defended him on the basis of the 'sound accounting' he espoused, not recognizing that the reason they thought his accounting was sound was that it reflected what they were doing.

The controversy, as I saw it, was whether Grady did a good job because his *product* was 'sound accounting' or because his *process* was anthropology. I opted for the process. If one included human flesh on the inventory of victuals for cannibals, it is likely that cannibals would think that one had proposed a 'sound diet' because it reflected what they were doing. If one recommended that they become vegetarians for health reasons, they would probably reject it as being too 'radically different' from current generally accepted dietetic practices.

Such disagreement continues to the present time albeit in a slightly different form. The 'positive accounting theorists' *define* accounting theory as that which explains and predicts accounting practices. They deny that it is possible to judge 'sound accounting' because such judgements are normative and therefore the *only* question is what accountants do, not whether what they do is sound.

Everyone would also agree that, by including human flesh on the inventory of victuals for cannibals, one had compiled an accurate inventory because it reflected what cannibals do. After that agreement, however, there is a chasm. Positive cannibal theorists would prohibit one from recommending the addition or substitution of vegetables in the diet because such recommendations are normative and therefore unscientific, regardless of the amount of scientific evidence regarding the nutritional qualities of vegetables. This 'normative theorist' would say that the positive theorists are studying what cannibals eat as contrasted to nutritionists who are studying nutritional effects of what one eats. Thus, the distinction is the subject matter one has selected for study, not scientific positivism versus non-scientific normativism.

If we make that distinction, it would alleviate, perhaps eliminate, the continuing conflict of normative versus positive, a priori versus empirical, social recorder versus asset recorder, and so forth.

17 It seems that 'social-recorder' differs from 'inductivist' in several ways, including Demski being critical of textbooks that have a 'tendency to tell the student how the accounting ought to be done' whereas Littleton, an early inductivist and leading proponent of the method, supplemented observations of practice with justifications for the purpose of teaching students how accounting ought to be done:

> [Accounting] methods devised by many different people were used [and became] generally accepted accounting principles. Teachers of bookkeeping and later accounting and auditing found it necessary to supplement the accumulated rules and descriptions of procedure by explanations and justifications. This was done in order that study should be something more than the memorizing of rules. Hence it is appropriate to say that both the methods of practice and the explanations of theory were inductively derived out of experience.
> (Littleton 1953: 185)

Ijiri (1975: 28), a leading modern inductivist, is even more direct, saying that 'the purpose of such an [inductive] exercise is to highlight where changes are most needed and where they are feasible'.

18 Instead of the usual form of *argumentum ad ignorantiam* (*N* is *X* because no one has proved that *N* is not-*X*) the form of this argument is: A knows *N* is *X* because we are ignorant of whether *N* is *X* or *N* is not-*X*. This is an especially noxious error when it is extended to claim that B does not know that *N* is not-*X* because we are ignorant of whether *N* is *X* or not-*X*. In the absence of even attempting to qualify or disqualify A or B as authorities, the choice of A over B is groundless.

19 An appropriate name for one who studies ornithologists would be 'ornithologist-ologist'. For that reason, I have previously suggested that accounting be renamed 'plutology' (from Plutus, god of wealth, hence the study of wealth and wealth changes including profit) because the study of plutologists would become plutologist-ology, the structure and repetitiveness of which might cause plutologist-ologists to pause long enough to think about what they are doing. Then when Watts and Zimmerman (1979) present the case that self-interest motivates plutologist-ologists (and Peasnell and Williams (1986) present a rebuttal) they would be called 'plutologist-ologist-ologists'. A planned paper of mine will present the case that Watts and Zimmerman were seeking their self-interest when they wrote 'The demand for and supply of accounting theories: the market for excuses'; so my paper ('The demand and supply of accounting papers: the market for hubris') will be plutologist-ologist-ologist-ology. We may be on to an all-day sucker here.

An equally important reason for the name change is that it would allow my next book to be *Principia Plutometrica* which title would befit the exalted plutometrician I expect to become, leaving behind my present, ignoble status as a normativist and my former, equally ignoble status as an apriorist.

20 There are also instances of arguments that a full or deep understanding of a discipline cannot be obtained without including practitioners of that discipline in the many things to be studied. For example, it is argued that one will not have a full understanding of geometry without studying practitioners of geometry (surveyors and other earth measurers) *in addition* to studying the earth, the rules of thumb used by Babylonians and Egyptians, the idealized concepts and the life and times of Euclid, as well as Descartes, Gauss, Lobachevsky, and others, topology, history, and other related topics. However, to the best of my knowledge no one has ever suggested that the study of geometry be *restricted* to the observation of the practices of surveyors and other geometricians. Nor

has anyone ever alleged that it would be normative to improve or correct the then current earth measurement methods.

21 Dewey illustrates the productivity of winnowing the good from the bad practices with the history of mathematics:

> Men began with counting and measuring things just as they began with pounding and burning them. One thing, as common speech profoundly has it, led to another. Certain ways were successful – not merely in the immediately practical sense, but in the sense of being interesting, of arousing attention, of exciting attempts at improvement. The present-day mathematical logician may present the structure of mathematics as if it had sprung all at once from the brain of a Zeus whose anatomy is that of pure logic. But, nevertheless, this very structure is a product of long historic growth, in which all kinds of experiments have been tried, in which some men have struck out in this direction and some in that, and in which some exercises and operations have resulted in confusion and others in triumphant clarifications and fruitful growths; a history in which matter and methods have been constantly selected and worked over on the basis of empirical success and failure.
>
> (Dewey 1963: 93)

Had there been a 'social recorder perspective' or a 'positive theory' of counting and measuring, the assessment of the practices would have been proscribed – it would have been considered 'normative' to decide success and failure of matter and method. The prescription of a 'positive-scientific' description would, in essence, prescribe the status quo ante.

Dewey's assessment of the distinction follows:

> The parrot-like repetition of the distinction between an empirical description of what is and a normative account of what should be merely neglects the most striking fact about thinking as it empirically is – namely, its flagrant exhibition of cases of failure and success – that is, of good thinking and bad thinking.

I agree. It is not the simple-minded distinction between the descriptive and prescriptive for the purpose of sanctioning one and censuring the other that is important but rather the cogency of the argument for the prescriptions and the adequacy of the evidence for the descriptions.

22 Hempel recognized early on that the analytic–synthetic distinction presents some formidable difficulties, even contributing to the explication of those difficulties (1965: 101ff), which weaken the verifiability theory of meaning but he maintains that 'the empiricist criterion of meaning is basically sound' and that its 'application has been, on the whole, enlightening and salutary'. I agree, and I think its application would be particularly enlightening and salutary in accounting.

Compare the contrast of arbitrary to right *or* wrong in Note 4 to the contrast of meaningless to true *or* false in Hempel and others in the philosophy of science literature.

23 There is now little dispute about the fact of divorce but there remains dispute about whether the effect of the divorce is good or bad. Hall, an eminent practitioner, and Demski, a well-known theorist, describe the divorce in a remarkably similar manner. Hall (1987: 31–2) writes about

the growing gap between practice and the 'theory as advanced in articles' and notes that it would be reasonable to 'question whether the subject matter [of those articles] was accounting'. Demski (1987: 89) contrasts the contents of a journal at two dates, saying that the 'first [1964] list of articles speaks to how to do the accounting or how to analyze some particular (investment) decision' whereas the 'second [1986] list speaks to something else, perhaps asteroids'. The second level of humour in Demski's joke is that many practitioners would take it seriously, agreeing that current accounting research is in outer space, being conducted by space cadets, and needs to be brought down to earth. Equally intense, if less colourful, disdain for practice is expressed by many academics.

Many practitioners who are concerned about the divorce plead for more applied or practical research. Many academics are pleased with the divorce, seeing it as a triumph of pure research. I agree that there is a problem but I don't see it stemming from the tension between pure and applied research. Instead I see it as the direct result of the complete divorce of subject matters.

Hall (1987: 35) is not one of the practitioners who expresses disdain for theory although he does plead for clearer expression of theory. I join in that plea. Perhaps we accountants could adopt what Chalmers (1976: xi) called a 'noteworthy feature of the Popperian school' namely 'the pressure it put on one to be clear about the problem one was interested in and to express one's views on it in a simple and straightforward way'. It seems to me that some accountants think that being understood is incompatible with being scientific or scholarly and therefore they are deliberately obscure. Is it possible to be *that* obscure accidentally?

24 Michael Power (personal communication) kindly pointed out that 'it is simply not clear from the paper that such an ontology of accounting phenomena is obvious'. I agree. I hasten to rectify that omission by noting that a central purpose of this chapter is to show the absence of ontology of 'historical costs' and therefore that they are modern fantasies to be shed in the same way that our ancestors shed medieval fantasies. In place of such fantasies we should ground accounting in what every plain man can see, measuring and generalizing the obvious things to be measured and generalized.

In other works I have suggested that we account for one of the 'ordinary notions' of economics, namely prices. In economics there is no question about the ontology of prices, although of course there might be many questions about the amount of a particular price, as was made clear by Leontief:

> As an empirical science, economics dealt from the outset with phenomena of common experience. Producing and consuming goods, buying and selling, and receiving income and spending it are activities engaging everyone's attention practically all the time. Even the application of the scientific principle of quantification did not have to be initiated by the analyst himself – measuring and pricing constitute an integral part of the phenomena that he sets out to explain.
>
> (Leontief 1982)

Conspicuous by its absence from this list of the 'phenomena of common experience' is historical costs. Since prices are inevitably included and historical costs are inevitably omitted when economists make such lists, I find it odd to require argument for the ontology of the ordinary notion of price and not to require argument for the ontology of the extraordinary notion of historical costs.

I suspect that the reason for this oddity is another instance of equivocation regarding 'historical costs' similar to that discussed on p. 126. A clue supporting that suspicion can be found when Power accepts the traditional way of framing the question of valuing cars and buildings as a choice of 'either selling price, replacement cost or *actual* historic cost' (Power 1986: 391, emphasis added) thereby apparently questioning the ontology of current purchase and selling prices by contrasting them to the actual, granting the ontology of historic costs (amounts paid) by characterizing it as actual, and then extending that grant, via equivocation, to historic costs (calculated amounts).

25 Peasnell distinguishes science from a 'service activity' when he writes:

> Accounting is not a science, it is a service activity [and] . . . should be equated with fields like medicine, technology and the law [that] . . . make use of scientific (i.e. empirical) knowledge – they often contribute to it – but their principal concern is with doing a particular job of work, fulfilling a social need.
>
> (Peasnell 1978: 220–1)

I fully agree and, except for the name 'service activity', I have drawn similar comparisons and suggested that we pattern ourselves after such service activities, especially medicine and engineering. What I mean when I suggest that accounting move toward a science is simply that it take the first step by switching from calculating numerals to measuring (observing) and reporting some kind of verifiable magnitude, such as prices. If we do this, perhaps we can play the role of a Tycho Brahe to an accounting Johannes Kepler. Although we cannot be sure that an accounting Kepler will appear if we do measure, we can be sure that one will not appear if we continue to calculate. If Tycho had calculated the 'historical positions' of the planets instead of measuring them, Kepler would not have had a data base to use to compare to his conjectured calculations, which comparison were necessary to convert some of the conjectures to the famous laws.

REFERENCES

Accounting Research and Terminology Bulletins (1961) final edition, New York: American Institute of Certified Public Accountants.

Boulding, K.E. (1958) *The Skills of the Economist*, Cleveland: Howard Allen.

Butterworth, J.E., Gibbins, M. and King, R.D. (1982) 'The structure of accounting theory: some basic conceptual and methodological issues'. in S. Basu and J.A. Milburn (eds) *Research to Support Standard Setting in Financial Accounting: A Canadian Perspective*, proceedings of the 1981 Clarkson Gordon Foundation Research Symposium. Toronto: Clarkson Gordon Foundation.

Chalmers, A.F. (1976) *What is this Thing called Science? An Assessment of the Nature and Status of Science and its Methods*, St Lucia: University of Queensland Press, second edition.

Christenson, C. (1983) 'The methodology of positive accounting', *Accounting Review*, January.

Demski, J.S. (1987) '(Theoretical) research in (managerial) accounting', in B.E. Cushing (ed.) *Accounting and Culture: Plenary Session Papers and Discussants' Comments from the 1986 Annual Meeting of the American Accounting Association*, Sarasota, Florida: American Accounting Association.

Dewey, J. (1963) 'The significance of logical reconstruction', in R. Jager (ed.) *Essays in Logic: From Aristotle to Russell*, Englewood Cliffs: Prentice-Hall.

Einstein, A. (1954) *Ideas and Opinions*, New York: Crown Publishers.

FASB (Financial Accounting Standards Board) (1983) *Accounting Standards: Statement of Financial Accounting Concepts 1–4*, Stamford, Connecticut: FASB.

—— (1984) *Statement of Financial Accounting Concepts No. 5*, Stamford, Connecticut: FASB.

Grady, P. (1965) *Inventory of Generally Accepted Accounting Principles for Business Enterprises*. Accounting Research Study No. 7, New York: American Institute of Certified Public Accountants.

Hall, W.D. (1987) *Accounting and Auditing: Thoughts on Forty Years in Practice and Education*, Chicago: Arthur Andersen & Co.

Hatfield, H.R. (1924) 'An historical defense of bookkeeping', *Journal of Accountancy*, April.

Hempel, C.G. (1965) *Aspects of Scientific Explanation and Other Essays in the Philosophy of Science*, New York: Free Press.

—— (1967) *Fundamentals of Concept Formation in Empirical Science*, Chicago: University of Chicago Press.

Ijiri, Y. (1975) *Theory of Accounting Measurement*. Studies in Accounting Research No. 10, Sarasota, Florida: American Accounting Association.

Kline, M. (1972) *Mathematical Thought from Ancient to Modern Times*, New York: Oxford University Press.

Leontief, W. (1982) Letter to the Editor, *Science*, 9 July.

Littleton, A.C. (1953) *Structure of Accounting Theory*, Monograph No. 5, Sarasota, Florida: American Accounting Association.

Luchins, A.S. (1942) 'Mechanization in problem solving', in J.F. Dashiell (ed.) *Psychological Monographs: The Effect of Einstellung*, 54 (6), Evanston: American Psychological Assoc.

Lyas, C. (1984) 'Philosophers and accountants', *Philosophy*, 59 (227): 99–110.

Mill, J.S. (1909) *Principles of Political Economy: With Some of Their Applications to Social Philosophy*, New York: Colonial Press.

Moonitz, M. (1961) *The Basic Postulates of Accounting*. Accounting Research Study No. 1, New York: American Institute of Certified Public Accountants.

Peasnell, K.V. (1978) 'Statement of accounting theory and theory acceptance: a review article', *Accounting and Business Research*, 8(31): 217–25.

Peasnell, K.V. and Williams, D.J. (1986) 'Ersatz academics and scholar-saints: the supply of financial accounting research', *Abacus*, 22(2): 121–35.

Power, M. (1986) 'Taking stock: philosophy and accountancy'. *Philosophy*, 61 (237), 387–94.

Sprouse, R.T. and Moonitz, M. (1962) *A Tentative Set of Broad Accounting Principles for Business Enterprises*. Accounting Research Study No. 3. New York: American Institute of Certified Public Accountants.

Stamp, E. (1981) 'Why can accounting not become a science like physics?' *Abacus*, Spring 17(1): 13–22.

Staubus, G.J. (1987) 'The Dark Ages of cost accounting: the role of miscues in the literature'. *Accounting Historians Journal*, Fall: 1–18.

Sterling, R.R. (1970) 'On theory construction and verification', *Accounting Review*, July.

—— (1979) *Toward a Science of Accounting*, Houston: Scholars Book Co.

—— (1982) 'Discussant's comments', in S. Basu and J.A. Milburn (eds) *Research to Support Standard Setting in Financial Accounting: A Canadian Perspective*, proceedings of the 1981 Clarkson Gordon Foundation Research Symposium, Toronto: Clarkson Gordon Foundation.

—— (1988) 'Confessions of a failed empiricist', *Advances in Accounting*, Vol. 6. JAI Press.

Thomas, A.L. (1969) *The Allocation Problem in Financial Accounting Theory*, Studies in Accounting Research No. 3, Sarasota, Florida: American Accounting Association.

—— (1974) *The Allocation Problem in Financial Accounting Theory, Part Two*, Studies in Accounting Research No. 9, Sarasota, Florida: American Accounting Association.

Watts, R.L. and Zimmerman, J.L. (1979) 'The demand for and supply of accounting theories: the market for excuses', *Accounting Review*, 54(2): 273–305.

—— (1986) *Positive Accounting Theory*, Englewood Cliffs: Prentice-Hall.

Whitehead, A.N. (1967) *Science and the Modern World*, New York: The Free Press.

Whittington, G. (1987) 'Positive accounting: a review article', *Accounting and Business Research*, Autumn issue.

Wolk, H.I., Francis, J.R., and Tearney, M.G. (1984) *Accounting Theory: A Conceptual and Institutional Approach*, Boston: Kent Publishing Co.

Ziman, J. (1978) *Reliable Knowledge: An Exploration of the Grounds for Belief in Science*, Cambridge: Cambridge University Press.

7 Accounting and language

Colin Lyas

> I dreamed a motto for a sober philosophy: neither a be-all nor an end-all be.
>
> (Austin 1961)

One way in which a subject like accounting can become philosophical is this: a discipline, be it literary criticism, linguistics, physics, psychology or accounting is furnished with a set of terms with which its practitioners handle their subject matter: terms like 'ironic', 'meaning', 'cause', 'behaviour', 'historic cost', 'true' and 'fair'. Given this we can distinguish two activities: one is the *use* of certain terms by the practitioners of a discipline, as when a critic talks about a poem as ironic, or a psychologist speculates about the cause of a certain piece of behaviour, or an accountant calculates a historic cost. The other activity is a *higher order* reflection on the terms that are being used by practitioners in which one asks such things as: do they have a precise meaning? Are they consistently used? Are they ambiguous? What, if anything, is the truth value of statements in which they are used? How, if at all, is that truth value to be determined?

When such higher-order enquiries occur in, say, mathematics, religion or psychology, we get what is called the philosophy of religion, the philosophy of mathematics and philosophical psychology. Philosophy, in this sense, is a matter of conceptual analysis, and any discipline which uses concepts, including accounting, will have this philosophical dimension.

No discipline worth bothering about can seek to evade such conceptual enquiries. For first, these enquiries constitute the hygiene of the reasoning of a discipline. Without them we are prey to the loose, the ambiguous, and the down-right slovenly. Nor need these conceptual enquiries be thought necessary but unexciting. We need only recall that physics took a new departure because Einstein asked himself questions about the concept of simultaneity as used by physicists, and that mathematics likewise altered when people started thinking about the concept of number instead of taking it for granted.

Conceptual enquiries of the kind that I have mentioned are essential to the well-being of accounting. That kind of involvement of philosophy with accounting, however, needs to be distinguished from another. The difference may be brought out by noting that the kinds of conceptual enquiries of which we have so far spoken are both descriptive and internal to the activity of accounting. By this I mean that to determine how a term like 'historic cost' is used one must study how *accountants* use this term in practice. If the term has more than one meaning, that can only emerge from a descriptive study of what goes on in accounting: it was such a study that led Stamp to distinguish 'two possible concepts of capital maintenance' (Stamp 1980, para. 27). And, as Sterling rightly points out, (this volume p. 126), to the extent that I have not grasped the way in which accountants use the term 'historic cost', so I have not understood the meaning of that term. (If asked why I made a mistake here, I can only reply as Dr Johnson did when asked how he came to define 'pastern' as 'knee of a horse': 'Ignorance, ma'am, pure ignorance'.)

Suppose now, the conceptual enquiry has laid bare how accountants use their terms. It would now seem that a further task lies open to the 'philosopher' of accounting. For she or he might go on to talk critically of certain accounting practices as they evidence themselves in the use of certain of the concepts of accounting. Sterling for example, (this volume p. 127), commends my use of 'what was paid' instead of the 'equivocal "historic cost"' as something that would avoid a 'long-standing, pernicious error'.

Here we are not describing what goes on in accounting but evaluating the nature and role of certain concepts used in its practice. The question then arises 'from what point of view does that evaluation come?' The simplest answer derives the unsatisfactory nature of certain activities within accounting from an understanding of what accountancy is about. This the critic does by beginning with an understanding of the ends that accounting by definition sets out to achieve and by showing that certain particular activities within accounting practice are either not the most efficient means to those ends, or are such as wholly to frustrate their achievement. For example, when the legislature of the United Kingdom altered the law so as to require the disclosure of reserves it was presumably from a belief that the practice of not disclosing them went against the purposes for which accounts are presented. Again, when in a striking paper Sterling argues that accounting numerals do not represent phenomena, this can be a criticism only if it is thought to be an aim of the accountant to present a representation of phenomena.[1] The goal of evaluative accounting theory, is, then, to lay bare any contradictions between, on the one hand, what accounting as an activity demands of its practitioners and, on the other, the practices that practising accountants actually pursue. Again, as we shall see, no discipline can neglect such theory. Only constant vigilance can ensure that such contradictions do not emerge.

As an outsider, what I find interesting and heartening is the measure of agreement in stating the goals of accounting. (In pleasant contrast to one of my specialisms, art.) In his *Corporate Reporting* Stamp offered:

> To provide adequate information about the real performance of an enterprise to all potential users who need such information to make decisions.
>
> (Stamp 1980: 4)

He later (1980: 33) replaces 'potential' by 'legitimate' and with that amendment it is not difficult to trace the steps which take us from his formula to section 228(2) of the Companies Act 1985 which requires that the published financial statements of companies incorporated in Great Britain show a true and fair view of the state of affairs of the company and its results. (Stamp, incidentally (1980: 4) thought such brief statements unhelpful. He may have been influenced in this by the difficulties of fleshing out such formulae. That does not show the uselessness of a briefly formulated and accurate statement of the aims of accountants. The formula tells us precisely what it is that we have to flesh out. Without it, we can't even begin.)

We have now seen that in order to determine the nature of the operative concepts in accounting we have to study the operations of accountants. The concepts of accounting are internal to accounting. We have also seen that in evaluating the concepts of accounting we have to start with an understanding of the aims of accounting. That, too, is discovered by seeing what accountants agree their task to be. Philosophy enters this apparently self-contained world not merely in the form of conceptual analysis but in a more dramatic and disturbing way. For the very statement of the aims of accounting, namely, to give a true and fair account of some reality, is loaded to the gunwales with a philosophical cargo of millenia of discussions about truth, reality, justice and fairness. Thus, for example, the concept of an accountant as reporting on a reality *out there*, independently of her or his own or his or her client's wishes, like a thing of brute nature, tangles with the belief that economic reality is a social *construct*. Again, to talk of the requirement to give a 'true' account is to become involved with centuries of increasingly sophisticated discussion of what truth is, and how, and in what ways it is, if at all, to be determined. Yet again, to talk of the requirement to give a 'fair' account, is to invite the question 'Fair by what competing philosophical account of fairness?'

I can imagine two responses to this. One is to flinch in the face of the thought that to be an adequate accounting theorist one needs to have mastered philosophy as well. For reasons that will become clearer, I do not think that thought is correct. The other response will be impatience. Accounting can't wait. It can't wait as a practice for the problems of philosophy to be resolved before it takes some stance on what is just fair and true. Nor can hard-pressed individual accountants wait for this (and even less have they time to get to work on the full-time study of philosophy). So although there is a clear leakage of philosophy into accounting, there is a problem of how that leakage is to be handled in a way that does not hamstring the need of accounting theorists to handle practical exigencies.

At this stage I must interpolate something more personal. Eddie Stamp did not take long to convince me, when we first met as colleagues at Lancaster University, that philosophy leaked into accounting. He took much longer to persuade me to write about this. My ignorance of accounting literature (which I find additionally shameful, in view of the evident acquaintance of so many accounting theorists with literature of my subject) held me back for a long while. What in the end persuaded me to become involved with these matters was their connection with a question that had taxed me for a long time, namely the question: what relevance does academic philosophy have to problems, the solutions to which have consequences for practice? For example, the answer to the question 'Is abortion wrong?' has consequences for practice, as do the answers to the questions 'Is it right to eat animals?' and 'Can a balance sheet that does not disclose reserves be called true and fair?'.

The question which taxed me has become more urgent for a British academic. For increasingly the demand has been placed upon us to demonstrate the relevance, in some sense never clearly formulated, of our subject specialities. Sometimes the test of relevance is crudely how much revenue for our host institutions we can pull in. Sometimes the test is what we are doing to improve the efficiency of industry.

Whatever the particular form the relevance requirement takes, it breeds a general demand that each of us specify some problem which there is an urgent need to solve for the national well-being, the solution of which we then undertake to provide. That demand is reinforced by recent developments in philosophy itself. For in the latter half of this century the kind of philosophy with which I grew up, the philosophy of Russell, Austin, Ryle, and Wittgenstein, has been fiercely criticized for having nothing to do with the great issues of human life. The following comment by Herbert Marcuse is not untypical:

> The contemporary effort to reduce the scope and truth of philosophy is tremendous, and the philosophers themselves proclaim the modesty and inefficacy of philosophy. It leaves the established reality untouched; it abhors transgression. Austin's contemptuous treatment of the alternatives to the common usage of words and his defamation of what we 'think up in our armchairs of an afternoon'; Wittgenstein's assurance that philosophy 'leaves everything as it is' – such statements exhibit, to my mind, academic sado-masochism, self-humiliation and self-denunciation of the intellectual whose labour does not issue in scientific, technical or like achievements.[2]
>
> (Marcuse 1972: 141)

Philosophers beguiled or intimidated by all this then form a certain conception of the task of philosophy. Its task is to take some pressing issue about which there is unresolved debate, for example, euthanasia, vivisection, abortion, capital punishment, fairness and distribution, human rights, and then, from some Archimedean point, informed by a special philosophical expertise, to offer a solution.

That conception of philosophy excites scepticism for a number of reasons. First philosophers themselves are divided, often bitterly so, as to whether that conception of the task of philosophy is coherent. There are, for example, those, of whom I am not one, who wholeheartedly endorse Richard Rorty's view that 'edifying philosophy aims at continuing a conversation rather than at discovering truth'. On that view we have to:

> drop the notion of the philosopher as knowing something about knowing which nobody else knows so well . . . [and] . . . drop the notion that his voice always has an over-riding claim on the attention of the other participants in the conversation. It would be to drop the notion that there is something called the 'philosophical

> method' or 'philosophical technique' or 'the philosophical point of view' which enables the professional philosopher, *ex officio*, to have interesting views about, say, the respectability of psychoanalysis, the legitimacy of certain dubious laws, the resolution of moral dilemmas, the 'soundness' of schools of historiography or literary criticism and the like.
>
> (Henry 1936)

Second, scepticism about the conception of philosophy that I have described is excited by evidence that some of its most emphatic advocates do not give it the allegiance one would expect. Thus Marcuse, for all his trenchant assertions of the duty of philosophy not to leave existing reality untouched, can yet say:

> The transformation of a given status is not, of course, the business of philosophy. The philosopher can only participate in social struggles insofar as he is not a professional philosopher.
>
> (Marcuse 1968: 180)

And that merely continues a tradition that began with Marx's assertion that philosophers have tried to understand the world, whereas the problem is to change it.

Finally, if the conception of philosophy as possessing some method for the solution of the kinds of problems I have mentioned were correct, one might expect some disputes to have been resolved. What we have, however, is the unending stridency of debate, with the voices of philosophers no less strident than those of any other participants. There are philosophers who are for the state ownership of the means of production, philosophers who are against it; philosophers who are for affirmative action, those who are against it, and so on, and so on. What we have is what MacIntyre calls 'conceptual incommensurability'. In those arguments between philosophers:

> The rival premises are such that we possess no rational way of weighing the claims of one against the claims of the other. . . . It is precisely because there is in our society no established way of deciding between these claims that moral argument appears to be necessarily interminable. From our rival conclusions we can argue back to our rival premises; but when we do arrive at our premises argument ceases and the invocation of one premise against another becomes a matter of pure assertion and counter-assertion. Hence perhaps the slightly shrill tone of so much moral debate.
>
> (MacIntyre 1987: 8)

This leaves the question, if philosophy does not offer solutions to the sorts of issues I have mentioned, what does it do? What contribution can it make? What is its place in debates in, say, medical ethics and accounting theory? What indeed is its place in culture?

Sterling (this volume p. 127) suggests one answer:

> Philosophers' propensity to use clear, simple terms is a major reason that I welcome their examination of accounting. . . . More generally, philosophers' appreciation of the connection of clarity of language to clarity of thought (and communication) is the reason for welcoming them to accounting. Accountants seem to lack such appreciation and the result is the perpetuation of a number of errors and fallacies that can be traced directly to linguistic turbidity.

That may be true. My students tell me not merely that after reading Kant nothing else ever seems difficult to understand, but that after a course in philosophy they become more aware of the illogicality and obscurantism of much that is said, both professionally and non-professionally in their culture. (Not that that awareness always helps them: such is the state of that culture that those who point out, however tactfully, the illogicality and obscurity of its idols, both academic and non-academic, often suffer in consequence.)

If I am not happy with Sterling's generous reason for wishing philosophers to turn to accounting, it is because the skills he mentions seem to me to have nothing intrinsically to do with philosophy, no more than, as his quotation from Popper (this volume p. 124) makes clear, critical thinking is the exclusive preserve of philosophy. That as a matter of fact philosophers tend to possess more eminently the skills mentioned by Sterling, says more about the deplorable standards of argument and expression in other disciplines than it does about the nature of philosophy. The skills he mentions are the patrimony of every human being. Every academic discipline ought to foster and insist upon them, and to root out slovenly habits of thought and expression. When that happens, then if the main reason for welcoming philosophers into the study of accounting were their greater skills in detecting weak and turbid thought, there would no longer be any special reason for their presence: whereas I think that even in that more rational world there still would be a reason for thinking that accounting theory could not do without philosophy. For philosophical considerations intrude into the foundations of accounting because, as we have seen, a financial report is required to give a true and fair view of the state of a company, and 'true' and 'fair' are terms with a philosophical baggage. That remains the case even if all illogicality and turbidity were expunged from human thought and expression.

By way now of throwing light on the way in which discussions in philosophy might bear on issues in the foundations of accounting theory, I wish now to sketch a view of language which, if correct, might illuminate the ways in which problems about truth and fairness can arise and be determined in the practice of accounting.[3]

The first thing I wish to do is to draw attention to what I shall call a 'naturalistic' view of language.

The essence of that view is that our language develops over millenia to fit our needs. As something arises that we need to mark off, so we develop, by a linguistic reflex, as it were, a way of marking it off. For example, as we developed the need to articulate our pains and emotions to others, so we developed the expressive means by which to do so. Just so, terms like 'just' and 'fair' emerged in order to mark distinctions that it seemed important to us to make. So did terms like 'true'. 'If these words have a use', Wittgenstein remarks, 'it must be as humble a one as that of the words "table", "lamp", "door"' (Wittgenstein 1967, para. 97):[4] and by that he means, in part, that these important looking words do not fit into the language in some special way, but, like all our other words, are related to human needs, interests, feelings and practices. And, it follows, that to understand the meaning of any term is to understand those human interests, needs and practices in the context of which it arose and into which it fits. So, Wittgenstein writes, 'to imagine a language means to imagine a form of life' (1967, para. 19). From this it follows that

> For a *large* class of cases – though not for all – in which we employ the word 'meaning' it can be defined thus: the meaning of a word is its use in the language.
>
> (Wittgenstein 1967, para. 43)

The best statement I know of the view that I wish to adopt, and one that hints at complexities to be developed, is contained in this famous passage from J.L. Austin:

> Certainly ordinary language has no claim to the the last word, if there is such a thing. It embodies, indeed, something better than the metaphysics of the Stone Age, namely, as was said, the inherited experience and acumen of many generations of men. But then, that acumen has been concentrated primarily upon the practical business of life. If a distinction works well enough for

> practical purposes in ordinary life, (no mean feat, for ordinary life is full of hard cases) then there is sure to be something in it, it will not mark nothing: yet this is likely enough to be not the best way of arranging things, if our interests are more extensive and intellectual than ordinary. And again, that experience has been derived only from the sources available to ordinary men throughout most of civilised history: it has not been fed from the resources of the microscope and its successors. And it must be added, too, that superstition and error and fantasy of all kinds do become incorporated in ordinary language and even sometimes stand up to the survival test (only, when they do, why should we not detect it?). Certainly, then, ordinary language is *not* the last word: in principle it can everywhere be supplemented and improved upon and succeeded. Only remember, it *is* the *first* word.
>
> (Austin 1961: 133)

Our language develops, then, to match our needs. Yet we have problems with it. One arises in the following way: we may use a word with no sense of strain in the traffic of life. This is how even children can operate with terms like 'know', 'true', 'fair', 'time'. Then, as Wittgenstein put it, 'language goes on holiday'. Instead of *using* a term like 'time', which we do without strain every waking day, we ask 'What is time?' and don't know what to say.

This tendency to think about our ordinary language, and to mischaracterize it, was, Wittgenstein thought, a potent source of philosophical problems. In this chapter, however, another kind of problem about our language interests me.

Let us first remember that we grow into our language. As we do so, we learn something about the conditions under which the language speaking community of which we are to be members applies its terms. We learn, for example, something about the conditions under which it is appropriate to use terms like 'dog', 'time', 'car', 'person', 'art' and the like. We learn, too, such things as the conditions under which it is appropriate to say something like 'the pain is in his knee'. Unless there were such conditions of use, agreed in the language community, meaningful talk would not be possible. Hence some of the force of Wittgenstein's claim that 'if language is to be a form of communication, there must be agreement not only in definitions . . . but also in judgments' (1967, para. 242).

Some puzzlements, including some important ones arise *within* a mastered use of language. To be puzzled as to why the car won't start is to be puzzled within a non-contested understanding of the term 'car'. Some puzzlements, however, arise not *within* our shared understanding but *about* it.

For example, in the face of contingencies not envisaged as our language evolved, our normal criteria for saying something can be pulled apart by borderline cases. Thus as we learn our language we are likely to come to believe that a pain is located within a body and at the place at which the person having the pain locates it. This governs our normal talk about the pains of others. Then, however, an amputee locates a pain where her or his foot *was*. In such a case we may be torn between the inclination to say that a pain *must* be within the body of the person having it (so that the pain *cannot* be where the foot *was*), and the inclination to say that the sufferer is the last authority on where her or his pain is located (even if that sufferer locates it outside the body).

As Austin notes, such cases are particularly likely to arise as scientific discoveries impinge upon a language that developed in advance of those discoveries. Thus our criteria of personal identity refer to both bodily and mental continuity. Our language for speaking of persons evolved in situations in which those two continuities normally go together. This is the same person as I meant yesterday if this person is mentally and physically continuous with the person I met yesterday. As science evolves, however, and it becomes plausible to posit cases of brain division, brain transplantation and brain repatterning, our normal criteria come under strain and we may become confused as to how these new cases should be described. Moreover a lot depends on what we now say. For all sorts of reasons we need to know who's who.

Deep puzzlements may, then, emerge as scientific advances impinge upon our ordinary speech dispositions. (Consider here the question 'Are tables really solid, given what physicists have told us about their structures?') A deep puzzlement may also emerge, as Austin reminds us, 'when our interests are more extensive . . . than ordinarily'. I have in mind here the case in which we learn a term like 'fair' in the school playground or the pub dominoes school and are then asked to consider the application of this term to a complicated case in accounting practice. (Is a balance sheet that does not disclose reserves 'fair'?) Even when we understand the case we might be unclear what should be said. Here the projection of our mastered competence into new areas is attended by the possibilities of uncertainty.

I want to say a little more about this latter case and in so doing I want to introduce the second component of my account of language, namely the claim that our use of our language is projectively creative.

I have said that we grow into our language by learning the conditions under which people use terms like 'dog' and 'time'. In learning these conditions we come into possession of a set of rules and conventions which define the place of a word in the system of the language. What we have to remember (and what, as I have argued elsewhere, structuralism forgot (Lyas, forthcoming)) is that this set of rules and conventions has an openness which has as its counterpart the creativity that we must show in every use of the words of our language.

Suppose, for example, I have learned the word 'deep' according to the codes and conventions that give meaning to that element of my language. For example, I have learned to use 'deep' in talking of ponds and oceans. Then, one day, with no apparent sense of linguistic strain, I say, 'I felt the slight deeply'. What is more, no one seems surprised, even though I have gone beyond the rules I learned for the application of the word 'deep'. And so it is throughout our lives: feelings are deep, people feel blue, musical notes are high, music is sad and so on.

That is to say, as Croce was among the first fully to realise (Croce 1992), our use of words in speaking our language is creative. Indeed unless it were, it would not be the speaking of language. Consider the difference between, on the one hand, learning a phrase book for a foreign language and only being able to produce by rote such phrases as 'my postillion has been struck by lightning', and, on the other, speaking a language. Even my use of a term like 'dog' has creatively to be extended from the contexts in which I learned its use in order to talk of dogs quite unlike the one in whose presence I may first have learned the term.

What guarantees the possibility of speaking meaningfully, and thus of sanity and community, is that our lives run together. When, having learned 'deep' with respect to ponds, I talk about my feelings as 'deep' I can *speak* in so doing only because others find that a natural projection of language, too. When that community ends, comprehension ends (and vice versa). Stanley Cavell puts the matter precisely in the following passage:

> We learn and teach words in certain contexts, and then we are expected, and we expect others, to be able to project them into further contexts. Nothing ensures that this projection will take place (in particular not the grasping of universals nor the grasping

> of books of rules) just as nothing will ensure that we will make, and understand, the same projections. That on the whole we do is a matter of our sharing routes of interest and feeling, modes of response, sense of humour and significance and of fulfilment, of what is outrageous, of what is similar to what else, what a rebuke, what forgiveness, of when an utterance is an assertion, when an appeal, when an explanation – all that whirl of organism Wittgenstein calls 'forms of life'. Human speech and activity, sanity and community, rests on nothing more, but nothing less than this.
>
> (Cavell 1966: 160–1)

If this, however briefly told, is something like the true story of our use of the words of our language, then there seem to me to be important corollaries.

First, it will I hope be clear why philosophers, though they may be in a position to explain how deep puzzlements about the use of such terms as 'person', 'fair', and 'wrong' may arise are, as individual members of the speech community, in no very strong position when it comes to resolving those puzzlements.

For example, suppose the puzzlement to be whether the eating of animals is wrong. Here the question is whether a term, 'wrong', which may have a generally agreed use in characterizing, say, the unjustified killing of one person by another, is to be extended to talk in the same sense of the killing of a non-human animal for the purposes of human consumption. Now, no declaration by any one philosopher that this *is* wrong will ensure that the term 'wrong' will be so extended. Whether it is projected into the new context of animal-eating will depend on whether enough people see a point in so extending it. Just so, the word 'vivid' learnt in the context of colour will be extended to cover metaphors not because I alone so use it, but because when I do see the point in so extending it, others follow me. The problem with the use of 'wrong' to cover the consumption of animals is that while many people *do* see the point of this way of talking, many do not. These views, as MacIntyre put it in the passage I quoted earlier, seem to be incommensurable, just as are views about abortion, affirmative action, euthanasia and vivisection. In that situation the demand that one show one's relevance by actually settling some problems is likely to find philosophers wanting.

What can philosophy offer in such situations? One thing is a clear account of the nature of these intractable disputes and how they arise from contrary projections of our language. Second, it is possible to lay bare just what the dispute is and what premises the contrary conclusions depend upon. Sometimes this will actually clear the way for progress. For example, if it emerges after analysis that someone is defending capital punishment on the grounds that this is the best deterrent, then that defence rests upon a factual matter and is undermined to the extent that the facts are not as the argument maintains. Third, and this has an important bearing on what I shall say about the true and fair doctrine, progress may be possible even if it should emerge that various parties just see the matter differently. For the way someone views something is open to influence. The influence here seldom consists in deductive argument (since the two parties will merely fall out over the premises). Rather it is more like the kind of reasoning that occurs in the law and in art. Two people may disagree about the proper characterization of Mahler. They might just agree to differ, but they seldom do. One will draw analogies between Mahler and some other composer about the merits of whom both agree, will draw attention to details that the other may have missed, will hum certain parts in a certain way or with a certain gesture of the hands. And possibly after a while the other (who is trying the same thing) may say, 'Yes, now I see it'. Sometimes time is enough, so that on returning to a work after an interval of time we just see what the other wished to make clear to us. And in the law, too, an advocate may try to argue that the case in question is analogous in this and that way to one that was dealt with earlier in such and such a way. And a judge, in a way exactly analogous to the way in which we project our language forward to cover new cases, finds the *ratio applicandus* which allows him to apply an existent law to a new case. So, too, when the difference is over whether animal-eating is wrong, the discussion may proceed by this kind of analogizing dialectic.[5] The main difference between such *philosophical* discussions and the analogous legal ones is that the former can continue indefinitely, the latter have, and have to have, a terminating procedure.

I shall now try to apply some of these thoughts to problems about the true and fair doctrine. I shall, while in all probability displaying that ignorance of accounting which Sterling gently but rightly attributes to me, scratch the surface of this matter by referring to an exchange between B.A. Rutherford and I.C. Stewart (Rutherford 1985; Stewart 1988).

That we are here dealing with something at the very root of accounting is clear. Leach asserts, for example, that the true and fair view provides the 'ultimate foundation' for financial reporting (Leach

1981: 7). The question Rutherford raises is how the practitioner is to be guided by the requirement that the published affairs of companies shall show a true and fair view of the state of affairs of the company and its results. He argues that the law, by and large, is no help; the ordinary meanings of 'true' and 'fair' don't help when the complex affairs of modern business concerns are at issue; text book definitions are contradictory; professional judgement is too subjective; reference to user need does not yet give sufficiently concrete guidance to those who have to judge what shall be reported. But the practitioner must have guidance: for the mere imperative 'be true and fair' is useless without some decision procedure for determining what is, in the relevant context, true and fair. In the same way, the imperative 'don't publish pornography' was useless before the Obscene Publications Act of 1959 actually defined what that involved. Indeed, one of the motive forces of that Act was the desire of book publishers to know in advance what to avoid. Just so, the practitioner wants to know in advance what she or he is being required to judge when required to judge truth and fairness (particularly if, as with pornography, litigation follows errors of judgement).

Rutherford's suggestion is that:

> In searching for a frame of reference within which current practice might be said to be conducted, perhaps the most obvious candidate would be the corpus of generally accepted accounting principles.
>
> (Rutherford 1985: 491)

Although there is something right about this, for it is in the principles by which they proceed that the profession's operative understanding of the terms 'true' and 'fair' is displayed, I am wary of this proposal because of the bluntness with which the rationality of generally accepted principles has been attacked (Sterling, this volume, *passim*).

Rutherford himself recognizes the mutability of such principles. He writes:

> Principles would drop out of the corpus as they ceased to be generally acceptable and new principles could enter the corpus as they won acceptance.
>
> (Rutherford 1985: 492)

But now I find an awkward tension in Rutherford's paper. For the reference to generally accepted principles was made *faut de mieux* (1985: 491) and in the absence of any satisfactory definition of the notions of truth and fairness in reporting that exists outside and 'transcendent' to generally agreed practice and by which that practice could be regulated. But now we are told that a principle could drop out if it ceased to be generally acceptable. Presumably ceasing to be generally acceptable is not a matter simply of going out of fashion, in the way that kipper ties and Oxford bags ceased to be generally acceptable. Rather it must be a matter of a hitherto generally accepted principle ceasing to be generally acceptable for a reason. That reason must be that by some standard independent of the set of generally applied principles, this or that member of the set fails to preserve truth and fairness. But then it might seem that there must already be a transcendent and operative understanding of the true and fair doctrine existing independently of generally accepted principles, and by which the adequacy of these principles is evaluated. But if there is such a thing, what becomes of the claim that *faut de mieux* the generally accepted principles are all that we have?

There is, however, something right in Rutherford's approach, and in particular in his scepticism about 'transcendent' definitions of 'true' and 'fair' which exist apart from, and which regulate, practice. I shall try to say what this is using some of the points I have earlier made about language.

I have to say right away that part of the story seems to me to go like this: there were in the school yard, during the division of the Sunday dessert and on the games field uses of the terms 'true' and 'fair'. The uses of these terms in accounting theory grew from and are related to these. These accounting uses are, to use my earlier terminology, projections into a new area, without change of meaning, of terms whose use is as humble as that of 'table', 'lamp' and 'door'.

I therefore find it astonishing that it has apparently been argued that the traditional model of accounting, which is true and fair according to the express declaration of the law, 'is wholly at odds with the *ordinary* meaning of truth and fairness, so that the legislature must have in mind some other meaning for TFV' (Rutherford 1985: 484). I am tempted to say that if the legislature did not wish to suggest a connection with what is customarily meant by 'true and fair', it was extraordinarily perverse of it to use those words, particularly when, as Chastney argues (1975) the courts would normally turn to ordinary meanings when asked to clarify hitherto legally undefined terminology. Moreover, I suspect users of accounts, me included, will be as disappointed to find that the truth and fairness guaranteed them by their auditors has nothing to do with our ordinary understandings of truth and fairness as the religious would on being told, as philosophers of religion sometimes tell them, that the use of the terms 'wise', 'good', and 'loving' when used of God have no connection of meaning with those terms used of those around us, and for all we know might signify something very unpleasant indeed. There must be some point that I have missed here. Other than that I can only think that there has been a faulty argument. Thus Rutherford remarks (1985: 484) that 'it does not seem likely that ordinary usage could solve the complex problems of treatment and disclosure that arise out of the activities of modern business enterprises'. That is true, if it means that a person who had only used the term 'fair' to characterize the transactions of the playground and the distribution of the Christmas pudding would be hopelessly lost when asked if a complex report on the complex activities of a business concern were fair. But it does not follow from that that when that report is called 'fair' the term is being used in a different sense from its ordinary one. To put it technically, the *extension* of the term (the range of things it covers) may have expanded: but its *intension*, what it says about them, has not.

Be that as it may. It remains the case that when an accountant uses the word 'fair' she or he projects into a new domain, and without change of meaning, a term which has been mastered in the ordinary language. When the affairs of companies and the commercial life of nations were simpler, most educated people could have seen the point of this and understood what was going on. As those affairs become more complex, so greater knowledge and experience are required to see the point of using a familiar word of the ordinary language in a new context. That is why those who have stressed that professional judgement is integral to decisions about truth and fairness, are right. (Although, as we shall see, this does not help decide what to do when professional judgements diverge. But it is important to emphasize that it is differences between *professionals* that is at issue.)

In this projection of ordinary language accounting does not differ from, for example, art criticism. A term like 'melancholy', widely understood in ordinary parlance, may be used of a complex painting or piece of music, where considerable experience and skill may be required to see the justification for this attribution, and where there may be doubt and confusion about the projection. It will not follow that the meaning of 'melancholy' now has nothing to do with its ordinary use.

How are we able to make such projections and understand others who make them? Here Rutherford is entirely right that 'transcendental' definitions existing apart from practice will not help. It is tempting to think that if I only had a *definition* of 'melancholy' or 'fair', I would then have a rule for the use of such terms. I could then understand and decide the question of the appropriateness of all their future uses, which would flow from the definition I now possessed as water from a reservoir: as if, as Wittgenstein (whose *Philosophical Investigations* explore these matters at masterly length) put it, 'the future development must in some way be present in the act of grasping the use' (1967: 197). But a transcendent definition won't do. If, suppose correctly, I define 'melancholy' as 'gently sad', and am in doubt as to whether this picture is or is not melancholy, then the definition will be of no help: for if I am in doubt whether this picture is melancholy, and if 'melancholy' means 'gently sad', then to the extent that I am in doubt whether it is melancholy I will also be in doubt as to whether it is gently sad. The same will go for any transcendent definition of 'true' and 'fair'.

How then can we make and understand new projections of our familiar language, often into technical contexts?

One thing we may need is experience (which is why the opinions of ignoramuses who haven't even tried to understand and gain the necessary experience can be ignored in both art and accounting). There is such a thing as informed (professional) judgement. Beyond that we are left with the brute fact, as my quotation from Cavell makes clear, that we do sometimes see the point of projecting a word into a new context, and when others see as we do, then sense is made in the public domain of that projection.

But now, it can rightly be said that I have left the crucial matter unresolved. What are we to do when professional judgements are in genuine and honest disagreement about whether this or that contributes to or detracts from the truth and fairness of a report? This, on my account, is to be construed as a genuine difference as to whether the term 'fair', say, is or is not extendable without change of meaning to cover a new case. How is this to be resolved?

To begin with, if my analogies with art and the law have been apposite, there will be initial room for debate in which the various parties attempt to get others to see things from a particular point of view. Past cases will be cited and efforts will be made to show that present cases are analogous to them. Stewart is right here to cite J.L. Lucas's description of this process as 'dialectical':

> Its logic, instead of being deductive logic, where premises necessitate their conclusions, is a logic of one side of an argument

against another, of pros and cons, of proposals and objections, of *prima facie* cases which may be countered, and presumptions that may be rebutted.

(Stewart 1988: 120)

If these sorts of discussions were to occur in a philosophical debate, 'conversation' could continue indefinitely. The exigencies of accounting practice mean that the debate cannot continue indefinitely, so that some means must be found of ending it.

It might of course be that the dialectic I have mentioned *does* end in an agreement in which one side gets the other to change a way of seeing the matter. That is not guaranteed, however. It therefore necessarily follows, since the disagreement must be resolved, and since the dialectic cannot be guaranteed to resolve it, that there must be some body (or somebody) empowered to reach a resolution. That indeed points in the direction of an Accounting Court. (Rutherford, (1985: 483–4) seems right to query any use of non-specialist legal bodies to resolve matters: they are likely 'to rely on accountants to provide the raw material from which a legal explication could be fashioned'. Since one ends with those with accounting expertise, one might as well start there.)

About that Court, however constituted, I make one small comment. It is tempting to think that such a court would reach a decision that would declare one party right in its projection of the term 'fair' into a new context. That doubtless is how the matter will be presented (just as the Supreme Court of the United States is supposed to say who is right in the interpretation of the constitution). I doubt, for reasons MacIntyre has rehearsed, that this is what an Accounting Court will actually do. For the views between which it arbitrates will both represent a sincerely held way of seeing the matter, ways which may reflect the lack of consensus in a society with a plurality of values. In that case the job of the Court is not to be right, but to be what MacIntyre calls 'a peacemaking or truce keeping body' which keeps 'the peace between rival social groups adhering to rival and incompatible principles of justice by displaying a fairness which consists of even-handedness in its adjudications'. (This, he argues, is how the Supreme Court acted in the *Bakke* case when, with some inconsistency, it forbade precise ethnic quotas for admission to higher education, but allowed discrimination in favour of previously deprived minority groups (MacIntyre 1987: 253ff).)

I conclude this chapter with an unscientific postscript about the role of accounting theory and philosophy in institutions of learning such as universities.

Two things have emerged from my earlier discussion as obvious targets for accounting research, both of which preserve a close bond between theory and practice. One is the dialectical discussion of the appropriateness or inappropriateness of projecting the terms 'truth' and 'fairness' into new areas. Another will be the constant task of rigorously measuring practices against one's general understanding of what the aims of accounting are in order to determine whether those practices most efficaciously achieve those aims and in order to ensure that those practices do not actually frustrate the purposes for which accountancy as a profession exists.[6] All this is doubtless a platitudinous statement of what the researchers already do (when teaching and other duties allow them time).

There is, however, one more, crucial duty owed by theorists in universities and other such institutions. This is to *prevent closure*. The tendency is for practices and procedures to settle into a comfortable, unquestioned rut, partly because this is more comfortable, more convenient, and less intellectually wearing. That being so it is important that there be ways of keeping institutions and practices under constant surveillance, to ask awkward questions, to think the dangerous. Often this will pay no immediate dividends (no more than did the early discovery of super-conductivity). So it is useless to ask what the immediate cash value of this activity is. But without that constant challenge, there will be no growth but only ossification and stagnation.

That critical reflection by theorists of accounting on the practices of accounting and their foundations will undoubtedly focus from time to time on the ways in which, as I have put it, concepts with a history and a use in philosophy 'leak' into the theoretical foundations of accounting. When that happens then philosophers may become involved. If they do it will not be as *authorities* possessed of a knowledge and a methodology which will allow them to solve problems that others find vexing. It will be as what Rorty calls 'kibitzers':

> Philosophers often do have interesting views upon such questions, and their philosophical training as philosophers is often a necessary condition for their having the views they do. But this is not to say that philosophers have a special kind of knowledge about knowledge (or anything else) from which they draw relevant corollaries. The useful kibitzing they can provide on the various topics I just mentioned is made possible by their familiarity with the historical background of arguments on similar topics, and,

most importantly, by the fact that arguments on such topics are punctuated by stale philosophical clichés which the other participants have stumbled across in their reading, but about which professional philosophers know the pros and cons by heart.

(Rorty 1980: 393)

It is perhaps appropriate that I should end a memorial piece for Eddie Stamp by mentioning the duty of those in universities to keep the spirit of critical scrutiny of our institutions alive, particularly at a time when the abolition by government decree of tenure is likely to dampen that spirit. For I have known no one who exceeded Professor Stamp in the determination to keep the customs, practices and activities of our culture under constant critical scrutiny. Nor have I known anyone who exceeded the Socratic passion, which is the mark of the true philosopher, with which he fulfilled what he took to be the duty of each of us to discover and reveal the truth, however painful and uncomfortable that truth might be, and however unpopular those who uncovered it might become.

NOTES

1 Sterling (1988), although I have only an unpublished copy of it.
2 For some discussion of this silliness see Lyas (1982).
3 I owe the origins of my thoughts about the relevance of the analysis of language use to the study of accounting to some conversations, many years ago, with Roger Mace.
4 All editions of this work have identical paragraph numbers.
5 For a working example see Clark (1984). Note particularly the introduction.
6 Earlier versions of this chapter contained a section, omitted for reasons of space, which justified the notion of accounting as a profession by using the distinction between practices and institutions and between internal and external goods. That will have to form the body of another paper. In the interim see MacIntyre (1987, chapter 14).

REFERENCES

Austin, J.L. (1961) *Philosophical Papers*, Oxford: Clarendon Press, p. 133.
Cavell, S. (1966) 'The availability of Wittgenstein's later philosophy' in G. Pitcher (ed.) *Wittgenstein*, London: Macmillan, pp. 160–1.
Chastney, J.G. (1975) *True and Fair View: History, Meaning and Impact of the Fourth Directive*, Research Committee Occasional Paper No. 6, London: Institute of Chartered Accountants in England and Wales.
Clark, S. (1984) *The Moral Status of Animals*, Oxford: Oxford University Press.
Croce, (1992) *The Aesthetic*, Cambridge: Cambridge University Press.

Henry, W. (1936) *Stabilizing Accounting*, New York: Harper & Bros.

Leach, R. (1981) 'The birth of British accounting standards', in R. Leach and E. Stamp (eds) *British Accounting Standards: The First Ten Years*, Cambridge: Woodhead-Faulkner.

Lyas, C. (1982) 'Herbert Marcuse's criticism of "Linguistic" philosophy', *Philosophical Investigations*, July.

—— (forthcoming) *The Rehumanisation of Art*.

MacIntyre, A. (1987) *After Virtue*, London: Duckworth.

Marcuse, H. (1968) *Negations*, London: Penguin.

—— (1972) *One Dimensional Man*, London: Abacus.

Rorty, R. (1980) *Philosophy and the Mirror of Nature*, Oxford: Blackwell.

Rutherford, B.A. (1985) 'The true and fair doctrine: a search for explication', *Journal of Business Finance and Accounting*, Winter issue.

Stamp, E. (1980) *Corporate Reporting: Its Future Evolution*, Toronto: Canadian Institute of Chartered Accountants.

Sterling, R. (1988) 'Confessions of a failed empiricist', *Advances in Accounting*, vol. 6, JAI Press.

Stewart, I.C. (1988) 'The explication of the true and fair view: a comment', *Journal of Business Finance and Accounting*, Spring issue.

Wittgenstein, L. (1967) *Philosophical Investigations*, 3rd edition, Oxford: Blackwell.

8 Paradigms, research traditions and theory nets of accounting[1]

Richard Mattessich

This chapter examines whether such ideas as Lakatos' research programmes, Balzer's and Stegmüller's theory nets, or Bunge's family of research fields, can meaningfully be applied to modern accounting theory and agency-information analysis. This investigation confirms, for contemporary accounting, the existence of two or three competing research traditions or theory nets (each connecting several special theories or theory elements). The chapter starts from some attempts by the late John Butterworth (see Butterworth and Falk (1983)) to distinguish between different accounting paradigms which here will be combined to entire research traditions. Before doing this, I attempt to clarify some of the differences and similarities between related methodological ideas offered by such divergent philosophers as Balzer, Bunge, Lakatos, Laudan, Sneed and Stegmüller.

INTRODUCTION

During the last decade or so, distinct research tendencies have manifested themselves in accounting (cf. Mattessich, 1984a and 1991c). These tendencies rest partly on ideas developed in Germany and the USA during the early part of this century, partly on ideas introduced relatively recently on the American continent. I am basing this survey of research tendencies on the following paradigms postulated by Butterworth,[2] but shall transform and elaborate them into various phases of three distinct research traditions, and shall also take the pertinent German literature into account:

1 Valuation I (present value and current cost theories)
2 Valuation II (theory of risk sharing)
3 Valuation III (theory of financial markets)

4 Stewardship I (historical acquisition cost theory)
5 Stewardship II (agency theory)
6 Stewardship III (theories of asymmetric information).

Previous attempts to formulate different accounting paradigms can be found by Wells (1976), by the American Accounting Association (1977)[3] and, above all, by Belkaoui (1981) who, apparently inspired by AAA (1977), distinguishes in both editions of his textbook the following six paradigms:

1 The inductive–anthropological paradigm: Hatfield (1927), Gilman (1939), Littleton (1953), Paton and Littleton (1940), Ijiri (1975), Gordon (1964), Watts and Zimmerman (1978).
2 The deductive ideal income paradigm: Paton (1922), Canning (1929), Sweeney (1936), MacNeal (1939), Alexander (1950), Edwards and Bell (1961), Moonitz (1961), Sprouse and Moonitz (1962).
3 The decision theoretic paradigm: Sterling (1970, 1972), Beaver *et al.* (1968).
4 The capital market paradigm: Gonedes (1972), Gonedes and Dopuch (1974), Beaver (1972).
5 The behavioural paradigm: Bruns (1968), Hofstedt and Kinard (1970), Birnberg and Nath (1967).
6 The information economic paradigm: Feltham (1968), Crandal (1969), Feltham and Demski (1970).

As interesting as this categorization may be, it constructs the various paradigms on the basis of different perspectives (from which accounting has been illuminated during recent decades) rather than on more fundamental criteria. But above all, Belkaoui's classification scheme is less suited than that of Butterworth and Falk (1983) to derive from it a limited number of global theories or research programmes in the sense of Lakatos (1983), or theory nets of Stegmüller (1979, 1983, 1986), or the families of research fields of Bunge (1983b, 1985a).

Yet, apart from this superimposed scheme, the question arises whether Butterworth and Falk (1983) were dealing at all with paradigms in the commonly understood sense. At best these seem to be merely *potential* paradigms, or those of a *methodological* nature.[4] Although the theoretical representation of accounting has been beset by conflicts between various camps, it is doubtful whether in our discipline the differences of opinions are crucial or basic enough to speak of rivaling paradigms in the scientific sense in which Kuhn (1962) employed this term. Such scientific rivalry may exist between one or the other of those Butterworth paradigms, *but hardly between all six*. Even more decisive is the fact that several of these paradigms are so closely connected with each other that the gaps between them are minor evolutionary jumps rather than revolutionary upheavals. The recent development of accounting can possibly be better understood by organizing the Butterworth paradigms into a small number of research traditions and theory nets. This is the newest methodological trend, and consists in the recognition that beyond specific theories and paradigms lies a more general and unifying framework, revealing the fundamental invariances of a certain research tradition. Indeed, Laudan (1977) calls it a research tradition while Lakatos (1983) refers in this context to a research programme, Stegmüller (1979, 1983, 1986) speaks of a theory net or theory complex, and Bunge (1983b, 1985b) of a family of research fields.

We therefore ask the following question: can the evolution of accounting be represented as a competition between two or three scientific research traditions? The combination of the first three Butterworth paradigms (valuations I, II, III) seems to make sense, since all three cases regard the evaluation of assets, equities and income as the primary function of accounting – we may therefore speak of a valuation research tradition. Similarly, it is possible to combine the last three Butterworth paradigms to a stewardship research tradition, since all of them regard allocation and the monitoring as well as the evaluation of stewardship as the primary function of accounting. Such a classification is not only based on the fundamental distinction between *valuation* and *allocation* (as competing *primary* functions of accounting), but would also reduce the fragmentation of accounting theory to a single dichotomy between two camps: on one side would be those who find the major function of financial accounting in the income and profitability measurement by means of discounted net cash flows or the current valuation of assets and equities. This would serve foremost the temporary investors, developers and speculators. In the other camp would be those who regard financial accounting as monitoring the stewardship of management for the sake of shareholders, particularly the more permanent and major shareholders. Thereby priority is given to income measurement on the basis of accrual accounting and the matching of costs against revenues.

But the urgent quest to give financial accounting a *purpose orientation*, rather than imposing upon it a monolithic goal limitation, suggests or even necessitates a third alternative: the information-strategic research tradition or programme. It focuses not on a single major accounting goal, but emphasizes the need for different accounting models matched to different information objectives. This third programme would, for example, pay equal attention to agency-information analysis, on one side, and to the capital asset pricing model, on the other. Towards the end of this chapter this third, more programmatic, tradition will be discussed. However, for the time being we concentrate on the controversy between the stewardship research tradition, so significant for conventional accounting practice, and the valuation research tradition, which during the last two decades succeeded in replacing the former in many academic circles. For the sake of a better understanding, I shall discuss each one of those two traditions in three phases, every one of which, in turn, approximates one of the Butterworth paradigms and may well constitute a theory element in Stegmüller's (1979, 1986) sense. Yet before discussing them, it seems appropriate to discuss concisely (in the next section) recent shifts in the general methodology and philosophy of science.

LAKATOS'S RESEARCH PROGRAMMES, STEGMÜLLER'S THEORY NETS, AND BUNGE'S FAMILIES OF RESEARCH FIELDS

The demise of positivism, and to some extent of Popper's falsificationism, during the last three decades or so, created an epistemological vacuum which was, and still is, difficult to fill. Although there was no lack of candidates promoting alternative philosophies (e.g. Toulmin (1953), Hanson (1958), Kuhn (1962), Feyerabend (1965, 1975) – for an overview see Suppe (1974)), hardly any of them could command the confidence and respect which either neo-positivism or falsificationism commanded from the 1920s to the 1960s. Nevertheless there is one book which, for over two decades, stirred the minds of philosophers and scientists more than any other: Thomas S. Kuhn's *Structure of Scientific Revolution* (1962). Kuhn's view certainly became the most widely quoted and debated of the novel epistemological theories of science and also found some response in the accounting literature (e.g. Wells (1976), AAA (1977), Belkaoui (1981), Mattessich (1979a, 1984a)). However, it also created much reaction; and presently it seems that some choice or combination of the more recently developed views of Lakatos (1970, 1983), Stegmüller (1976, 1979, 1983, 1986), Laudan (1977), and Bunge (1983a,b, 1985a,b) could explain the epistemology and methodology of science on a more rational basis. Since these relatively recent methodologies have hardly been mentioned in the accounting literature, they deserve to be taken into consideration here.

Lakatos's evolutionary programmism

For a quick understanding of Lakatos's (1983) view, the following five items might serve as a summary:

1 Lakatos's notion of a 'scientific research programme' is the basic unit of epistemological appraisal (amounting to an evolutionary interconnection of various related theories, in contrast to individual hypotheses or isolated theories).
2 The 'hard core' (the set of basic laws) of a research programme is either irrefutable or very hard to refute (negative heuristics) because it is sheltered by a protective belt of auxiliary hypotheses (positive heuristics) which bear the brunt of the testing and get adjusted and readjusted (e.g. Newton's three laws of mechanics are regarded as such an irrefutable hard core). Therefore, not the emerging anomalies but the auxiliary hypotheses dictate the choice of the problems to be solved, and continuing confirmations keep a research programme going.
3 The distinction between 'progressive' and 'degenerative' research programmes facilitates their appraisal and ultimate acceptance or rejection. While a progressive programme is capable of generating novel facts and auxiliary hypotheses, a regressive one lacks these features, it stagnates, and finally has to be rejected. However, since degenerating research programmes occasionally have a *comeback* (see Lakatos (1983: 113)), it is difficult to determine when a research programme has ceased to 'bud'. Thus Lakatos rejects in most cases Popper's criterion of 'crucial experiments' and the instant rationality based on a single refutation.
4 Lakatos also prefers a 'theoretical or methodological pluralism' to Kuhn's 'theoretical monism'. He regards Kuhn's scientific paradigms as approaching a dogmatic *Weltanschauung* which must be avoided through methodological tolerance (for further criticism of Lakatos's theory as well as Kuhn's, see Laudan (1977: 73–8)).
5 Lakatos makes a somewhat more complicated distinction between the 'internal' and the 'external' history (or influence) of a research programme. What may be deemed to be an external influence for Popper, Kuhn, or others (e.g. priority disputes), Lakatos may interpret as an internal influence (for him priority disputes are vital internal problems).

Although Lakatos complains that for Kuhn there can be no logic but only a psychology of discovery, he adds that:

> Kuhn is right in objecting to naive falsificationism, and also in stressing the *continuity* of scientific growth, the *tenacity* of some scientific theories. . . . But Kuhn overlooked Popper's sophisticated falsificationism and the research programme he initiated. Popper replaced the central problem of classical rationality, the old *problem of foundations*, with the new *problem of fallible–critical growth*, and started to elaborate objective standards of this growth. In this paper I [Lakatos] have tried to develop his programme a step further. I think this small development is sufficient to escape Kuhn's strictures.
>
> (Lakatos 1983: 90–1, footnote omitted)

Stegmüller's epistemological structuralism

While Lakatos's proposal is admittedly an attempt to further develop, and thus to rescue, important aspects of Popper's view, Stegmüller's proposal might be interpreted as a refinement of Kuhn's exposition, but is certainly much more than that. Yet apart from terminological differences and the degree of formalism, we find sufficient similarities between Lakatos's and Stegmüller's methodology[5] (especially the similarities between research programmes and theory nets) to regard them as closely related if not identical, and shall usually address them as 'research traditions'. My preference for Laudan's (1977) terminology is prompted by the fact that it seems to fit best the particular situation of accounting; but there is no denying that we are here dealing with two or three nets of more specific theories (or 'theory elements' in Stegmüller's recent versions). On the other hand, Stegmüller admits that he seriously considered using the phrase 'to hold a research programme' instead of his formulation of 'holding a theory' (see Stegmüller 1979: 61). And, as Stegmüller remarks at the same place, Lakatos in turn pointed out that 'his own concept of research programme was "reminiscent" of Kuhn's notion of normal science'. Furthermore, Stegmüller emphasizes that in the *sophisticated* version of falsificationism (which Lakatos adopts from Popper and then adapts for his own purpose), neither individual hypotheses nor theories but 'theory nets' (in Stegmüller's sense) are compared and related to each other.

Of course, there remains an epistemological, perhaps even an ontological, difference between Lakatos's research programmes and

Stegmüller's theory nets. The former contain theories that possess truth values, while the latter's theories, theory nets and theory complexes (which are a further generalization) are all mathematical structures to which no truth values (only *preferences* based on specific goals) can be assigned. However, this difference is not as crucial as it might seem at a first glance, because even in Stegmüller's scheme the individual hypotheses contained in a theory do possess truth values.

Other major features of Stegmüller's approach

Theoretical core and intended applications

The two components of a theory (more recently called 'theory element') are considered to be a permanent theoretical *core* and a set of *intended* (empirical) *applications*. The core in turn consists of a set of models containing the fundamental law as well as a set of possible models containing the conceptual apparatus including the *theoretical terms* (which play such a crucial role in the Sneed–Stegmüller theory), furthermore a set of partial possible models excluding the theoretical terms (together with a reduction function enabling such exclusion), and finally a set of constraints linking various theory elements with each other. In time, more and more theory elements emerge all through specialization of either the core or the intended applications or both during Kuhn's phase of *normal* science. A scientific revolution, however, would require a change of the fundamental law and hence of the core.

Special theories or theory elements

Usually there is not one intended application of a theory but there are many such applications which often overlap to some degree. The double-classification syndrome, for example, did not only find application in financial and managerial accounting but could successfully be applied in the matrix algebra of inter-industry analysis, in national income accounting and several other areas. And in physics Newton not only applied his theory to planetary motions, but also to falling and pendulating objects on earth, as well as to ocean tides, etc.; he even hoped it could be applied to optics. But when Maxwell's electromagnetic wave theory of light proved that this 'intended' application of Newtonian mechanics was not permissible, it did not constitute a rejection of Newtonian physics, but was considered merely an instance of limitation. The formulation of the special theories or theory elements for the purpose of specific applications may remind the reader of the positivistic notion of *interpretation* of the general theory.

The rejection of a theory does *not* depend on Popper's naive refutation; it occurs through dislodgement *as soon as a better theory is available* but not before – this is another important instant where Stegmüller, Lakatos, and possibly Bunge approach each other.

Theoretical vs. non-theoretical terms

The distinction between *theoretical and non-theoretical* terms is no longer absolute (in contrast to the neo-positivistic distinction between theoretical and observational terms), but now is considered to be dependent on the specific theory (e.g. such terms as weight, mass, value, or utility may be theoretical notions in one theory but non-theoretical notions in another). For example in a theory T, belonging to the stewardship programme, the *book value* arises as a residual (e.g. of acquisition cost minus depreciation) out of this very theory. Thus, it seems that the book value cannot be determined without this theory, and would be called a *T-theoretical* variable by Sneed (1971) and Stegmüller (1975, 1979, 1986); the market value or the present value, however, might be *T-nontheoretical* variables because they might be measurable without the aid of theory T. But if we take another theory I, this time belonging to the information strategic programme (see 'Research tradition No. 3', pp. 202f.), in which the *book value*, the *market value* as well as the *present value* might not be measurable outside this more comprehensive theory, then *all three* of these values would be *I-theoretical* (although only the first remains *T-theoretical*). A clear distinction between theoretical and non-theoretical terms might not be possible before clarifying the related distinction between *conceptual representation* and the *reality* behind it or its absence – for several pertinent studies see Balzer and Mattessich (1991) and Mattessich (1990, 1991a,b).

Threefold immunity

There exists, according to Stegmüller (1975: 520–3), a threefold *immunity* of theories against empirical refutation.

First of all, the core of a theory (representing the analytical aspects and corresponding to Kuhn's 'theory matrix') can be expanded by further theory elements thus creating a larger theory net. In a way this net is open, since it cannot be known in advance how far it can be further expanded. If at some intermediate stage a theory element does not explain or predict satisfactorily, this may be due to the fact that the researcher failed in correctly formulating the appropriate theory element (this refers to Kuhn's assertion that in normal science it is the skill of the researcher that is being tested not the theory).

Second, the set of intended applications (reflecting the *empirical* aspects of a theory and corresponding to Kuhn's 'exemplars') too is an *open set*. Should the researchers consistently fail to apply such a theory to a particular area (e.g. Newton's theory as applied to the problem of electromagnetic waves), this would, in contrast to Popper's interpretation, not constitute a rejection of the theory but a mere setting of its boundary.

The third type of theory immunity is complex and can here only be hinted at. Its reason lies in Sneed's (1971) rejection of the absolute, positivistic *criterion of theoreticity*, and in accepting a *relative* criterion that is context dependent (as previously mentioned). 'This kind of theory-dependent T-theoretic variable makes it impossible to empirically refute laws containing such variables' (Stegmüller 1975: 522). He also mentions the irrefutability of Newton's second law (force = mass × acceleration) as an example of this third type of irrefutability.

Although accountants have, so far, paid little heed to these particular notions of research programmes, theory nets, etc., economists have found these ideas useful. The well-known historian of economic thought, Mark Blaug (1983, 1980) for example, sympathizes with the idea of research programmes, and Hausman (1984: 22), an epistemologist of economics, points out that Lakatos's methodology has influenced many economists. And Stegmüller, who originally began as an economist, edited with some of his collaborators a book on the application of his ideas to economics: Stegmüller *et al.* (1982). For further economic and accounting applications of this theory see Balzer (1982), Hamminga (1983), Stegmüller (1986, chapter 14), and Balzer and Mattessich (1991).

Bunge's critical scientific realism

While most philosophers write primarily for other philosophers, Bunge's (1974a,b, 1977, 1979, 1983a,b, 1985a,b) epistemological and methodological explorations seem to be directed primarily to empirical scientists. And since many of them have, like Bunge, a strong realist bias, his criticism of Lakatos and Stegmüller, as well as his own proposal, deserve some examination.

Bunge's attitude towards Thomas Kuhn's philosophy is fairly favourable. He agrees with most aspects of Kuhn's methodological dogmas, his notions of paradigm, exemplars and their consequences as well as with his distinction between normal versus extraordinary science.[6] But Bunge criticizes Kuhn's insufficient clarity or precision:

> Kuhn's (1962) modern classic had the merit of bringing it [extraordinary research] to the fore. What remains problematic are the very notions of a conceptual framework and of a paradigm, and of a revolution in it. Neither of these notions has been elucidated carefully, either by Kuhn or by his followers or critics (see e.g. Lakatos and Musgrave (1970)).
>
> (Bunge 1983b: 175–6)

> Kuhn's most important contributions to a methodology are perhaps his ideas that in every science there is a permanent tension between tradition and change, and that negative evidence is treated differently by normal research and by extraordinary research. . . . The second idea is more original: it is that, whereas normal research attempts to *accommodate* negative evidence to the ruling conceptual framework, extraordinary research uses such anomalies to *undermine* the framework.
>
> (Bunge 1983b: 178–9)

Indeed, Bunge subsequently presents his own answer according to which *extraordinary research need not be revolutionary*: 'it may ensue in an epistemic counterrevolution, i.e. a partial return to an earlier conceptual framework' (Bunge 1983b: 178) – note the similarity with Lakatos's 'comeback' of a research programme. Our ensuing examples from accounting theory (particularly the emergence of agency-information analysis as a partial return to the traditional stewardship paradigm) offers excellent illustration for such a counterrevolution or comeback (see pp. 181 and 186).

Another aspect of Kuhn's work which Bunge criticizes is the acclaimed 'incommensurability' between different paradigms – Kuhn believes that 'operations and measurements are paradigm-determined' (1962: 125), and that 'after a scientific revolution many old measurements and manipulations become irrelevant and are replaced by others instead' (ibid. p. 128). This point has been contemplated by many philosophers (including Stegmüller (1983: 1064; 1986, chapter 10)), but Hacking's (1983: 65–74) pertinent analysis offers the best illustrations. Hacking (another *realist*) distinguishes *different* *kinds* of incommensurabilities: the first kind is *topic-incommensurability*; it occurs when 'the successor theory (T^*) totally replaces the topics, concepts and problems of T (the previous theory' (ibid. p. 69)). Hacking calls his second category *dissociation*: here he points out that 'some theories indicate so radical a change that one requires something far harder than mere learning of a theory' (ibid. p. 69). He compares, for example, our modern theories with those of Paracelsus (1493–1541) and states that 'the contrast between ourselves and Paracelsus is *dissociation* . . . Paracelsus lived in a different world from ours' (ibid. p. 71). Finally, Hacking presents his *meaning-incommensurability* according to which such theoretical, unobservable entities as, for example, '"mass" in Newtonian theory would not mean the same as "mass" in relativistic mechanics. "Planet" in Copernican theory will not mean the same as "planet" in Ptolemaic theory, and indeed the sun is a planet for Ptolemy but not for Copernicus' (p. 72). Bunge's attitude toward Lakatos's methodology is much less enthusiastic than toward Kuhn's; above all, he criticizes the former's 'hazy notion of research programme' (Bunge 1983b: 163). But of greater interest is Bunge's reaction towards the Sneed–Stegmüller approach. It begins with a short review of Stegmüller's (1976) book, and raises the following complaint about the Sneed–Stegmüller theory:

1 It eschews meta-mathematical considerations.
2 It identifies theories with uninterpreted theories and defines their applications as models in the model-theoretic sense.
3 It cannot explain how one and the same formalism can be assigned a number of different factual interpretations.
4 It sees no need to provide a semantic theory elucidating factual interpretation.
5 Its dogmatism and neglect of evidence (e.g. narrowness of illustrations) for or against this structurist view.
6 It takes unwarrantedly for granted that Kuhn's hypotheses have been borne out by historical case studies.

This review closes with the following words:

> The new philosophy of science advanced in this work is at least as remote from living science as any of the rival views criticized in it.
> (Bunge 1978)

Many years later Bunge continues in a similar tone.

> The models built in factual science and technology are radically different from those studied by model theory, a branch of logic.

> . . . This is the *logical* concept of a model, and must be sharply distinguished from the *epistemological* concept of a model as a conceptual representation of concrete things of a narrow kind. . . . But whether logical or epistemological, all such models are conceptual: real things are not models of anything, but instead the objects of modeling. (The statement that the real world is a model of some theory makes sense only in a Platonic ontology.) This terminological remark had to be made in view of the widespread confusion between the two kinds of model introduced by the so-called set-theoretic semantics of science (e.g. Sneed, 1979; Stegmüller, 1976).
>
> (Bunge 1983a: 337)

> A related view is *formalism*, according to which model theory, i.e. the semantics of mathematics, suffices to analyze factual theories (Sneed, 1979, Stegmüller, 1976). The upholders of this view have probably been misled by the ambiguity of the term 'model', which in mathematics designates an example of an abstract theory, whereas in science and technology it designates a specific theory. Consequently they ignore the concepts of reference and representation, central to the semantics of factual theories, and they cannot explain why factual theories cannot be validated or invalidated by purely mathematical considerations.
>
> (Bunge 1983a: 355)

And two further years later:

> The failure to distinguish the logical from the epistemological concepts of model (as in Sneed 1971 and Stegmüller 1976) has given rise to an utterly artificial philosophy of science. (See Truesdell 1984 for proof that this philosophy is remote from real science.)
>
> (Bunge 1985a: 47)

But, as I see it, Truesdell's (1984) often sarcastic remarks and objections towards the approach of Sneed, Stegmüller and other 'Suppesians' (Sneed was a student of Patrick Suppes who is the spiritual father of the logical or epistemic structuralists) are primarily based on their, according to Truesdell, inadequate understanding of classical particle mechanics, its mathematical structure, and its proper representation. Thus Truesdell's review is hardly based on a general epistemological inadequacy that necessarily would affect the application of the Sneed–Stegmüller framework to other disciplines.

Some of Bunge's objections to structuralism might be due to

misunderstandings, and others due to a different philosophic outlook (realist versus idealist). Indeed Bunge relegates the Sneed–Stegmüller theory to Pythagoreanism or to formalism, since Stegmüller (e.g. 1983: 1037–8) regards an 'empirical phenomenon as a model of the theory'. Bunge rightly attacks this view with the objection that 'real things are not models of anything, but instead are the objects of modeling' (Bunge 1983a: 337). Hence Bunge claims that those theorists 'ignore the concepts of reference and representation, central to the semantics of factual theories, . . . they cannot explain why factual theories cannot be validated or invalidated by purely mathematical considerations' (Bunge 1983a: 355). Bunge offers us something like a reinterpretation of the Sneed–Stegmüller approach in the following sentences:

> Then the set of consequences of the union of T [a general theory] and S_i [a set of specific hypotheses] is the ith T-model, or $M_i(T)$. And the set of all T-models will be called the T-family, or $F(T) = \{ M_i(T) \mid 1 \leq i \leq n \}$. Perhaps this is what Sneed (1979) has in mind when he states (wrongly) that a theory is composed by its hard core and the set of its applications.
>
> (Bunge 1983b: 163)

Does Bunge mean that his general theory T corresponds to the Sneed–Stegmüller theory core? Does Bunge furthermore mean that his $F(T)$ would be comparable to their intended applications, provided the latter were regarded as something conceptual instead of something concrete? It seems that in both references, the one referring to Sneed and the previous one referring to Lakatos, Bunge does not so much criticize those ideas in themselves, as their particular formulations and the restriction to pure formalism.

Furthermore, Bunge (1983b: 176) envisages for every theory a 'conceptual framework' containing not only the general, formal, and specific background, but also other aspects such as the *problematics*, the *fund of knowledge*, and the *research goals*. This affords a richer vision, and can further be extended to what Bunge calls a *family of research fields* by taking into consideration (in addition to the conceptual framework) the research community, the society, and the universe of discourse (see Bunge 1983b: 198). But it must be pointed out that in a more recent version Stegmüller (1986, chapter 3 ff.) indicates some structuralistic research which has already taken several of those aspects into consideration.

Further aspects of Bunge's criticism might also be redundant in the face of Stegmüller's (1986) latest presentation. This revised and expanded version of the structuralist theory is quite up-to-date, taking recent contributions by many structuralists, as well as some criticism by others, into consideration. Although it neither mentions such major criticism as Bunge's (1978, 1983a,b, and 1985a) nor Truesdell's (1984), it may have taken some of their criticism into account. For example, the statement that an 'empirical phenomenon is a model of the theory' to which Bunge objected, has been reformulated (Stegmüller 1986: 45) and now says: 'that the empirical structure *e* can be complemented to a possible model in such fashion that the latter turns out to be a model of the theory'. No longer is the variable *e* (supposedly representing reality) addressed by Stegmüller as an empirical phenomenon, but as an empirical *structure*; there can be no doubt that the mental replication and approximation of such a structure is conceptual. Thus it is questionable whether Bunge's previously mentioned objection still applies to this improved formulation.

Structuralism versus realism?

However, as to the broad philosophic differences between realists and structuralists, no reconciliation – as, for example, attempted by Niiniluoto (1984) – is made by Stegmüller (1986). On the contrary, a separate chapter (chapter 11 with major reference to some works by Sneed (1981, 1983), Putnam (1980, 1982), Niiniluoto (1981, 1983), and others) is devoted to discuss and clarify those differences. According to this presentation the conflict between scientific realism and structuralism can be found in the following three items (K1 to K3):

> K1 The structuralist reconstruction of theories is such that the empirical claims of those theories contain logical forms which considerably deviate from the logical forms encountered in the traditional literature. This degree of divergence is deemed to be strong enough by realists to reject structuralist reconstructions.
>
> (Stegmüller 1986: 328 (translated))

A major thesis of the epistemological structuralists is the claim that the traditional term 'theory' is too vague, as it can mean at least three different things:

1 A set of *empirical claims* or hyotheses; or
2 A *theory element* consisting of a logical structure called the core, and of a set of 'intended applications'; or

3 A *theory net* (or theory complex) consisting of many connected theory elements.

The structuralists try to clarify the situation by imposing a very specific logical structure upon a 'theory' (see K1), and not only make a strict distinction between logical and descriptive variables, but also between the theoretical core and its 'intended applications' (the latter are supposed to be the empirical part; but as they form the subset of a set of conceptual models, this subset as well as its members appear to be purely conceptual, and should rather be called 'partial models intended *for* application'). Furthermore, a structure is imposed upon the core (an ordered tuple or vector) consisting of a set of models M (containing the fundamental laws), a set of possible models M_p (containing the conceptual framework *including* the theoretical terms), a set of partial possible models M_{pp} (*excluding* theoretical terms), a reduction function r (reducing M_p to M_{pp}), and a set of constraints C or Q (connecting various theory elements with each other). Thus they reject the traditional and simplistic logical form in which empirical claims are presented.

> K2 The structuralist difference between theoretical and non-theoretical elements (of the models of a theory) contain an ontological distinction of the entities or properties (magnitudes) which the theory discusses. Realism rejects the idea of such a distinction.
>
> (Stegmüller 1986: 128–9 (translated))

K2 is admittedly imprecise, but Stegmüller seems to mean that the realists are deemed to attribute *existence* not only to the non-theoretical but also to the theoretical terms whereas the structuralist regards only the latter as real.

> K3 According to the structuralist view, it is possible that the meaning of theoretical terms changes in the course of 'normal' as well as 'revolutionary' development. Realism rejects this view.
>
> (Stegmüller 1986: 328–9 (translated))

This refers to the context-dependence of the structuralist notion of theoretical terms previously discussed. But I wonder whether scientific realists, like Bunge, Hacking and Niiniluoto, would agree to this threefold characterization (K1 to K3) and its arguments. Furthermore, if philosophers could succeed in finding some kind of common ground with regard to theory nets or research traditions, the new methodology might have much greater chance of being accepted and applied by empirical scientists.

RESEARCH TRADITION NO. 1 (STEWARDSHIP PROGRAMME)

Accounting, being an applied science, has to replace the structuralists' 'fundamental law' by the *primary function* (with its basic principles). This function, according to tradition, is the principal's monitoring of stewardship. The latter is carried out by the various managerial and sub-managerial echelons. Thus, the information provision for short- and middle-term investment is relegated to financial analysis including capital budgeting, and becomes a mere *secondary* function of accounting. For the realization of this tradition a model type emerged, which Butterworth originally called 'stewardship paradigm I' and which will be discussed and elaborated as the first phase (or 'theory-element') of the stewardship tradition.

First phase: the plain periodization approach

This approach arose out of the view that the monitoring of managerial stewardship can be fulfilled best by the *'appropriate' allocation of cost and revenues to a particular period.*

Hence we find the following well-known principles in the foreground of this model:

1 The historical or *acquisition cost basis*.
2 The periodical allocation of costs and revenues via *matching* one with the other.
3 The *allocation* of depreciable asset costs over an estimated time of useful life.
4 The assumption of *on-going enterprise*.
5 The *stewardship function* which dominates this and the other two phases of this particular programme.

The periodization approach has been dominating accounting practice for a considerable time, and was supported and elaborated by Schmalenbach (1919) and his followers (e.g. Kosiol (1956, 1970, 1978)) in the German literature, and by Paton (1922) in the Anglo–American literature. Further interpretations of this model type are to be found by the AAA (1936, 1941, 1948), by Sanders *et al.* (1938), as well as by Paton and Littleton (1940). In more recent times Ijiri (1967, 1981) has been its most prominent proponent. Butterworth and Falk (1983) also counted Mattessich (1964b) into this category, but I regard my efforts as belonging to the third research programme (see pp. 202f.) which Butterworth and Falk (1983) did not treat as a separate paradigm or programme.

An essential aspect of the periodization approach lies in the fact that valuation is not perceived as the primary function of accounting but of the market. This is manifested in various slogans such as 'the accountant is not an appraiser' or 'the accountant ought to report facts and not opinions'. The function of accounting therefore lies in the 'digestion' of data resulting from various business transactions. Hence cost aggregates become the cornerstone, and consistency, objectivity, cost verification, etc. its basic principles.

In reference to Paton's (1922) first attempt of postulation, Butterworth and Falk (1983) raise the following question: from whence are the foundations of accounting derived? Since it does not seem possible to find an empirical–scientific basis, those authors speak of the '*ex cathedra* character' of such foundations. This characterization is understandable in the face of accounting theory as generally practised, but some proponents of the third research programme might disagree. They believe that a general accounting theory can be developed which will permit them to match a specific information purpose to a specific accounting model on the basis of analytical as well as empirical foundations (see pp. 204f.).

Second phase: the original agency approach

The first publications analysing systematically the problems of work and management contracts seem to be those of Coase (1937) and Herbert Simon (1951).[7] Yet, these publications found little echo, and it took some two decades until a more widely accepted theory of the principal-agency relations evolved. In economics it was the paper by Alchian and Demsetz (1972), and in business administration a subsequent paper by Jensen and Meckling (1976) which provided the actual launching basis. Shortly before, *special aspects* of similar contracts were analysed in two fundamental papers by Mirrlees (1971, 1976) as well as Spence and Zeckhauser (1971). The integration of all those and a considerable number of later research efforts led to that which nowadays is known as 'agency theory'. But there is an essential difference between this *original*, predominantly descriptive agency theory and the subsequent, predominantly analytical agency theory which we address as agency-information analysis to be discussed in the next section as the third phase of the stewardship research programme.

The central problem of the original agency theory lies in the *costs* caused by the potential goal conflict between principal and agent (e.g. monitoring of agent's activity, profit reduction due to a different value judgement between the two parties, forgoing of actions preferred by agent in consideration of the principal's different preferences – in the last case, for example, the agency costs are borne by the agent). Closely related to this problem is the search for a *motivational contract which enables risk sharing between principal and agent that hopefully is Pareto-optimal.* Thereby the accounting-information system employed plays a vital role. In this way the agent (whose activity cannot always be observed) will be motivated such that his interest coincides with that of the principal (*self-enforcing* contract); and furthermore the 'agency costs' shall be reduced to a minimum. Finally, it is to be expected that the agency costs grow to a lesser degree than the agent's share in the firm – but the more the motivational incentive decreases, the higher the costs of monitoring the agent will be.

In the realm of finance, agency theory tried to analyse the motivations and relations caused by certain shifts between internal and external financing in order to search for an optimal financing ratio. Such a finance theory seems to be more realistic than the theory of Modigliani and Miller (1958) which neglects this kind of optimization problem.

But Butterworth and Falk (1983) have pointed out that within the predominantly descriptive approach of Jensen and Meckling (1976), it was neither possible to examine the equilibrium conditions of such a contract model, nor certain consequences (e.g. bonding and monitoring features voluntarily accepted by the agent) which possibly might arise from this theory.

Butterworth also includes two well-known publications by Watts and Zimmerman (1978, 1979) in this second phase or paradigm. These two authors put special emphasis on the 'positive' nature of their theory to distinguish it strictly from the preceding normative phase. Although this positive theory is strongly oriented towards 'political phenomena' (as for example the *legislation* of accounting standards), it tries for this very reason to connect agency theory with accounting and the *political costs* connected with it. This theory has been criticized by Christenson (1983), Mattessich (1984a: 77–80), and Peasnell and Williams (1986). Also Butterworth and Falk (1983) hold that the Watts and Zimmerman theory lacks any relevant, theoretical economic foundation. Finally, the publication by Holthausen and Leftwich (1983) which supplied early empirical tests to the agency theory, are included in this phase.

Third phase: the agency-information approach

This third phase of the stewardship paradigm arose out of the combination of descriptive agency theory, on one side, and information economics, on the other. The latter was developed by Marschak (cf. 1974) and others in the 1950s and 1960s, and applied to accounting by Butterworth (1967, 1972), Demski (1972), Demski and Feltham (1972, 1976), Feltham (1967, 1968, 1972), Feltham and Demski (1970), and many others (for references to the pertinent German literature see Ballwieser (1985)).

For years there did not exist much contact between descriptive agency theory and information economics, but with increasing formalization of the former, both camps became aware for the need of a close cooperation or even an amalgamation of both research areas. For this reason we speak in the following of agency-information analysis when referring to the analytical approach of agency theory. Its core is to be found in the contractual relations and the risk sharing between the *principal* and the *agent.*

Depending on the type of employment contract, management's share on the total enterprise profit (before its remuneration) might span a wide spectrum limited by two extremes: on the one side we find a *fixed managerial salary* (under full monitoring of the manager's activity by the principal), whereby the total remaining profit goes to the principal who bears all the risk (principal is risk neutral, agent is risk averse), whereas the other extreme is found in the *renting of the business by the agent* such that the principal receives a fixed rent, and the agent, who bears all the risk, pockets the remaining profit (principal is risk averse, agent is risk neutral). There exist many types of contracts between these extremes, the most interesting of which leads to a Pareto-optimal profit and risk sharing between the two parties in accordance with classical marginal economic theory (principal and agent are both either risk neutral or risk averse). All these are 'first-best solutions' and of less practical interest than the so-called 'second-best solutions' because only the latter offer means to cope with two crucial issues:

1 The problem of *moral hazard*: since the full monitoring of the agent's activity by the principal is often not feasible (and since

agency-information analysis assumes that each party maximizes its own expected utility) the agent's optimal actions may not coincide with those actions optimal for the principal.

2 The problem of *adverse selection* of revealed information: in many situations there exists an asymmetry of information between principal and agent (usually but not always in favour of the agent). So for example the manager may have an information advantage over the principal due to the former's better or more specialized training and experience; or in the case of an insurance contract the insured person (principal) may have better information about his own health than the insurer (agent) in spite of a required medical examination. (Another favoured example is the secondhand car market – see Akerlof (1970).) If, therefore, one party withholds some information which otherwise would lead the other party to choose a different contract or action, namely one less favourable to the first but more favourable to the second party, then this adverse selection of information impedes a first-best solution.

A major task of agency information analysis, therefore, is to find conditions under which a Pareto or quasi-Pareto optimal contract between both parties can be obtained. That is to say, one searches for an incentive and risk-sharing scheme which is mutually satisfactory for both parties. Such an analysis would take care of both the problem of moral hazard as well as that of adverse selection. But the literature dealing with the latter has become comprehensive enough to speak of a 'theory of asymmetric information' as well as of a 'contract theory', both of which are closely related or a part of agency-information analysis. Butterworth and Falk (1983) even speak occasionally of an 'asymmetric information paradigm' as well as of a 'contracting paradigm'. Here again, the aim is the *efficient* contract that leads to a compromise between two opposing tendencies: on the one side one has to find an efficient risk sharing between principal and agent; on the other side, it is necessary to motivate the manager sufficiently to act in the interest of the principal – indeed, research has shown that contracts which are risk efficient are inefficient as regards motivation (cf. Butterworth and Falk 1986: 22).

For the further understanding of this phase or theory element we illustrate by means of three simplified models the way in which the information economic approach and the original agency theory were synthesized to agency-information analysis. Information economics is taken to be the natural extension of statistical decision theory, whereby the decision theoretical model has become enriched by the notion of 'information' or 'signal'. This yields the following information:

Basic model of information economics

$$E\,(u|\eta^*) = \max_{a(y),\,\eta} \sum_s \sum_y u(a(y), s) \bullet p(y|s, \eta) \bullet p(s)$$

$$= \max_\eta \sum_y \max_a \sum_s u(a, s) \bullet p(s|y, \eta) \bullet p(y)|\eta)$$

Explanation of symbols for this and the following two models:

a	Action or effort of agent (* refers to optimal action), often as a function of y.
argmax	Refers to the maximization of an argument with possibly *several* maxima.
$d(a)$	Agent's disutility caused by effort a.
$E(u\|\eta^*)$	Expected value of utility u, given optimal information system η^*.
$E(u\|\bullet)$	Principal's expected value utility given some variables.
$E(\eta^*)$	Principal's expected value of optimal information system η^*.
η	Information system.
$p(y \mid s,\eta)$	Probability of information y, given state s, and η.
$p(s)$	Probability of state s (sometimes conditioned on y and η).
s	State s.
y	Information.
$u(a(y), s)$	Utility as a function of y and s.
u_p or u	Utility of principal (usually as a function of some variables).
u_A or u	Utility of agent (usually as a function of some variables).
u_A^{min}	Agent's minimum acceptable utility.
$x(a, s)$	Outcome (profit) as a function of a and s.
$z(\bullet)$	Agent's reward for effort a (usually as a function of some variables).

Basic agency model

$$E_p(u_p|a^*, z^*) = \max_a \sum_s u_p(x(a, s) - z(x(a,s))) \bullet p(s)$$

subject to:

$$\sum_s u_A\,(z(x(a,s))) \bullet p(s) - d(a) \geq u_A^{min}$$

$$a \in \operatorname{argmax} \sum_s u_A\,(z(x(a,s))) \bullet p(s) - d(a)$$

This formulation regards the situation *from the point of view of the principal*, but it is possible to formulate it similarly from the agent's point of view; thereby goal function and constraints become reversed and slightly modified. In our situation, the principal's utility (after deduction of agent's reward) is to be maximized. The constraints refer to the agent's opportunity costs (offering his services in a free market) and to the maximization of his own utility respectively.

Basic model of agency-information analysis

$$E_P(u_P|a^*, z^*, \eta) = \max_{a,z,\eta} \sum_s \sum_y u_P(x(a,s) - z(y)) \bullet p(y|a,s,\eta) \bullet p(s)$$

subject to:

$$\sum_s \sum_y u_A(z(y)) \bullet p(y|a,s,\eta) \bullet p(s) - d(a) \geq u_A^{min}$$

$$a \varepsilon \operatorname{argmax} \sum_s \sum_y u_A(z(y)) \bullet p(y|a,s,\eta) \bullet p(s) - d(a)$$

The amalgamation of the original agency model with the information economic model can be discerned through the enrichment of the information signal variable y and the information system variable η – as shown in the agency-information model. The goalfunction of principal P maximizes his utility expectation through the choice of an optimal contract with the agent A (stipulating the optimal information system η^*, and the optimal agent's reward z^*) in such a way that the optimal action a^* will be chosen by A. The constraints correspond to the previous model, modified by the enrichment mentioned above.

Through elimination of more and more restrictions, on one side, and further enrichments of the model, on the other, many variations of this basic agency-information model are possible.

This stewardship research programme (which during the 1970s seemed to be pushed aside by the valuation-investment programme) has now in its third phase, as a consequence of agency-information analysis, experienced a genuine renaissance. This rueful return to the stewardship programme illustrates Lakatos's belief in the new 'budding' of what was believed to be an already 'degenerate' research programme; it is also an admission that stewardship (i.e. the provision of information for establishing an efficient contractual basis) belongs to accounting's most important functions (cf. Butterworth, *et al.* 1982). Such a contract should be capable of reducing the agency costs to a minimum (apart from residual costs, which do not necessarily have to be carried by the principal) and enable a mutually satisfactory position for both parties. Yet it must be taken into consideration that the capital risk need not only rest on the shoulders of principal and agent; it may also rest on those of other investors and creditors. The contracts with the latter (e.g. bond indentures) might possibly be incorporated into a sophisticated agency-information model under consideration of market equilibrium. Credit contracts may be represented as contingent claims towards the assets of the borrowing person or firm. This is the starting point of 'contingent claims analysis' in which the price of the assets is determined by such stochastic processes as logarithmic-normal diffusion. Black and Scholes (1973) have pioneered an equilibrium model for stock options under simple capital structure of the pertinent enterprise. This work was extended and further developed by Merton (1973a, b, 1974, 1976), Brennan and Schwartz (1977, 1978, 1979), Cox and Ross (1976a,b) and others, and was also supplied to other areas. For a survey of contingent claims analysis we refer to Hughes (1984); for the application of agency theory to the area of finance we refer to Barnea *et al.* (1985); and for the application to accounting, several papers in Mattessich (1984a and 1991c) offer an appropriate overview: Feltham (1984) Baiman (1982) and Butterworth *et al.* (1982). In each of these areas the agency-information analysis was instrumental in clarifying specific problems.

RESEARCH TRADITION NO. 2 (VALUATION-INVESTMENT PROGRAMME)

This tradition regards the 'correct' or 'approximately correct' economic evaluation of the assets and equities as the primary purpose of accounting. Behind this, however, stands the quest for an 'economically correct' income determination and optimal capital disposition. The capital theory of Böhm-Bawerk and Irving Fisher was applied to accounting in Canning's (1929) fundamental work, and in a somewhat modified way through the current value theory of Schmidt (1921, 1929). The latter can be interpreted as an objectified realistic compromise of this basically subjective approach. Again we encounter three phases (or theory elements) in the actual attempt to describe this tradition.

First phase: the present value and current value approach

Occasionally one encounters opposition to the historical cost and accrual approach (of the stewardship tradition) which merged during the nineteenth century. This has had practical as well as theoretical roots: the latter is to be found in capital theory, the former in the promotion of replacement costs by American as well as German railway companies – for details see Seicht (1970: 511), Boer (1966), and Mattessich (1982b: 349–50). In the accounting and business literature this approach seems first to be discussed by Fäs (1913) – see Seicht (1970: 330); later on we find it by Paton (1918), and possibly by Limperg – see Van Seventer (1975: 68) who claims that Limperg conceived this approach between 1917 and 1918. Yet, the first systematic exponent of it is Schmidt (1921, 1929) and after him Canning (1929) for whom the replacement value is a kind of objective substitute for the true economic present value. Apart from the fact that this approach shall serve (temporary) investors (cf. Staubus 1961), this phase is split into two camps. On one side stand the defenders of the current entry value approach (replacement value), like AAA (1957), Edwards and Bell (1961), and Sprouse and Moonitz (1962) as well as those of the current exit value approach, as MacNeal (1939), Chambers (1966) and Sterling (1970). On the other side are the proponents of the capital theoretic approach (for whom the present value forms the centre of attention, for example Hansen (1962), Honko (1959), Albach (1965), and Seicht (1970: 558–619).

Butterworth and Falk (1983) characterize this 'paradigm' through the present value which, however, as they point out, may be substituted in situations of uncertainty by the current value. Our objection to this substitution possibility lies in the notion that every investment or disinvestment decision requires a subjective as well as an objective evaluation (i.e. the juxtaposition of a personal estimation with a market situation). This means that, at least in such situations, the latter cannot be regarded as a substitute for the former; this is in agreement with other authors – e.g., Chambers, Sterling, etc. – who, for example, would object to the use of net realizable values (NRV) as a substitute for present values (PV).

Second phase: the risk sharing approach

This phase is also based on neo-classical economic theory and its extension by Arrow and Debreu (1954), but above all, on modern portfolio theory (Markowitz 1952 and Fama 1965) as well as on the capital asset pricing theory of Sharpe (1963, 1964) and Lintner (1965). Within the area of accounting Butterworth originally emphasized the research by the following authors: Hakansson (1969), Demski (1973), Garman and Ohlson (1980) as well as Ohlson and

Buckman (1980). This second phase also stresses the valuation of market predictions and similar information as well as its effect upon our discipline. Furthermore, it introduces stochastic processes into accounting. Finally, it takes into consideration the evaluation of securities in accord with modern finance theory with its distinction between unsystematic risk ($\beta = 1$) – which is unique to each security and can be eliminated by portfolio diversification – on one side, and systematic risk ($\beta > 1$ for securities the returns of which are expected to be more volatile, and $\beta < 1$ for securities the returns of which are expected to be less volatile than the market portfolio), on the other side. Therefore, the pioneering work of Ball and Brown (1968) ought to be mentioned in this connection; it was the first well grounded accounting publication which took into consideration the correlation between published profits and stock prices. Benston's (1967) study was a year earlier, but its results and presentation were less articulate).

Other works which in this context are most significant are those by Hakansson *et al.* (1982) and Ohlson (1987, 1988, 1990). Previous publications concerning the value of public information contradicted each other: e.g. Hirschleifer (1971) showed that public information has no value under perfect competition; whereas Marshall (1974) and others demonstrated that (under certain assumptions) public information may have value even under perfect competition. The papers by Hakansson *et al.* (1982) and Ohlson (1987, 1988, 1990) not only reveal the necessary and sufficient conditions under which public information (for perfectly competitive markets) has value, but also unites and reconciles in an elegant mathematical way the literature which previously appeared to be contradictory.

Third phase: the capital market approach

This phase is closely tied to the preceding one. While Butterworth originally tried to distinguish these two phases by two paradigms, he seems later to have combined them (see Butterworth and Falk 1983). The basic premises are those of the preceding approach but enriched by the further assumption that the pertinent security yield possesses a probability distribution (which, however, need not be observable). The information of the security market is considered to have value if it helps to improve the estimation of the actual yield. A further underlying assumption is market efficiency with regard to the financial statement information. Therefore, phase 3 is mainly an application of newer, especially empirical, insights of finance literature gained in the wake of further developments of the Sharpe–Lintner capital asset pricing models. A frequently mentioned pioneering work is that by Ball and Brown (1968) which showed that the changes of stock prices highly correlate with the (unexpected) profit changes of the pertinent firms. Further publications to be taken into consideration are those by Beaver (1968, 1981), Gonedes and Dopuch (1974), as well as other empirical studies – for a concise survey see Clarkson and Mattessich (1984: 361–89). But no phase of this research programme offers well formulated relations for choosing the optimal accounting system.

THE THIRD RESEARCH TRADITION (INFORMATION-STRATEGIC PROGRAMME)

Whether one is justified or not to talk in this case about a separate research tradition might be a point of controversy; perhaps it would be more appropriate to talk about the 'programme for a research programme or tradition'. Although one repeatedly encounters in the literature the quest for different accounting models suited to different information needs, there hardly exists agreement on how such a purpose-oriented theory can systematically be developed, and in which way the system structure can be matched to the pertinent information purpose. We seem to be in a dilemma: on one side, most experts agree that so-called general purpose systems satisfy only very simple accounting needs; on the other side those experts join opposing groups each of which pursues only a single, one-sided direction. The major impediment towards the development of such a purpose-oriented theory seems to be the '*ex cathedra* character' of most foundations of accounting which Butterworth and Falk (1983) criticize explicitly. However, to understand our objection to this criticism it must be taken into consideration that the foundations of science in general are subject to a similar *ex cathedra* aspect. Furthermore, the justification for the use of any instrument lies in the fulfillment of its purpose. And the construction and evaluation of this instrument must begin and end with the purpose and the degree of its fulfillment within a long-range cost–benefit context. And we do not require an instrumental philosophy to recognize that both accounting as well as science in general are instruments in this sense.

In this connection the reader ought to be reminded that Bertrand Russell (1948), who endeavoured to formulate the foundations of science and of knowledge in general, had to abandon the quest for an absolute foundation of science, and had to be satisfied with formulating fairly pragmatic postulates. In other words, he had to substitute the epistemic question 'what are the foundations of science?' with the pragmatic question 'which assumptions do we accept when doing science?' (cf. Mattessich 1978a: 176–9). Similarly, I abandoned the search for any absolute foundation of accounting over twenty years ago, and tried to answer the following question: 'which assumptions do we accept when applying any kind of double-classification accounting system?' (cf. Mattessich 1964b, 1970). Hence this kind of question is primarily directed towards the *basic assumptions* and only secondarily towards the *foundations* of accounting. Of course, one may object that an attempt to start from the more or less consciously adopted assumption of current accounting practice implies that the latter is considered satisfactory. If this implication should hold, then there can be little objection to infer inductively from accounting practice its basic assumptions, from which in turn major theorems and other consequences may be deduced. However, this would be too simplistic a solution. Even if the majority of public accountants and other preparers of accounts would regard present-day accounting as satisfactory, there may be many academics, investors, consumers, etc. who may not be satisfied with present-day accounting. Our presumption is that this dissatisfaction is most likely directed to specific models and hypotheses but not to the basic premises of accounting that hold for various social statistical systems all over the world. Any formulation of the truly basic assumptions from such an overall point of view should then make it easier to find further potential or intended applications (in the sense of Sneed (1971) and Stegmüller (1979, 1986)), needed for specific situations.

Thus our problem falls into two tasks:

1 The *formulation of the basic assumptions* (which hopefully would come close to my own formulations (cf. Mattessich (1964b: 176–9));
2 The more difficult task of formulating auxiliary or specific hypotheses for a series of different applications, each optimally or quasi-optimally suitable for a particular information purpose (see Balzer and Mattessich 1991).

Beyond this constant flux and search for new applications and improvements of specific accounting hypotheses, there also is the possibility to subject the basic assumptions themselves in the long-run to scrutiny and possible improvement. Of course, to a modest degree, a purpose-orientation of accounting has been available for a considerable time; the distinction between financial accounting and cost or managerial accounting is the most obvious example. But the information-strategic programme aims not only at a richer diversification but, above all, at a much better theoretical justification of its diverse categories and articulations (cf. Mattessich 1978b).

J.M. Clark (1923) might be regarded as the father or precursor of this third research programme; his slogan 'different costs for different purposes' sets the stage and points in the direction which I and a few others have tried to pursue.[8] Other proponents of a purpose-oriented accounting are: Le Coutre (1949), Spacek (1962), Backer (1966), Heinen (1978), possibly Schneider (1981, particularly on p. 405 ff), and Hamel (1984). Further publications about objectives of accounting are to be found by Stützel (1967), Beaver and Demski (1974), Cyert and Ijiri (1974), Cramer and Sorter (1974), above all the Trueblood Report of the AICPA (1973), the UK Accounting Standards Committee's 1975 discussion paper *The Corporate Report* (with which Eddie Stamp was much involved), FASB (1979), Stamp (1980: 32–8), and Griffin (1982).

Butterworth and Falk (1983) classified my own work (Mattessich 1964b) under the stewardship paradigm I (though with reference to some 'refinements'); but I personally regard myself as being associated with the third research programme. Since the early 1960s I have attempted to bring more clarity into this programme by two major steps, first by formulating the basic assumptions of accounting as presently practised on the micro- and macro-level and second, by strictly distinguishing between the basic uninterpreted or semi-interpreted theory, on one side, and the purpose-oriented interpretations for different intended applications (see Mattessich 1964b, 1970, 1972, 1979b, as well as 1984a: 1–45) on the other side. The introduction of additional auxiliary hypotheses in the case of new applications of a basic theory is generally accepted in modern science, and may correspond to the introduction of new theory elements in the Sneed–Stegmüller methodology previously discussed. But I believe that this kind of 'specific interpretation' or expansion of the theory net assumes particular significance in the applied sciences, to which I count medicine, engineering, and the administrative sciences including accounting because of their special teleologic status. The purpose orientation of all applied sciences creates methodological problems hitherto insufficiently explored (e.g. instead of the 'fundamental law' the 'purpose' may serve as the invariant nucleus of a theory net; for other problems see Mattessich (1978)). Surprisingly, those endeavours took little root in the academic community, in spite of the fact that the need for purpose-orientation is often acknowledged in the literature and even materializes in actual practice. In the USA and in Canada the standards established by FASB (1979, 1984a,b) (but now abandoned) and CICA (1982), to my mind result in the introduction of greater purpose-orientation into the accounting systems of American business. These current cost accounting standards were much more than mere inflation accounting; they serve a series of different information purposes (e.g. income measurement on the basis of *nominal* and *real* financial capital maintenance, as well as *physical* capital maintenance – each of these bases serves a different decision goal).

Academically even more rewarding, and hopefully more enduring than the above mentioned legislation of current cost methods, was the attempt to introduce statistical methods (by Trueblood and Cooper (1955) and others) and, on a more general level, the introduction of rigorous analytical methods to accounting (Mattessich 1957, 1964b). At first, only a few authors followed this course, e.g. Charnes *et al.* (1959), Bierman *et al.* (1961), Williams and Griffin (1964), Ijiri (1965, 1967). Today the analytical methods are not only an important and integral part of current accounting research, but significant papers such as that by Hakansson *et al.* (1982), have grown on this soil fertilized by some of us over twenty years ago. It is hoped that the highly analytical agency-information analysis and its adaptation to accounting, as well as the structuring of accounting traditions, will contribute to the purpose orientation of accounting theory. Although individual phases or theory elements were not shown for this research tradition, they do exist and extend into managerial accounting, budgeting, even macro-accounting – this new trend is indicated by the pioneering work of Johnson and Kaplan (1987). This offers a more integrated picture without which our discipline remains a half-way house.

CONCLUSION

Accounting research can be illuminated from different angles and classified in a great variety of schemes. It may seem that this chapter is but another such attempt of classification. I hope it is more than that. The crucial point of our distinction between three accounting research traditions lies in its being based on the latest research results of methodology and the philosophy of science. This goes beyond Thomas Kuhn's popular but somewhat simplistic picture of a dominating paradigm. It is important to recognize two things: first, that accounting, like many other scientific endeavours, consists of different research traditions that compete with each other, and not a single dominating paradigm (emerging from the struggle between a preceding, obsolete paradigm and several new competitors). Second, and perhaps more importantly, that each research tradition constitutes an entire network of theory elements which, in a way, also compete with each other (but in a more moderate or secondary fashion) because each of these theory elements is based on one and the same fundamental law or premise, and because each element is a further specialization or articulation of the basic theory element from which it evolves chronologically. This chapter is a first attempt to show that such a scheme, developed on the basis of other scientific disciplines, may be valid for accounting.

Attempts of rigorous logical-structuralist reconstructions of theories and their networks from various fields, including accounting, have already been made (see Stegmüller 1986, Balzer *et al.* 1987, and Balzer and Mattessich 1991). This chapter is more informal and does not go that far; but a more formal treatment is feasible. Indeed, the best chance for a more rigorous treatment of accounting networks might be the close cooperation between a philosopher of science with expertise in the logical reconstruction of theories and an accountant versed in formalization and axiomatization. It is for this reason that Balzer and I have embarked upon such a project (see Balzer and Mattessich 1991) which, however, thus far deals mainly with the input–output aspects of accounting (see also Mattessich 1987a, 1989) without any expansion into finance and agency theory. Hopefully our project can be extended in the way sketched in this chapter. Such an interdisciplinary effort might put a stop to the lengthy search for the appropriate axiomatization of accounting theory (as surveyed, for example, by Willett (1987)), by revealing its logical structure as well as its empirical claims in a clearer and more generally acceptable way than previously done.

But since my past analytical efforts (cf. Mattessich 1957, 1964a,b) were not quite in vain and have helped to create the basis for computerized budgeting and various accounting simulations – as nowadays most successfully applied in such best-selling microcomputer spreadsheet programs as Visi-Calc, Super-Calc, Lotus 1–2–3, etc. (see Leech 1986) – there exists some precedent for the usefulness of analytical endeavours in accounting.

To avoid misunderstanding, something else has to be added. Some experts may argue that there exist many more research traditions than here indicated; that, for example, behavioural accounting has here been neglected as a special tradition. Such an objection not only constitutes a misunderstanding of this chapter, but also of the nature of behavioural accounting. The latter is not a research tradition in the sense of a theory network consisting of a variety of interrelated theory elements, but an empirical methodology to complement the theoretical or analytical approach independent of the particular research tradition involved.

Elsewhere I have argued, first, that each research tradition must be pursued through analytical *as well as* empirical research, and second, that only when analytical and empirical accounting research begin to complement each other in a similar fashion (as theoretical and experimental physics) will accounting theory be on a more secure foundation than is presently the case (cf. Mattessich 1991c: 11, 41, endnote 21). Obviously, an applied science like accounting cannot expect to attain the same degree of collaboration or matching between its theoretical and empirical research as encountered in the pure sciences. But occasionally some giving and taking between analytical and behavioural accounting research has already occurred, and it can only be hoped that such cooperation can be extended on a broad front.

APPENDIX
DIMENSIONS OF MULTI-PERSON INFORMATION ECONOMIC MODELS

1 Number of persons
  - Small number (game-theoretic model)
  - Large number (equilibrium model)

2 Transferability of claims to outcomes
  - Transferable
  - Non-transferable (transferability either prohibited or not enforceable)

3 Variety of transferable claims available
  - Complete (security market is sufficiently flexible to satisfy all combinations of investment needs)
  - Incomplete due to exogenous restrictions
  - Incomplete due to insufficient information

4 Alternative actions in transferable claims models
  - Pure exchange models (no choices); firm's actions are exogenously determined and cannot be influenced by creating new information
  - Production models (actions are collective choices, e.g. manager and principal decide in cooperation, or decisions in a planned economy)
  - Agency models (individual choice, e.g. by manager)

5 Direct preferences for actions in agency models
 None (manager has no particular preferences)
 Disutility expressing manager's efforts is taken into consideration
6 Similarity of preferences for actions in non-transferable claims models
 Strictly independent (e.g. manager has different preferences than principal)
 Strictly identical (e.g. principal and agent have same preference structure)
 Strictly opposite (preferences of agent harm preferences of principal and vice versa)
7 Action commitments in non-transferable claims model
 Non feasible
 All feasible (purely cooperative model)
 Some feasible
8 Similarity of prior beliefs.
 Homogeneous (principal and agent use same probability distribution)
 Heterogeneous (*p* and *a* use different probability distribution)
9 Timing of information distribution
 Pre-commitment (see also Baiman 1982: 276–7)
 Pre-decision (see also Baiman 1982: 277–8, 279–80)
 Post-decision (see also Baiman 1982: 270–6, 278–9)
10 Extent of information distribution
 Public report
 Private acquisition
 Private acquisition prior to public report
11 Extent to which private information is revealed
 None revealed
 Fully revealed
 Partially revealed
12 Selection of information system
 Exogenous
 Endogenous
13 Number of periods
 Single period
 Multiple periods

Source: this is a somewhat extended version of Feltham's (1984a: 183–4) Table I, adapted with permission of the author and the publisher (copyright Canadian Certified Public Accountants Research Foundation).

NOTES

1 This is an extended version of a paper of mine published under the title 'An applied scientist's search for a methodological framework' (1987) in P. Weingartner and G. Schurz (eds) *Logic, Philosophy of Science and Epistemology* (Proceedings of the 11th International Wittgenstein Symposium) Vienna, Hölder-Pichler-Tempsky, pp. 243–62 and reproduced with permission of the Hölder-Pichler-Tempsky Publishing House. Financial support from the Social Sciences and Humanities Research Council of Canada is gratefully acknowledged.

2 Those *six* paradigms were presented by Butterworth in an Accounting Faculty Seminar in autumn 1983 at the University of British Columbia. Meanwhile different drafts of this paper (by Butterworth and Falk) have appeared until its ultimate version was published as chapter 2 ('Information attributes of the contractual paradigm') of Butterworth and Falk (1986: 9–29). However, in this last version only the following *four* paradigms are mentioned: A. The discount money-value paradigm (corresponding to Valuation I), B. The stewardship paradigm (corresponding to Stewardship I), C. The capital market paradigm (combining valuation II and III, and, quite unexpectedly, Stewardship II), and D. The contracting paradigm (corresponding to Stewardship III). From the viewpoint of this chapter, the original presentation is more meaningful, but since it is not available in print, we shall always refer to the original presentation *together with* the final version as: Butterworth and Falk (1983).

3 Two excellent review articles of this Report were written by Peasnell (1978) and Hakansson (1978).

4 About the possibilities and difficulties of formulating paradigms in accounting and business administration see Mattessich (1979a) and the different contributions of the anthological proceedings by Fischer-Winkelmann (1982).

5 Stegmüller, for example, points out that 'Lakatos anticipated the [Stegmüller's] distinction between theories and empirical claims of theories *in our sense*, but that he was not consistent in his terminology. Whenever he speaks of *theories as members of a sequence* with the sequence representing a research programme [footnote omitted], his "theories", correspond to our "empirical-hypothetical claims"' (Stegmüller 1979: 60–1).

6 Cf. Bunge 1983a: 224–5, 1983b: 129, 163–4, 175.

7 For further details see Mattessich (1984b).

8 Staubus (1987) blames J.M. Clark for our 'dark ages of cost accounting'; but this hardly affects our issue. Staubus merely concludes 'that instead of "different purposes", Clark should have stressed proper identification of the object of costing in each case' (Staubus 1987: 7), instead of neglecting the 'object-of-costing concept'.

REFERENCES

AAA (American Accounting Association) (1936) 'A tentative statement of broad accounting principles underlying corporate financial statements', *Accounting Review*, June.

—— (1941) 'Accounting principles underlying corporate financial statements', *Accounting Review*, June.

—— (1948) 'Accounting concepts and standards underlying corporate financial statements', *Accounting Review*, June.

—— (1957) *Accounting and Reporting Standards for Corporate Financial Statements*: 1957 (Revised 1957).

—— (1977) *A Statement on Accounting Theory and Theory Acceptance*, Sarasota, Florida: AAA.

AICPA (American Institute of Certified Public Accountants) (1973) *Report of the Study Group on the Objectives of Financial Statements*, (Trueblood Report), New York: AICPA.

Akerlof, G. (1970) 'The market for "lemons": qualitative uncertainty and the market mechanism', *Quarterly Journal of Economics*, 89, August: 488–500.

Albach, H. (1965) 'Grundgedanken einer synthetischen Bilanztheorie', in: *Zeitschrift für Betriebswirtschaft*, 31(1): 21–31.

Alchian, A. and Demsetz, H. (1972) 'Production, information costs, and economic organization', *American Economic Review*, 62 December: 777–95.

Alexander, S.S. (1950) 'Income measurement in a dynamic economy' *Five Monographs on Business Income*, Study Group on Business Income, New York: American Institute of [Certified Public] Accountants. (Reprinted by Scholars Book, Lawrence, Kansas, 1973)

Arrow, K.J. and Debreu, G. (1954) 'Existence of an equilibrium for a competitive economy' *Econometrica*, 22(2): 256–90.

Backer, M. (1966) 'Accounting theory and multiple reporting objectives' M. Backer (ed.) in *Modern Accounting Theory*, Englewood Cliffs, New Jersey: Prentice Hall, pp. 439–63.

Baiman, S. (1982) 'Agency research in managerial accounting: a survey', *Journal of Accounting Literature*. (Reprinted in R. Mattessich (ed.) *Modern Accounting Research: History, Survey and Guide*, Vancouver, British Columbia: Canadian Certified General Accountants' Research Foundation pp. 251–94.)

Ball, R., and Brown, P. (1968) 'An empirical evaluation of accounting income numbers', *Journal of Accounting Research*, Autumn: 159–78.

Ballwieser, W. (1985) 'Informationsökonomie, Rechnungslegung und Bilanzrichtlinien-Gesetz', *Zeitschrift für betriebswirtschaftliche Forschung*, 1: 47–66.

Balzer, W. (1982) 'Empirical claims in exchange economics', in W. Stegmüller, W. Balzer and W. Spohn (eds) *Philosophy of Economics*, New York: Springer Verlag, pp. 16–40.

Balzer, W. and Mattessich, R. (1991) 'An axiomatic basis of accounting: a structuralist reconstruction', *Theory and Decision* 30: 213–43.

Balzer, W., Moulines, C.U. and Sneed, J.D. (1987) *An Architecture for Science*, Dordrecht, Netherlands/Boston, Massachusetts: D. Reidel.

Barnea, A., Haugen, R.A. and Senbet, L.W. (1985) *Agency Problems and Financial Contracting*, Englewood-Cliffs, New Jersey: Prentice Hall.

Beaver, W.H. (1968) 'The information content of annual earnings announcements', *Empirical Research in Accounting,* Supplement to *Journal of Accounting Research*, 67–92.

—— (1972) 'The behavior of security prices and its implication for accounting research (methods)', in American Accounting Association, *Report of the Committee on Research Methodology in Accounting*, supplement to vol. 47, *Accounting Review* pp. 407–37.

—— (1981) *Financial Reporting: An Accounting Revolution*, Englewood Cliffs, New Jersey: Prentice Hall.

Beaver, W.H. and Demski, J.S. (1974) 'The nature of financial objectives: a summary and synthesis', *Studies in Financial Accounting Objectives*, supplement to vol. 12, *Journal of Accounting Research*, pp. 170–87.

Beaver, W.H., Kennelly, J.W. and Voss, W.M. (1968) 'Predictive ability as a criterion for the evaluation of accounting data', *Accounting Review*, October: 675–83.

Belkaoui, A. (1981) *Accounting Theory*, San Diego: Harcourt Brace Jovanovich, (second edition 1985).

Benston, G.J. (1967) 'Published corporate accounting data and stock prices', *Empirical Research in Accounting*, supplement to *Journal of Accounting Research*, 5: 1–14, 22–54.

Bierman, H., Fouraker, L.E. and Jaedicke, R.K. (1961) *Quantitative Analysis for Business Decisions*, Homewood, Illinois: R. Irwin.

Birnberg, J.G. and Nath, R. (1967) 'Implications of behavioral science for managerial accounting', *Accounting Review*, July: 468–79.

Black, F. and Scholes, M. (1973) 'The pricing of options and corporate liabilities', *Journal of Political Economy*, May/June: 637–59.

Blaug, M. (1983) *Economic Theory in Retrospect*, Cambridge: Cambridge University Press paperback edition (first published by Cambridge University Press, 1978).

—— (1980) *The Methodology of Economics*, Cambridge: Cambridge University Press.

Boer, G. (1966) 'Replacement accounting: a historical look', *Accounting Review*, January: 92–7.

Brennan, M. and Schwartz, E. (1977) 'Convertible bonds: valuation and optimal strategies for call and conversion', *Journal of Finance*, December: 1699–715.

—— (1978) 'Finite difference methods and jump processes arising in the pricing of contingent claims: a synthesis', *Journal of Finance and Quantitative Analysis*, September: 461–74.

—— (1979) 'A continuous time approach to the pricing of bonds', *Journal of Banking and Finance*, July: 133–55.

Bruns, Jr, W.J. (1968) 'Accounting information and decision making: some behavioral hypotheses', *Accounting Review*, July: 469–80.

Bunge, M. (1974a) *Semantics I: Sense and Reference*, vol. 1, *Treatise on Basic Philosophy*, Dordrecht, Netherlands/Boston, Massachusetts: Reidel.

—— (1974b) *Semantics II: Interpretation and Truth*, vol. 2, *Treatise on Basic Philosophy*, Dordrecht, Netherlands/Boston, Massachusetts: Reidel.

—— (1977) *Ontology I: The Furniture of the World*, vol. 3, *Treatise on Basic Philosophy*, Dordrecht, Netherlands/Boston, Massachusetts: Reidel.

—— (1978) 'Review of Stegmüller, Wolfgang. The structure of dynamic theories, 1976', *Mathematical Review*, 55(2) February: 330, item 2480.

—— (1979) *Ontology II: A World of Systems*, vol. 4, *Treatise on Basic Philosophy*, Dordrecht, Netherlands/Boston Massachusetts: Reidel.

—— (1983a) *Epistemology I: Exploring the World*, vol. 5, *Treatise on Basic Philosophy*, Dordrecht, Netherlands/Boston, Massachusetts: Reidel.

—— (1983b) *Epistemology II: Understanding the World*, vol. 6, *Treatise on Basic Philosophy*, Dordrecht, Netherlands/Boston, Massachusetts: Reidel.

—— (1985a) *Epistemology II: Philosophy of Science and Technology*, vol. 7/I, *Treatise on Basic Philosophy*, Dordrecht, Netherlands/Boston, Massachusetts: Reidel.

—— (1985b) *Epistemology III: Philosophy of Science and Technology*, vol. 7/II, *Treatise on Basic Philosophy*, Dordrecht, Netherlands/Boston, Massachusetts: Reidel.

Butterworth, J.E. (1967) 'Accounting systems and management decision: an analysis of the role of information in the managerial decision process', PhD dissertation, University of California, Berkeley.

—— (1972) 'The accounting system as an information function', *Journal of Accounting Research*, Spring: 1–27.

Butterworth, J.E. and Falk, H. (1983) 'The methodological implications of a contractual theory of accounting', working paper (1983) University of British Columbia. Published in revised form in J.E. Butterworth and H. Falk (eds) (1986) *Financial Reporting – Theory and Application to the Oil and Gas Industry in Canada*, Hamilton, Ontario: Society of Management Accountants of Canada, pp. 9–29.

—— (1986) *Financial Reporting – Theory and Application to the Oil and Gas Industry in Canada*, Hamilton, Ontario: Society of Management Accountants of Canada.

Butterworth, J.E., Gibbins, M. and King, R.D. (1982) 'The structure of accounting theory: some basic conceptual and methodological issues', *Research to Support Standard Setting in Financial Accounting: A Canadian Perspective*, Toronto: Clarkson Gordon Foundation. (Reprinted in R. Mattessich (ed.) *Modern Accounting Research: History, Survey and Guide*, Vancouver, British Columbia: Canadian Certified General Accountants' Research Foundation, pp. 209–50.)

CICA (Canadian Institute of Chartered Accountants) (1982) 'Reporting the effects of changing prices', *CICA Handbook*, Toronto: CICA, section 4510.

Canning, J.B. (1929) *The Economics of Accountancy*, New York: Ronald Press.

Chambers, R.J. (1966) *Accounting, Evaluation and Economic Behavior*. Englewood Cliffs, New Jersey: Prentice Hall. (Reprinted 1975, in Accounting Classics Series, Houston: Scholars Book Co.)

Charnes, A., Cooper, W.W. and Miller, N.H. (1959) 'Applications of linear programming to financial budgeting and the costing of funds', *Journal of Business*, January: 20–46.

Christenson, C. (1983) 'The methodology of positive accounting', *Account-*

ing Review, 58, January: 1–22. (Reprinted in R. Mattessich (ed.) *Modern Accounting Research: History, Survey and Guide*, Vancouver, British Columbia: Canadian Certified General Accountants' Research Foundation, pp. 131–49.)

Clark, J.M. (1923) *Studies in the Economics of Overhead Costs*, Chicago: University of Chicago Press.

Clarkson, P. and Mattessich, R. (1984) 'A review of market research in financial accounting', in R. Mattessich (ed.) *Modern Accounting Research: History, Survey and Guide*, Vancouver, British Columbia: Canadian Certified General Accountants' Research Foundation pp. 361–89.

Coase, R.H. (1937) 'The nature of the firm', *Economica*, November: 386–405.

Cox, J. and Ross, S. (1976a) 'A survey of some new results in financial option pricing theory', *Journal of Finance*, May: 383–402.

—— (1976b) 'The valuation of options for alternative stochastic processes', *Journal of Financial Economics*, 3: 145–66.

Cramer, Jr. J.J. and Sorter, G.H. (eds) (1974) *Objectives of Financial Statements*, vol. 2 Selected Papers, New York: American Institute of Certified Public Accountants.

Crandall, R.H. (1969) 'Information economics and its implications for the further development of accounting theory', *Accounting Review*, July: 457–66.

Cyert, R.M. and Ijiri, Y. (1974) 'Problems of implementing the Trueblood Objectives Report', *Studies on Financial Accounting Objectives* Supplement to vol. 12, *Journal of Accounting Research*, pp. 29–42.

Demski, J.S. (1972) *Information Analysis*, Reading, Massachusetts: Addison-Wesley, (second edition 1980).

—— (1973) 'Rational choice of accounting method for a class of partnerships', *Journal of Accounting Research*, Autumn: 176–90.

Demski, J.S. and Feltham, G.A. (1972) 'Forecast evaluation', *Accounting Review*, July: 533–66.

—— (1976) *Cost Determination: A Conceptual Approach*, Ames, Iowa: Iowa State University Press.

—— (1978) 'Economic incentives in budgetary control systems', *Accounting Review*, April: 336–59.

Edwards, E.O. and Bell, P.W. (1961) *The Theory and Measurement of Business Income*, Berkeley: University of California Press.

Fama, E.F., (1965) 'The behavior of stock market prices', *Journal of Business*, 38, January: 34–105.

Fäs, E. (1913) *Die Berücksichtigung der Wertverminderung des stehenden Kapitals in den Jahresbilanzen der Erwerbswirtschaft*, Tübingen.

FASB (Financial Accounting Standards Board) (1979) *Statement of Financial Accounting Standards No. 33: Financial Reporting and Changing Prices*, Stamford, Connecticut: FASB.

—— (1984a) *Statement of Financial Accounting Standards No. 82: Financial Reporting and Changing Prices: Elimination of Certain Disclosures*, amendment of FASB Statement No. 33 Stamford, Connecticut: FASB.

—— (1984b) *Proposed Statement of Financial Accounting Standards: Financial Reporting and Changing Prices: Current Cost Information*, Stamford, Connecticut: FASB.

Feltham G.A. (1967) 'A theoretical framework for evaluating changes in accounting information for managerial decisions', PhD dissertation, University of California, Berkeley.

—— (1968) 'The value of information', *Accounting Review*, October: 684–96.

—— (1972) *Information Evaluation*. Sarasota, Florida: American Accounting Association.

—— (1984) 'Financial accounting research: contributions of information economics and agency theory', in R. Mattessich (ed.) *Modern Accounting Research: History, Survey and Guide*, Vancouver, British Columbia: Canadian Certified General Accountants' Research Foundation pp. 179–207.

Feltham, G.A. and Demski, J.S. (1970) 'The use of models in information evaluation', *Accounting Review*, October: 623–40.

Feyerabend, P.K. (1965) 'Problems of empiricism', in R. Colodny (ed.), *Beyond the Edge of Certainty*, Englewood Cliffs, New Jersey: Prentice-Hall, pp. 145–50.

—— (1975) *Against Method*, London, New Left Books.

Fischer-Winkelmann, W.F. (ed.) (1982) *Paradigmenwechsel in der Betriebswirtschaftslehre*, Munich: Institut für Kontrolling, Hochschule der Bundeswehr.

Garman, M.B. and Ohlson, J.A. (1980) 'Information and the sequential valuation of assets in arbitrage-free economies', *Journal of Accounting Research*, Autumn: 420–40.

Gilman, S. (1939) *Accounting Concepts of Profit*, New York: Ronald Press.

Gonedes, N.J. (1972) 'Efficient capital markets and external accounting', *Accounting Review*, January: 11–21.

Gonedes, N.J. and Dopuch, N. (1974) 'Capital-market equilibrium, information production and selecting accounting techniques: theoretical framework and review of empirical work', *Journal of Accounting Research*, Supplement: 48–129.

Gordon, M.J. (1964) 'Postulates, principles and research in accounting', *Accounting Review*, April: 251–63.

Griffin, P.A. (1982) *Usefulness to Investors and Creditors of Information Provided by Financial Reporting – A Review of Empirical Accounting Research*, Stamford, Connecticut: Financial Accounting Standards Board.

Hacking, I. (1983) *Representing and Intervening*, Cambridge: Cambridge University Press.

Hakansson, N.H. (1969) 'An induced theory of accounting under risk', *Accounting Review*, July: 495–514.

—— (1978) 'Where are we in accounting: a review of "Statement on Accounting Theory and Theory Acceptance"', *Accounting Review*, 53: 717–25. (Reprinted in R. Mattessich (ed.) *Modern Accounting Research: History, Survey and Guide*, Vancouver, British Columbia: Canadian Certified General Accountants' Research Foundation pp. 69–76.)

Hakansson, N.H., Kunkel, J.G. and Ohlson, J.A. (1982) 'Sufficient and necessary conditions for information to have social value in pure exchange', *Journal of Finance*, December: 1169–81.

Hamel, W. (1984) 'Ansatzpunkte Strategischer Bilanzierung', *Zeitschrift für betriebswirtchaftliche Forschung*, 11, November: 903–12.

Hamminga, B. (1983) *Neoclassical Theory Structure and Theory Development*, New York: Springer Verlag.
Hansen, P. (1962) *The Accounting Concept of Profit. An Analysis and Evaluation in the Light of the Economic Theory of Income and Capital*, Copenhagen.
Hanson, N.R. (1958) *Patterns of Discovery*, Cambridge: Cambridge University Press.
Hatfield, H.R. (1927) *Accounting: Its Principles and Problems*, New York: D. Appleton.
Hausman, D.M. (ed.) (1984) *The Philosophy of Economics – An Anthology*, Editor's introduction, Cambridge: Cambridge University Press.
Heinen, E. (1978) 'Supplemented multi-purpose accounting', *International Journal of Accounting*, 14(1), Autumn: 1–15.
Hirschleifer, J. (1971) 'The private and social value of information and the reward to inventive activity', *American Economic Review*, September: 561–74.
Hofstedt, T.R. and Kinard, J.C. (1970) 'A strategy for behavioral accounting research', *Accounting Review*, January: 38–54.
Holthausen, R. and Leftwich, R. (1983) 'The economic consequences of accounting choice: implications of costly contracting and monitoring, *Journal of Accounting and Economics*, August: 77–117.
Honko, J. (1959) *Yrityksen Vuositulos. The Annual Income of an Enterprise and its Determination. A Study from the Standpoint of Accounting and Economics*, Helsinki: Oy Weilin & Goos.
Hughes, J.S. (1984) *A Contracting Perspective on Accounting Valuation*, Sarasota, Florida: American Accounting Association.
Ijiri, Y. (1965) *Management Goals and Accounting for Control*, Chicago: Rand McNally.
—— (1967) *The Foundations of Accounting Measurement*, Englewood Cliffs, New Jersey: Prentice-Hall.
—— (1975) *Theory of Accounting Measurement*, Studies in Accounting Research, No. 10, Sarasota, Florida: American Accounting Association.
—— (1981) *Historical Cost Accounting and its Rationality*, Vancouver: Canadian Certified General Accountants' Research Foundation.
Jensen, M.C. and Meckling, W.M. (1976) 'Theory of the firm: managerial behavior, agency costs, and ownership structure', *Journal of Financial Economics*, October: 305–60.
Johnson, T. and Kaplan, R. (1987) *Relevance Lost: The Rise and Fall of Management Accounting*, Cambridge, Massachusetts: Harvard Business School Press.
Kosiol, E. (1956) 'Pagatorische Bilanz', *Lexikon des kaufmännischen Rechnungswesens*, 3: 2085–120.
—— (1970) 'Zur Axiomatik der Theorie der pagatorischen Erfolgsrechnung', *Zeitschrift für Betriebswirtschaft*, 22: 135–62.
—— (1978) *Pagatoric Theory of Financial Income Determination*. Urbana, Illinois: Center for Education and Research in Accounting.
Kuhn, T.S. (1962) *The Structure of Scientific Revolutions*, Chicago: University of Chicago Press, 1962 (second edition 1970, University of Chicago Press).
Lakatos, I. (1970) 'Falsification and the methodology of scientific research

programmes', in I. Lakatos and A. Musgrave (eds) *Criticism and the Growth of Knowledge*, Cambridge: Cambridge University Press, pp. 91–196.

—— (1983) *The Methodology of Scientific Research Programmes, Collected Philosophical Papers*, vol. I, J. Worrall and G. Currie (eds), Cambridge: Cambridge University Press, paperback edition (originally published 1978, Cambridge University Press).

Laudan, L. (1977) *Progress and its Problems*, Berkeley: University of California Press.

Le Coutre, W. (1949) *Grundzüge der Bilanzkunde – Eine totale Bilanzlehre*, vol. 1, fourth edition, Wolfenbüttel.

Leech, S.A. (1986) 'The theory and development of a matrix-based accounting system', *Accounting and Business Research*, Autumn: 327–41.

Lintner, J. (1965) 'The valuation of risky assets and the selection of risky investments in stock portfolios and capital budgets', *Review of Economics and Statistics*, February: 13–37.

Littleton, A.C. (1953) *Structure of Accounting Theory*, Monograph No. 5, Sarasota, Florida: American Accounting Association.

MacNeal, K. (1939) *Truth in Accounting*, Philadelphia: University of Pennsylvania Press.

Markowitz, H. (1952) 'Portfolio selection', *Journal of Finance*, March: 77–91.

Marschak, J. (1974) *Economic Information, Decision and Prediction*, 3 vols., Dordrecht/Boston: D. Reidel.

Marshall, J. (1974) 'Private incentive and information', *American Economic Review*, 64, June: 373–90.

Mattessich, R. (1957) 'Towards a general and axiomatic foundation of accountancy – with an introduction to the matrix formulation of accounting systems', *Accounting Research*, 8(4): 328–55. (Reprinted in S.A. Zeff (ed.), *The Accounting Postulates and Principles Controversy of the 1960s*, New York: Garland Publishing.)

—— (1964a) *Simulation of the Firm through a Budget Computer Program*, Homewood, Illinois: R. Irwin.

—— (1964b) *Accounting and Analytical Methods*, Homewood, Illinois, R. Irwin. (Reprinted in Accounting Classics Series, Houston, Texas: Scholars Book Co, 1977.)

—— (1970) *Die Wissenschaftlichen Grundlagen des Rechnungswesens*, Düsseldorf: Bertelsmann Verlag.

—— (1972) 'Methodological preconditions and problems of a general theory of accounting', *Accounting Review*, July: 469–87.

—— (1978a) *Instrumental Reasoning and Systems Methodology*, Dordrecht Netherlands/Boston, D. Reidel; (paperback edition, 1980, Dordrecht: Reidel).

—— (1978b) 'Instrumentelle Bilanztheorie: Voraussetzungen und erste Ansätze', *Zeitschrift für betriebswirtschaftliche Forschung*, 30 (10/11), October/November: 792–800.

—— (1979a) 'Konfliktresolution in der Wissenschaft – Zur Anwendung der Methoden von Thomas Kuhn, Sneed und Stegmüller in den Sozial-und Wirtschaftswissenschaften', in G. Dlugos (ed.), *Unternehmungsbezogene Konfliktforschung: Methodologische und Forschungsprogrammatische Grundfragen*, Stuttgart: Poeschel Verlag pp. 253–72.

—— (1979b) 'Instrumental aspects of accounting', in R.R. Sterling and A.L. Thomas (eds), *Accounting for a Simplified Firm: Seventeen Essays Based on a Common Example*. Houston, Texas: pp. 335–51.

—— (1980) 'On the evolution of theory construction in accounting: a personal account', *Accounting and Business Research* (UK) special issue on accounting history, Spring: 158–73. (Reprinted in R. Mattessich (ed.) *Modern Accounting Research: History, Survey and Guide*, Vancouver, British Columbia: Canadian Certified General Accountants' Research Foundation pp. 27–57.)

—— (1982a) 'Axiomatic representation of the systems framework: similarities and differences between Mario Bunge's world of systems and my own systems methodology', *Cybernetics and Systems*, 13: 51–75.

—— (1982b) 'On the evolution of inflation accounting – with a comparison of seven models', *Economia Aziendale*, 1(3), December: 349–81.

—— (ed.) (1984a) *Modern Accounting Research: History, Survey and Guide*, Vancouver, British Columbia: Canadian Certified General Accountants' Research Foundation. (Revised edition, 1989, Vancouver, Canadian Certified General Accountants' Research Foundation.)

—— (1984b) 'Agency-information analysis and the new science of management decisions', in J.P. Brans (ed.) *Operational Research '84*, Amsterdam: North-Holland/Elsevier pp. 77–89.

—— (1987a) 'Prehistoric accounting and the problem of representation: on recent archeological evidence of the Middle-East from 8000 B.C. to 3000 B.C.', *Accounting Historian's Journal*, Fall: 71–91. (Reprinted in T.A. Lee (ed.) *The Closure of the Accounting Profession*, New York: Garland Press.)

—— (1987b) 'An applied scientist's search for a methodological framework', in P. Weingartner and G. Schurz, *Logic, Philosophy of Science and Epistemology*, Vienna: Hölder-Pichler-Tempsky, pp. 243–62.

—— (1989) 'Accounting and the input–output principle in the prehistoric and ancient world', *Abacus*, Fall: 74–84.

—— (1990) 'Epistemological aspects of accounting', *Praxiology* (formerly published by the Polish Academy of Sciences). (Reprinted in *Keiri Kenkyu*, Autumn: 3–30.)

—— (1991a) 'Social reality and the measurement of its phenomena', *Advances in Accounting*, 9: 3–17.

—— (1991b) 'Social versus physical reality in accounting, and the measurement of its phenomena', in B. Banerjee (ed.) *Contemporary Issues of Accounting Research*, Calcutta: Indian Accounting Association's Research Foundation, pp. 1–30.

—— (ed.) (1991c) *Accounting Research in the 1980s and its Future Relevance*, Vancouver, British Columbia: Canadian Certified General Accountants' Research Foundation.

—— (1991d) 'Counting, accounting, and the input–output principle', in O.F. Graves (ed.), *The Costing Heritage*, Harrisonburg, Virginia: Academy of Accounting Historians, pp. 25–49.

Merton, R. (1973a) 'Theory of rational option pricing', *Bell Journal of Economics*, Spring: 141–82.

—— (1973b) 'An intertemporal capital asset pricing model', *Econometrica*, September: 867–87.

—— (1974) 'On the pricing of corporate debt: the risk structure of interest rates', *Journal of Finance*, 29: 449–70.

—— (1976) 'Option pricing when underlying stock returns are discontinuous', *Journal of Financial Economics*, 3: 125–44.

Mirrlees, J. (1971) 'An exploration in the theory of income taxation', *Review of Economic Studies*, April: 175–201.

—— (1976) 'The optimal structure of incentives and authority within an organization', *Bell Journal of Economics*, 7(1): 105–31.

Modigliani, F. and Miller, J. (1958) 'The cost of capital corporation finance, and the theory of investment', *American Economic Review*, June: 261–97.

——(1963) 'Corporate income taxes and the cost of capital: a correction', *American Economic Review*, June: 433–43.

Moonitz, M. (1961) *The Basic Postulates of Accounting*, Accounting Research Study No. 1, New York: American Institute of Certified Public Accountants.

Niiniluoto, I. (1981) 'The growth of theories: comments on the structuralist approach', in J. Hinitka, K. Gruender, and E. Aggazzi (eds) *Pisa Conference Proceedings 1980*, Dordrecht: Reidel, pp. 4–47.

—— (1983) 'Theories, approximations, and idealizations' *Proceedings of the 7th International Congress of Logic, Methodology, and Philosophy of Science*, vol. 3, Abstracts of section 6, pp. 4–7. Salzburg.

—— (1984) *Is Science Progressive?* Dordrecht: D. Reidel.

Ohlson, J.A. (1987) 'On the nature of income measurement: the basic results', *Contemporary Accounting Research*, Fall: 1–15.

—— (1988) 'The social value of public information in production economies', in G.A. Feltham, A. Amershi, and W.T. Ziemba (eds) *Economic Analysis of Information and Contracts*, Boston: Kluwer Academic Publishers, pp. 95–119.

—— (1990) 'A synthesis of security valuation theory and the role of dividends, cash flows, and earnings', *Contemporary Accounting Research*, Spring: 648–76. (Reprinted in Mattessich (ed.) *Accounting Research in the 1980s and its Future Relevance*, Vancouver, British Columbia: Canadian Certified General Accountants' Research Foundation, pp. 157–81.)

Ohlson, J.A. and Buckman, A.G. (1980) 'Toward a theory of financial accounting', *Journal of Finance*, May: 537–47.

Paton, W.A. (1918) 'The significance and treatment of appreciation in the accounts', in G.H. Coons (ed.) *Michigan Academy of Science, Twentieth Annual Report*, Ann Arbor, Michigan. (Reprinted in: S.A. Zeff (ed.), *Asset Appreciation, Business Income and Price-Level Accounting: 1918–1935*, New York: Arno Press, pp. 35–49.)

—— (1922) *Accounting Theory*, New York: Ronald Press.

Paton, W.A. and Littleton, A.C. (1940) *An Introduction to Corporate Accounting Standards*, Monograph No. 3, Sarasota, Florida: American Accounting Association.

Peasnell, K.V. (1978) 'Statement of accounting theory and theory acceptance: a review article', *Accounting and Business Research*, 8 Summer: 217–25.

Peasnell, K.V. and Williams, D.J. (1986) 'Ersatz academics and scholar-saints: the supply of financial accounting research', *Abacus*, 22(2): 121–35.

Putnam, H. (1980) 'Models and reality', *Journal of Symbolic Logic*, 45: 462–82.

—— (1982) *Vernunft, Wahrheit und Geschichte*, German translation by J. Schulte of: *Reason, Truth and History*, Frankfurt: Suhrkampverlag.

Russell, B. (1948) *Human Knowledge: Its Scope and Limits*, New York: Simon & Schuster.

Sanders, T.H., Hatfield, H.R. and Moore, U. (1938) *A Statement of Accounting Principles*, New York: American Institute of [Certified Public] Accountants.

Schmalenbach, E. (1919) 'Grundlagen dynamischer Bilanzlehre', *Zeitschrift für handelswissenschaftliche Forschung* (now: *Zeitschrift für betriebswirtschaftliche Forschung*), pp. 1–60, 65–101.

Schmidt, F. (1921) *Die organische Bilanz im Rahmen der Wirtschaft.* Leipzig *Die organische Tageswertbilanz* (third edition, Leipzig, 1929; unchanged reprint, Wiesbaden: Betriebswirtschaftlicher Verlag Dr Th. Gabler, 1953).

Schneider, D. (1981) *Geschichte betriebswirtschaftlicher Theorie*, Munich: R. Oldenbourg Verlag.

Seicht, G. (1970) *Die Kapitaltheoretische Bilanz und die Entwicklung der Bilanztheorien*, Berlin: Duncker & Humblot.

Sharpe, W.F. (1963) 'A simplified model for portfolio analysis', *Management Science*, January: 277–93.

—— (1964) 'Capital asset prices: a theory of market equilibrium under conditions of risk', *Journal of Finance*, September: 425–42.

Simon, H. (1951) 'A formal theory of employment relation', *Econometrica*, 19: 293–305.

Sneed, J.D. (1971) *The Logical Structure of Mathematical Physics*, Dordrecht: D. Reidel. (Second edition, 1979, Dordrecht: Reidel.)

—— (1981) 'Conventionalism in kinetic theory', *Proceedings: Second Annual International Symposium on Philosophy*, Autonomous University of Mexico.

—— (1983) 'Structuralism and scientific realism', *Erkenntnis*, 19: 345–70.

Spacek, L. (1962) 'Comments', appended to R.T. Sprouse and M. Moonitz *A Tentative Set of Broad Accounting Principles for Business Enterprises*, New York: American Institute of Certified Public Accountants, pp. 77–9.

Spence, A.M. and Zeckhauser, S. (1971) 'Insurance, information and individual action', *American Economic Review*, 61, May: 380–90.

Sprouse, R.T. and Moonitz, M. (1962) *A Tentative Set of Broad Accounting Principles for Business Enterprises*, Accounting Research Study No. 3, New York: American Institute of Certified Public Accountants.

Stamp, E. (1980) *Corporate Reporting: Its Future Evolution*, Toronto: Canadian Institute of Chartered Accountants.

Staubus, G.J. (1961) *A Theory of Accounting to Investors*, Berkeley: University of California Press.

—— (1987) 'The Dark Ages of cost accounting: the role of miscues in the literature', *Accounting Historians Journal*, Fall: 1–18.

Stegmüller, W. (1973) *Theorie und Erfahrung – Zweiter Halbband: Theorien Struktur und Theoriendynamik*, Heidelberg: Springer Verlag.

—— (1975) *Hauptströmungen der Gegenwartsphilosophie*, Stuttgart: Kroner, vol. II.

—— (1976) *The Structure and Dynamics of Theories*, Berlin/New York: Springer Verlag.

—— (1979) *The Structuralist View of Theories*, New York: Springer Verlag.

—— (1983) *Erklärung, Begründung, Kausalität*, vol. I, part G, (Studienausgabe), second revised edition, Berlin: Springer Verlag.

—— (1986) *Theorie und Erfahrung: Vol. II/Part 3 – Die Entwicklung des neuen Strukturalismus seit 1973*, Berlin: Springer Verlag.

Stegmüller, W., Balzer, W. and Spohn, W. (eds) (1982) *Philosophy of Economics*, Berlin/New York: Springer Verlag.

Sterling, R.R. (1970) *Theory of the Measurement of Enterprise Income*, Lawrence, Kansas: University Press of Kansas.

—— (1972) 'Decision-oriented financial accounting', *Accounting and Business Research*, Summer: 198–208.

Stützel, W. (1967) 'Bemerkungen zur Bilanztheorie', *Zeitschrift für Betriebswirtschaft*, 37: 314–40.

Suppe, F. (ed.) (1974) *The Structure of Scientific Theories*, Urbana: University of Illinois Press.

Toulmin, S. (1953) *The Philosophy of Science*, London: Hutchinson.

Trueblood, R.M. and Cooper, W.W. (1955) 'Research and practice in statistical applications to accounting, auditing, and management control', *Accounting Review*, 30: 221–9.

Truesdell, C. (1984) *An Idiot's Fugitive Essays on Science*, New York: Springer Verlag.

Van Seventer, A. (1975) 'Replacement value theory in modern Dutch accounting', *International Journal of Accounting Education and Research*, 1(1), Autumn: 67–94.

Watts, R.L. and Zimmerman, J.L. (1978) 'Towards a positive theory of the determination of accounting standards', *Accounting Review*, January: 112–34. (Reprinted in R. Mattessich (ed.) *Modern Accounting Research: History, Survey and Guide*, Vancouver, British Columbia: Canadian Certified General Accountants' Research Foundation, pp. 81–102.)

—— (1979) 'The demand for and the supply of accounting theories: the market for excuses', *Accounting Review*, April: 273–305. (Reprinted in R. Mattessich (ed.) *Modern Accounting Research: History, Survey and Guide*, Vancouver, British Columbia: Canadian Certified General Accountants' Research Foundation, pp. 103–29.)

Wells, M.C. (1976) 'A revolution in accounting thought?', *Accounting Review*, 51, July: 471–82. (Reprinted in R. Mattessich (ed.) *Modern Accounting Research: History, Survey and Guide*, Vancouver, British Columbia: Canadian Certified General Accountants' Research Foundation, pp. 47–57.)

Willett, R.J. (1987) 'An axiomatic theory of accounting measurement', *Accounting and Business Research*, Spring: 155–71.

Williams, T.H. and Griffin, C.H. (1964) *The Mathematical Dimension of Accounting*, Cincinnati: South-Western Publishing Co.

9 Achieving scientific knowledge: the rationality of scientific method

R. Murray Lindsay

It was with great anticipation that I left Canada in the fall of 1985 to pursue a PhD at the University of Lancaster under the tutelage of Professor Edward Stamp (and David Otley). Unfortunately, fate was unkind: just a few short months after my arrival Professor Stamp passed away.

In spite of our brief acquaintance, I am quite certain that Professor Stamp would approve of the spirit of this chapter. Shortly before he died, I had a meeting with him to discuss my thesis topic. I told him of my serious reservations about the way management accounting research was being conducted. He listened patiently, and after some reflection began to tell me how the life of a critic was a difficult road to follow. However, he encouraged me to pursue the topic if I felt able to make a contribution; it was, he said, my duty. I hope this chapter discharges some of that duty.

INTRODUCTION

> It is criticism that, recognizing no position as final, and refusing to bind itself by the shallow shibboleths of any sect or school, creates that serene philosophic temper which loves truth for its own sake, and loves it not less because it is unattainable.
>
> (Oscar Wilde, cited in Radnitzky and Bartley 1987: 279)

Over the last decade numerous articles have emphasized the methods of the humanities (i.e. 'qualitative' models) and increased doubts as to the appropriateness of the 'natural scientific' model (essentially the use of inferential statistical procedures based on 'objectively' obtained data) in organizational research (e.g. Mintzberg 1979, Colville 1981, Hopwood 1983, Tomkins and Groves 1983, Kaplan 1984, 1986). Although one can share in the concern for the generally poor rate of progress in behavioural accounting (see Colville 1981) which, undoubtedly, has motivated many to adopt such positions, the switch from quantitative to qualitative research methods is in itself unlikely to improve matters greatly.

Three reasons underlie this gloomy prognosis. First, research practices in accounting currently operate within the philosophical context or meta-methodology[1] of (neo)-justificationism, namely the doctrine of establishing knowledge claims as true (or probably true), secured on the basis of some infallible *authority*. Until accounting researchers break free from the justificationist shackles guiding their research practices, little if any (real) progress is envisaged.[2] Second, this meta-methodology is antithetical to an appreciation of the essence of the scientific approach, the consequence of which is that researchers adopt vulgarized conceptions of science and continually (mis)place their faith in obtaining *the* method which will deliver them instant, meaningful results.[3] Statistical thinking and practice in the social sciences provides a good example of this point (Acree 1978, Gigerenzer *et al.* 1989):

> Leaders of influential schools in the social sciences have sincerely believed that real science is done by putting masses of quantitative data through a statistical sausage-machine, and then observing the Laws which emerge. From such caricatures of the process of scientific inquiry are derived criteria of adequacy which enforce an apparently rigorous procedure of research, but whose results can but rarely escape vacuity.
>
> (Ravetz 1971: 158)

Third, some 'informed' students of research method, in (correctly) recognizing that scientific theories cannot be conclusively proved or disproved, have altogether given up the idea that science is a rational activity. For them, the choice between theories is ultimately determined by the subjective values and wishes of individual scientists. Pursued to its logical conclusion, this relativist account of science implies that our research conclusions are inherently non-objective. The following passage by Kirk and Miller in a book entitled *Reliability and Validity in Qualitative Research* aptly expresses the writer's concern with this position:

> In response to the propensity of so many nonqualitative research traditions to use such hidden positivist assumptions, some social scientists have tended to overreact by stressing the possibility of alternative interpretations of everything to the exclusion of any effort to choose among them. This extreme relativism ignores the

> other side of objectivity. . . . It ignores the important distinction between knowledge and opinion, and results in everyone having a separate insight that cannot be reconciled with anyone else's.
>
> (Kirk and Miller 1986: 15)

This chapter represents a response to Christenson's (1983: 2–3) call for accounting researchers to be more self-conscious about methodology. Its aim is to provide accounting researchers with an in-depth examination of the foundations of methodology and a more appropriate view of the development of scientific knowledge.

The chapter proceeds in the following manner. In the section 'The justificationist quest for a theory of rationality' the justificationist 'solution' to the 'rationality problem' in science is examined. This examination is important because, even though justificationism has been philosophically refuted, its inductivist variant still remains to retain a stranglehold on accounting research practices. Following this, a *non*-justificational meta-methodological theory of knowledge, based on Popper's 'critical rationalism', is discussed in the section 'The rationality of scientific method'. The aim here is to argue that the *rationality* of scientific claims derives from the indefatigable use of *criticism*, not from providing positive, justifying reasons for their support.

The section 'The nature and production of scientific knowledge' comprises the bulk of the chapter. This analysis is fully consistent with the fact that: observation is theory impregnated and does not deal with a fixed, objective reality (Hanson 1958, Kuhn 1970, Chalmers 1982); theory appraisal involves value judgments (Ravetz 1971, Howard 1985); scientific conclusions are inherently fallible, although their acceptance is not necessarily irrational or relativistic (Popper 1963, Phillips 1987); and that the practice of successful science does not depend on finding some single and ideal algorithm or method (Ravetz 1971, Hines 1988: 660–1). All of these points, of course, contradict the inductivist view of science which underlies so much accounting research (Chua 1986).

The lessons obtained from this examination are twofold. First, scientific facts are complex intellectual constructions which exhibit the three attributes (or tests) of (a) 'significance' (i.e. they are considered important enough by other members of the scientific community to warrant continued research), (b) 'stability' (i.e. empirical reproducibility), and (c) 'invariance' (i.e. portability from one research programme to others). Second, scientific knowledge does not derive from the single efforts of isolated scientists, but rather stems from the *social* process of criticism or testing administered by the scientific community.

In the fifth section 'The lack of a critical attitude in the social sciences' (pp. 239–40) it is argued that the social sciences generally, and accounting research in particular, do not appear to be operating under a critical and fallibilist meta-methodology. Conclusions, and implications for accounting research strategy and policy, follow in the last section (pp. 242–5).

THE JUSTIFICATIONIST QUEST FOR A THEORY OF RATIONALITY

> It seems extraordinary that so many people who like to think of themselves as plain, down-to-earth, practical men should dismiss the critical examination of models as an unpractical activity. If you don't drag out into the light the pre-suppositions of your thinking you remain simply the prisoner of whatever the reigning authority in the matter at issue happens to be. Thus the model of your age, or the model of your day, becomes your cage without you even realizing it.
>
> (Magee 1979)

The quest for rationality in science

Walter Weimer (1979: 3) writes that one can view the historical development of the philosophy of science as the (unsuccessful) quest for a theory of rationality that would justify science as being a legitimate source of knowledge (cf. Bartley 1964, 1982b: 138, 148, Popper 1963: 3–32, Suppe 1977: 652, 716). As Rudolf Carnap (1967: xvii), a leading member of the Vienna Circle, expressed this thesis: 'It must be possible to give a rational foundation for each scientific thesis'.

Epistemologies were developed in response to a need to answer one fundamental question: what is the nature and source of the *ultimate authority* which can justify scientific inference as a legitimate source of knowledge? The force underlying this search was compelling. Failure to find an answer would make it irrational to believe that science holds a privileged status over other competing sources of belief (e.g. astrology, religion, voodoo, etc.) in *guaranteeing* the validity of its claims. Scientific imperialism would therefore cease. Scientific knowledge would be left without a rational foundation, and belief in it, as with all other competing claims to knowledge, would become nothing more than irrational commitment (Bartley 1964:

5–7); 1982b: 134–5). To use Bertrand Russell's (1961: 646) colourful phrase, there would be 'no intellectual difference between sanity and insanity'.

Historically, justificationism sought *the* ultimate source of knowledge in the intellectual intuition of clear and distinct ideas or in sense experience. In both variants, knowledge was fused with *proof* and *authority* — the cardinal tenets of justificationism (Bartley 1964, 1982b). According to the justificationist account, to accept a proposition in science is to accept it as proven; and to reject a proposition is to reject it as provenly false. After the recognition of the untenability of apodictic knowledge, the later switch to neo-justificationism required propositions that were only (probably) highly probable. Inductivism, with its focus on the accumulation of objective, value-free facts derived from sense experience, has increasingly become the ruling methodology since the seventeenth century (see Chalmers 1982).

The justificationist stranglehold

The inductivist methodology, in either its classical or neo-classical (probabilistic) forms, was the incumbent philosophy of science until the 1960s. Today, inductivism, as a theory of knowledge, belongs to the history of the philosophy of science (Suppe 1977: 632, Christensen 1983: 7). The relinquishment of inductivism by philosophers is most clearly explained in terms of its faulty justificationist underpinning. As Chalmers (1982: xvi), Kuhn (1970), Maxwell (1975), Lakatos (1970: 92–5), Popper (1959: 29–30, 1963: vii, 3–30), and Weimer (1979) argue (to name a few of the many philosophers advocating non-justificationist meta-methodologies), no ultimate sources of knowledge exist which allow scientific theories to be proven true (or even probably true; see Salmon 1967: 132): any attempt at justifying statements will lead either to infinite regress or apriorism. As Bartley explains, the *limits of rationality* preclude any other view:

> Any view may be challenged by questions such as 'How do you know?', 'Give me a reason', or 'Prove it!'. When such challenges are accepted by citing further reasons that justify those under challenge, these may be questioned in turn. And so on forever. Yet if the burden of justification is perpetually shifted to a higher-order reason or authority, the contention originally questioned is never effectively defended. One may as well never have begun the defense: an infinite regress is created. To justify the original

> conclusion, one must eventually stop at something not open to question *for which one does not and need not provide justificatory reasons*. Such a thing – e.g. a standard, criterion, authority, basic presupposition, framework, way of life – would mark the halting point for rational discussion, the limit of rationality.
>
> (Bartley 1987a: 207–8; emphasis in original)

In short, truth is above human authority (Popper 1963: 27, 29). Human knowledge will *always* be ultimately unjustified and unjustifiable (in the philosophical sense of being proven or probable) (Miller 1987: 345). Consequently, if there is any rationality that attaches to scientific claims, it is not of the justificationist variety.

However this may be, the most widely accepted conception of science in the social sciences still considers the inductivistic methodology, including its implicit justificationist meta-methodology, to be correct for science (Weimer 1979, Bartley 1982a: 260, Colville 1981, Birnberg and Shields 1989: 55).[4] Moreover, even though justificationism has been philosophically refuted, the justificationist stranglehold remains and 'plays a central role in modern and contemporary discussions of epistemology' (Suppe 1977: 717). As Grover Maxwell (1975: 112) explains, despite the fact that most contemporary philosophers and methodologists accept the arguments against justificationism, it seems that many 'proceed to forget, ignore, or repress some of them at crucial junctures in the development of their own "solutions"' to the rationality problem. Indeed, Bartley, who has studied the issue of rationality in some depth, goes so far as to suggest that justificationism – with its focus on true belief – *is* the praxis of western philosophies:

> Most western philosophies – philosophies of science as much as philosophies of religion – sponsor *justificationist metacontexts of true belief*. They are concerned with how to justify, verify, confirm, make firmer, strengthen, validate, vindicate, make certain, show to be certain, make acceptable, probabilify, cause to survive, defend, particular contexts and positions.
>
> (Bartley 1982b: 128; second emphasis removed)

Conclusion

Popper denies that we must continue to be, in principle, imprisoned by these same (justificationist) prison walls. Although we can never, *in toto*, escape from our conceptual prisons, Popper writes (1983: 16ff.) that we can escape the old walls for newer and perhaps wider confines by recognizing or becoming aware of the prison walls that bind us, i.e. our language, assumptions, and points of view; for our imprisonment largely consists in our intellectual blindness to the prison walls. The aim of this section has been to provide such an awareness. As Popper (1963: 122) notes, before we can criticize a tradition and possibly reject it, we have to know of and to understand the tradition.[5]

The next section, based on Karl Popper's *non*-justificationist meta-methodology, provides a replacement framework. Popper's work represents the first non-justificationist philosophy of criticism in the history of science (Bartley 1964: 23, Weimer 1979). He has written extensively and critically on the (neo)-justificationist theory of rationality in the course of presenting his own philosophy; indeed, his analysis of the justificationist meta-methodology provides one of the main pillars of his philosophy (Lakatos 1968: 318n). This point is noted because, although Popper's falsificationist methodology has been severely criticized (e.g. Hines 1988), his non-justificationist theory of rationality remains a comparatively little explored area despite its importance to his philosophy (Bartley 1982b: 122).

THE RATIONALITY OF SCIENTIFIC METHOD

> So my answer to the questions 'How do you know? What is the source or the basis of your assertion? What observations have led you to it?' would be: 'I do *not* know: my assertion was merely a guess. Never mind the source. . . . But if you are interested in the problem which I tried to solve by my tentative assertion, you may help me by criticizing it as severely as you can . . . .'
>
> (Popper 1963: p. 27)

The gem in Popper's philosophy lies in his comprehension that rationality in science cannot consist in justifying theories as true or probably true but rather that a solution to the problem of rationality requires a reformulation of the problem – an escape, if you like, from our justificationist prison walls. Since truth is beyond human authority, Popper realized that the best we can do is to weed out false ideas, and this requires replacing the question of the sources of knowledge by an entirely different question: 'How can we hope to detect and eliminate error' (Popper 1963: 25). His answer is 'by criticizing our theories' (p. 26). In a sentence then, for Popper 'knowledge is not provable, but is improvable, improvable through criticism' (Watkins 1978: 4).

Rationality is therefore located in criticism and not in justification (Bartley 1987a, cf. Popper 1959: 16). In other words, *critical reasons*, rather than positive, justifying reasons, underlie our comparative *preference* for theories. Popper's position on this matter has been given as follows:

> From a rational point of view we should not 'rely' on any theory, for no theory has been shown to be true, or can be shown to be true. . . . But we should *prefer* as basis for action the best-tested theory.
>
> In spite of the 'rationality' of choosing the best-tested theory as a basis of action, this choice is *not* 'rational' in the sense that it is based upon *good reasons* for expecting that it will in practice be a successful choice: *there can be no good reasons* in this sense, and this is precisely Hume's result.
>
> (Popper 1979: 21–2, emphasis in original)

In principle, the possibility of criticism is unlimited (i.e. our critical reasons are also open to criticism).[6] However, there is no infinite regress because the aim or pretence of justifying has been abandoned (Bartley 1964: 28–9, 1987a); we simply stop when we cannot offer any more responsible criticism, at least for the time being. To quote Popper:

> The empirical basis of objective science has thus nothing 'absolute' about it. Science does not rest upon solid bedrock. The bold structure of its theories rises, as it were, above a swamp. It is like a building erected on piles. The piles are driven down from above into the swamp, but not down to any natural or 'given' base; and if we stop driving the piles deeper, it is not because we have reached firm ground. We simply stop when we are satisfied that the piles are firm enough to carry the structure, at least for the time being.
>
> (Popper 1959: 111)

It is this point that lies at the heart of the difference between justificatory and critical frameworks (Popper 1983: 29).

As Bartley (1964: 22–4, 1987a) tells it, Popper's innovation lies in *un*fusing the idea of criticism from the idea of justification and abandoning the latter entirely. Under justificationist philosophies of criticism, to criticize a view is to see whether it can be justified by some rational criterion or authority. On the other hand, Popper's non-justificationist philosophy of criticism separates the two notions and treats criticism as an *alternative* to justification. This point is crucial because the simplicity of Popper's solution has caused many to miss its full significance and novelty,[7] and has led to unwarranted criticism of his falsificationist methodology.[8]

Based on the foregoing, science's rationality problem is now capable of solution. Simply put, scientific statements derive their rationality by virtue of the scientific community operating under the 'critical attitude' (cf. Popper 1959: 16), namely engaging in sincere attempts to reduce error through the willingness and commitment to submit all ideas, institutions, traditions and theories to critical examination and appraisal because of the recognition that *all* viewpoints are limited and fallible (Bartley 1982b: 123). It is this feature of science that provides scientific statements with their *objectivity* (cf. Popper 1959: 44n*1) and it is this, Popper has argued, that demarcates science from non-science:

> The distinction between the dogmatic and critical thinking, or the dogmatic and the critical attitude, brings us right back to our central problem [of demarcation]. For the dogmatic attitude is clearly related to the tendency to *verify* our laws and schemata by seeking to apply them and to confirm them, even to the point of neglecting refutations, whereas the critical attitude is one of readiness to change them – to test them; to refute them; to *falsify* them, if possible. This suggests that we may identify the critical attitude with the scientific attitude, and the dogmatic attitude with the one which we have described as pseudo–scientific.[9]
>
> (Popper 1963: 50; emphasis in original)

Moreover, and perhaps more important, criticism underlies the *growth* of scientific knowledge:[10]

> Criticism of our conjectures is of decisive importance: by bringing out our mistakes it makes us understand the difficulties of the problem which we are trying to solve. This is how we become better acquainted with our problem, and able to propose more mature solutions.
>
> (Popper 1963: vii)

Perhaps it should be noted that Popper does not stand alone in this characterization of scientific method. The eminent orthodox philosopher of science, Ernest Nagel, concurs with Popper on this point. For Nagel (1961: 13), as for Popper, 'the practice of scientific method is the persistent critique of arguments'. In an article entitled the 'Nature and aim of science', Nagel highlights the fact that:

> It is of primary importance . . . to regard [scientific] explanatory systems, not as a body of fixed and indubitable conclusions, but rather as the corrigible products of a continuing process of inquiry that involves the *indefatigable use of a distinctive intellectual method of criticism*. It is this logical method which is the special glory of modern science as well as the spiritual foundation of every genuinely liberal civilization. There are no reasonable alternatives to it for arriving at responsibly supported conclusions about the world men inhabit and men's place in it.
>
> (Nagel 1967: 13; emphasis added)

The 'organized skepticism' of David Krathwohl (1985: 21), former president of the American Educational Research Association, also succinctly describes Popper's notion of the critical attitude underlying the 'method' and rationality of science. He writes:

> Organized skepticism is a basic norm that makes science a unique source of knowledge. It is the responsibility of the community of scientists to be skeptical of each new knowledge claim, to test it, and to try to think of reasons that the claim might be false – to think of alternative explanations that might be plausible as the one advanced. This challenge to new knowledge is *sought* in science rather than avoided as it is in other methods.
>
> (Krathwohl as cited in Phillips 1987: 63–4)

Unfortunately, the simplicity and elegance of Popper's result appears to have impaired its lessons for epistemology. For example, because of a confusion between methodology (i.e. the logical characterization of its methods) and meta-methodology (i.e. the philosophical theory dealing with how and why a methodology is held) science is typically distinguished from non-science by its empirical method, which is essentially inductive, proceeding from observation or experiment. As Morris Cohen (1931: 115) put it: 'Scientific method is popularly associated with the cult of induction'. But, although common (see Ravetz 1971, Colville 1981, Bartley 1982a), this viewpoint is a patently false characterization of the scientific method. The unquestionable importance of observation and experiment does not stem from their authority to *justify* claims to know, but rather because they represent a manifestation of the critical attitude – the commitment to *test* all claims (cf. Popper 1963: 128, 197, Magee 1971: 73, Bartley 1982b: 127).

THE NATURE AND PRODUCTION OF SCIENTIFIC KNOWLEDGE

The previous analysis, general in its orientation, has indicated that the essence of science is its critical attitude (a meta-methodology). None the less, it would be misleading not to acknowledge the significance of methodological precepts in science (although it is important to appreciate that their role is prophylactic and not heuristic).

The aim of this section is to provide a more detailed account of the nature and production of scientific knowledge and, in so doing, indicate how methodology and the critical attitude enter into the development of scientific knowledge. This discussion is based upon Ravetz's *Scientific Knowledge and its Social Problems*. The reader is forewarned that Ravetz's depth and complexity of argument cannot possibly be recast here and what follows is necessarily a condensed account. (Unless otherwise noted, page references which follow are to that, 1971, book.)

The nature of criteria of adequacy

If we accept the fact that it is impossible to prove or probabilify a single result in science, then we arrive at two results of enormous importance. First, far from examining conclusions for their truth or probable truth, we can only impose criteria for judging their *adequacy*. It is only in this context that methodological considerations validly surface. Second, the difference between mature and immature disciplines does not rest in the logical aspects of their arguments and conclusions, but in the particular circumstances of their development (p. 155). Specifically, the mature disciplines have *developed*, throughout the centuries, criteria of adequacy (methodology) to guard against pitfalls which can vitiate the conclusions obtained. This subsection will examine the nature of criteria of adequacy. There are seven points to this examination.

First, the criteria of adequacy associated with a discipline are directly relevant to the strength that the discipline attains (pp. 155–6). Criteria of adequacy signpost pitfalls that lurk in every stage of obtaining a scientific conclusion. They provide a warning that unless the work is done rigorously, in a particular way, conclusions are problematic. Consequently, progress will only occur when a discipline's criteria of adequacy do their job well. As Ravetz puts it: 'The failure of facts to be achieved is an effect of undetected pitfalls' (p. 156).

Second, it is scientists who erect criteria of adequacy – not philosophical analyses. As the noted physicist Max Born writes:

> I believe that there is no philosophical highroad in science, with epistemological [methodological] signposts. No, we are in a jungle and find our way by trial and error, building our road *behind* us as we proceed. We do not *find* signposts at crossroads, but our own scouts *erect* them, to help the rest.
>
> (Born 1943: 44, cited in Nash 1963: 168)

Third, erecting signposts, and therefore obtaining facts, takes time: there are no short cuts! Inevitably, textbooks vulgarize rational reconstructions of important scientific discoveries (see pp. 203–8). This tends to disguise the fact that today's mature sciences have benefited enormously from the dismal failures of the work of earlier generations of scientists:

> The stumbling way in which even the ablest of the scientists in every generation have had to fight through thickets of erroneous observations, misleading generalizations, inadequate formulations, and unconscious prejudice is rarely appreciated by those who obtain their scientific knowledge from textbooks. It is largely neglected by those expounders of the alleged scientific method who are fascinated by the logical rather than the psychological aspects of experimental investigations.
>
> (Conant 1951: 44, cited in Nash 1963: 157)

In other words, the close-up perspective of science reveals that progress is 'sporadic, laborious, [and] tortuous' (Nash 1963: 157).

Fourth, a discipline's criteria of adequacy are not static: they can change over time (Hacking 1981: 142–3), and indeed they must change. A deep innovation in science necessarily involves an innovation in methods and the development of new criteria of adequacy to circumvent the pitfalls associated with these new methods (pp. 172, 266).

Fifth, criteria of adequacy are not infallible: there is no test to establish their validity. Their acceptance is based on the experience of the scientific community with respect to the performance of the criteria in providing for stable (i.e. repeatable) conclusions in an extensive class of inquiries (cf. Nagel 1939: 192).

Sixth, each area of inquiry needs to have a methodology tailored to its own specific circumstances. This is because criteria of adequacy must be 'intimately related to the characteristic pitfalls of the problems investigated in the field; and these will be very particular to it, in its objects of inquiry, its sources of data, its tools, and its patterns of argument' (Ravetz 1971: 157). The practice of science is essentially a skill based on 'craft' knowledge: a personal, tacit knowledge built up through the long-term experience of working and struggling with the objects of inquiry (Polanyi 1962, Ravetz 1971). It is this point about methodology that legitimates pleas for the use of qualitative research methods in accounting research, and not some false characterization of science which we have attempted to ape in the past.

Finally, it would be misleading not to note the subordinate role that methodology plays to ideas in the growth of scientific knowledge. Methodology tell us how to criticize hypotheses. It does not, of course, tell us how to arrive at them (Andreski 1972: 108; Nagel 1961: 12).

The development of scientific knowledge

This discussion leads us to the following paradox: scientific knowledge results from a process (including its methodology) which is not 'scientific' in character (pp. 146, 180). As Ravetz describes it: 'the certainty and objectivity of scientific knowledge [dissolve into] a set of intuitive judgments based on principles which frequently cannot even be made explicit, let alone defended or tested' (p. 155).[11] The key to understanding this paradox is that we must eradicate ourselves from the 'cumulative' or building-block conception of science. While history provides abundant evidence to suggest that the knowledge produced in the mature sciences can be described as cumulative (in some sense of the word), progressive, impersonal and, to some extent, permanent, this observation must be seen as the result of a complex and ever-changing process of the social activity of science which has little, if anything, in common with the widely-held 'cumulative' conception of science. Specifically, facts do not occur as a consequence of one person's investigation, but instead are the result of the *social* phase of 'testing' the solution through its use over an *extended* period of time. The remainder of this subsection will examine this point.

Scientific facts are not immutable. They are *intellectually constructed assertions* about the objects of inquiry which result from viewing the world through a particular perspective (in Kuhn's terms, through a 'disciplinary matrix' (Suppe 1977: 149)). Hence, their relation to the external world is neither immediate nor certain (Kuhn 1970, Ravetz 1971: 202). However, contrary to what some might argue, this result need not be interpreted as suggesting that acquiring genuine knowledge is impossible. As Ravetz explains: once 'we appreciate that each object of scientific inquiry carries with it a complex burden of meaning, *derived from its history of use and adaptation*, the way is open for showing how genuine knowledge of the external world is possible' (p. 202, emphasis added). The essence of Ravetz's argument for understanding the nature and production of scientific knowledge appears in the italicized portion of this quotation. This will now be considered.

On Ravetz's account, a scientific fact is characterized by three defining properties. First, a published research report must pass the research community's 'test of significance' in order for it to take on a life of its own (pp. 183, 188):

> The automatic, communal test of value yields a negative result when a particular paper happens to be of interest to absolutely no one. As a candidate for the status of scientific knowledge, it has then been killed. It may continue its career in a political function, as an entry in the scientist's list of publications, but as a contribution to the advancement of knowledge it has died, precisely because it is unwept, unhonored, and unsung.
>
> (Ravetz 1971: 184)

This test of value is of crucial importance in that a field's health and future prospects depend on it (p. 159). In the main, it addresses whether the work will or does advance knowledge of the discipline's objects of inquiry, either directly or through suggested descendant-problems (p. 162). Clearly this consideration involves a *value judgement* which is both tacit in nature and fallible.

Second, 'solutions' must be capable of reproduction and use by others (p. 188) – otherwise they are useless for subsequent work. Not surprisingly, this common-sense requirement is fully appreciated in mature sciences (but see Collins 1985). For example, Popper writes of the standard procedure, one of attitude it might be said, whereby no physicist would offer for publication a finding he could not repeat:

> We do not take even our own observations quite seriously, or accept them as scientific observation, until we have repeated and tested them. Only by such repetitions can we convince ourselves that we are not dealing with a mere isolated 'coincidence'. . . . Every experimental physicist knows those surprising and inexplicable apparent 'effects' which in his laboratory can perhaps even be reproduced for some time, but which finally disappear without

> trace. Of course no physicist would say in such a case that he had made a scientific discovery. . . . No serious physicist would offer for publication, as a scientific discovery, any such 'occult effect', as I propose to call it – one for whose reproduction he could give no instructions. The 'discovery' would be only too soon rejected as chimerical, simply because attempts to test it would lead to negative results.[12]
>
> (Popper 1959: 45)

Third, and most important of all to our discussion, results must be 'invariant'. Because our scientific understanding of the world is achieved through the creation of complex intellectual constructions, it is necessary that a result can be used in applications other than those peculiar to its own construction or invention; in particular, that it can live on through its descendants:

> When a solved problem has been presented to the community, and new work is done on its basis, then the objects of investigation will necessarily change, sometimes only slightly, but sometimes drastically. In a retrospect on the original problem, even after a brief period of development, its argument will be seen as concerning objects which no longer exist. There is then the question of whether it can be translated or recast so as to relate to the newer objects descended from the original ones, and still be an adequate foundation for a conclusion. If not, then the original conclusion is rejected as dealing with non-objects, or ascribing false properties to real objects. But if such a translation or recasting is possible, then the original solved problem is seen to have contained some element which is invariant with respect to the changes in the objects of investigation.
>
> (Ravetz 1971: 189)

This requirement recognizes that the theory-dependence of observation results in many 'solutions' being bound too closely to the circumstances of their production and, hence, illusory.

Based on this examination it is now possible to outline the nature of how scientific knowledge comes to be. Central to Ravetz's analysis is the idea that attaining knowledge is inextricably linked to the growth of scientific knowledge, a theme encountered throughout contemporary philosophy of science (see Suppe 1977).

To survive as an object of interest, a fact must result from a problem of novelty or depth which acts as a heuristic and as a challenge to further work (p. 233), for 'a problem known to be solved is a dead problem' (p. 192; cf. Popper 1963: 240). This is because 'facts stay alive only as long as they are useful in new contexts' (p. 209) or in providing materials for further investigations (p. 305). As Ravetz (p. 199) puts it: 'An interesting fact presents a challenge: if it is in conflict with other accepted results, one or the other must be rejected or modified; and if it promises further advances, it calls for its own improvement' through its extension.[13] Consequently, by the defining requirement of their survival, facts underlie the growth and not merely the retention of knowledge.

Thus we see that in order for facts to acquire the status of scientific knowledge they must remain alive. This can only occur if they survive through their progeny by virtue of some of their strands remaining invariant. It is this property of invariance that explains how scientific knowledge develops its tough fabric, so resistant to trivial refutations and simple revolutions (p. 192): certain strands of a particular fact have had to survive the processes of selection, testing, and transformation of content and function, characteristic of the evolutionary nature of scientific knowledge. Furthermore, it is in this sense, and only in this sense, that science may be said to be cumulative. To recapitulate:

> Such, then, is the character of a unit of scientific knowledge. It may appear to be a very untidy and also imperfect sort of thing to enjoy such a status. But the processes which have operated to create this family have at the same time eliminated a host of competitors. The particular fact survives only because it is capable of breeding hardy descendants, who find niches in so many areas of science that the continuous displacement of problems and whole fields, while modifying its members, do not destroy the integrity of the family as a whole. To reduce the body of scientific knowledge to such elements may seem to dissolve its unity, and indeed to destroy its reality, leaving only a heap of pragmatically justified tools. But the destruction is only of certain ideal knowledge: one which demands that for it to be real, it must be clear, distinct, and eternal. Such knowledge of the external world may exist in the mind of God; but it is clearly beyond the capacity of human beings, who derive their knowledge of the external world ultimately from particular interactions with it, observed through the senses. That which we can recognize as scientific knowledge has achieved its state only by surviving a long series of ruthless selections, and of drastic changes in the meaning of its objects.
>
> (Ravetz 1971: 234–5)

In this way we come to resolve the paradox of knowledge. Although in the short-run scientific inquiry is very subjective, personal, and highly fallible, scientific knowledge obtains its 'tough fabric' by virtue of the complex social processes that act upon results over time to transform them into something that exceeds anything that could be achieved by a single effort (p. 236). In this regard, Lakatos (1970: 174) is surely correct in stating that 'Minerva's owl flies [only] at dusk'.

The role of the critical attitude in the production of scientific knowledge

All that remains is to clarify the role of the critical attitude in the production of scientific knowledge.

We have seen that facts do not occur as a consequence of one person's investigation, but instead are the result of the social phase of 'testing' the solution (i.e. for 'significance', 'stability' and 'invariance') through its use over an extended period of time. This is the commonly considered aspect of the critical attitude – the criticism administered by the collective effort of the scientific community. However, Ravetz also identifies individual self-criticism as an additional component of the critical attitude.

Scientific work is a craft skill whose quality cannot be routinely appraised. Although scientific work is judged by referees in relation to the discipline's criteria of adequacy, in the final analysis it is easy to find ways of formally satisfying such tests while producing vacuous results. Consequently, only the scientists themselves are in a place to judge the adequacy of the work performed, for only they, through their intimacy with their materials, can assess their quality.

This second component can therefore be described as the possession of an attitude, whereby scientists are willing to submit their materials, for example, methods, evidence, argument and conclusions, to the harshest test possible – one's own criticism. It manifests itself through an overriding commitment to the quality and trustworthiness of the work performed. It is the embodiment of the ethic which is based on the 'uncompromising, indefatigable pursuit of truth' (Born 1963).

It would, of course, be extremely naive to think that all scientists, by the very fact of being a scientist, are paragons of virtue. Clearly this is not so for the simple reason of their humanity. Moreover, while self-criticism is extremely important and desirable, it is limited by our unconscious biases which must inevitably occur simply as a result of pursuing a matter in a certain way (see Nagel's comments below). Put succinctly: what we see is what we don't see. However, forces at the level of the scientific community counteract such limitations in individual self-criticism. Commensurate with our analysis of knowledge, objectivity in science does not result from the individual scientist attempting to be 'objective' – this is not only impossible (Cohen 1931: 81, Nagel 1961), it may even be harmful to science (see Popper 1963: 312n, 1975: 245ff., Lakatos 1970). Rather, scientific objectivity is closely bound up with the *social* aspect of the 'scientific method', with the fact that all statements can be inter-subjectively tested and scrutinised (Popper 1959: 44–5).

The following passage by Nagel explains how scientific objectivity comes to be, even though all scientists operate under various forms of bias:

> For the most part we are unaware of many assumptions that enter into our analyses and actions, so that despite resolute efforts to make our preconceptions explicit some decisive ones may not even occur to us. But in any event, the difficulties generated for scientific inquiry by unconscious bias and tacit value orientations are rarely overcome by devout resolutions to eliminate bias. They are usually overcome, often only gradually, through the self-corrective mechanisms of science as a social enterprise. For modern science encourages the invention, the mutual exchange, and the free but responsible criticisms of ideas; it welcomes competition in the quest for knowledge between independent investigators, even when their intellectual orientations are different; and it progressively diminishes the effects of bias by retaining only those proposed conclusions of its inquiries that survive critical examination by an indefinitely large community of students, whatever be their value preferences or doctrinal commitments.
>
> (Nagel 1961: 489–90)

We may therefore state that while individual self-criticism is highly desirable, it is not indispensable, providing that the critical attitude operates at the level of the scientific community (cf. Popper 1975: 239–40).

Today, however, scientists find themselves operating within an environment in which they must publish or perish. Moreover, it is also an environment where philosophy and religion no longer dominate the thinking of scientists; instead, we find that money and power often provide the overwhelming source of inspiration for many individuals. Both money and power may now be obtained through the practice of 'successful' science, and 'success' tends to be defined in terms of the quantity rather than the quality of publications.[14] It is therefore not surprising to find a growing number of reports which argue that the critical attitude is being totally abandoned, let alone compromised.[15] One can only hope that this does not apply to all the members of a particular field, particularly to the leadership which is responsible for defining and applying the professional ethic (p. 303); for if it does, then 'the outlook for science is grim' (p. 311). Ravetz explains the problem in more detail:

> Reforming a diseased field, or arresting the incipient decline of a healthy one, is a task of great delicacy. It requires a sense of integrity, and a commitment to good work, among a significant section of the members of the field; and committed leaders with scientific ability and political skill. No quantity of published reports, nor even an apparatus of institutional structures, can do anything to maintain or restore the health of a field in the absence of this essential ethical element operating through the interpersonal channel of communication.
>
> (Ravetz 1971: 179)

THE LACK OF A CRITICAL ATTITUDE IN THE SOCIAL SCIENCES

It is the writer's contention that the social sciences are not operating within the requisite critical attitude. Not only do we find journals inundated with pointless publications (Andreski 1972), we also find that the social sciences are fixated with finding *the* method which will snatch them from their obscurity and immaturity and deliver them authenticity (Ravetz 1971, Bartley 1982a: 260). The recent calls for qualitative research methods may be seen as another indication of this point.

The lack of a critical attitude is well illustrated in the following passage by the economic methodologist, Mark Blaug (1976: 173). He writes: 'Much empirical work in economics is like "playing tennis with the net down": instead of attempting to refute testable predictions, economists spend much of their time showing that the real world bears out their predictions, thus replacing falsification, which is difficult, with confirmation which is easy'.[16] In his follow-up comment to this citation by Blaug, Charles Christenson (1983: 19), in criticizing Watts and Zimmerman's highly influential 'positive accounting theory' programme, writes that 'the work of the Rochester School is certainly no exception to this "general trend"'. Blaug's view finds general support in the numerous practices which are antithetical to the critical attitude (e.g. Lakatos 1970: 176n, Meehl 1967, 1978, 1986, Greenwald 1975, Burgstahler 1987).

However, perhaps the most telling indication of the situation in accounting is provided by David Burgstahler's article in *The Accounting Review*. In choosing a research project Burgstahler argues that the researcher will choose the project which maximizes expected utility. In the course of his analysis Burgstahler notes that:

> Under some circumstances, researchers could also have a high utility for rejecting a true hypothesis. For example, researchers may have a high utility for publishing [statistically] significant, but incorrect, results if subsequent results which contradict the original results are not likely to be published until after some decision affected by publication (e.g. tenure) has been made. Alternatively, for very costly tests, there may be little chance that a replication contradicting the results will ever be conducted and published to reveal an error. Even if subsequent tests reveal that the [null] hypothesis is true, the impact on the original researcher's reputation and wealth may be small as long as there is no evidence of deceit or incompetence.
>
> (Burgstahler 1987: 212)

Two points may be noted from this quotation. First, notice how the ethical component of the critical attitude – the 'uncompromising, indefatigable pursuit of truth' – is completely missing in this description. The name of the game is simply publication and the rewards that publication brings; it is not about creating knowledge, nor about producing quality in one's work, nor about taking pride in one's work. As Burgstahler states: 'the utility of each state/outcome combination depends primarily on the product of the reward to publication and the probability of publication' (Burgstahler 1987: 211; cf. Abdel-Khalik and Ajinkya 1983: 382, Willmott 1983: 403n, Burgstahler and Sundem 1989: 86). Anthony Hopwood concurs. In explaining how the academic control system has shaped behavioural accounting research (BAR), he writes that:

> A concern with ease, speed and the immediate publishability rather than the substance of the research still bedevils the area, although in this respect it certainly is not unique.
>
> (Hopwood 1989: 12–13)

Second, and more importantly, notice that there does not appear to be an environment where one can expect others, *in the ordinary course of things*, to provide criticism through further testing of the solution and its materials, or by attempting to extend the work (for which failure might cast doubt on the original solution). In this regard, how many comments on articles or repetitions of studies does one find in accounting journals? As Burgstahler and Sundem (1989: 90) write: 'Accounting journals seldom publish replications'.[17] Repetitions are considered to be 'inferior' (Umapathy 1987: 170) and of 'low prestige' (Campbell 1986: 122). This is completely unlike the situation existing in the successful (physical) sciences where significant findings get repeated, either deliberately or in the course of successive experimentation, hundreds of times (Campbell 1969: 427–8; 1986: 122).

This latter result is a manifestation of the wider problem, that accounting researchers fail to operate within the perspective of a research programme whereby subsequent experiments are dedicated towards solidifying (eliminating plausible rival hypotheses), generalizing and exploring new consequences of previous research results on the path to *developing* comprehensive explanatory theories. Instead, as Burgstahler and Sundem (1989: 86) have observed, they operate on the basis of 'many small, one-shot research projects'. This has led some commentators to state that BAR is 'unfocused' (Hofstedt 1976), 'shapeless' and 'fragmented' (Colville 1981: 120), and 'disjointed' (Caplan 1989: 115). Collins explained the situation this way:

> Behavioural accounting research can be characterized as lacking in continuity. That is, researchers seem to carve out islands of knowledge which seem unrelated and sometimes contradictory.
>
> (Collins 1978: 331)

Nor do matters appear to be much better in financial accounting. Dyckman *et al.* (1978: 79), in their review and evaluation of experimental and survey research in financial accounting, complain of the lack of ties to the work of others, and urge researchers to replicate findings and explore variables further.

Other signs also indicate that accounting researchers are not operating within the context of Popper's critical attitude. Like many disciplines in the social sciences (see Acree 1978, Johnstone 1986, Gigerenzer *et al.* 1989), the test of significance has been institutionalized in accounting research as the *sine qua non* of the scientific method.[18] The procedure virtually defines the process of forming hypotheses, conducting experiments and, most importantly, analysing results. Yet, in many applications, null hypothesis testing represents the practice of *pseudo*-science because it is non-critical (Lindsay 1989); it provides an extremely weak test for a hypothesis to survive (Meehl 1967, 1986, Freedman *et al*. 1978: 492).

Furthermore, accounting researchers are generally unconcerned with the validity and reliability of their measurement instruments; they appear to operate under the positivistic notion that constructs are isomorphic with operational measures. Rarely does one see a researcher attempting to improve materially upon a previously used measurement instrument. Nor do researchers attempt critical triangulation (multiple measures or manipulations) to assess potential validity threats (see Cook 1983: 84). Instead, they appear content with using measurement instruments developed by others, usually in other disciplines. In fact, one gets the distinct impression that as long as researchers note the weaknesses of their instruments in the 'Limitations section' – no matter how serious those limitations – their scientific duty will have been discharged.[19] This is not the practice of critical science!

CONCLUSIONS AND IMPLICATIONS

Three conclusions follow from this analysis. First, given our understanding of what the scientific method really is – the possession of the critical attitude – we should not expect the recent calls for the full scale adoption of qualitative research approaches in accounting *in themselves* to lead to an improvement. Such arguments merely substitute one source of authority for another and thus the justificationist meta-methodology will still remain to provide the context in which these methods will be used and abused.

Second, there is no reason why social sciences should not be scientific in much the same sense that physical sciences are. As Phillips (1987: 49, 64–5) explains, given the old and discredited view of the 'natural scientific method' (i.e. inductivism), it was no doubt quixotic to suppose that the social sciences could be like the physical sciences. The fact of the matter is that not even the physical sciences could be scientific in this vulgarized sense (for this account of the physical sciences is inappropriate). (See Chapter 10, this volume, by Philip Stamp.) However, if Popper is right in stating that the possession of the critical attitude is the basis of all scientific inquiry, then there is no bar in principle to the social sciences and accounting research being naturalistic endeavours. As Popper (1960: 2) has noted:

> Whether a student of method upholds anti-naturalistic or pro-naturalistic doctrines . . . will depend on his views about the methods of physics. I believe this latter point to be the most important of all. And I think that the crucial mistakes in most methodological discussions arise from some very common misunderstandings of the methods of physics.

D.T. Campbell's (1986: 131) conclusion (in a hermeneutic oriented analysis) aptly summarizes this discussion. He writes:

> There are social, psychological, and ecological requirements for being scientific that are shared by successful physical sciences and unsuccessful sciences. The relative lack of success of the social sciences, as well as possibilities for improvement, are understandable in terms of these requirements.

Third, as argued earlier, there is no sign of accounting researchers conducting their research within the context or meta-methodology of the critical attitude. Thus while some, including the writer, might find the second conclusion above to be highly encouraging, this third one is not: 'the absence of a critical attitude among the members of a scientific community is a *cause* of a degeneration into vacuity and corruption' (Ravetz 1971: 277n; emphasis in original). Consequently, the outlook for the future, sad to say, appears grim (cf. Campbell 1986: 122).

In an attempt to improve matters, this chapter closes with some comments regarding accounting research strategy and policy.

The foregoing analysis indicates that we must construct an environment which allows the critical attitude to develop in accounting. The following question, stated in its general form, is therefore paramount: 'How can our lives and institutions be arranged so as to expose our positions, actions, opinions, beliefs, aims, conjectures, decisions, standards, frameworks, ways of life, policies, traditional practices, etc. . . . to optimum examination, in order to counteract as much error as possible?' (Bartley 1987a: 213). In putting this maxim into practice, we must develop research methods and approaches, along with institutions, that will contribute to such an environment. Three points follow.

First, repetition (broadly defined) must be granted the status of a methodological imperative by researchers, editors and funding agencies (see Campbell 1986). It cannot be overemphasized that a single study is 'nearly meaningless and useless in itself' (Ravetz 1971: 174, 374, Yates 1951, Taveggra 1974: 397, Kempthorne 1978: 10, Abdel-

Khalik and Ajinkya 1983, Ehrenberg 1983, Lovell 1983, Mayo 1983: 324, Guttman 1985, Nelder 1986). That so many studies in accounting are observational (survey) in nature (Hopwood 1989: 6, Dyckman *et al*. 1978: 82) should surely serve to underscore the appropriateness of this conclusion (cf. Cook 1983: 90).

There are indications, however, that the importance of repetition is sometimes acknowledged. For example, the review papers by both Dyckman *et al*. (1978) and Burgstahler and Sundem (1989) stress the need for repetition, as do Abdel-Khalik and Ajinkya (1983). Perhaps more significantly, the editorial policies of the journal *Behavioural Research in Accounting* and the *British Journal of Management* (under the general editorship of David Otley) explicitly state that repetitions would be published as research notes. Clearly this was a constructive step; however, relegating repetitions to second class status (i.e. as notes) will do little to dispel the inferiority complex that surrounds them.[20] Unlike disciplines in the natural sciences, accounting lacks a pedigree of knowledge or a body of reliable methods of inquiry from which to establish new 'facts'; consequently, repetition (broadly defined) is every bit as important as 'novel' research in our quest to build a reliable body of 'facts' *and* methods. Campbell (1986: 130) goes so far as to advocate the establishment of more journals dedicated to critique and rebuttal.

Second, the research community must identify those areas which are significant[21] enough to warrant the devotion of sufficient resources to test properly for the stability (reproducibility) of a result by means of undertaking several studies performed under different conditions, perhaps with different instruments at different sites, and with different researchers. As Nelder (1986: 113) puts it: 'Looking for reproducible results is a search for significant *sameness*, in contrast to the emphasis on the significant *difference* from the single experiment'. Moreover, and perhaps more importantly, in the aim of establishing and maintaining a disputative scholarly community for each problem area, scholars from various perspectives or traditions should attempt to repeat studies (cf. Hopwood 1989: 13, Burgstahler and Sundem 1989: 92, Cook 1983: 89, Abdel-Khalik and Ajinkya 1979, 1983, Willmott 1983: 403), a point underscoring the utility of having a journal dedicated to critique and rebuttal. This is D.T. Campbell's advice:

> Even though the epistemology of some versions of these ['qualitative'] movements deny the relevance, there should be replication efforts and sequential studies guided by rival interpretations of

> prior studies. I join D'Andrade [1986] in affirming my faith that these approaches have much to offer the validity-seeking social sciences that is not precluded by their relevance for other epistemologies and goals.
>
> (Campbell 1986: 130)

The methodological warrant for such triangulation (across methods) is that each perspective is unique, subject to its own tradition and consequent biases and limitations.

Third, once it appears that a stable effect has been obtained, the next step is to explore new consequences. These follow from attempts to extend the research programme's empirical domain and to develop theoretical explanations that explain the results uncovered in earlier exploratory research.[22] These theories can then be the subject of further investigation designed to assess their adequacy and to provide for their improvement by detecting their weak spots, and to extend the theoretical domain into new problem contexts.

In conclusion, it must be appreciated that this approach is laborious and cannot be expected to produce quick results. In this regard there is a potential conflict between the social constraints which force upon us the pretence of maturity in order to obtain legitimization, and scholarly requirements for integrity and thoroughness (see Ravetz 1971, chapter 14). The guiding principle must be *veritas temporis filia* – truth is the daughter of time (Ravetz 1971: 149n). The following passage by the sociologist Paul Lazarsfeld is as apt to accounting researchers as it was to sociologists when it was written in 1948:

> But sociology is not yet in the stage where it can provide a safe basis for social engineering. . . . It took the natural sciences about 350 years between Galileo and the beginning of the industrial revolution before they had a major effect upon the history of the world. Empirical social research has a history of three or four decades. If we expect from it quick solutions to the world's greatest problems, if we demand of it nothing but immediately practical results, we will just corrupt its natural course.
>
> (Lazarsfeld quoted in Ravetz 1971: 385n, emphasis removed)

Current publication and promotion practices, with their emphasis on 'novel' research and prolific publication, also conflict with this approach. Clearly the often voiced appeals for changes in the academic control system must be heeded if we are to witness any real changes in research practices and attitudes.

The 'method' of real rather than pseudo-science has been described. The choice is ours to make.

ACKNOWLEDGEMENTS

I would like to acknowledge the helpful comments provided by Simon Archer, George Murphy and Ken Peasnell on earlier versions of this chapter. I am particularly grateful to Michael Mumford for the careful reading and detailed comments he provided.

NOTES

1 The term 'meta-methodology' is due to McMullin (1978). His threefold distinction between method, methodology and meta-methodology is drawn upon (with slight adaptations in definitions), whereby method is the specific technique used in conducting research; methodology, the fundamental principles of reasoning which guide and control the inquiry in providing the basis for which various types of propositions are accepted or rejected into the scientific body of knowledge (cf. Machlup 1978: 55–6); and meta-methodology, the epistemological *context* in which the methodology is placed, i.e. how and why the methodology is used.

2 To take a specific example, Lindsay (1988) argues that the history of the prolonged and continued misuse of tests of significance in the social sciences (see Morrison and Henkel 1970) is a manifestation of researchers operating within a justificationist meta-methodology (cf. Gigerenzer 1987).

3 For example, Abdel-Khalik and Ajinkya view the scientific method 'as being synonymous with "verification"' (1979: 9, 1983) – a meta-methodology that was abandoned by philosophers in the early part of this century. They also consider 'that the notion of verification . . . is essentially based on deductive logic and in that sense is "scientific"' (1983: 378). Properly speaking, the hypothetico-deductive model of scientific explanation, a model which is prevalent in accounting research (Chua 1986: 608), is not deductive but inductive (Salmon 1967: 18–19). Obtaining a successful prediction offers no *logical* bearing on the truth of a theory because the candidate theory will be one among an indefinitely large number of mutually incompatible theories, each of which will explain or imply the data equally well (Maxwell 1975: 124–5, Hines 1988: 657n).

4 Presently, the inductivistic framework centres on statistical inference. In this connection Acree (1978: 32) states: 'We can no longer imagine doing without statistical inference, because we can no longer imagine an alternative *episteme*'. See also Gigerenzer (1987) and Gigerenzer *et al.* (1989).

5 Hopwood (1989: 12) stressed this point in accounting.

6 At the meta level, even the principle of the critical method itself is not exempt from criticism (Popper 1966: 379, 1963: 122, Bartley 1964, 1987a: 212).

7 Bartley (e.g. 1962, 1964, 1982b, 1987a,b) has developed and generalized Popper's meta-methodology into a full blown theory of rationality called comprehensively critical rationalism (CCR) or, more recently, pancritical rationalism. CCR has led to a considerable body of literature expounding its merits and problems in the three decades since its inception. For the

interested reader, the volume edited by Radnitzky and Bartley (1987, Part II) provides a useful starting point to this literature.

8 For example, once one fully appreciates this discussion, the attacks on Popper for being a 'naive falsificationist', i.e. for claiming that we can infallibly refute a theory, are unfair. Popper clearly appreciates that any 'falsification' decision is fallible. See Popper's *Realism and the Aim of Science* (section 22) which is the first volume of Popper's *Postscript to the Logic of Scientific Discovery*. The book was written in 1956 but only published in 1983. See also Bartley (1987a: 212–13).

9 The problem of demarcating science from pseudo-science was considered by Popper to be one of the fundamental problems of epistemology (Bartley 1982b: 193; see Popper 1963, chapter 1, especially p. 42). As is well known, Popper's demarcation criterion is a theory's testability or falsifiability (Popper 1963: 37, 255–6; Miller 1982: 22–3). However, Bartley (1982b: 189–201) argues that Popper's demarcation criterion is confusing, its development over the years inconsistent, and it is responsible for creating some anomalies in his philosophy, all largely the result of the fact that Popper did not fully appreciate that his earlier work constituted a shift from justificationism to a critical and fallibilist meta-methodology. This, Bartley argues, has led his 'testability' solution to be 'frequently, and wrongly, presented by him and others, *as if* a solution to the [problem of induction]'. (Bartley 1982b: 194; emphasis in original).

10 Although this point is not always appreciated by discussants of Popper's philosophy, in the main Popper's philosophy represents an attempt to deal with the 'critical problem of epistemology' – the problem of the growth of knowledge (Popper 1959: 15; see the prefaces in his 1959 and 1963). The titles of his two classics reflect this viewpoint: *The Logic of Scientific Discovery* and *Conjectures and Refutations: The Growth of Scientific Knowledge*. Lakatos (1968) gives this aspect of Popper's philosophy good coverage.

11 The basic idea behind craft or tacit knowledge is that we know more than we can articulate. As Collins *et al.* (1986) describe it: 'humans have ways of using components of knowledge without knowing how they use them or even that they use them'.

12 Recent events with respect to the so-called discovery of cold fusion by Pons and Fleischmann bear out Popper's comments. An article appearing in the Canadian newspaper, *The Globe and Mail* (11 May 1989: A1–2), reported that Stanley Pons was not offered tenure at the University of Alberta in 1984 because of the concern that he published too much, too soon. As one university official put it: 'He was too fast on the draw. He didn't do that extra experiment that one wants to do to verify'. The inability of the scientific community to reproduce the result would seem, at least for the moment, to vindicate the university's decision.

13 This discussion has a meaningful translation into the field of management accounting. David Otley's (1978) study, essentially a repetition of Hopwood (1973), had a significant influence upon subsequent work in the area (Lord 1989: 138) for just such reasons: it contradicted Hopwood's results and led to a decade of further research attempting to explain the conflicting results. One may add, however, that no study has ever attempted to establish the stability of either the Hopwood or Otley

results as they pertain to the (alleged) different environments associated with their respective studies. In effect, we may have been occupying ourselves with the consequences of non-objects. This point is noted because, at least for the *Journal of Accounting Research*, papers of this nature are no longer being accepted, due, in part, to the mixed and conflicting results that have been obtained (private correspondence with the editor, Katherine Schipper).

14 Lakatos's (1978: 216n) discussion on wastepaper-baskets is descriptive of the current situation. He writes: '"Wastepaper-baskets" were containers used in the seventeenth century for the disposal of some first versions of manuscripts which self-criticism – or private criticism of learned friends – ruled out on the first reading. In our age of publication explosion most people have no time to read their manuscripts, and the function of wastepaper-baskets has now been taken over by scientific journals'. Christenson (1983) cites this passage in criticizing the Rochester school.

15 Examples are Broad and Wade's *Betrayers of the Truth: Fraud and Deceit in the Halls of Science* (1982) and Colman's *Facts, Fallacies and Frauds in Psychology* (1987).

16 Blaug's use of the words 'refute' and 'falsification' in the cited quotation have falsificationist overtones and may distract readers from appreciating the paper's salient point which is that we must replace our confirmationist meta-methodology with a fallibilist one and appreciate the implication that this switch entails, i.e. the necessity of employing criticism. More specifically, it is Popper's non-justificationist meta-methodology and not his falsificationist methodology that is being advanced in this paper. In this regard it may be useful to clarify a potential worry with some readers. Employment of the critical attitude does not necessarily imply the wholesale rejection of a research programme when inconsistent 'facts' are obtained (a view many attribute to Popper; but see Popper 1963: 246, 312n, 1975: 245–6, Magee 1971: 72, Miller 1982: 25). The acceptance and rejection of theories more properly rests with a logic of discovery rather than with a logic of justification (see Lakatos 1968).

17 In a survey of empirical planning and control articles published in *Accounting, Organizations and Society*, *Journal of Accounting Research* and *The Accounting Review* for the years 1970 to 1987 inclusive, the author could only classify 4 out of 43 studies as repetitions – and most of these would be more properly considered as extensions or generalizations (see Lindsay 1988).

18 Burgstahler and Sundem (1989: 90) write: 'in the U.S. BAR seems to have gone too far toward requiring papers to use empirical analyses with rigorous statistical tests to be published. A reviewer for a major accounting journal once wrote that a particular BAR paper was not "research" because no hypotheses were tested'. The author's study (described in Note 17) indicates the extent of the reliance that accounting researchers place on tests of significance. A total of 3082 tests were performed in the 43 studies surveyed. Of these, 1871 focused directly on the status of the major hypotheses investigated. This translates into an average (median) of 43.5 (20) major tests of significance per article. Note, these statistics are conservative: researchers clearly undertake more tests than they report.

19 This discussion of measurement stems from the survey referred to in Note 17. As such, it may not be appropriate to generalize this conclusion to all research in accounting.

20 In 1975 the editors of the *Journal of Political Economy* announced that their standard submission fee would be waived and publication expedited for notes submitted to a newly established Confirmation and Refutation section. However, Lovell (1983: 11 fn. 22) writes that in spite of this encouragement very few articles have appeared in this section.

21 Campbell (1986: 128–9) provides two useful criteria for determining the significance of a problem: 'If you are wrong about this, who, if anyone, will notice?'; 'Who will try to check by replicating?'

22 In this connection, Burgstahler and Sundem (1989: 86) are surely correct in stating that much of BAR 'is (or should be) still exploratory'. Operating under the false pretence of hypothesis testing (perhaps to acquire more scientific legitimacy (see Willmott 1983: 403n)) when data should be used for the *formation* of hypotheses can do little good and much harm (see Lindsay 1989).

REFERENCES

Abdel-Khalik, A.R. and Ajinkya, B.B. (1979) *Empirical Research in Accounting*, Accounting Education Series, vol. 4, Sarasota, Florida: American Accounting Association.

—— (1983) 'An evaluation of "the everyday accountant and researching his reality"', *Accounting, Organizations and Society*, 8: 375–84.

Acree, M.C. (1978) 'Theories of statistical inference in psychological research: a historico-critical study', Unpublished Phd dissertation, Clark University.

Andreski, S. (1972) *Social Sciences as Sorcery*, London: André Deutsch.

Bartley, W.W., III (1962) *The Retreat to Commitment*, New York: A.A. Knopf.

—— (1964) 'Rationality versus the theory of rationality', in M. Bunge (ed.) *The Critical Approach*, New York: The Free Press, pp. 3–31.

—— (1982a) 'A Popperian harvest', in P. Levinson (ed.), *In Pursuit of Truth*, Brighton: Harvester Press, pp. 249–89.

—— (1982b) 'The philosophy of Karl Popper, part III: rationality, criticism, and logic', *Philosophia*, 11: 121–221.

—— (1987a) 'Theories of rationality', in G. Radnitzky and W.W. Bartley III (eds) *Evolutionary Epistemology, Theory of Rationality, and the Sociology of Knowledge*, La Salle, Illinois: Open Court, pp. 205–14.

—— (1987b) 'A refutation of the alleged refutation of comprehensively critical rationalism', in G. Radnitzky and W.W. Bartley III (eds), *Evolutionary Epistemology, Theory of Rationality, and the Sociology of Knowledge*, La Salle, Illinois: Open Court, pp. 313–41.

Birnberg, J.G. and Shields, J.F. (1989) 'Three decades of behavioral accounting research: a search for order', *Behavioral Research in Accounting*, 1: 23–74.

Blaug, M. (1976) 'Kuhn versus Lakatos, or paradigms versus research programmes in the history of economics', in S.J. Latsis (ed.), *Method and Appraisal in Economics*, Cambridge: Cambridge University Press pp. 149–80.

Born, H. (1963) 'Review of *The Scientist Speculates: An Anthology of Partly-Baked Ideas*', *Bulletin of the Atomic Scientists*, (May 1963), pp. 30–1. (Book edited by I.J. Good, published by Basic Books, New York.)

Born, M. (1943) *Experiment and Theory in Physics*, Cambridge: Cambridge University Press.

Broad, W. and Wade, N. (1982) *Betrayers of the Truth: Fraud and Deceit in the Halls of Science*, London: Century Publishing Co.

Burgstahler, D. (1987) 'Inference from empirical research', *Accounting Review*, January: 203–14.

Burgstahler, D. and Sundem, G.L. (1989) 'The evolution of behavioral accounting research in the United States, 1968–1987', *Behavioral Research in Accounting*, 1: 75–108.

Campbell, D.T. (1969) 'Reforms in experiments', *American Psychologist*, 24: 409–29.

—— (1986) 'Science's social system of validity – enhancing collective belief change and the problems of the social sciences', in D.W. Fiske and R.A. Shweder (eds), *Metatheory in Social Science: Pluralisms and Subjectivities*, Chicago: University of Chicago Press, pp. 108–35.

Caplan, E.H. (1989) 'Behavioral accounting – a personal view', *Behavioral Research in Accounting*, 1: 109–23.

Carnap, R. (1967) *The Logical Structure of the World: Pseudoproblems in Philosophy*, translated by R.A. George, 2nd. edition, London: Routledge & Kegan Paul, 1967, second edition. (First published as *Der Logische Aufbau der Welt*, (1928), Hamburg: Felix Meiner Verlag.)

Chalmers, A. (1982) *What is this Thing Called Science? An Assessment of the Nature and Status of Science and its Methods*, second edition, Milton Keynes: Open University Press.

Christenson, C. (1983) 'The methodology of positive accounting', *Accounting Review*, January: 1–22.

Chua, W.F. (1986) 'Radical developments in accounting thought', *Accounting Review*, October: 601–32.

Cohen, M.R. (1931) *Reason and Nature: An Essay on the Meaning of Scientific Method*, New York: Harcourt, Brace & Co.

Collins, F. (1978) 'The interaction of budget characteristics and personality variables with budgetary response attitudes', *Accounting Review*, April: 324–35.

Collins, H.M. (1985) *Changing Order: Replication and Induction in Scientific Practice*, London: Sage Publications.

Collins, H.M., Green, R.H. and Draper, R.C. (1986) 'Where's the expertise?: expert systems as a medium of knowledge transfer', in M. Merry (ed.) *Expert Systems: Proceedings of the Fifth Technical Conference of the British Computer Society Specialist Group on Expert Systems* (University of Warwick, December 17–19, 1985), Cambridge: Cambridge University Press.

Colman, A.M. (1987) *Facts, Fallacies and Frauds in Psychology*, London: Hutchinson.

Colville, I. (1981) 'Reconstructing "behavioral accounting"', *Accounting, Organizations and Society* 6: 119–32.

Conant, J.B. (1951) *Science and Common Sense*, New Haven, Connecticut: Yale University Press.

Cook, T.D. (1983) 'Quasi-experimentation: its ontology, epistemology, and methodology', in G. Morgan (ed.), *Beyond Method: Strategies for Social Research*, Beverly Hills, California: Sage Publications, pp. 57–73.

D'Andrade, R. (1986) 'Three scientific world views and the covering law model', in D.W. Fiske and R.A. Shweder (eds), *Metatheory in Social Science: Pluralisms and Subjectivities*, Chicago: University of Chicago Press; pp. 19–41.

Dyckman, T., Gibbins, M. and Swieringa, R. (1978) 'The impact of experimental and survey research', in A.R. Abdel-Khalik and T.F. Keller (eds), *The Impact of Accounting Research on Practice and Disclosure*, Durham, North Carolina: Duke University Press, pp. 48–105.

Ehrenberg, A.S.C. (1983) 'We must preach what is practiced', *American Statistician*, 37: 248–50.

Freedman, D., Pisani, R. and Purves, R. (1978) *Statistics*, New York: W.W. Norton.

Gigerenzer, G. (1987) 'Probabilistic thinking and the fight against subjectivity', in L, Krüger, G. Gigerenzer and M.S. Morgan (eds), *Probabilistic Revolution: Ideas in the Sciences*, Cambridge, Massachusetts: MIT Press, pp. 11–34.

Gigerenzer, G., Swijtink, Z., Porter, T., Daston, L., Beatty, J. and Krüger, L. (1989) *The Empire of Chance: How Probability Changed Science and Everyday Life*, Cambridge: Cambridge University Press.

Greenwald, A.G. (1975) 'Consequences of prejudice against the null hypothesis', *Psychological Bulletin*, 82: 1–20.

Guttman, L. (1985) 'The illogic of statistical inference for cumulative science', *Applied Stochastic Models and Data Analysis*, 1: 3–10.

Hacking, I. (1981) 'Lakatos's philosophy of science', in I. Hacking (ed.) *Scientific Revolutions*, New York: Oxford University Press, pp. 128–43.

Hanson, N.R. (1958) *Patterns of Discovery*, Cambridge: Cambridge University Press.

Hines, R. (1988) 'Popper's methodology of falsificationism and accounting research', *Accounting Review*, October: 657–62.

Hofstedt, T.R. (1976) 'Behavioral accounting research: pathologies, paradigms and prescriptions', *Accounting, Organizations and Society*, pp 43–58.

Hopwood, A. (1973) *An Accounting System and Managerial Behaviour*, London: Saxon House.

—— (1983) 'On trying to study accounting in the context in which it operates', *Accounting, Organizations and Society*, 8: 287–305.

—— (1989) 'Behavioral accounting in retrospect and prospect', *Behavioral Research in Accounting*, 1: 1–22.

Howard, G.S. (1985) 'The role of values in the science of psychology', American Psychologist, March: 255–65.

Johnstone, D.J. (1986) 'Tests of significance in theory and practice', *Statistician*, 35: 491–8.

Kaplan, R. (1984) 'The evolution of management accounting', *Accounting Review*, July: 390–418.

—— (1986) 'The role of empirical research in management accounting', *Accounting Organizations and Society*, 11: 429–52.

Kempthorne, O. (1978) 'Logical, epistemological and statistical aspects of nature–nurture data interpretation', *Biometrics*, 34: 1–23.

Kirk, J. and Miller, M.L. (1986) *Reliability and Validity in Qualitative Research*, London: Sage Publications.

Krathwohl, D. (1985) *Social and Behavioral Science Research*, San Francisco: Jossey-Bass.

Kuhn, T. (1970) *The Structure of Scientific Revolutions*, 2nd edition, Chicago: University of Chicago Press.

Lakatos, I. (1968) 'Changes in the problem of inductive logic', in I. Lakatos (ed.), *The Problem of Inductive Logic*, Amsterdam: North Holland pp. 315–417.

—— (1970) 'Falsification and the methodology of scientific research programmes', in I. Lakatos and A. Musgrave (eds) *Criticism and the Growth of Knowledge*, Cambridge: Cambridge University Press, pp. 91–196.

—— (1978) *The Methodology of Scientific Research Programmes, Collected Philosophical Papers*, vol. 1, J. Worrall and G. Currie (eds), Cambridge: Cambridge University Press.

Lindsay, R.M. (1988) 'The use of tests of significance in accounting research: a methodological, philosophical and empirical inquiry', unpublished PhD dissertation, University of Lancaster.

—— (1989) 'Reconsidering the status of tests of significance in management accounting research', working paper, College of Commerce, University of Saskatchewan.

Lord, A.T. (1989) 'The development of behavioral thought in accounting, 1952–1981', *Behavioral Research in Accounting*, 1: 124–49.

Lovell, M.C. (1983) 'Data mining', *Review of Economics and Statistics*, February: 1–12.

Machlup, F. (1978) *Methodology of Economics and Other Social Sciences*, New York: Academic Press.

McMullin, E. (1978) 'Philosophy of science and its rational reconstructions', in G. Radnitzky and G. Andersson (eds), *Progress and Rationality in Science*, Dordrecht: D. Reidel, pp. 221–52.

Magee, B. (1971) *Modern British Philosophy*, London: Secker & Warburg.

—— (1979) *Men of Ideas*, New York: Viking Press.

Maxwell, G. (1975) 'Induction and empiricism: a Bayesian-frequentist alternative', in G. Maxwell and R.M. Andersson (eds) *Induction, Probability and Confirmation*, Minneapolis: University of Minnesota, pp. 106–65.

Mayo, D.G. (1983) 'An objective theory of statistical testing', *Synthese*, 57: 297–340.

Meehl, P.E. (1967) 'Theory testing in psychology and physics: a methodological paradox', *Philosophy of Science*, 34: 103–15. (Reprinted in D.E. Morrison and R.E. Henkel (1970) *The Significance Test Controversy – A Reader*, London: Butterworth, pp. 252–66.)

—— (1978) 'Theoretical risks and tabular asterisks: Sir Karl, Sir Ronald, and the slow progress of soft psychology', *Journal of Consulting and Clinical Psychology* 46: 806–34.

—— (1986) 'What social scientists don't understand', in D.W. Fiske and R.A. Shweder (eds), *Metatheory in Social Science*, Chicago: University of Chicago Press, pp. 315–38.

Miller, D. (1982) 'Conjectural knowledge: Popper's solution of the problem of induction', in P. Levinson (ed.), *In Pursuit of Truth*, Brighton: Harvester Press, pp. 17–49.

—— (1987) 'A critique of good reasons', in J. Agassi and I.C. Jarvie (eds), *Rationality: The Critical View*, Dordrecht: Martinus Nijhoff, pp. 343–58.

Mintzberg, H. (1979) 'An emerging strategy of "Direct" research', *Administrative Science Quarterly*, December: 582–9.

Morrison, D.E. and Henkel, R.E. (eds) (1970) *The Significance Test Controversy – A Reader*, London: Butterworth.

Nagel, E. (1939) 'Probability and degree of confirmation', in *Principles of the Theory of Probability*, vol. 1, no. 6, *International Encyclopedia of Unified Science*, Chicago, pp. 60–74. (Reprinted in M.H. Foster and M.L. Martin (eds) (1966) *Probability, Confirmation, and Simplicity: Readings in the Philosophy of Inductive Logic*, New York: Odyssey Press, pp. 184–94.)

—— (1961) *The Structure of Science: Problems in the Logic of Scientific Explanation*, London: Routledge & Kegan Paul.

—— (1967) 'The nature and aim of science', in S. Morgenbesser (ed.) *Philosophy of Science Today*, London: Basic Books, pp, 3–13.

Nash, L.K. (1963) *The Nature of the Natural Sciences*, Boston: Little, Brown & Co.

Nelder, J.A. (1986) 'Statistics, science and technology',*Journal for the Royal Statistical Society* (presidential address) A 149: 109–21.

Otley, D.T. (1978) 'Budget use and managerial performance', *Journal of Accounting Research*, Spring: 122–49.

Phillips, D.C. (1987) *Philosophy, Science, and Social Inquiry*, Oxford: Pergamon Press.

Polanyi, M. (1962) *Personal Knowledge*, London: Routledge & Kegan Paul.

Popper, K.R. (1959) *The Logic of Scientific Discovery*, London: Hutchinson.

—— (1960) *The Poverty of Historicism*, London: Routledge & Kegan Paul, second edition.

—— (1963) *Conjectures and Refutations*, London: Routledge & Kegan Paul.

—— (1966) *The Open Society and Its Enemies*, Vol. 2, London: Routledge & Kegan Paul, fifth edition.

—— (1975) 'The Rationality of Scientific Revolutions', in R. Harré (ed.) *Problems of Scientific Revolution: Progress and Obstacles to Progress in the Sciences*, the Herbert Spencer Lectures 1973, pp. 71–101. (Reprinted in *Scientific Knowledge*, J.A. Kourany (ed.), (1987), pp. 235–52.)

—— (1979) *Objective Knowledge: An Evolutionary Approach*, revised edition, Oxford: Clarendon Press.

—— (1983) *Realism and the Aim of Science*, W.W. Bartley (ed.), London: Hutchinson.

Radnitzky, G. and Bartley, W.W. III (eds) (1987) *Evolutionary Epistemology, Theory of Rationality, and the Sociology of Knowledge*, La Salle, Illinois: Open Court.

Ravetz, J.R. (1971) *Scientific Knowledge and Its Social Problems*, New York: Oxford University Press.

Russell, B. (1961) *History of Western Philosophy*, London: George Allen & Unwin, second edition.

Salmon, W. (1967) *The Foundations of Scientific Inference*, Pittsburgh: Pittsburgh University Press.

Suppe, F. (1977) 'Critical introduction and afterword', in F. Suppe (ed.),

The Structure of Scientific Theories, 2nd edition, Urbana: University of Illinois Press.

Taveggra, T.C. (1974) 'Resolving research controversy through empirical cumulation', *Sociological methods and research*, 2: 395–407.

Tomkins, C. and Groves, R. (1983) 'The everyday accountant and researching his reality', *Accounting, Organizations and Society*', 8: 361–74.

Umapathy, S. (1987) 'Unfavorable variances in budgeting: analysis and recommendations', in K.R. Ferris and J.L. Livingstone (eds) *Management Planning and Control*, revised edition, Beavercreek, Ohio: Century VII Publishing Co., pp. 163–76.

Watkins, J. (1978) 'The Popperian approach to scientific knowledge', in G. Radnitzky and G. Andersson (eds), *Progress and Rationality in Science*, Dordrecht: D. Riedel, pp. 23–44.

Weimer, W. (1979) *Notes on the Methodology of Scientific Research*, Hillsdale, New Jersey: Lawrence Erlbaum Associates.

Willmott, H.C. (1983) 'Paradigms for accounting research: critical reflections on Tomkins and Groves' "Everyday Accountant and Researching His Reality"', *Accounting, Organizations and Society*, 8: 389–405.

Yates, F. (1951) 'The influence of *Statistical Methods for Research Workers* on the development of the science of statistics', *Journal of the American Statistical Association*, 46: 19–34.

10 In search of reality

Philip Stamp

INTRODUCTION AND ACKNOWLEDGEMENTS

The article which follows has endured several transformations since David Tweedie first mooted to me the idea of this commemorative volume. The original plan was that I should include a large amount of material from my father's unpublished work, as well as the background material behind his attack on the 'scientization' of accounting. I myself was quite heavily involved in the discussions surrounding the latter, since my father wished to know a great deal about how 'real' sciences like physics operated.

The resulting first version of this article (Feb 1989) was very long, and contained a large amount of historical and biographical material. This led to a second version which cut out all of this material and left an essay comparing 'scientific reality' (exemplified by physics and linguistics) with 'accounting reality'. However, at 100 pages this was still too long, and so the present and final third version has had most of the explanatory material, on quantum mechanics and Chomskyian linguistics, cut back. This step was taken very reluctantly, since trying to compare accounting with the sciences in the absence of such material (by, for example, looking instead at the philosophy of science), is, as Voltaire noted, like outside tourists speculating on what goes on inside the sultan's harem (see Note 58)! To make up for these lacunae, I have referenced some pedagogical books and articles (although there are very few in linguistics), but readers wishing to really get to grips with some of the arguments may wish to have a copy of one of the earlier versions of the present essay, and I would be perfectly happy to send these.

In what is left I have tried to deal with two main questions, viz., 'is it conceivable that accounting could become a science?', and if so, 'what is the "reality" (or realities) that underlie the objects of various sciences, and towards which scientific inquiry seems to be directed?'.

It is, of course, not at all obvious that 'accounting reality' may have anything much to do with physical reality.

Of course to address these questions requires a detour into science, which I have made from my point of view as a practising scientist. Two examples are picked; physics, because it is usually referred to as the model science, and because I am a physicist; and linguistics, because it is a fledgling science which has certain important similarities to accounting. These examples allow us to get to a grip on the kinds of reality one deals with in science, in a very 'hands on' way, i.e., by looking at the real thing. After extracting some home truths from this discussion, we are in a position to look at the candidature of accounting for a position as a future science. In 'Science, reality and accounting' (pp. 285–96) I explain why, although such a candidature is perhaps not completely untenable, the present proposals for the evolution of accounting towards scientific status seem to be hopelessly inadequate, and indeed completely misunderstand what would be required.

As a physicist it is rather difficult for me to go beyond this critical role (for more constructive ideas see version I of this article – these of course are not mine but my father's), but I hope that I can at least have succeeded in clarifying a few issues from 'the other side'!

During the writing of this article I received help, encouragement and ideas from a number of people. I would particularly like to thank Ken Peasnell, who responded so positively at the beginning to David Tweedie's idea for this volume, and gave me access to ICRA's files during the month of October 1986 (on which parts of version I of this article were based); and Michael Mumford, who put so much effort into getting everything organized, edited, and published, and without whom the project would never have seen completion. Useful comments on linguistic questions (in particular, Japanese syntax) were made by Tony and Haruko Leggett (and my discussion of physical reality bears the unmistakeable imprint of Tony Leggett's fundamental contributions to our understanding of quantum physics). Steve Zeff, Colin Lyas, Michael Mumford, John Cope, and Ken Peasnell all gave me useful hints on parts of my father's work. The enormous task of typing version I was undertaken at the Institute of Theoretical Physics in Santa Barbara by Kit Barbieri, who not only typed it but also found it interesting! The article is dedicated to my father's memory.

Pinning down reality

> Humankind cannot stand too much reality
>
> (T.S. Eliot)

> Ces parfums d'herbe et d'étoiles, la nuit, certains soirs où le coeur se détend, comment nierais-je ce monde dont j'éprouve la puissance et les forces? Pourtant toute la science de cette terre ne me donnera rien qui puisse m'assurer que ce monde est à moi. Vous me le décrivez et vous m'apprenez à le classer. Vous énumérez ses lois et dans ma soif de savoir je consens qu'elles soient vraies. Vous démontez son mécanisme et mon espoir s'accroît. Au terme dernier, vous m'apprenez que cet univers prestigieux et bariolé se réduit à l'électron. Tout ceci est bon et j'attends que vous continuez. Mais vous me parlez d'un invisible système planétaire où des électrons gravitent autour d'un noyau. Vous m'expliquez ce monde avec une image. Je reconnais alors que vous en êtes venus à la poésie: je ne connaîtrai jamais. Ai je le temps de m'en indigner? Vous avez déjà changé de théorie. Aussi cette science qui devait tout m'apprendre finit dans l'hypothèse, cette lucidité sombre dans la métaphore, cette incertitude se resout en oeuvre d'art.
>
> (Camus)

In this section, which constitutes the major part of the chapter, we are going to look at some of the ontological questions that crop up in science. We are, in short, going to examine what sort of picture we get of 'reality' from science, and what sort of idea scientists *need* about reality in their work. A lot of discussion will be given of physics, partly because most non-scientists and philosophers use physics as a model for science (as well as many scientists working outside physics), and also because the author is a professional physicist.

However in 'Reality in language' (pp. 278–85) I will look at the discipline of linguistics (particularly Chomskyian linguistics) as a fledgling science. This is not simply to provide an antidote to physics, but also the problems of this subject seem to this writer to more closely resemble those of economics or accounting than do those of physics.

REALITY IN PHYSICS

Whenever discussions about science arise, either amongst philosophers of science or other non-scientists, it is quite remarkable how often the attention of the participants seems to settle almost exclusively on physics. This tendency has been very strong in the accounting literature,[1] and seems to me to be quite misplaced, first because physics is a highly evolved science dealing with a very different subject matter (so that the problems and issues are and always have been quite different, and hence the methodologies employed), and second because almost none of the literature in the philosophy of science (let alone accounting) makes any attempt to come to grips with the fundamental 'reality problems' in physics (or even to show awareness of their existence!); and these problems seem rather particular to physics alone.[2]

Nevertheless, so much attention demands a fairly thorough response from a physicist, and so I will try here to explain in some detail what 'physical reality' looks like to modern physics, and why the problems associated with it are so tricky (and presently unresolved). The relationship to other sciences, and to accounting, will then be more easily explored. This section is written for a non-mathematical layman – however I would insist that any reader, trying to properly understand what is said, should go to some of the references cited.

Before starting let me say that I will seldom refer, in connection with physical reality, to either Newtonian mechanics or classical special relativity. It has been the fashion (at least until recently) for philosophers of science to base their arguments around these two sub-fields of physics, but this seems to me to be a colossal mistake. One has very little trouble identifying the fundamental entities in these theories, and specifying how a very limited sort of reality is to be defined in terms of them.[3] But this is because they are too simple – trying to give a proper discussion of physical reality on this basis would be like trying to discuss 'astronomical reality' (i.e. cosmology or modern astrophysics) on the basis of medieval astronomical ideas.[4]

In fact the present view of physical reality is very delicate, and so we now take a good look at how physicists attempt to deal with it.

Quantum reality

Now for most physicists, a *certain kind* of view about physical reality is a fairly secure part of their working lives, in the same way as a 'common sense' view of reality remains unquestioned by most of us during our ordinary daily lives.[5] Physicists believe that it is meaningful to divide up the universe into various sub-components or 'systems', which have complicated internal interactions and also interact among each other. In the simple old days, of course, these systems could be reduced to the fundamental point particles, which had no self-interactions, but since the mid-nineteenth century this picture has become far more complex.[6]

In modern physics the basic entities are *fields*, which interact with each other and also have complicated self-interactions. A simple example (the first discovered, in the early nineteenth century) is the electromagnetic field. However, any attempt to perturb it causes excitations of the field to propagate through spacetime: if these are weak perturbations, the excitations will have a simple character.

In general these fields exist in four-dimensional spacetime,[7] and they (and hence the state of the entire universe) are then specified if we know the values (or components) of the fields throughout spacetime.[8] Now these fields will evolve in spacetime, either very simply in the absence of interactions (according to some kind of 'wave equation') or else in a very complicated way in the presence of either self-interactions or interactions between fields. The fundamental notion of 'interaction' is introduced in much the same way as done originally by Newton for point particles. There, point particles moved in 'straight lines' at constant velocity unless interacted upon, in which case they were accelerated. Likewise, fields evolve simply unless interactions intervene. The apparent circular reasoning, whereby in Newtonian mechanics the interactions are defined by the resulting accelerations while the accelerations are the result of the interactions, was short-circuited by Newton by noting that a point particle is completely specified by its mass M, which is *constant* and is moreover the constant of proportionality between force and acceleration (we speak here of the inertial mass). Then we can define interactions and corresponding forces independently of the resulting accelerations, in terms of 'test particles'. Likewise, in modern theory, the 'free fields' have a kind of mass and can be probed locally by other 'test fields'.[9]

Actually this probing is usually described as being done by 'test charges' – so that a probe of the electromagnetic field, for example, is made by using hypothetical (or real) electric charges.

But wait a minute – if 'everything' is made up of fields, where do the particle-like charges come in?

This is where the awful Medusa's head of quantum mechanics enters the picture. We shall see shortly what is awful about it, but first we take a look at how it affects our fields. Looking first at the electromagnetic field, we recall from elementary physics that in *classical* (i.e. pre-quantum) electromagnetism, energy moves around in space in the form of wave-like excitations of the field (at least for weak disturbances). If we now introduce quantum mechanics, one of the consequences of 'quantizing' the field is that its excitations take on a dual character, behaving like particles if we probe the electromagnetic field *locally* (i.e. in a small region of spacetime) or like waves if not (the particle-like excitations of the electromagnetic field are called 'photons').

This duality is quite general – all the 'particles' one has ever heard of are just local excitations of some field. Electrons are excitations of the electronic field, protons of the protonic field, and so on (of course, a protonic field is actually a complex composite field – it is made up from interacting quark fields and mesonic fields, with side-effects coming from electronic, electromagnetic, and other fields. But this takes us off our point!).

So far, so good. Now the *vast majority* of physicists spend most of their time exploring various facets of these fields and their interactions. This is not usually done directly unless one is specifically interested in the 'bare' fields. More usually in physics one is interested in the extraordinarily complex world which results when they interact together on all levels from the very small (sub-nuclear physics) to the very large (astrophysics and cosmology). In between one finds a huge range of different worlds, from that of atoms and molecules, which when combined en masse exhibit an endless variety of collective behaviour, covering chemistry and biological systems as well as the more exotic superconductivity and superfluidity; through the gamut of large-scale classical processes (of great complexity in, say, meteorological processes) and our world of tables, chairs, metals, etc. (which behave classically en masse but need quantum mechanics to be explained in detail); and on to the stars.[10]

Naturally, to understand all of this, whole hierarchies of concepts and levels of description have been invented to describe the collective behaviour of the fields. Mainstream physics then proceeds by trying to precisely formulate such concepts, exploring their consequences and testing out the ideas with various experiments (or vice versa, experiments may indicate new paths for theoretical work). The result is a continuous dialogue on many different levels (in which, incidentally, experiment and theory are very often in disagreement – but this almost never leads, à la Popper, to any 'refutation' of theory by experiment, but merely to a refinement of both. The real world of physics research is not nearly so clean as Popper would have it[11]). Particle theorists also try to push back still further the curtain surrounding these fields, from time to time revealing new ones – much of the time they are using concepts derived from studies of collective phenomena to do this.

This, then is the reality of modern physics research – and in its essential method, it is not obviously radically different from, say, biological or medical research. It all seems so simple (as well as being so messy!).

However, if we want to look for trouble, we don't have to try very hard or look very far. All we have to do is ask direct questions about *physical reality*. We then land ourselves in one of the most fascinating and perplexing debates ever seen, which reaches to the very heart of our most cherished common-sense ideas of reality. For it turns out that despite its fantastic success in explaining virtually every phenomenon to which it has been applied (and revealing many new worlds to us), the fundamental principles of quantum mechanics are *not properly understood at all*. The implications for anyone asking questions about any kind of reality, accounting or otherwise, are very important, for as we shall now see, the essential problems arise precisely in the understanding of *physical reality*.[12]

To do this I must first summarize, very briefly, the central features of quantum mechanics. It is essential for any readers unfamiliar with physics to see how the following ideas are fleshed out in practice – otherwise they will be unable to appreciate how violent an assault they constitute on our common sense. A very good introduction for the layperson is provided by Feynman[13] ch. 6; or see the extended version of this article.[14]

The first point to make is that the fields which lie at the basis of all physics are *not directly observable at all*.[15] They are often called 'amplitudes', and if we imagine a simple scalar field $\psi(r,t)$ (a function of space-time coordinates (r,t)) then the '*modulus squared*'[16] of ψ, i.e. $|\psi(r,t)|^2$, represents a *probability* $P(r,t)$. In fact $P(r,t)$ is the probability of observing the system, described by the field $\psi(r,t)$, at position r at time t.

Thus the basic entities describing all physical systems lead to mere probabilities of observation! Ignoring here the problem that this seems to render physics hopelessly anthropocentric, we go on to the even more curious behavior of $\psi(r,t)$ itself. This 'amplitude' is a '*complex*' function[17] of its variables, and when combining them one adds them. This latter feature means that once the amplitude of one field becomes correlated with that of any other, then these correlations are never lost – even if they become widely separated. This latter feature is sometimes called 'non-separability' of two quantum systems.

The consequences can be extraordinarily bizarre. Thus, for example, the amplitudes for a system to behave in two quite different ways can 'interfere' with each other, even to the extent of mutually cancelling. Yet these amplitudes do not refer to actual events, but only to their *possibility*.

In fact the situation[18] is rather as though what one does on a certain day depends not only on the actual door by which one leaves one's house in the morning, but also on the *possibility* that one might have left through the other door. In quantum mechanics, one must always consider all possible sequences of events, including the ones that do not in the end occur, because these *potential* events influence what *actually* happens. This is true even when the different sequences of events are widely separated (i.e. 'separable').

Strange paradoxes arise from the situation. Thus, Schrödinger noted[19] that quantum mechanics allowed states of, e.g., a cat, in which interference occurred between amplitudes representing a live cat and a dead cat – so the summed state was not one or the other, but both! Modern theory has shown in great detail[20] that while such strange superposed states do not occur for cats, they certainly can for some other very large objects. Hence, we have a blatant paradox, since common sense tells us that large bodies are in only one state at any one time.

Perhaps the most painful paradox was noticed by Einstein.[21] The non-separability noted above means that one cannot even talk about the state of some system in nature without also including all other systems with which this system may have previously established correlations. These other systems may be anywhere else in the universe now (or even have ceased to exist).

A simple example of the 'Einstein–Podolsky–Rosen' (EPR) class of paradoxes is provided by the following. We imagine two systems, each exactly the same, and very simple; we can describe their quantum state by a simple unit vector (we call it the *spin*, and denote it by Σ). This can be imagined as a point on a sphere, such that the direction of this point from the centre of the sphere gives the direction of Σ.

Now we let the two systems (call them A and B) intersect, so that after the interaction, the spins are oppositely correlated; Σ_B is forced to be opposite to that at Σ_A, so that $\Sigma_B = - \Sigma_A$. Now we let them separate (let B go sailing off to Mars, for example).

So, we then ask, suppose we wish to know the state of B, after it is on Mars, and way beyond our reach? Well, since we know that $\Sigma_B = - \Sigma_A$, it should suffice to measure Σ_A, and then we shall know Σ_B. But now comes a catch. We can set up a measuring apparatus which measures whether Σ_A is 'up' or 'down' (we represent this by '$| A \uparrow \rangle$', or '$| A \downarrow >$'). But, you may say, what if it is not 'up' or 'down', but pointing off sideways? This is the first mistake – the spin is not *anything* yet, according to quantum mechanics; except that it is opposite to Σ_B! Moreover, because of this funny idea of adding or 'superposing' states, it turns out that a sideways state can actually be represented in terms of a superposition of 'up' and 'down' states (thus, for example, a 'right-pointing state', $| \rightarrow >$, can be written as:

$$| \rightarrow > = \frac{1}{\sqrt{2}} (| \uparrow > + | \downarrow >).$$

Another way of saying this is that the 'up' and 'down' states 'interfere' to form an np state).

Let us continue, however, and make the measurement. Imagine that we find that Σ_A is 'up'. Then we can certainly say, from this moment on, that Σ_B is 'down', even though it is on Mars, and beyond the reach of any signals or intersection from Σ_A telling it to *be* down.

But now comes the full paradox. Supposing, at the very last moment, we suddenly switch over our apparatus so that it measures 'left' or 'right'. Quantum mechanics tells us we *must* get one result or the other – there is no choice about this.

Unfortunately this leaves the spin on Mars in a real pickle; $\Sigma_B = - \Sigma_A$, and so it must also be either 'left' or 'right' (thus, if we find $|A\rightarrow>$, we *must* find $|B\leftarrow>$). Therefore the resulting state of B, and indeed the possible states at its disposal, depend on a measurement taking place on the earth, beyond any possible interaction or other means of actually communicating what was *actually* done, to Σ_B (no signal or interaction can travel faster than light).

Readers are asked to reflect very seriously on the implications of these results, since they show quite unambiguously that we cannot say that some system *is* in a state, or indeed use the verb 'to be' in the way that common sense prescribes, when talking about quantum-mechanical systems.[22] And it is crucial to take account of the generality of quantum mechanics in judging these paradoxes. Quantum mechanics, in one way or another, describes the entire known universe, from the most microscopic scales imaginable to the supergalactic scale. Thus we cannot evade these paradoxes – even we ourselves are encompassed by this theory. It is true that on the large scale, quantum-mechanical interference effects are often 'washed out', by thermal noise and so forth. But not always, and recent experiments have concentrated on realizing these paradoxes on a *macroscopic* scale, involving objects on the mm or cm scale.[23]

The philosophical implications are enormous. The most fundamental 'physical reality' we have is given to us by quantum mechanics, since it is our fundamental physical theory. There is no chance whatsoever that the peculiar features described above will be suppressed in some future theory, since they have been observed experimentally, in ways which agree beautifully with the theory. In fact the surprising consequences of quantum theory have been observed in fantastic abundance, in realms which were thought to be way beyond the purview of science only seventy years ago.

Thus anyone seriously concerned with physical reality, either directly as physicists, or indirectly as, say, accounting theorists interested in physics as a model science, simply must face up to the fact that 'physical reality' is now essentially quantum reality, at bottom. And yet quantum reality is nothing but a sphinx. It is utterly irreconcilable with common-sense views about the physical world, according to which some system *is* in some state, at any particular moment; in quantum mechanics we are not even allowed to use the verb 'to be' in the usual way!

Now in order to elude this quantum-mechanical miasma, the accounting theorist may well try one of the following two arguments:

1 Perhaps we should not pay so much attention to physics after all, if it leads to so much trouble; or
2 If we are only interested in physics as a model of a science, then why not choose some earlier version of pre-quantum physics? Or choose some branch of physics which looks more like accounting, such as meteorology (in which quantum mechanical effects are washed out)? We can then use this as a model for accounting theory.

Argument 1 will recur often in this essay. Argument 2 is more specific, and so we deal with it now.

Meteorology

Let us now turn away for a while from quantum mechanics, and towards a point which one constantly has to deal with in the comparison of physics with other sciences, or non-science. The following argument is made: 'Okay, the *fundamental* reality may be very strange, but for *some* purposes one only has to deal with the "secondary" reality of our macroscopic *classical* world, with its simple concepts of particles, forces, lengths, times, energy, etc., from which we derive ideas like pressure, temperature, weight, and so on.

Now the basic laws here are very simple (and deterministic!), and can be verified on simple systems – we may then extrapolate them to extremely complex systems like the weather, or economic entities, etc.; the same simple laws are valid, and can be applied here using detailed and complex calculations via powerful computers, and so on. Hence we ought to be able to understand "phenomenon X" in a scientific way, provided we have the basic laws.' We may call this the 'simple can explain complex' argument.

Now this argument is to some extent an article of faith, which underlies much of biology, medicine, and economics at this time. It depends very much on the success of physics in extrapolating simple physical laws to complex phenomena. But just how great has been this success, and does it justify the faith of biologists and economists?

The example of the earth's weather well illustrates here what ought to be a number of home truths. For meteorology does consist in applying simple laws concerning gases being heated, water vapour, and various gravitational, rotational, and other forces, and does not directly involve quantum mechanics. Very powerful computers are used to apply these laws to the complex real world. It is commonly assumed, on this basis, that weather prediction is then just a question of sufficiently detailed models of the earth, and sufficiently powerful computers (and this idea is commonly advanced even by meteorologists).

Unfortunately the idea is fundamentally *wrong*, for two reasons. First, the climatic system is in fact an 'open system' – it is acted upon (and reacts back upon), essentially the entire universe. The sun heats it and the sea; energy and particles are constantly exchanged between the atmosphere, the solar wind, and deep space, either directly or via the earth's magnetic field; this exchange reaches down through the atmosphere to the complex interacting system of sea and land; and all of these are subject to huge solar and lunar tidal forces. These two celestial bodies are influenced in their motion by the planets, interstellar matter and fields, the galactic motion, and so on. Second, the climatic system is a good example of a non-linear dynamical system, in which even infinitesimal changes in initial conditions or parameters can induce huge changes in the subsequent evolution of the system, even over fairly short time scales. It is sometimes said, to illustrate this, that 'the flap of a butterfly's wing today in Japan may cause a hurricane next month in Texas'.

To the reader unfamiliar with non-linear dynamical systems this statement may seem extraordinary. It is possible to catch a little of the flavour of the subject by considering a much simpler problem, the famous 'three-body problem' in classical Newtonian gravitation. Consider two planets orbiting around the sun – we ask what is their long-time dynamical behaviour, and whether two initially stable orbits will remain stable.

To understand the difficulty of this problem (which was only solved in the 1960s, after two centuries of effort by mathematicians) we notice that over long periods of time, even very weak perturbations between the two planets can be magnified enormously provided they add up 'synchronously'. This requires that the planets meet each other (i.e. find themselves in the same parts of their respective orbits) at periodic intervals. If t_1 and t_2 are initial periods of these orbits, synchronicity can be approximated arbitrarily closely after n_1 orbits of planet 1 and n_2 orbits of planet 2, just by requiring that the fraction n_1/n_2 approximate t_2/t_1 arbitrarily closely (so that after n_1 orbits of planet 1, it finds itself very close to planet 2, which has just accomplished n_2 orbits).

But now we can approximate any ratio t_2/t_1 (rational or irrational) as closely as we want by fractions n_1/n_2, because the rational numbers (i.e. fractions) are *infinitely dense on the line* (i.e. in any section of the real line, no matter how small, there are always an infinite number of rational numbers n_1/n_2). Of course, to really closely approximate t_2/t_1, we may need rather large values of n_1 and n_2. This means that this 'resonant interaction' between the two planets will take a long time to build up – but its ultimate effect can be as large as we like, if we wait long enough. From this informal discussion the *perturbation* of one planet on the other (and vice versa) will be seen (at least for mathematically-minded readers) to have the form

$$V(t) \sim \sum_{n_1} \sum_{n_2} V_{n_1 n_2} \frac{e^{i(n_1\Omega_1 + n_2\Omega_2)t}}{n_1\Omega_1 + n_2\Omega_2}$$

where $\Omega_1 = 1/r\pi t_1$ and $\Omega_2 = 1/2\ \pi t_2$ are the orbital frequencies of the planets.

Now in fact in our own solar system one can see these effects over even a few centuries. Thus the ratio of Saturn's orbital period t_2 to Jupiter's period t_1 is roughly 5/2; Jupiter orbits the sun every 11.88 years, Saturn every 29.46 years. Hence there is a short resonance period of roughly sixty years (plus an infinite number of longer ones).

What is very remarkable about this is that if the ratio of the periods was *exactly* a fraction, the perturbations would be infinitely large over a long period of time. Thus, quite fascinatingly, we see that the structure of the perturbation expression is quite different depending on whether the ratio $t_1/t_2 = \Omega_2/\Omega_1$ is *rational* or *irrational* – even though we can arbitrarily closely approximate a rational by an irrational, and vice versa.

Now of course to go beyond this perturbation theory is rather difficult – but in general one finds the following. There are regions of 'parameter space' (the initial parameters being, for example, Ω_1, Ω_2, and the interaction between the planets) in which the effect of these perturbations is to completely destabilize the orbits and other regions where they remain stable. In many parts of the parameter space, these two kinds of regions are mixed together in a 'fractal' or 'Cantor set' structure of infinite complexity, rather like the way the rational numbers and irrational numbers are mixed together on the line. Then the smallest perturbation in initial conditions (or the smallest perturbation from outside) is sufficient to move the system from a stable to unstable evolution, or in general to change its evolution by an arbitrarily large amount. Thus if the system is in a region of parameter space like this its dynamical evolution is utterly unpredictable *in principle* – despite being deterministic! In fact we have *no idea* whether our solar system is in such a region or not (although it is *probable* that it is not – in a sense which is rather technical to define).

Now these fractal features of the parameter space are common to virtually all non-linear equations. This has led to an explosion of interest in physics and mathematics in methods and ideas capable of handling them, in topology, catastrophe theory, number theory, and so on. So far, the methods are only useful for simple problems, and suffice to show us the 'topology' of the parameter space – which regions are stable, and which are not, etc.

A system like the real climatic system is at the opposite extreme – the number of different factors or variables entering the relevant equations is essentially infinite, not two or three as in our example above. And we have not the faintest idea what is the topology of this infinite parameter space, although it is surely unbelievably complex.

And so we see the true meaning of the remark about the butterfly – it can tip the climatic system from one kind of behaviour to a quite different one, and simple meteorological models bear this out.

Moreover it will not take much thought now to see that the private thoughts of a single individual on earth,[24] let alone a magnetic storm on a far-off star (another climatic system!) will have a far larger effect in general on the earth's climate than a butterfly – the energy exchange is so much larger. This point will come up again in our discussion of accounting.

Thus we come to the conclusion that non-linear systems like

the weather, despite being deterministic (if we ignore quantum mechanics) are nevertheless unpredictable in principle. Moreover we see that *it is certain* that weather prediction will *always* remain guesswork for more than a couple of weeks (which is, incidentally, a good argument for leaving the earth's ecosystem alone). To use the terminology favoured in the accounting literature, weather forecasting will always remain an 'art'. This is fundamentally because of its non-linear character, and the quite fascinatingly complex behaviour inherent in this non-linearity.[25]

Now in fact *virtually all complex systems in nature* have this non-linear character. However in physics one seeks out systems which do not, or else which interact very weakly with their surroundings (they are 'almost closed'). This is what enables us to give a detailed account of them – they constitute 'test systems' or benchmarks for our theories and experiments,[26] at least over short time-scales. In the absence of such systems, it is difficult to see how physics could have started. We note also that it is not a priori obvious that laws for simple systems ought to be always extrapolable to complex systems, and we are very lucky that this method has worked so well so far.[27] The current problems in quantum mechanics, and also some problems in biology, have encouraged a number of people to wonder how long it will continue. It is then interesting to ask how one might proceed if this were not the case, or if we were dealing with a realm in which *all* sub-systems were strongly coupled to each other and to their environment. I shall be arguing on page 291 that this is very nearly the case in accounting, i.e. that almost all accounting entities are strongly coupled to their financial environment, and that the financial system is a very open one.

Laws or conventions?

Let us now turn to some questions of a more philosophical nature, which concern all of the different theories in physics (past or present), and are thus relevant to the discussion of scientific method in most other sciences. The first question we address is to what extent the 'laws' of physics may be regarded as 'conventions', fixed by the decisions of, for example, committees or established practice, as opposed to objective natural laws, referring to a physical reality independent of man in such a way that we have no choice in the way that we formulated them.

That we should ask such a question at all may seem extraordinary to many non-scientists. After all, is there not a crucial difference between the natural law of physics and the normative prescriptions of, for example, law or accounting?

Well of course there are very important differences, and certainly no physicist would imagine that physical laws do anything but to say how nature *is*, rather than how it *ought* to be. Nevertheless, and without in any way trying to belittle this crucial distinction, it is important to note that in a certain sense all physical laws are a kind of convention, so that the question as formulated above is ill-posed. It is even the case that some decisions about physical laws at any particular time are the result of previous historical accident and scientific consensus.[28]

The point is really the following (and it was first clearly made nearly a century ago by Poincaré);[29] the way we define our fundamental quantities, and then the relationships between them (the latter as physical laws or corollaries of them) is not given inevitably to us, much as the way we do mathematics, or speak a language, is not written in the sky for us. In fact all of these are the results of *convention*, decided either formally (in the case of physics conventions, this is usually done by committees appointed by IUPAP – the 'International Union of Pure and Applied Physics', in liaison with similar bodies in chemistry, astronomy, and biology), or by informal consensus.[30] Similarly, linguistic conventions are usually decided by precedent and 'common usage', and more or less formalized in dictionaries (whose definitions are decided upon by precedent and committee). Occasionally certain bodies will try and *impose* conventions upon science or language; the result is usually either retrograde (as in Lysenkoism) or laughable (as in the efforts of the Academie Française to 'purify' French). Conventions can only work if they conform with daily use, in science as in language.

We can see how this works out in physics via simple examples. Consider, for example, the definition of velocity as $V = dr/dt$. Now originally the length was decided by one convention (a standard metre bar in Paris) and the time by another (a very refined pendulum clock). Now, however, it is the velocity of light which is decided by convention (the velocity of light c = 299,792,458 metres/second, *by definition*) and also the measure of time (1 second = 2.3528716431 $\times 10^{15}$ vibrations of a caesium atomic clock). Thus previously the units of length and time were 'fundamental' and decided by committee, and the velocity then a derived quantity! Note that the new metre is not exactly the same as the old, but is very close to it.[31]

One then goes on to assume the *additivity* of lengths (thereby putting them into correspondence with the real number system), and so on.[32] Now we see that conventions come in because, for example, we *decide* to fix the relationship between time and the position of a pendulum (or the wave function of an atomic clock) such that the pendulum (or the atom) beats out constant time. We decide that the number of beats $N(t)$ after a time t will be proportional to t; $N(t) = \alpha t$.

Suppose, however, we decided to fix $N(t) = \beta t^2$. Then there would be no inconsistency, *provided* we changed all of the other equations in physics accordingly. The main criterion which then decides how we write our laws, and fix our units, is that of formal simplicity and elegance, as clearly recognized by Poincaré – obviously writing $N(t) = \beta t^2$ would hopelessly complicate the structure of physical theory.[33]

Now this conclusion may unnerve some non-scientists. After all, what has happened to 'natural laws' in this picture (to say nothing of physical reality!)? The answer to this would appear to be twofold.

First, we are obviously very severely constrained in the different kinds of formal system we may choose from by experimental and other facts, usually to the extent that one formulation of physical theory seems much more compelling than the others (but let us again recall the very important way in which the historical development of theory influences this formulation). There is then a strong psychological tendency on the part of physicists (and others) to then associate the elements of such a formulation with 'elements of reality', without perhaps examining this association too closely. This tendency is strongly reinforced by the enormous power of modern physics.

Second, and perhaps more importantly, this arbitrariness is just a fact of life. It is in fact an essential feature of all formal languages that this question of conventions should arise. This is very clearly seen in mathematics and formal logic, where such problems can be enunciated very precisely. Any formal system, defined solely via axioms and rules of symbol manipulation, can be 'mapped' onto many others. Often such mappings are used to 'interpret' the first system – the symbols and manipulation rules of the first system are given a semantic component (or 'interpretation', or 'meaning') by their correspondence with symbols and manipulation rules of the second. In physics, we have mappings between physical objects and formal mathematical objects. Now of course this means that we can map physical quantities onto mathematical systems in many different ways, and this is just Poincaré's point – but we see it is a general feature of formal systems and transformations between them.[34]

Thus we see that even if we ignore quantum mechanics and stick to simple physics, we find a 'conventional' component to physical theory. However, far from being a problem, this seems to me to be an essential and inescapable part of science – a 'fact of life'. Moreover the freedom we have to develop new ways of looking at nature (within the constraints she offers, given by way of empirical observation) is not only part of the philosophical process since time immemorial, but an essential part of any creative activity. Its importance in theoretical physics perhaps explains why physicists are more at home in music, literature, or art than they might be in business or accountancy.[35] It, and the fundamentally ineluctable nature of physical reality, have often produced a highly mystical attitude towards epistemological and ontological questions on the part of theoretical physicists. It is hard to imagine accounting or management theory (at least in their present state in Western countries) producing a similar effect!

Measurements

The important rule of measurements in the art of the experimental scientist has from time to time led to much discussion of their epistemological place in various sciences, most notably in the discussions of logical positivists in the early part of this century. Although these discussions now seem curiously simple-minded,[36] they were nevertheless useful in focusing attention on this particular aspect of scientific practice, and it is important to understand their place in modern physics. This can be largely accomplished by looking at a good dictionary, or simply a little reflection, on the words 'measure' and 'measurement'. Notice first that in everyday life one can measure in two important and distinct senses. One measures the height of a garage, by, for example, noting the length of its shadow with the sun at a certain angle. The measure of the garage height is then derived from direct measures of the shadow length and the solar angle. But one also says, for example, 'The Apollo missions provide a good measure of US technological advance in the 1960s', or 'Cleopatra's love for Antonius was without measure'. Here 'measure' is being used metaphorically, and more literal substitutions would be 'indication' and 'limit' in the two respective cases. Clearly science is only concerned with the first use of 'measure'.

And yet, in the accounting literature and elsewhere, one repeatedly finds 'measure' being used where one should be saying 'estimate', 'calculate', or even 'count'. One does not 'measure' the inventory or cash flow of a company – one can add it up or count it directly, or estimate it (by, for example, statistical analysis of an inventory survey) or calculate it (on the basis of certain assumptions and estimates already made).

This distinction is important, particularly in view of the tendency to introduce words like 'measure' into the vocabulary of many subjects to make them sound more scientific.[37] Thus, despite the common use of the terms 'measure' or 'measurement' in accounting, it seems to this author that there is no operation whatsoever in accounting that could be described as a 'measurement', in the sense used by physicists, or biologists, or geologists, and so on. To measure in science (and, actually, in the everyday sense described above) *necessarily* involves the physical operation of comparison of the quantity being measured with some standard, in the sense alluded to in the previous sub-section. This can be done directly, as in the measure of a table length with a metre rule, but is more commonly done indirectly – the garage height above was indirectly measured via two direct measures and a simple calculation. The vast majority of measurements in science, most particularly in physics, are very indirect comparisons with standards, involving long chains of deductions, calculation, and many different standards. Typical examples are the distance to the nearest star, the diffusion rate of oxygen in blood, or the age of a rock.[38] These examples do not involve counting (one does not 'measure' the number of Jupiter's satellites) or estimation (one does not 'measure' the size or age of the universe) and calculation only enters at an intermediate stage.

Note, incidentally, the essential role that theory plays in measurement. Even in direct measurements, theory enters via our choice of conventions for the various standards and the relations between them. Indirect measurements involve a far larger theoretical component – one must rely on a huge corpus of interrelated theory to derive the quantities one is really investigating (or 'measuring') from the raw experimental output of voltages, elapsed times, etc. Thus even in direct measurements it is not even possible to conceive of or define a measurement outside the context of some theory. It is in this sense that one often says that a theory in science embodies its own means of verification, by defining and giving meaning to measurements within its domain of application. Now since most measurements in science are highly indirect, we see that any apparent inconsistency between theory and experiment in, say, physics, can in principle call into question most of physics, as well as many other more or less articulated assumptions about the particular experiment and how theory should be applied to it. This clearly makes a nonsense of any philosophy of science which treats measurements as the primal stuff of scientific investigation, or which argues that experiments can 'falsify' theories. Inconsistency between theory and experiment is a daily occurrence in laboratories, because of our imperfect understanding of both – and the dialogue between them is essential not just to the working of science, but to the very definition of measurements, which *always* come laden with theory.

Ontological questions

I have already noted the common belief that our ideas about reality should be based on some notion of physical reality; and we have seen how this belief leads one onto treacherous ground. This is not simply because quantum mechanics renders physical reality very mysterious. It is also because no matter how the paradoxes of quantum mechanics may end up being resolved, its fundamental features of interference and non-separability will remain. Thus we cannot expect physical entities ever again to have the simple materialistic properties usually accorded to them, and anyone trying to compare, for example, accounting entities with physical entities as though the latter were simply materialistic is in big trouble.

However, one may object, why tie ourselves to simple materialism? After all, in many cultures and at many different epochs, primacy has been given to 'mental' rather than 'physical' entities, and, in many more, no distinction has been made between them at all. So we have no reason to believe that in some future science, the objects of biology or physics will not find themselves united, and having a very different ontological status from that of today.

From this standpoint it is not entirely obvious that modern science actually demands adherence to any particular kind of materialism. In fact the majority of scientists have adopted one or other of two attitudes towards this kind of ontological question, at least in their daily work.

Perhaps the most widespread view dates very much from the Renaissance and is that of Cartesian dualism. This holds that, despite all our present understanding of, for example, the physical basis of perception right up into the brain, nevertheless visual sensations must eventually reach 'the mind', which involves mental sensations in a quite different mental realm. Our very language practically enforces the idea of an essential subject, the 'self', to which we attribute consciousness of sensations, and which is implied in all sentences involving mental phenomena.[39] Of course many philosophers over the millenia have tried to avoid the assumption that mental events should be contingent on a 'self', or even on any subject at all; and they have gone to the extent of altering the rules of language to do so. But the idea is very strongly imbedded in Western thought, and clearly dates to well before its first really clear expression by Descartes.[40]

The impact on all our ideas should be obvious – in science perhaps the most important result has been the way we think about scientific or experimental observation. Cartesian dualism, and the primary place it gives to mind as opposed to matter, strongly encourages one to doubt the evidence of one's senses, even to the point of lurching into solipsism (indeed Descartes himself seemed to have avoided this fate only by invoking the existence of God, a rather common ploy in those days). Strange as it may seem to the non-scientist, the desire to make experimental science 'objective' has made scientists very suspicious of their senses, and of ideas about 'reality', so that only measurable or verifiable assertions about the world are permissible in experimental science. The situation is quite different in theoretical science, or in mathematics, where one can play at will with objects which may be unobservable in principle (i.e. the ψ-function) or not exist at all (as with mathematical objects); in the mental realm one is supposedly safe from Cartesian doubt.[41] Of course the objectivity of science in no way circumvents solipsism or Cartesian doubt (we could all be but hallucinations in the mind of, for example, God), but it certainly diminishes its force. Nevertheless whenever problems arise in science, one sees many scientists almost instinctively distinguishing mind from matter – the oft-repeated invocations of 'consciousness' to alleviate or 'solve' the measurement paradoxes are a good example.

In stark contrast is the viewpoint, gaining influence at the present time, that *all* events, physical or mental, must eventually be reducible to physics. According to this scenario (call it 'materialistic monism', for lack of a better name), mental phenomena are merely very complicated aspects of physical reality. Thoughts, for instance, should be generally regarded as 'logical constructs' (in the sense employed by, for example, A.J. Ayer[42]) from intricate physical processes occurring in the brain (and even outside it, in principle). This point of view is being articulated more and more in the new fields of artificial intelligence and 'neural network' theory, where one commonly regards mental processes as being extremely complex patterns of electrical and chemical activity which are stored or excited in the vast array of multiply-connected non-linear synaptic and neuronic elements in the brain. The extremely rapid recent progress in these fields is making it clear that such non-linear networks possess the storage capacity, stability over time, recall power, and learning ability that we commonly associate with mind, and one can easily see how even more complex thoughts and feelings, and *even the very idea of the 'self'*, would simply be associated with electrical processes in such networks.[43]

This point of view can be very persuasive – it has the advantage of dissolving many of the paradoxes which arise in a dualistic approach – and is also *scientifically useful*, because it leads to the development of *new* and *detailed* theoretical ideas, which are fast approaching the stage where they may be applicable to neurological phenomena (as opposed to just computers). It also highlights the limitations inherent in mental processes, by tying them to physical processes occurring in the brain; within such a scheme it is easy to see how 'complete knowledge' or understanding of something, on the part of a mind, is a chimera.[44] Moreover mental acts, being mere aspects of physical phenomena, will inevitably influence and be influenced by other physical phenomena, *at the same time*, in distinct contrast to the 'passively observing mind' of Cartesian dualism.

It is easy to see why this idea is more palatable to biologists than physicists at the present time – but notice that this is mainly because physicists have quantum mechanics to remind them of the pitfalls involved in a simple materialistic view of physical reality, and because biology refuses to deal with most mental phenomena. More importantly, we see that the kinds of question that someone working in this area will ask depend crucially on which philosophical point of view they start from (to say nothing of their answers!). Since the monistic viewpoint gives biologists more to do (and more of a feeling that they are looking at deep questions), it is a popular one. *But it is only one possible starting point*. There are many others, most of them provided for us in one form or another by philosophy already, and just waiting to be used and transformed by some area of scientific inquiry.

Thus when one now comes to ask how *philosophers* look at reality, the answer is 'in many different ways'. The point of this sub-section is not to attempt a philosophical analysis of reality (for which a philosopher would be better qualified!), but simply to emphasize how useful to science such enquiries may be and how important a role they play in science – the more, the merrier. Of course one must also remember the enormous influence that science has had on philosophy, upon which much more has been written – but this is another subject.

Having noted that philosophy does not treat questions about reality quite so lightly or simply as some scientists, and that philosophers have developed many different ideas about reality, we are then naturally led to ask – which of the ideas about reality developed in philosophy are *compatible* with, or capable of forming an underlying basis for, modern science?

The answer in the case of physics should be clear already. Because of quantum mechanics and its paradoxes, we simply don't know. In the case of classical mechanics or special relativity, a simple mechanistic philosophy of the kind already developed by Democritus or Leucippus is good enough for most purposes – but we have seen that it is virtually impossible to avoid quantum mechanics except by restricting ourselves to the most banal questions.

I should emphasize at this point that merely because we do not know what is the physical reality lying behind quantum mechanics, this does not mean physicists don't believe it is there! In fact they are *sure* of it! This seems to be common to all scientific inquiry – one must believe in some 'reality', which is 'out there', waiting to be discovered!

In biology, many questions about simple processes can be answered in a more or less mechanistic way. However a glance at any book dealing with the deep issues of biology will show the reader that such an approach is untenable in general (see the books mentioned in Notes 2, 12 and 14), even if we ignore the obvious connection with physics. The general question of what kind of 'biological reality' is emerging in the late twentieth century is most fascinating (and perhaps most easily answered in terms of the somewhat abstract reality of the 'gene' – a reality supposedly reducible to that of physics[45]) but we have no space to look at it here.

Nevertheless, before we turn to sciences quite different from physics and biology, it is useful to ask in just what way they should be viewed as scientific. This of course is a question much discussed in philosophy and philosophy of science, with increasing realization that the answer is far from simple. Without wishing to go too deeply into any of the issues, I hope that the foregoing discussion has made at least some of the following points clear:

1 Although a casual glance at physics might indicate that physical theory is firmly based on a bedrock of 'measurements', which confirm or deny 'physical laws', the true picture is rather different. Even in the very rare cases where experiment and theory are in close contact, disagreement between them almost never leads to a

breakdown of theory, but rather to a closer examination of the many assumptions or approximations involved in both. The symbiosis between the two is so complex that physicists rarely attack the roots of their discipline; almost all their work is concerned with management of the growth of the outlying branches.

2 The most crucial feature of this symbiosis is that *no scientific assertion or activity can mean anything outside the context of theory*. This point is so important that it deserves almost endless repetition (and it has been oft repeated by, for example Kuhn). In physics, measurements or experiments *cannot even be defined* outside the appropriate theoretical framework.

3 It will become somewhat clearer in our discussion of linguistics that the emphasis of much of philosophy of science on measurement and experimentation is misplaced, and comes from paying too much attention to physics. One has only to think of, for example, evolutionary biology or population biology to see this. Until recently, controlled experimentation had little place in either of these disciplines – and the widespread acceptance of Darwinian theory, even by 1900, had much more to do with its explanatory power (and its later explanation in terms of genetic theory[46]) than any conceivable measurements or experiments. Even now, almost all our understanding of, and belief in, the basic tenets of evolution theory, comes from the mathematical modelling of species evolution, in ways similar to modelling in mathematical economics.

To those who still persist in allocating a primary place to physics in this discussion, I would then ask – what role has experimentation or measurement ever had in the almost universal acceptance of general relativity, within a few years of its publication in final form in 1916? The experimental (or rather, *observational*) evidence for this theory is still extremely slender, and only came at the end of the 1960s with the discovery of pulsars. In fact, of course, physicists believe in general relativity because of its logical, philosophical, and aesthetic appeal.

4 Even the emphasis on 'laws' is misplaced. There are no 'laws' of evolution, only an explanatory theory, a way of unifying our diverse observation of nature past and present, and expressing in a general way how models of species development and differentiation will work.

5 Nor are 'numbers' necessarily important (although this is obviously not true in physics). This will become clearer in our examination of linguistics, but I repeat again that much of the power of

evolution theory lies far from the quantitative realm. The revolutionary changes in our understanding and interpretation of fossils at the end of the nineteenth century had little to do with numbers.

6 One thing that does seem to be absolutely necessary is the belief or faith that behind the objects of investigation of the science concerned, there is some appropriate 'reality', independent of our conventions and rules. Otherwise, for example, 'empirical testing' would be quite meaningless. Nevertheless we do *not* necessarily know what it is!

7 Finally, we have seen that even in the 'hard science' of physics, an important role is played by conventions, committees, and consensus (see pages 268–71). This is even more true in biology.

Now one point which we have not yet addressed is what (if anything) makes a particular domain of inquiry ripe for, or amenable to, scientific investigation. This is one excuse for turning now to the study of human language and the new 'science' of linguistics.

REALITY IN LANGUAGE

Some of the discussion in the last section indicates how various philosophical preconceptions enter into the everyday language used by physicists and other scientists – and a change in these preconceptions would involve, among other things, a change in this language.

It is then unfortunate how little attention is payed by scientists to the linguistic shackles within which they work. In fact the tendency in recent years has rather been for physicists to ridicule modern philosophy and the philosophy of language. It is thus rather ironic that developments in linguistics in the last thirty years have led many linguists to claim that linguistics is now well on the road to becoming a science, if it is not one already.

This claim is going to be taken seriously here. If justified, it should be of considerable interest to us. This is not just because of the philosophical liberation it implies (either from materialistic monism or Cartesian dualism, as well as from associations of science exclusively with phenomena in the material world, and with numbers and experiments). I shall also endeavour to show that linguistics as a developing discipline may have some useful liberating lessons to offer to accountants or economists.

Modern linguistics – the 'Chomskyian revolution'

An enquiry into language seems a priori rather hopeless. Language is perhaps the most complex and diverse phenomenon we are *capable* of understanding, given the restrictions on our own thoughts and expressions of them by language itself. In saying this we recognize from the outset that a proper enquiry into human languages must include *all* of them, including presumably even formal languages like mathematics or music (although these are not usually regarded as part of linguistics!). This requirement is even more evident once one starts to make generalizations from a study of human languages to draw conclusions about 'human nature' (as linguists and philosophers are wont to do).

The important developments in linguistics to which I refer begin essentially with Chomsky, but they have roots in much earlier attempts to make linguistics 'scientific', as it moved away from its philosophical origins.[47] This was particularly evident in the methodology of American linguistics at the turn of the century, with an emphasis on field work and the taxonomic cataloguing of phonetic structures and syntax (particularly for the rapidly disappearing American Indian languages). Thus theory took a back seat, and this tendency was radically enhanced by the early twentieth century work of Bloomfield and followers. Ironically, this was not Bloomfield's intention – his well-known book[48] was a self-conscious attempt to turn linguistics into a descriptive empirical science. But, fatally, he adopted a behaviourist philosophy in doing so – meaning that language was to be analysed solely in terms of physical stimuli and the responses to them, and all 'data' not directly 'observable' or 'measurable' were to be held irrelevant or meaningless.

Of course this is not the removal of theory, but simply the replacement of complex ideas, about the meanings of words and the structure of language, with a very much simpler 'black box' approach. Some readers (like myself) may find it extraordinary that such 'black box' ideas could ever be taken seriously (most physical systems, even very simple ones, cannot be so described!). Nevertheless they were much in harmony with pre-war 'hard verification' positivism, and with contemporary developments in psychology and anthropology, where the idea was to 'strip away theory' as much as possible from empirical investigation – to 'scientize' linguistics.[49] In the process, all questions of semantics and the meaning of phrases, as well as most theoretical questions about the formal structure of languages, were dismissed completely.

That the result was quite vacuous was the obvious point made by Chomsky in a well-known attack[50] on B.F. Skinner, published in 1959. His lasting contribution to linguistics began two years earlier with the publication of *Syntactic Structures*, a small book[51] which was largely a condensation of an earlier unpublished manuscript.[52] And yet this work, while breaking away from the behaviourist stranglehold, did not neglect the appropriation and refinement of some of its tools (as well as those of analytic philosophy). The 'Chomskyian revolution' that followed was as much a technical one as a conceptual one. But the crucial change was that the tools, elaborated and properly formulated, were now in the service of a *theory*.

The elaboration of Chomsky's ideas since 1957 has had an enormous impact on linguistics and philosophy (some of which can be traced in the notes to this sub-section). Here we concentrate on the main question, namely the extent to which the theory has transformed linguistics into a science.

The most successful part of Chomsky's theory is the first developed, which concentrates on syntax (i.e. the formal structure of languages). In the Appendix (p. 296) an example is given of the use of 'transformational grammar', the basic syntactical tool in Chomsky's theory (the reader may find it helpful to read the Appendix at this juncture). In this example, one sees all of the key features of transformational grammar. 'Strings' of symbols are generated by formal rules to make 'deep structures', which can then be turned into phrases in some language by inserting 'lexical items' (e.g., words). This generative process is creative and inexhaustible – a finite set of rules and lexical items can generate an infinite number of phrases. The 'deep structures' can be viewed as merely a stage in the formal generation of phrases, but in fact they are inevitably associated with some *invariant* linguistic reality, and we shall return to this point.

That the theory is purely formal at this state begs a lot of questions. But before we address these, notice some of the advantages of this approach. In fact the transformational grammar possesses a number of features which are essentially *scientific*.

In the first place we do *have* a theory, which has been elaborated *formally* so that both its operation and domain of application are fixed rather precisely (at least so far); moreover this domain of application is apparently very large and non-trivial, so that the theory is very *rich*, and thereby claims to unveil, in an *unambiguous* way, a hitherto unknown 'reality' (of deep structures and generative rules) which suggest further undiscovered facts about the structure of the human mind (see section 'Quo vadis?' on p. 281. The theory also claims to elucidate previously inexplicable facts (whose importance was not always previously recognized), such as the 'creativity' of human language – that it 'makes infinite use of finite means' (von Humboldt).

All of these features are those one associates with a scientific theory. Perhaps most interesting of all, in view of the complete lack of numbers, measurements, or 'laws' in the theory is that it is in a form in which it is applicable to the real world (of linguistic phenomena) and is *empirically testable*, up to a point. This testing is not, to be sure, done with numerical experiments, but rather by comparing the structures generated with features of real spoken and written language. More ambitious projects involve, for example, machine translation of languages, and related mathematical work in ciphering. We return to the testing of linguistic theory at the end of this section.

From a physicist's point of view, all of this has the right 'smell'. The theory has the right mix of generality within prescribed limits, with the precision which makes it unambiguous and susceptible to critical analysis, and even empirical test.

A further quality of transformational grammar, and one characteristic of *all* good scientific ideas or theories, is that it suggests bold and general hypotheses. Chief amongst these hypotheses are those which attempt to link up the linguistic structures of transformational grammar with putative biological or mental 'structures'.

To clarify this point somewhat, we note two features of the kind of theory we are dealing with. First, the linguistic rules we are using are indeed very *species-specific* – it is clear that animals or computers use very different rules. In fact so far they are much more than species-specific, but language-specific (to the extent that we can define a language better than 'a dialect with an army and a navy'). In fact the deep structures as we have defined them will vary considerably from one spoken language to another, and the rules we have given here would be quite inappropriate to, for example, Japanese. They would be even more inappropriate to the languages of mathematics and music (which may not be armed, but can certainly be used to communicate – and are generative).

Thus clearly if we wish to establish a link between linguistic structures and mental structures, or simply find linguistic structures common to all humans, we must go beyond the rules and deep structures we have so far. The search for a set of linguistic rules and structures common to all humans is known under the somewhat pretentious epithet of 'the search for a *universal grammar*'.[53]

Quo vadis?

The attempt to go beyond syntactical structure to some more universal theory of linguistic structure (or 'grammar') is not solely motivated by grandiose ambition. It is also forced on linguists by the open nature of language itself. In fact it is impossible to prevent semantic considerations (i.e. those related to the 'meaning' of phrases) from entering into syntax. This is most easily seen by noting that, so far, we have done nothing to prevent our generative grammar from producing nonsense sentences; but in fact semantics reaches far deeper than this, into the very heart of syntax.

Consider for example, the well-known nonsense sentence 'colourless green ideas sleep furiously'. There is no grammatical problem here, only a semantic one. We can only reject this phrase because it has no meaning.

Now one might try and simply ignore this, by taking the purist attitude that one's job is simply to generate sentences, regardless of their meaning. I will not stop here to ask whether it is possible to do this (i.e. whether it is possible to rigorously separate syntactic and semantic components of a language in this way), but merely note that such an attitude is *unscientific*. If linguistics aspires to be a science, it must strive to go beyond syntax. The simplest way to see this is to note that if one tries to maintain that transformational grammar will eventually lead to a 'universal grammar', then one must find a way of translating between different human languages, at the very least. Otherwise the assertion of universality is untestable! And yet we cannot translate unless we know the meaning of the words! The 'universal grammar' is an empty idea unless we can test it, for we have very little a priori evidence to suggest that such a thing should exist (and *no* biological evidence).

The reaction of the Chomsky school to this has been to steadily enlarge the scope of linguistic enquiry to include the extralinguistic factors which inevitably enter into any consideration of the meanings of words. Unfortunately this forced search for a universal grammar now leads us into a far wider realm, consisting of all the concepts and objects of language, and the entities in nature (or elsewhere) to which they refer. In the 'systems' language so beloved by members of this school, the linguists are trying to devise formal language systems which describe not only the system of human languages, but also a far, far larger system including all relevant extralinguistic factors. Such an effort is clearly self-defeating – not only do we have no inkling of how to formalize this larger system, but we expose ourselves completely to the most devastating of Gödel's proofs.[54] For he showed that any attempt to devise a formal 'metasystem' trying to formally encompass a 'larger' system was doomed to failure. One finds that the metasystem will be riddled with inconsistent and/or undecidable propositions. These ideas refer solely to formal systems – but that is what linguists are trying to make of language. (Note, incidentally, that Gödel's ideas are well known as practical problems in robotics and cryptography, for essentially the same reasons.)

This points the way to a fundamental flaw, not just in the quest for universal grammar, but in the almost universally unquestioned hypothesis that 'the human linguistic faculty is unique', or that 'language and creativity in language are what distinguish humans from animals or robots'. Recall that Descartes[55] felt it was obvious that one could distinguish between people and animals/robots by observing their actions and responses to questions. Chomsky has made it abundantly clear that he is of the same opinion,[56] feeling that it is the creativity of human language that makes it unique. Yet it should be utterly obvious that no such judgement is permissible unless we have a theory of 'universal grammar' which not only encompasses all human language (all *possible* human languages) but also all possible non-human languages! Such a theory is impossible *in principle* for us if we allow non-human languages which break the putative rules which describe *human* universal grammar. It seems to then be very obvious to anyone listening to, say, recordings of the sounds of whales communicating, that a substantial amount of information is being exchanged (the musical quality is enough to indicate this), and that we have not the slightest idea what this might be. The *obvious* explanation for this, *within the very framework that Chomsky has advocated*, is that something is being communicated, very possibly in a creative manner (if such a concept is relevant), but that it is being done within a formal linguistic framework which is (at present anyway) inaccessible to us.[57]

So we seem to be in a quandary – the attempt to formalize the study of human language, to make it scientific, inexorably forces us into the arms of Gödel and the unfathomable limits to human understanding. What do we do now? And has anything been achieved at all?

In fact things are not quite so bad. Transformational grammar has done a lot to systematize (if not explain) at least some important aspects of the incredibly wealthy structure in language. Some territory has been gained! But this limited success is typical of scientific advance – one searches for, and with a combination of luck, systematic work, and leaps of imagination, one unearths *underlying invariants*, or *unifying principles*. And it is equally typical of scientific advance that this success stimulates attempts to extend these principles beyond the terra firma which has been gained – often with embarrassing results. Just as Descartes vastly overreached himself (and the science of his day) with his theory of 'fluxions', Chomsky and his followers have gone way too far in their discussion of semantics, and the generalities of human (and other) languages. One must never forget that the class of *unsuccessful* would-be scientific theories is far larger (in principle, infinitely larger!) than the class of successful ones.[58]

This is particularly true when it comes to vague prognostications or 'sketches for future theories', such as the 'theory' of universal grammar.[59] This sort of thing runs counter to the very spirit of *discovery* (rather than forecasting) of science. And, in fact, none of the arguments for the existence of 'semantic structures', a 'semantic component', or a 'universal grammar', with some connection to mental or biological structures, have any force outside the 'black-box' paradigm.[60]

So, one obvious tactic that a would-be *scientific* linguist may think of employing is to stay with what has been established so far (i.e. the rules of transformational grammar), and then try testing these out in a limited way. One may imagine the analogy here with species classification. Clearly the *origin* of different species involves deep questions which were impossibly difficult for the taxonomists of the eighteenth century. But it did not stop them from classifying species, and this classification is still very useful – although it is constantly being modified as we learn more about the *evolution* of species.

In the same way we can imagine syntax as a taxonomy, subject to progressive revision as we learn more about its syntactical origins.

In fact this is very much what some schools of linguistics are doing these days. Typical programmes involve, for example, the attempt to systematically eliminate nonsense phrases from language (this being empirically testable), or trying to machine translate between languages. Even these programmes are very ambitious, but they have the great advantage that they are at all times restrained by empirical test. Moreover, they test any theories about grammar, whether these arise in the context of transformational grammar or not (the reader is encouraged to look at some of the recent literature on these topics). Notice, incidentally, that these programmes presuppose some kind of 'linguistic reality' behind the rules – a feature which is scientific – but this reality is clearly *semantic* in nature.[61,62]

So, finally, what have we learnt? We have taken a subject like linguistics, which is so different from physics that even fundamental categories of physics (of systems, interactions, etc.,) and the language associated with them, are inappropriate to linguistics. Nevertheless the subject can be developed, up to a point, in a reasonably scientific way, in the context of a formal and testable theory which has already offered new insights into the way we communicate.

To be sure, we are a long way from *linking up* linguistics with the mainstream of science. This mainstream has a chain or 'tree-like' structure, which runs from sciences like geology and biology down through chemistry to physics (and the mysteries of quantum mechanics!). These subjects are all linked, and it is usual to look at this linking in a way which envisions physics as the fundament or root of the whole structure (although, as I have already discussed, such a view is not necessarily correct). Now one can guess (as Chomsky has) how the linking up of linguistics might be accomplished – but guessing is one thing, and doing another! It seems difficult now to imagine what kind of subject linguistics will be (or what it will be called) when this linking up is finally achieved. Who could have foreseen modern physics in the writings of Galileo?

This ends our discussion of science *per se*. The non-scientific reader may feel a bit disoriented – the picture offered here of both 'hard' and 'soft' sciences is less limpid or secure than might be hoped or expected. If this is the impression I give, then so much the better. Perhaps the finest summary of our position ever given is that in the cave analogy of Plato – of helpless mortals fated only to watch the shadows of the fundamental 'ideas', projected from behind by the ineluctable light of reality. In this light, physicists and linguists are no different from anyone else, despite all the refinements of 'scientific method'.

Nevertheless we have had to cover all this ground, and we have gained something. Rather than a long discussion of contemporary philosophy of science, which is a constantly changing amalgam of fashionable ideas about science, I have chosen to display, as a kind of benchmark, the *real thing*, i.e. the present state of two would-be scientific disciplines, including their ugly and uncertain sides. There seems to be no other honest way to approach the question of whether accounting can be considered as a science, and if so, what is the 'accounting reality' with which it is trying to come to grips.

Science, reality and accounting

There's no accounting for taste.

(Anon.)

Our long survey of different kinds of science has at last brought us to accounting and economics, and the possibility that accounting might *become* a science. We are going to assume from the outset that it has not yet achieved this goal, in common with the majority of contemporary accounting theorists.

Why is this? One common popular view of accounting is summed up by Samuelson,[63] paraphrasing Schumpeter.[64]

> Accounting does not benefit from arithmetic; it is arithmetic – and in its early stages, according to Schumpeter, arithmetic is accounting, just as geometry in its early stages is surveying.

Perhaps so – but what do the numbers *represent* – if indeed anything? This question takes us straight to the heart of much of the debate in accounting theory (and to be fair, Samuelson has elsewhere given a simple review of some of this debate[65]). The problem is an accountant's one, and I will not try and discuss it in any detail here – suffice it to say that many of the numbers in accounting and financial reports depend on judgements or estimates of things which may not have yet occurred (and indeed may never do so). This renders some of these numbers rather arbitrary.[66] Other articles in this book by accounting theorists will cover some of this debate in more detail (and see also Notes 67 and 68 on attempted 'conceptual frameworks' for accounting, and Note 69). In this article I offer a scientist's view. Apparently such a view is desirable, since there is a belief among some accounting theorists that the conceptual problems of accounting could be *solved* if only it could be made into a science like, for example, physics.

ACCOUNTING AS A SCIENCE?

Now we have already seen, in the section on linguistics, how the blind application of naive 'black-box' ideas about science can lead a subject into sheer nonsense. Unfortunately in the twentieth century it has become very common to see 'science' and 'scientific' being used as buzzwords to describe everything from religions to Rice Krispies. Thus it is well to note the warning given (again by Samuelson[70]) against those economists who let themselves be too impressed by physics:

> There is really nothing more pathetic than to have an economist or a retired engineer try to force analogies between the concepts

> of economics and the concepts of physics . . . Nonsensical laws, such as the law of conservation of purchasing power, represent spurious social science imitations of the important physical law of energy conservation; and when an economist makes reference to a Heisenberg principle of indeterminacy in the social world, at best this must be regarded as a figure of speech or a play on words.

Notice that Samuelson does not believe that *no* aspect of human behaviour is amenable to scientific inquiry (and nor do I – see the last section!); certainly he believes economics to be something of a science.[71] But can accounting be one, and if so, how?

These are the two questions we address in this sub-section. Recently the idea has been promulgated, particularly by R. Sterling in the USA, that the 'scientization' of accounting is a worthy and attainable goal; and much of the argument has been by analogy with simple classical concepts in physics (like volume, length, etc.). Sterling has even proposed 'laws' of accounting, analogous to those in physics, and his ideas constitute a good starting point for our analysis. They are well set out in his book,[72] and also in articles written both before[73] and after[74] that book; and he returns to the fray in the present volume.[75]

Sterling begins by noting that issues in accounting theory never seem to get solved, but simply fade away, to later reappear under different names. However, he does not believe this to be an intrinsic feature of the discipline or its subject matter, but merely the result of a misconception. Apparently the widespread belief that accounting is an 'art', not amenable to scientific method, is false – and has led accountants into a morass in which accounting principles are nothing but *conventions*, decided by legal *fiat* or by endless committee meetings (of, for example, the FASB).

All of this, according to Sterling, will change if we simply *redefine* accounting as a science. For those unsure what this may entail, Sterling gives an example, which he calls 'Sterling's Definition', which says essentially that depreciation ought to be redefined as a 'measurable' attribute, namely, as 'the decline in the exit value of a productive asset' (the exit value being the expected selling price). 'Sterling's Law' then consists in the empirical proposition that the exit value V of an automobile depreciates exponentially,[76] so that $V = V_0e^{-\alpha t}$, where t is the time; he proposes a depreciation rate of 40 per cent per annum. This proposition is empirical because it can be tested by surveys of automobile exit values. The great advance provided by Sterling's Law is supposed to be that depreciation is no longer *allocated* (by convention) but corresponds rather to an empirical quantity, namely, the exit value. As such, Sterling compares his law to the law of mass conservation in physics – the two are presumed to have a similar epistemological status. Moreover, redefining various accounting notions so that they become 'measurable', in this sense, is supposed to change accounting from a subjective art into an objective science; and the relevant measurements are repeatedly compared to measurements of simple extensive quantities in physics like volume, length, or mass.[77]

What is a scientist to make of this? Sterling's traduction of the usual use of words like 'measurement', 'objective', or 'scientific law' have already been discussed by philosophers,[78] and my father has given a fairly comprehensive rebuttal of Sterling's ideas from an accounting standpoint.[79] However no scientist to my knowledge has commented on Sterling's ideas or the general question of whether one might scientize accounting, so I shall attempt to do so here.

First, a few general remarks. It seems to me that neither recurring controversy, nor the existence of conventions decided by consensus and/or committees, nor the presence or absence in a discipline of numbers, quantitative or non-quantitative 'laws', or 'measurements', have much to do with whether a discipline is scientific or not. I have already discussed most of these points (see pp. 268–71 and 276–8 for committees, conventions, and consensus; see p. 271 and p. 276 for irrelevance of numbers, measurements, and 'the flight from judgment into calculation' (Colin Lyas, Note 78) and p. 277 for 'laws'), and so will not repeat myself. As far as recurring issues are concerned, physical science is hardly immune to this phenomenon – one needs only to think of the controversies over 'action at a distance', or 'atomism' (i.e. whether nature has 'fundamental building blocks' or not), both as old as or older than ancient Greek philosophy,[80] to see that many of the fundamental issues in physics never die, but are continually being reborn under new names. This is true of almost *all* issues in biology!

In fact Sterling's claims are very reminiscent of the claims made by behaviourists in post-war linguistics, discussed in the section 'Reality in language' (p. 279). Moreover I suspect that most scientists would find them equally irritating – as with many claims made for social 'science', one senses that the attempt is being made to get something for nothing. To hear that all that is required is a 'change of definition', or a 'change in methodology' (as though the application of 'scientific method' were like a dose of aspirin); to see 'laws' made to appear out of the thin air of statistical analysis, or postulated in an *ad hoc* way (often by analogy with some law in a science like physics), in the absence of any real theory; nothing is more guaranteed to make scientists turn away in sheer boredom. As I have elaborated in the foregoing, scientific disciplines do not appear by magic, but involve *fundamentally new ideas and concepts*, which with great skill and insight must be transformed into a *theoretical framework*, which itself defines the application of the ideas and concepts. Typically such work takes decades or centuries.

This point has not been ignored by Sterling (cf. his reference to the 'theoretical import' of a concept, and his example of 'cephalic index' in this context[81]). But then where is the theory which is supposed to lead to 'Sterling's Law'? Or the empirical testing, that one might expect him to have presented, of the accuracy of this law?

In fact, quite apart from any criticisms one might have of Sterling's conception of science, it seems to me that *insofar as Sterling's law is testable it is manifestly wrong*.

Suppose, for example, we take Sterling's example of car depreciation. Now anyone who has bought and sold a car knows very well that its value (as defined by selling price) may depreciate (or even occasionally *appreciate*, particularly if it is old) in a way which depends on an awesomely large number of uncontrollable and unknown factors. Even an average over samples, each consisting of different makes of cars, sold in different regions, with differing climates, in differing economic conditions, is highly unlikely to show any obvious pattern, but rather large and fluctuating variations from sample to sample, and with large variances within any particular sample. For example, in France a Citroen CX20 will tend to depreciate slowly because it is a well-made family car, usually driven by respectable middle-class families; while a Citroen 2CV (the famous 'Deux Chevaux') may well depreciate rapidly in the first few years (it has a fairly fragile body) but thereafter very slowly (the motor lasts almost indefinitely). But depreciation will be slower in the South of France (better weather), except near the sea (salt erosion); in times of high inflation the 2CV exit value may rise, along with that of the CX20, but if this is accompanied by low economic growth or high unemployment, the 2CV exit values may rise faster than those of the CX20 (it is initially cheaper) or maybe slower (rich people suffer less in hard times); and so on, through the effects of air pollution legislation, the budget presented by the government to the Assemblée Nationale, petrol prices, the health of Mikhail Gorbachev, etc., etc.

Thus any attempt at a realistic model of car exit values must clearly be very sophisticated (one might imagine a Leontief-type input–output model, involving hundreds of economic factors influencing the exit value of a 2CV in various non-linear ways) and necessarily inaccurate. Indeed the situation seems reminiscent of weather prediction (where modern computers now take account of *trillions* of different factors), and Sterling's Law is then analogous to, say, the hypothesis that regardless of location on the earth, the time correlation average between cloud cover at time t_1 and time t_2, at this location, will decay exponentially as $e^{\beta(t_2 - t_1)}$. This is not only *not true*, but clearly a silly proposition – even the *statistics* of weather pattern evolution are not going to be that easy!

But in fact the situation is far worse in accounting than meteorology. One might imagine a peculiar sect of meteorologists whose only interest was to make up and test statistical assertions like the above. We know now that they would have no success, because of the inherently chaotic behaviour of non-linear systems such as the weather system, and it is doubtful who would be interested in their work anyway – it would not satisfy any 'user-needs', quite apart from its total lack of *theoretical import*. However in meteorology we do have the relevant equations (of heat transfer, gas motion, etc.) defined in terms of the relevant variables (pressure, temperature, humidity, reflectivity, solar radiation distribution, plant absorption coefficient, etc.), valid to a very good approximation, which numerically *do describe the state of the system we are interested in*. In accounting we do not even know how to accurately describe the 'financial state' of a business enterprise, which is what we are interested in! As we have already seen, the numbers in accounting do not necessarily represent this at all. Attempts like those of Sterling to make accountants talk about empirical quantities may seem laudable, but in the absence of any *theory*, his definition of depreciation has the same status as that of cephalic index – a number of no theoretical import. I thus have to say that I am at a complete loss to understand how an *ad hoc* law, proposed in the absence of any theory and in obvious contradiction with economic facts, should be taken seriously at all!

However (the reader may point out) surely I am just tilting here at a straw man – I still haven't tried to answer the two questions originally posed (*can* accounting become a science, and if so how?). Here it seems to me that a comparison of accounting with economics (and related disciplines such as population biology) is quite revealing, both in the possibilities, and fundamental difficulties, it suggests.

We have already, at numerous reprises, seen how accounting and economics depend on each other for basic information and concepts.

Economics depends on accounting information, and accounting, for its mere formulation, requires some economic theory. But now it is often claimed that 'economics is a science' – so why not accounting?

Let us first see in what sense economics is supposed to be a science. At first glance many of the models in mathematical economics seem rather like those of meteorology in their basic structure – both involve complicated non-linear equations coupling large numbers of variables, the latter being a function of time (and location, if one wants a really detailed economic model). The solutions will then often be very complex, with chaotic behaviour or worse, and a very complicated 'phase space', so complex that most economists never try to solve the dynamical equations, but look rather for certain characteristic features (stability, fixed points, extremum properties, etc.). This is true whether one is looking at decision theory, or wheat prices, or the stock market (although in the latter case one often looks at the 'discrete map' approximation to the dynamic equation).[82]

However there is a fundamental difference, which is immediately obvious when one looks at the nature of the disputes which arise in the two fields. In meteorology almost all disputes are essentially about the quality and applicability of various *approximation techniques* to the complex equations, in the full knowledge that the solutions are beyond the reach of any conceivable computer (even one quite literally as large as the universe). The approximations can be of many kinds, often involving various subsidiary *models* which attempt to simplify the problem. In the case of arguments, these models can be checked in various ways, by comparison with other approximations, or even with scaled-down laboratory experiments (and in a famous case, by comparison between observations of Jupiter's cloud motion, computer simulations, laboratory experiments, and theoretical analysis of a simple 'Taylor column' model – which turned out eventually to be inapplicable).

In economics, on the other hand, disagreement is usually centred around the applicability or meaningfulness of the models themselves, rather than the mathematical analysis applied to them. This problem cannot arise in meteorology, where one can, in principle, *derive* the models from the underlying known equations for the earth's climatic state (or else show that they are not derivable). There are no such underlying equations in economics, nor even a way of describing the economic state of the world. To put it another way, we do not have a handle on 'economic reality', in the sense of having some unambiguous formal way of describing the economic state of the world.

This should hardly come as a surprise – it has been re-expressed[83] by saying that while we can completely describe the climate in terms of the individual molecules on earth, which have a simple behaviour, the fundamental molecules of economics have minds of their own, and are hence unbelievably complex – indeed the reader constitutes one such molecule (as does Margaret Thatcher, who, as seen in Note 24, is one of the more influential molecules around). In fact, as noted on p. 264, meteorology is not quite so simple, since the earth's climatic system is fundamentally *open*, although apart from the solar influence the outside influences are weak (even though crucial in the *long term*).

Obviously the economic system is far more open – even a theory which took account of every conceivable economic index in the world (including, for example, the whereabouts of every single cent, penny, centime, etc., in all conceivable forms, in the world) would be a theory of a hopelessly open system, since it would not include a description of the *mental state* of individual people, which is clearly the main determining factor in economic changes (and, as we have seen, can even affect the climatic state).

In this case, why does mathematical economics work at all? After all, predictions of national trade deficits or unemployment rates, on the macroscopic scale, or, for example, gold, shares, or house prices on the microeconomic scale, are not complete nonsense – they work to some accuracy, at least on short time scales (of order months, or sometimes a year or two).

To answer this question in any general way seems well nigh impossible to me. Clearly the fact that one can predict unemployment rates in a country, a year hence, with an accuracy of ≈ 1 per cent of the total workforce is impressive, but it is also easy to argue that in any open system, no matter how complex or open, there will always be some global macroeconomic indices whose behaviour will be reasonably smooth and/or governed by simplifying conditions (such as, for example, some maximum principle), at least to a reasonable approximation. But there will be other indices which will not – nobody would think, for example, of trying to predict the Dow Jones index to 1 per cent accuracy over periods of more than a few weeks, let alone a year! These features are fairly general in the treatment of many different models of non-linear systems. And it must not be forgotten that while the successes of mathematical economics, in discussing certain models of certain aspects of economic behaviour, are quite remarkable, nevertheless most microeconomic phenomena are quite beyond any meaningful predictive analysis. If one thinks of the motion of a particular share price, for example, this seems rather clear. Getting back to accounting, it also seems clear that economic theory would not be capable of saying much more than an experienced businessman, no matter how sophisticated a model of the situation one might run through a computer. And such a model would lack the essential businessman's intuition about the best moves to make. Even though we might put a very sophisticated game theoretic program into the computing model, to simulate the various strategic alternatives open to the various parties involved, there is nothing to stop, say, a board of directors from simply changing the rules, by going outside any conceivable model of the situation. Hence the essential *creativity* involved in the real economic world of business enterprises – and this is perhaps the crucial and ineluctable difference between any meteorological system and the economic sphere. While the climatic system (and to a lesser extent certain macroeconomic indicators) are relatively unaffected by the exercise of human will and creativity (or only affected in simple ways), the microeconomic indicators relevant to a business enterprise, as well as other multifarious factors affecting its operation, are quite essentially dependent on individuals and their desires, emotions, and creative capacities.[84]

And so, in a way, we come full circle, for as discussed on p. 279, a very similar block lay in the way of ever describing language in the same way as one describes physical processes. And yet we saw that in a certain sense linguistics *could* become a science, by postulating the existence of linguistic 'structures', and showing how they constrain and explain at least the syntactical structure of language.

Thus it seems to me to be premature to say that accounting may *never* become a science in the way that we could imagine linguistics becoming one. But the time seems far off, since any conceivable theory of accounting will presumably have to depend on a far wider variety of 'deep structures' than the human language faculty, and there is hardly even a glimmer of such a theory at the present time.

THE QUEST FOR ACCOUNTING REALITY

Where then does this leave us in our search for the sphinx of reality? Let us briefly recap what we have learnt so far. We have seen that in subjects as disparate as biology and linguistics, various 'structures' or invariant underlying features are sought, and an attempt made ultimately to relate them to physical entities. The road to physics may be long – in linguistics it proceeds through language analysis to the postulate of underlying biological structures, through the gene, and molecular biology, until one arrives at the quantum mechanics of organic molecules. Nevertheless, this 'programme' for the construction of a scientific understanding of reality has had great successes, and it strongly influences everyday discourse about reality. In their everyday work, physicists talk about atoms, photons and nuclei as though they were simple entities having the same ontological status as bricks or marbles. Biologists and linguists follow suit with their genes and phonemes. More generally it is clear that on a superficial level, old ideas about 'substance', the 'aether', 'building blocks', etc. still guide the intuition and day-to-day activities of scientists.

Unfortunately, as we have also seen, the fact that, for example, physicists *talk* about quarks or gluons or superfluids as they were like marbles or beer (particularly in popular presentations) does not mean that they really *think* about them in this way. Indeed if we force a physicist to articulate his or her real way of looking at the basic entities of the subject, we find that the surface reality of particles or waves, spins, etc., is little more than a shorthand for the description of the unfathomable quantum-mechanical mystery lying beneath. This shorthand sounds almost like ordinary discourse, albeit with a rather arcane vocabulary – but in fact it is merely a code which masks the enigma from the uninitiated.

Thus one finds a yawning *duality* in the approach of physicists towards their own subject. In some ways the paradoxes of quantum mechanics have made this more obvious in physics than other subjects. But even in biology, where the crude materialistic vocabulary is most developed (one sometimes gets the impression that the 'organism' is built up like a Meccano set from the 'molecular building blocks') or in linguistics, with its cognitive structures, one is always aware of a substratum which is far more ethereal (even if one notices it only in the questions that biologists or linguists refuse to discuss!).

And so, marching along beside the powerful reductionism in science, which aims to construct everything from the building blocks of physics, we see a far more intangible substratum of presuppositions about the *reality beneath*, which strongly influence the development of our ideas, and without which it would be very difficult to unify or even make sense of the disparate aspects of our 'surface reality'.

Now it seems to me that one may also discern a similar substratum of reality in economics or accounting, but it is far more ghostly than anything we have seen so far. The reason is that there is no obviously simple or useful way of connecting economic or financial phenomena to the reductionist chain, leading back to physics, that we have discussed above. It is useful, in making this point, to compare mathematical economics with population biology. In the latter subject it is common to set up models involving distributions in time and space of the population density of various species – and then by building in simple hypotheses about the various species, such as their desire to eat (each other, or something else which is also in the model), to reproduce, to survive for as long as possible, etc., one may derive in a rather remarkable way, some of the more complex patterns of species evolution on earth;[85] with very sophisticated mathematical analysis being sometimes required. Often one may resort to game theory in setting up these models, in situations involving competing individuals or species.

Now we note that although the fundamental 'forces' driving the equations in these models (the various 'desires' of the individuals, for example) are not explained, and only defined in a simple way, there is usually a fairly clear connection with known biological processes, capable (at least in principle) of explaining the simple biological needs involved. This establishes the connection to the reductionist chain.

However, in economics, which also often involves similar genetheoretic or decision-theoretic models, the connection is very tenuous indeed. Nobody could really imagine (except perhaps Jim and Tammy Bakker) that we are endowed at birth with the 'profit motive'. Even what appear to be much more primitive desires, such as the desire to have a home (with or without cars and a swimming pool) can only be reasonably seen as the complicated result of various individual desires within the framework of a particular social arrangement (think of nomadic tribes). Moreover we have already seen that many economic phenomena, particularly on the microeconomic scale relevant to accounting, involve *in a quite essential way* a huge number of factors which are external to the microeconomic models which one may feasibly consider.

Thus it seems reasonable to assert that while we have a very interesting 'surface reality' in accounting and economics, consisting of goods, plant, people, financial transactions, etc., we can only organize this by excluding consideration of most of the 'elements' of this reality, leaving us with the stripped-down data of accounting. In doing so we pay a severe price – for not only do we leave many decisions about the meaningfulness of the entities involved (such as the legally-defined 'business enterprise') rather arbitrary (not to say allocation of costs, depreciation, etc.), but we also lose contact with the underlying, very complex, 'deep reality' of human desires and cognition, of climatic processes, of the countless other agents that underlie economic phenomena. In population biology there is no problem because we have found that only a few factors matter, when it comes to modelling evolution. In economics I have tried to argue that this is fundamentally not so, particularly on the microeconomic scale. The 'systems' with which accounting tries to deal, from corner stores to oil multinationals, are fundamentally *open systems, interacting strongly* with their environment *at all levels* (to make the analogy with physics).

This gloomy analysis of economic reality may satisfy neither the accountant nor the philosopher. To the optimistic accountant I can only give my encouragement in the search for a theory. To the philosopher my analysis will seem drastically over-simplified. In particular, most of my discussion of 'realities' makes them seem merely synonymous with 'internally consistent closed theories' (or, if not closed, connected to some other closed theory in a subsidiary way). However this is really how a scientist must look at reality – for every time theory changes, so must his/her way of looking at its fundament. Even if philosophy did not teach us how fragile was our sense of reality, the constant changing of scientific theory would serve to remind us. In this sense all the various realities that we grasp at must be viewed as mere conventions (personal or otherwise), as dust in the wind, or as Plato saw it, shadows on a cave wall.

Appendix: Transformational grammar

A proper description of these ideas would of course require many pages, and what I shall do here is simply outline how the theory may be viewed as *scientific* – even though, in my opinion at least, it is unlikely to be a correct theory in all its ramifications.

Chomsky started by trying to build a formal syntactical system which was capable of *generating* all the conceivable sentences in a language – and no more. This endeavour should be understood in the same way one understands any formal system, whether it be arithmetic, higher mathematics, the rules of chaos, or a computer or neural network – as a set of manipulation rules applied to a set of symbols, to produce 'strings' of symbols, starting from some set of initial strings. In mathematics the initial strings are known as the 'axioms', and the strings produced or *generated* using the manipulation rules are the 'formulae' or 'theorems' of the system – in general they will be infinite in number.[86] Moreover, *no 'meaning' whatsoever* is to be attached to these strings until they are 'interpreted' by mapping onto some other formal system – or, more generally, by making statements (i.e., strings) about the system or strings in it, in some higher *metasystem*. Thus, for example, upon examining the strings of a chess game (a formal system with strings expressed as a sequence of statements like [. . . 14.*K* → *Q*4; *KP* → *KP*5 . . .], as in the newspaper reporting of chess games), one may make meta-chess statements like 'White will win this game (string)'. This string would be generated in a formal system more complicated than chess, containing rules about winning and losing as well as rules enabling one to decide, for some strings, whether they will terminate and how. An *interpretation* of a chess string is provided by the equivalent sequence of moves on a chess board. The formal systems of mathematics are more elaborate than this – the symbols are *variables* (*x, y, z,* etc.), which range over, for example, the complex number system, itself generated by a simple set of axioms referring to these variables.[87]

Over the years the various efforts to devise a similar formal system

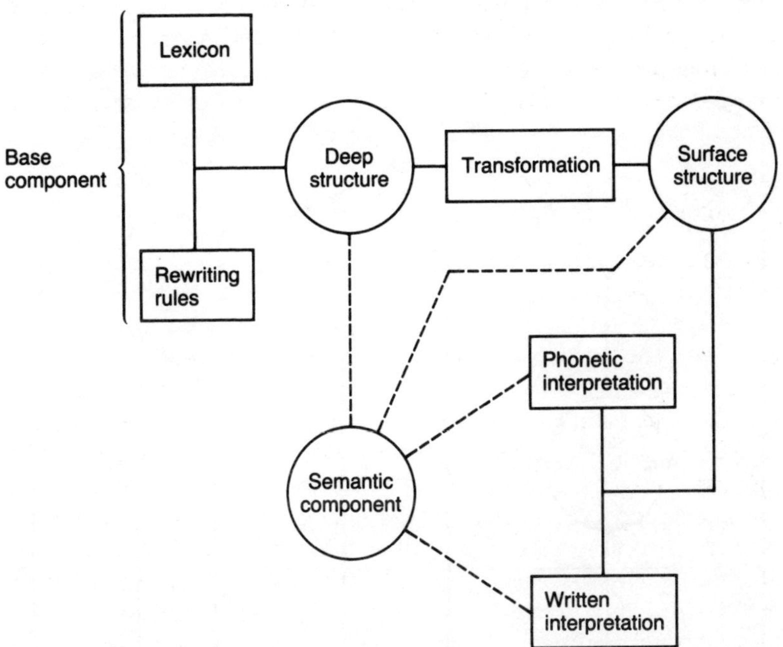

Figure 10.1 The basic structure of the 'standard theory' model of linguistic performance, roughly equivalent to that outlined by Chomsky (see Note 89). The terms used in the diagram are explained in the text

to generate language have very considerably elaborated Chomsky's initial attempts.[88] It is convenient for our purposes to discuss a particular model, which is similar to those of the 'standard theory', first outlined[89] by Chomsky in 1965. Models of this kind have the advantage of not being too complex, but still going beyond the initial work in incorporating semantic considerations into the formal syntactical system.[90]

The basic structure of the model we are going to deal with is illustrated in Figure 10.1, as a kind of flow diagram.[91] Roughly speaking the 'lexicon' is equivalent[92] to the 'set of symbols' in our formal system (a more precise analogy will appear shortly); these symbols are manipulated into 'strings' by the 'rewriting rules'. The set of 'initial strings' (or axioms) is essentially defined by the rewriting rules – they are rather abstract structures called 'initial phrase markers' which can be manipulated into 'deep structures' by the rewriting rules – at which point lexical items can be inserted.

What all this jargon means is best shown by an example. We are going to *generate* the following phrase (called P_9):

P_9 = 'Ken was asked by Phil to edit the book' (1)

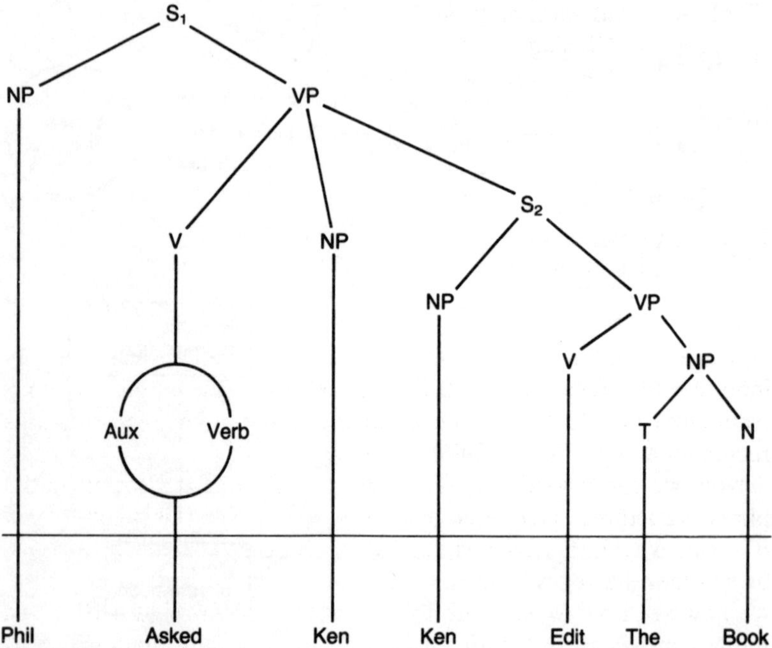

Figure 10.2 The 'deep structure' for the sentence of equation 1 represented graphically in 'tree' form

The relevant deep structure for P_9 is shown in Figure 10.2; it is a kind of 'tree' which results from the operation of the rewriting rules.[93] After inserting the appropriate lexical items in the deep structure, we will still need the transformation rules to derive P_9; this is discussed below.

Now to generate the tree of Figure 10.2 we need to know our rewriting rules. The rules I use are similar to those in *Syntactic Structures*[94] and are:

$$\begin{array}{l}
1\ \text{Sentence S} \rightarrow \left\{ \begin{array}{c} \text{NP + VP} \\ \{0\} \end{array} \right\} \\
2\ \text{VP} \rightarrow \text{Verb + NP + S} \\
3\ \text{Verb} \rightarrow \text{Aux + V} \\
4\ \text{V} \rightarrow \{\text{set of all verb infinitives: run, look, \ldots}\} \\
5\ \text{Aux} \rightarrow \text{Tense +} \left\{ \begin{array}{c} M \\ \text{have + en} \\ \text{be + ing} \end{array} \right\} \\
6\ \text{Tense} \rightarrow \left\{ \begin{array}{l} \text{Present} \\ \text{Past} \end{array} \right. \\
7\ \text{M} \rightarrow \{\text{ will, can, may, must, \ldots}\} \\
8\ \text{NP} \rightarrow \left\{ \begin{array}{l} \text{NP sing} \\ \text{NP plural} \end{array} \right. \\
9\ \text{NP sing} \rightarrow \left\{ \begin{array}{l} \text{N} \\ \text{T + N} \end{array} \right. \\
10\ \text{NP plural} \rightarrow \left\{ \begin{array}{l} \text{N + s} \\ \text{T + N + s} \end{array} \right. \\
11\ \text{T} \rightarrow \text{the} \\
12\ \text{N} \rightarrow \{\text{set of all nouns: dog, cat, \ldots}\}
\end{array} \qquad (2)$$

Now we see first that rules 1 and 2 alone can generate recursively an infinite set of trees (Figure 10.3); substituting 0 (the empty set) for S (sentence) in rule 1, at some point along the chain, will stop this recursion and produce a finite sentence.

Now we can regard the trees in Figure 10.3 as the set of 'initial phrase structures', generated by rules 1 and 2; from this point of view it is somewhat immaterial whether they are referred to as the axioms, or whether we regard the rules themselves as axioms. In any case, we now see how to generate the deep structure in Figure 10.2. An initial phrase structure with a main clause S_0 and subsidiary clause S_1 is generated, and then rules 3–6, 8, 9, 11, and 12 are applied (using the past tense for 'ask' which converts it to 'asked'). Note that rules

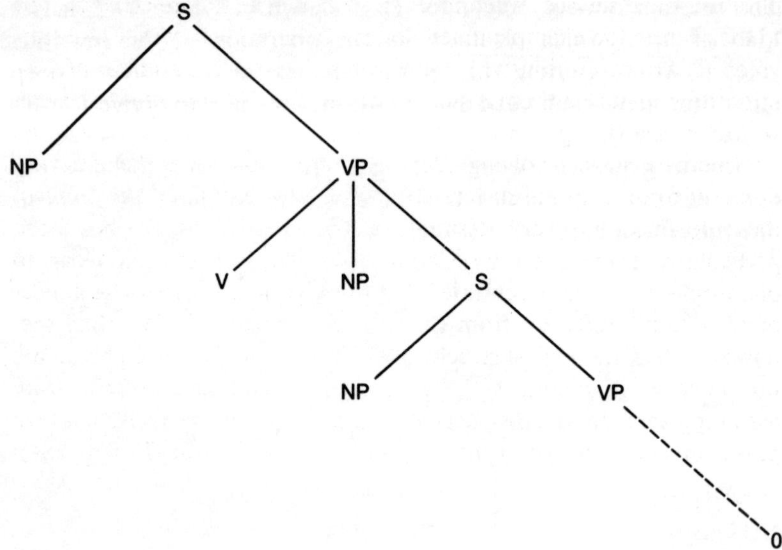

Figure 10.3 The set of deep structures generated by the rules in equation 2 illustrated in tree form *before* the application of the rewriting rules 3 to 11

4 and 12 draw upon the lexicon of verbs to nouns to fill in N and V – thus N and V behave like the variables *x, y, z* . . . in mathematics, and the lexicon is just the 'domain' of the variables, in the same way as, for example, the complex numbers can constitute the domain of the variables in mathematics.

So far, so good – we have generated a deep structure for P_9 in a generative manner. But now, in order to get to P_9, we need the 'transformation rules' (cf. Figure 10.1), which are responsible for the name 'transformational grammar' sometimes given to this kind of system. These rules act in general on the entire tree, rather than just parts of it – this distinguishes them from the rewriting rules. Without going through these rules in detail,[95] we can see what we need here – we must identify the second NP (noun phrase) in S_0 with the first NP in S_1 (with an obvious generalization to larger sentences) change the active verb in the dominant S_0 to passive, and add 'to' to the infinitive 'edit' in S_1.

Finally, if we wish to transform this 'surface structure' into a spoken phrase, we need a phonetic interpretation of it – see section 'Quo vadis?' on p. 281.

First, however, what have we come up with? So far our system is entirely *syntactical*, and capable of generating all sorts of nonsense phrases, at the surface structure level, such as 'The square circle walked to the silence' (an example much discussed in the 1960s was 'Colourless green ideas sleep furiously.'). However it does have a number of very interesting features. From a small number of rules and a finite lexicon we can *create* (i.e. generate) an infinite number of sentences, with an intermediate stage involving deep structures which may have a very different form from the surface structures we use in daily life. Both of these features are very desirable – the creative aspect has been particularly emphasized by Chomsky,[96] and it has been clear to philosophers for many centuries that the logical structure of sentences must be quite different from their surface structure.[97] We shall see, however, that the logical structure and deep structure of a phrase are not necessarily identical.[98] The reader should also refrain from assuming that the deep structure of a proposition is invariant as we pass from one language to another (see section 'Quo vadis?' on p. 281).

NOTES

1 Unfortunately, it seems that the tendency of some accounting theorists, to take examples from physics all the time, comes from an understanding of science derived from the philosophy of science literature. This literature has, very regrettably, ignored other fields like biology, as well as the more successful 'social sciences' (such as, for example, economics or linguistics). Worse still, very few philosophers of science actually understand modern physics properly at all.

I therefore earnestly hope that this section may help readers from fields outside physics to go to more original and authoritative sources (see Notes 2, 12, 14); some of these are eminently readable, and, moreover, *correct*.

2 Some helpful antidotes to ignorance are as follows. Books for the layman which discuss 'physical reality' and the problems at the basis of physics are, for example, A.I.M. Rae, *Quantum Physics: Illusion or Reality*? (Cambridge University Press 1986), or N. Herbert, *Quantum Reality* (Anchor/Doubleday, 1983). Two books which also describe, in a very readable way, the main branches of modern physics and the phenomena they deal with, are R.P. Feynman, *The Character of Physical Law* (MIT/BBC Publications, 1965), a remarkable survey of modern physics given in Feynman's famous relaxed style, and A.J. Leggett, *The Problems of Physics* (Oxford University Press, Oxford paperbacks 1987), an equally remarkable introduction to the *problems* of contemporary physics. This latter book is part of a series published for the seventy-fifth anniversary of Bertrand Russell's famous *Problems of Philosophy* (Oxford University Press paperbacks, first published 1912). Other notable books in this series are those dealing with the problems of biology (J. Maynard-Smith), of evolution (M. Ridley), and of mathematics (I. Stewart). All these books are strongly recommended for their introduction to the deep issues in

their fields, which make the nature of the subjects so much clearer than would a mere discussion of their successes.

Most of the popular 'glossy' books on contemporary physics are so superficial as to be useless, but the reader may glean something of its wide applicability from *The Quantum Universe* by A. Hey and P. Walters (Cambridge University Press 1987), which has many pretty pictures.

Finally, a book at introductory university level which gives a very beautiful explanation of how quantum mechanics *really works*, is R.P. Feynman, *The Feynman Lectures on Physics*, vol. III: *Quantum Mechanics* (Addison-Wesley 1965). This is the third book in the famous 'Feynman lectures' series, transcribed from recordings of his lectures.

3 Thus in special relativity, 'reality' is made up of point particles moving in a four-dimensional (and infinite) spacetime continuum; the rods and clocks used in the various 'Gedankenexsperimente' are constructed from these particles. Newtonian particles move in (3 + 1)-dimensional spacetime. A very simple book which explains all this is *Spacetime Physics* by E.F. Taylor and J.A. Wheeler (W.H. Freeman 1966), eschewing even elementary calculus in doing so.

4 And yet many of the discussions of physics in the accounting literature do just this! Thus Sterling seems to rely almost exclusively on examples of pressure, volume and length, spring tension, etc., which are if anything pre-Newtonian. One might argue that this is more appropriate to comparisons with accounting (regarded as either primitive/pre-scientific, or just intrinsically simple); this argument is dealt with in the section 'Science, reality and accounting' on p. 285).

5 Of course from time to time (or perhaps very often, depending on one's inclinations), we become much more aware of the deep mysteries lying just below the surface of ordinary life. If nothing else, traumatic events such as death must make us *wonder*. As we shall see, quantum mechanics has had just such a traumatic effect on physics.

6 Actually I am making things seem simpler than they are. The problem of the self interaction of the point electron in even classical electrostatics raises various paradoxes, which are merely made worse by going to classical electrodynamics (involving the electromagnetic field). A quite readable discussion of this appears in R.P. Feynman, *The Feynman Lectures on Physics*, vol. II, ch. 28 (see Note 2). In fact, point particles lead to insuperable problems in classical physics.

7 Two caveats here. First, in some recent theory this assumption is dropped; the fields are assumed to exist in a 'superspace' of more dimensions (presently thought to be ten), with the extra dimensions being observable only at very high energies (quite inaccessible to all actual or conceivable experiments!). Second, in general relativity, the spacetime metric is itself a field, which duly interacts with the other fields. A 'unified field theory' aims at unifying all of these fields into a single (very complicated) field. Such a theory seems rather remote to this author.

8 Most fields are not simple scalar (i.e. having a single numerical value at each point in spacetime), but vector or tensor, with many components at each point.

9 To avoid confusion, the notion of 'test' particles or fields in no way implies any actual or hypothetical measurement (even though this is how

such a measurement would be done – hence the name). A test particle is merely one that has a low enough mass or charge that it can be considered to leave undisturbed the other particles with which it interacts. In classical physics there is no need whatsoever to introduce 'measurements' as part of the logical structure of the theory. The same is not true at all of quantum mechanics, at least at the present time.

10 The extraordinary range of phenomena now treated by physics is solely a result of quantum mechanics; previously, classical physics was only capable of dealing with a very small range of phenomena in any detail, such as the motion of the planets, or pendula, or simple engineering problems. It is not widely realized among the public that the enormous changes that have taken place in the twentieth century in technology, biology, chemistry, medicine, and even mundane things such as modern architecture stem almost entirely from quantum mechanics, directly or indirectly. This is because we know of no phenomena whose detailed workings cannot be explained by quantum mechanics, except (possibly) for life itself, and general relativistic phenomena (note that most biologists *assume* that quantum mechanics will eventually explain life as well, once the enormous complexities of this 'collective phenomenon' have been tamed. Not all physicists would agree!). The contrast with pre-quantum science, whose purview was limited to a few rather simple natural phenomena, is quite stunning.

11 Or even as clean as Kuhn would have it. Kuhn still makes mainstream science sound like applied mechanics, with neat little problems to be solved. As pointed out by Colin Lyas (Note 78) accounting theorists who read too much early philosophy of science are in danger of missing the point made by Feyerabend (see, for example, P.K. Feyerabend *Against Method* (Verso 1975)) which is that 'anything goes' in much of science research – *provided it works*. This sometimes leads to very strange ideas – but that is science!

12 The Medusa's head at the heart of quantum mechanics is indeed 'physical reality'. However another useful metaphor that suggests itself in discussing this subject is that of the Sorcerer's Apprentice – we have been given a magic wand that illuminates everything it touches, and yet remains fundamentally inscrutable to us (and perhaps dangerous as well – it has given us nuclear weapons). From this point of view, quantum mechanics is quite unique in human intellectual history – it is by far the most successful theory ever invented in any domain, and yet, as one of its greatest-ever exponents put it, 'nobody understands it' (R.P. Feynman, *The Character of Physical Law*, BBC Publications (1965), ch. 6, p. 129). Even more remarkably, most of its founders (including Einstein, Planck, de Broglie, and Schrödinger) rejected it later as an incomplete theory! It seems to be a major failure on the part of philosophers that such a remarkable situation in the development of human thoughts should have received so little serious attention in the philosophical literature (but see Note 2 above).

13 See Note 12.

14 There exists an extended version of this article, in which I give a much more thorough discussion of the technicalities of both quantum mechanics and linguistic theory; anyone interested in a copy of this may

write to me for one. It also contains a large amount of historical material, including my father's notes for a book which he intended to write on accounting, science, and philosophy, and the relation to standards setting; and all the notes on the discussions of science and accounting which we had in 1979–83.

15 It is actually very common in physics (and other sciences) to find many quantities or entities which are in principle not measurable or not observable. Another notorious example is the quark (of which there are presently believed to be eighteen kinds); theory indicates these particles to be unobservable in principle, despite their role as the fundamental nuclear particle and the massive *indirect* evidence for their existence.

16 I remind the reader of some simple mathematics. The function $\psi(r,t)$ is *complex* in general – this means that for any particular coordinate value (r_0,t_0), $\psi(r_0,t_o)$ will be a complex number $\psi = a + \imath b$. Recall then that the modulus of ψ is $|\psi| = (a^2 + b^2)^{1/2}$, and we can rewrite ψ as $\psi = |\psi|e^{\imath\theta}$, where $\tan\theta = b/a$, and θ is the phase. These statements become clear in the usual Argand representation of complex numbers, where $|\psi|$ is the magnitude of ψ, and θ is the angle between the line from the origin to (a,b) in the 'complex plane', and the real axis.

The terminology 'probability amplitude' is confusing, since it is not $\psi(r,t)$ which is a probability, but its modulus *squared*. A better term for ψ is 'wave function'.

17 See Note 16.

18 See Notes 12 and 14.

19 Schrödinger, E. (1935) 'Die gegenwërtige Situation in der Quantenmechanik', *Naturwissenhaften* 23: 807 (translation (1980) The present situation in quantam mechanics', *Proc. Am. Phil. Soc.* 124: 323.

20 See, for example, A.J. Leggett, S. Chakravarty, A. Garg, M.P.A. Fisher and W. Zwerger (1987) 'Dynamics of the dissipative 2-state system', *Rev. Mod. Phys.* 59: 1 and references therein; Caldeira, A.O. and Leggett, A.J. (1983) 'Quantum tunneling in a dissipative system', *Ann. Phys.* (New York) 149: 374.

21 Einstein, A., Poldolsky, B. and Rosen, N. (1935) 'Can quantum mechanical description of physical reality be considered complete?' *Phys. Rev. Lett.* 47: 777.

22 Bell, J.S. (1966) 'On the problem of hidden variables in quantum mechanics' *Rev. Mod. Phys.* 38: 447, and (1964) 'On the Einstein–Podolsky–Rosen paradox' *Physics* 1.195; see also the very interesting book *Speakable and Unspeakable in Quantum Mechanics*, by Bell (Cambridge University Press, Cambridge, 1988).

23 See, for example, Martinis, J.M., Devoret, M.H. and Clarke, J. (1987) 'Experimental tests for the quantum behaviour of a macroscopic variable; the phase across a Josephson junction', *Phys. Rev.* B35: 4682 (1987), and references therein. See also, Aspect, A., Dalibard, J. and Roger, G. (1982) 'Experimental test of Bell's inequalities using time-varying analyzers', *Phys. Rev. Lett.* 49: 1804, and references therein.

24 Thus, (who knows?) maybe the recent and surprising change of heart by Margaret Thatcher on 'green issues' (who could have predicted it?) may lead to politicians taking the action which may save the earth's atmosphere from severe man-made damage. Who knows? Nobody, of course.

Incidentally, we can see how quantum mechanics will eventually raise its ugly head again. If the perturbations are small enough, they will have to be described quantum-mechanically. In fact, even if we had a complete description of the *universe* (which we assume quantum-mechanical), we would still have to take account of quantum-mechanical uncertainties, which would be enormously magnified as time went on. Too bad for omniscient beings!

25 I have been very briefly describing here the results of fairly recent advances in our understanding of non-linear dynamic systems. Ironically, they were inspired partly by a paper of E. Lorenz, (1963) 'Deterministic non-periodic flow', *J. Atmos. Sci.* 20: 130, 448, which analysed the infinitely complex behaviour available to a very over-simplified model of our climate. These advances have been described for the laymen in the widely-selling book *Chaos* by James Gleick (Viking, New York, 1987). Further aspects of the subject are discussed in, for example, I. Stewart, *The Problems of Mathematics* (OPUS/Oxford University Press 1987), chapters 13–16; M.V. Berry (1978) 'Regular and irregular motion', in S. Jorna (ed.) *Topics in Non-linear Dynamics*, *Am. Inst. Phys. Conf. Proc.* 46: 16–120, and V. Arnold, (1963) 'Small denominators and problems of stability of motion in classical and celestial mechanics', *Russ. Math. Surveys*, 18: 6, 85.

The knowledgeable reader will immediately see that I have given a much over-simplified discussion of the dynamics of non-linear systems such as the solar system. In particular, the real phase space will not be divided up into regions of rational and irrational frequency ratios, but in a much more sophisticated way, because of frequency-pulling, etc. (and one even finds rational period ratios to be stable rather than unstable). Nevertheless the basic idea, that there is a 'fractal' or 'Cantor set' structure to evolution of these systems, is quite faithfully portrayed by the discussion – and any reader who has seen the detailed Voyager 2 photographs of Saturn's rings will have an example of how this structure can be displayed on a planetary scale. There has been a recent vogue in 'fractals' – readers can find pictures in Gleick's book, as well as many other references.

That such *simple* classical systems can exhibit such complexity must make the reader wonder at the awesome possibilities open to complicated systems possessing many particles or degrees of freedom. This takes us into the field of 'condensed matter physics', which deals with subjects as varied as superfluids, stars, neural networks, polymers and macromolecules, or the early universe. As such its reach extends far into modern biology, and the interesting connections with parts of modern economics have been recently realized (see the section 'Science, reality and accounting', p. 285, and Notes 63 to 85). Among other things, condensed matter physicists try to explain 'emergent properties' of complex systems – properties which cannot be found in the building blocks of which the complex systems are made.

26 Note that these 'simple systems' can often be very complicated, particularly in modern condensed matter physics.

27 E.P. Wigner expressed this as the 'unreasonable effectiveness of mathematics in science', while according to Einstein, 'the most incomprehensible thing about the universe is that it is comprehensible'.

28 This is fairly obvious in the case of quantum mechanics, where for many years the 'Copenhagen interpretation' of Bohr held sway, and still underlies the way almost all textbooks on quantum mechanics are written; this interpretation was put together by Bohr in the course of a series of debates at successive Solvay conferences in 1927–30 (principally between Einstein and Bohr).

A much more striking example, of course, is provided by both theories of relativity, whose present form, presentation, and underlying philosophy owe so much to Einstein alone. Since much of modern physics is affected by special relativity, his influence has been very great.

29 H. Poincaré, *Science et Hypothése* (H. Poincaré, Paris 1899); English translation in London, 1905.

30 One of the principal jobs of IUPAP committees is to make decisions about the fundamental quantities and units, and how they should depend on each other. This demands a thorough review of current understanding of the logical structure of physical theory, and is not a trivial undertaking. These committees are greatly aided by bodies such as the National Bureau of Standards in the USA, or the National Physical Laboratory in Britain; final decisions are usually made in Paris.

31 The reasons for the redefinition are very complex, but one reason is roughly as follows: the metre bar was observed to be not exactly 'constant' in length (despite a highly controlled environment). More correctly one would say that the convention that it *was* constant led to very small variations over time in the laws of physics. Atomic clocks have fantastic stability over time (much more than metallic bars), and the velocity of light is known now to be a fundamental constant of nature (after Einstein), so that nothing can change it. Hence the redefinition.

32 The assumption of additivity of lengths presupposes Euclidean geometry, and fails in general relativity. Thus, near a neutron star, we could find that two metre bars placed end-to-end would not always match up to a 'two-metre' bar (depending on how the comparison was done).

33 This point came to the fore in the debate over general relativity. Many scientists, reacting against the strange ideas of non-Euclidean geometry, tried to rewrite general relativity in Newtonian form, with the introduction of extra forces. The hopeless complexity, formal inelegance, and arbitrary nature of the result meant it was quickly abandoned. (Similar things happened in special relativity, but in reverse chronological order.) General relativity theory is widely acclaimed as being one of the most aesthetically compelling theories ever invented, and this certainly had much to do with its rapid acceptance in physics, despite the almost total lack of experimental evidence for it until quite recently. Note that quantum mechanics does *not* have this formal elegance – but it works! Physicists are constantly looking for new formulations of existing theory – this sometimes opens the way to new theories.

34 This subject is dealt with more fully in the context of languages (p. 281). The reader may wonder what happens if we attempt, using a series of mappings, to map back onto the original system. The results are then fascinating and very profound; such mappings led Gödel to his monumental proofs on the limitations inherent in all formal systems of more than very elementary complexity (K. Gödel (1931) 'Über

unentschiedbake Sätze der Principia Mathematics, und verwandter Systeme', *Montasch. f. Math. u. Phys.* 38: 173. A good introductory book on this work is Nagel and Newman, *Gödel's Proof*, (Routledge & Kegan Paul, 1959). Ironically, Gödel's work on the foundations of mathematics drove him to a Platonic view of mathematical objects, in which they have as much claim to reality as any physical 'element of reality'. This view has had much influence on twentieth century American philosophy, particularly via W.V. Quine. According to it, it simply remains for us to 'discover' mathematical objects or theorems, in the same way as we discover physical objects or laws. Gödel's ideas are discussed later in this chapter.

35 Another important difference between the worlds of physics and business is simply that they involve the worship of different gods (Mammon, as opposed to a god of knowledge!).

36 Thus logical positivism, in either its hard or soft forms, is utterly incapable of even formulating many of the substantial questions arising in physics, treating them instead as 'meaningless'. Remarkably, its influence appears to hang on in several quarters (such as behavioural psychology, despite the apparently obvious flaws which have been repeatedly underlined in the literature – see, for example, N. Chomsky, Note 50). One can also see its unfortunate influence on the accounting literature.

37 Other examples of words susceptible to this tendency are, for example, 'law', 'calculate', 'predict', etc.

38 One might object that many measurements contain significant errors, which can often be roughly quantified, and which arise from imperfectly understood processes or external factors entering into the chains of reasoning involved in indirect measurements. In this case, where is the dividing line between measurements and estimates? But in fact there is no ambiguity, since once we start *estimating* errors, our final result then also becomes an estimate. Thus in geology, one really measures the fraction of Carbon-14 nuclei in rock samples of recent origin, and if there are large uncontrollable errors involved, one then *estimates* the corresponding age of the rock.

Note, incidentally, that the mere fact that scientists occasionally misuse the term 'measure' does not mean it lacks a specific and unambiguous meaning in science.

39 Interestingly, the concept of 'the self' is not so evident in many other languages (and of course any serious philosophical theory must show that its detailed arguments or assumptions do not depend on some arbitrary feature of a particular language. Rather ironically, this is not always true of the twentieth-century linguistic philosophers or philosophers of language – I return to this in the section 'Reality in language' p. 278). Thus in French, one can say 'l'être', but this is easily confused with its more general and correct usage as 'being' (as in 'the essence of being'). In Spanish, similar problems arise with 'el ser'. However I am told that in Sanskrit, roughly the same distinction is made between Ātman (self) and Sat (being) as in English; but here the distinction is supposed to be illusory.

40 It is perhaps a good idea here to see just what Descartes said. In Cartesian doubt, one must 'reject as though absolutely false everything which one could believe was quite indubitable'. Descartes then continues:

> Thus, since our senses sometimes deceive us, I wished to suppose there was nothing corresponding to that which they make us imagine. And because some men make errors in reasoning – even regarding the simplest matters of geometry – I adjudged myself as subject to error as others, and rejected all reasonings I had previously assumed demonstrated. Finally, accounting for the fact that all the experiences we have when awake may come to us when asleep, without any one being true, I resolved to pretend that all which had ever entered my mind was no more true than the illusions of my dreams.

But then Descartes goes on (these passages are from *Discours sur le méthode*, section IV, and translated by this author; E. Gilson (ed.), Paris, Urin, 1947) that 'this truth, *I think, therefore I am* was so solid and certain that all the most extravagant suppositions of the sceptics were incapable of upsetting it'.

Thus already we see a curious ambivalence about the sureness of *thoughts*. And Descartes very quickly decides that these are more sure than knowledge of, say, the body; his conclusion is:

> From this I knew that I was a substance, whose whole essence or nature is to think, and which to exist, needs no place and no dependence on any material thing. Thus *I*, that is to say my mind – that which makes me what I am – is entirely distinct from body; and moreover, the former is more easily known than the latter, whilst if the latter did not exist the former could be everything that exists.

Further on, in section V, Descartes makes it quite clear that this implies a fundamental distinction between animals and men, the latter being possessed of rational minds:

> It is practically impossible for there to be sufficient variety in a machine to make it act on all of the occasions of life in the same way that our reason makes us act.
>
> And by the same tests we can recognize the difference obtaining between men and animals.

Now we see how much of 'common sense' has been here articulated by Descartes. It is this author's experience, for example, that the majority of scientists and the overwhelming majority of non-scientists would agree with the last passage quoted. But this opinion nevertheless runs counter to the spirit of modern biology (and to me, quite frankly, seems to be nonsense – nothing from my knowledge and observation of animals, which to me clearly have thoughts and feelings, encourages me to believe that there is anything fundamentally different about their mental processes from those of humans). It seems that the true impact of evolution theory has yet to catch up with humanity (or vice versa)! See also Note 43 below.

41 Nevertheless if one adopts the 'Platonistic' viewpoint of Gödel, in which mental objects like sets have the same status as physical objects, there seems no way to justify this assertion.

42 A.J. Ayer, *Language, Truth, and Logic* (Penguin, first published 1936).

43 For some introductions to this, see, for example, D.W. Tank and J.J. Hopfield, *Scientific American* 257, No. 6 (Dec. 1987), p. 62; a more

technical book by several of the masters in this field is '*Spin Glass Theory and Beyond* by M. Mezard, G. Parisi, and M. Virasoro (World Scientific, 1987, with a reprint collection).

44 As a side note, it has always seemed to me that adopting this point of view entirely resolves any free will vs. determinism problems, since nobody can possibly be cognizant of, or have complete knowledge of, their own or anybody else's mental state or activity. This is quite aside from any Gödel-like objections that one might make to ideas about complete knowledge.

45 Emphasis on the gene as the fundamental structural unit of biology, capable of explaining all aspects of evolutionary biology, is particularly clearly articulated by Richard Dawkins in *The Selfish Gene* (Oxford University Press 1976), and *The Blind Watchmaker* (Penguin 1988).

46 See the books by Maynard-Smith and Ridley in Note 2, as well as Note 45. Note that the rise of evolutionary biology was quite independent of genetic theory – the early work of Mendel was unknown until decades after his death.

47 The reader is warned here that my main purpose in writing this section is to illustrate how it is conceivable that an essentially human activity be amenable to scientific inquiry, and so I make not even the slightest attempt to give a proper discussion of Chomskyian linguistics, or its place within linguistic theory or philosophy of language. Those who are curious and wish to find out more are referred to, for example, J. Lyons, *Chomsky* (Fontana 1970); J. Lyons (ed.), *New Horizons in Linguistics* (Penguin 1970); R.H. Robins, *A Short History of Linguistics* (Longman 1967); E. Sapir, *Language* (Harcourt, Brace and World, 1921); M. Piatelli-Palmarini, *Language and Learning* (Harvard 1980), and references therein. Finally, for an overall picture of English, try the very readable *The Story of English*, by R. McCrum, W. Cran and R. MacNeil (Viking/Penguin 1986).

Books about the history of various languages are also worth looking at; for example R. Burchfield, *The English Language* (Oxford University Press 1986), or P. Rickard, *A History of the French Language* (Hutchinson 1974).

More technically complete introductions are, for example, J. Lyons, *Language and Linguistics* (Cambridge University Press 1981); or the works of Chomsky himself.

48 L. Bloomfield *Language* (Holt, Rinehart & Winston 1933).

49 I use the verb 'to scientize' rather deliberately here – it is an ugly word, which describes an ugly idea.

50 N. Chomsky, *Language* 35, 26 (1959); reprinted in J.A. Fodor and J.J. Katz, *The Structure of Language: Readings in the Philosophy of Language* (Prentice Hall 1964). This article had considerable influence in 'calling the bluff' of behaviourism in linguistics and elsewhere – and behaviourism is now hardly taken seriously anywhere, even in the USA (for an exception to this rule, see for example, R. Epstein, R.P. Lanza and B.F. Skinner, *Science* 207, 543 (1980)).

51 N. Chomsky, *Syntactic Structures* (Mouton 1957).

52 N. Chomsky, 'The logical structure of linguistic theory' (unpublished 1955). This was later published by Plenum Press (1975), under the same title.

53 See, for example, J.J. Katz, *Philosophy of Language* (Harper & Row 1965) or J.J. Katz and P.M. Postal, *An Integrated Theory of Linguistic Description* (MIT Press 1964); J.J. Katz, *Semantic Theory* (Harper & Row 1972); N. Chomsky, *Language and Mind* (Harcourt, Brace & Jovanovich 1972).
54 See Note 34.
55 See Note 40.
56 See, for example, N. Chomsky, *Language and Mind* (Harcourt, Brace & Jovanovich 1972), chapters 1 and 3 or N. Chomsky, *Cartesian Linguistics* (Harper & Row 1966).
57 I find it hard to see why Chomsky has not realized this! Descartes at least had the excuse of being hamstrung by religious belief, but Chomsky is apparently in broad agreement with the idea that universal (human) grammar must find its explanation in biologically limited physical structures in the brain (the hypothesis behind, for example, neural network theory). Yet his discussions are totally unconvincing – most work he refers to concerns attempts to teach animals to use *human* language systems, or to analyse animal communication in ways rather specific to human language. This of course merely begs the question. He essentially dismisses the biological evidence and consensus that animal communication must, in some species, be very complex, and that it is not understood in any detail except very indirectly. In doing so he also dismisses without discussion the obvious explanation for the failure of the experiments to teach animals human language, and for us to decipher whale communication – that they can't understand us, nor we them, because we are biologically predisposed to communicate using different 'grammars'. I say 'the obvious explanation' because it is so obvious within the very theory of 'universal human grammar' that Chomsky is asking us to believe in!
58 Thus, although it is clear that the theory of 'fluxions' anticipated to some extent the idea of 'lines of force' (Faraday) or 'fields' (Maxwell), this is nothing to get excited about – the ideas were already 'in the air' (indeed, the magnetic lines of force were understood intuitively by ancient mariners). And Descartes vastly overreached himself trying to 'unify' all the 'fields' into a fluxion theory – he missed completely the differences between electromagnetic and gravitational fields (the former being unknown at the time), and ignored too much of the contemporary empirical evidence, and the deductions that should be made from it.

Unfortunately this approach had enormous influence on the continent in the eighteenth century, and seriously retarded the development of French and German science. One of the best-known scourges of Cartesian (and Leibnizian) thinking was Voltaire, whose writings on French philosophy (and the French in general) are an endless source of pleasure to the curmudgeon. Thus, on the subject of 'black-box' philosophies, he had the following to say:

> Les Philosophes qui font de systèmes sur la secrète construction de l'univers, sont comme nos voyageurs qui vont à Constantinople, et qui parlent du Sérail: ils n'en ont vu que les dehors, et ils prétendent savour ce que fait le Sultan avec ses favourites.

59 W.V. Quine gives a rather good description of what this kind of theory does in discussing 'mentalism', which, he says:

> Engenders an illusion of having explained something. And the illusion is increased by the fact that things wind up in a vague enough state to insure a certain stability, or freedom from further progress.

This is taken from his well-known book, *From a Logical Point of View* (Harvard University Press 1953).

60 It is useful, to bring home this point, to make some analogies with other complex systems. For instance, in neural network theory, the non-linear nature of circuits enables the creation of 'logical structures' (current patterns), under the influence of external stimuli, which can be said to have been 'latent' in the structure of the network (albeit in a *very* indirect way). But the situation is like that in meteorology where the climatic behaviour is 'encoded' in the few physical laws which describe the behaviour of various gases, liquids, and solids under the action of gravitational fields of the earth, sun, and moon (to a first approximation) and the radiation field of the sun. All of this is reducible to the two equations describing quantum electrodynamics and the gravitational field.

But picking out 'linguistic structures' is like picking out, say vortex motions in the atmosphere (tornadoes, thunderstorms, etc.). Trying then to extrapolate to a 'universal grammar', and then further to associate mental and biological structures, would be like trying to find some underlying fundamental structure in the physical laws which led uniquely to a description of the entire climatic system in terms of these – some kind of 'mirror' or corresponding 'vortex structure' in the laws. This is of course ridiculous.

Thus there is no a priori reason whatsoever to believe in mental or biological structures corresponding to syntactical ones.

61 See, for example, the collection of articles in *Computational Linguistics*, 11 (1): pp. 1–36, and 2–3: 91–183; and references therein.

62 An introduction to these ideas is given in the book by G. Leech, *Semantics* (Pelican 1981), although he goes a lot farther in introducing semantics than I am.

Rather amazingly, a considerable number of linguists try to invent reasons for *not* studying other languages, or for ignoring the problems that arise when one tries to translate between them. This further restriction of the domain of linguistic study seems to me to have no justification – not only does it single out one language at the expense of others, but it ignores the extensive relations between them, as well as the difficulty of properly defining a language in the presence of dialect, slang, etc.

63 P.A. Samuelson, Nobel Prize Lecture (reprinted in *The Collected Scientific Papers of P.A. Samuelson*, vol. 3, 1972; MIT Press).

64 J.A. Schumpeter (1933) *Econometrica*, 1: 5.

65 See in particular P.A. Samuelson, *Economics* (11th edition, McGraw-Hill, 1980), appendix to chapter 6. This appendix on the elements of accounting is actually a very nice short introduction, for the reader totally ignorant of accounting, of its basic ideas and a few of its problems. The book itself is of course very well known.

66 This point has of course been made many times in the accounting literature. One of the most influential works in recent years in accounting

theory was A.L. Thomas *The Allocation Problem in Financial Accounting Theory*, Part I (1969) and Part II (1974) (published by the American Accounting Association). These books give a powerful demonstration that many of the figures in a financial report, particularly allocations, deferrals and accruals, but also inventory and depreciation figures, are arbitrary to some degree, often a very large one.

On the sheer number of different ways of assigning figures, see E. Stamp, *The Future of Accounting and Auditing Standards* (ICRA Occasional Paper No. 18, University of Lancaster, 1979).

67 A number of well-known attempts are, for example, *The Corporate Report* (Accounting Standards Committee, London 1975); or *Corporate Reporting: Its Future Evolution* (Canadian Institute of Chartered Accountants, Toronto 1980). An account of how the second of these came to be written is in E. Stamp (1985) 'The politics of professional accounting research: some personal reflections', *Accounting, Organ & Society*, 10: 111.

68 For some interesting views on the progress made, see 'Accounting regulation in the US: the growing debate' (Keynote interviews by E. Stamp); published in the *International Accounting Bulletin* (London, January, 1984), and reprinted in *Edward Stamp Later Papers*' (M.J. Mumford ed., Garland 1988). Particularly critical is interview No. 3 with Lee Seidler.

69 See, for example, Notes 72 to 75 and 78 and 79.

70 See Note 63.

71 Indeed Samuelson is a rather good representative of the more optimistic kind of economist when it comes to its amenability to scientific inquiry. Some good examples of his views are 'Economic forecasting and science' (*Michigan Quarterly Review*, October, 1965), and 'Some notions on causality and teleology in economics' (D. Lerner ed. in *Cause and Effect*, New York Free Press 1965).

72 R. Sterling, *Towards a Science of Accounting* (Houston, Scholars Book Co. 1979).

73 R. Sterling 'Accounting at the crossroads', *J. of Accountancy*, August 1976 (and also in *World*, Spring 1976); R. Sterling 'Towards a science of accounting', *Fin. Analysts Journal* September/October 1975 (also in the *Arthur Andersen Chronicle* 36: 42, 1976).

74 R. Sterling 'Confessions of a failed empiricist'. (unpublished manuscript).

75 Chapter 6, this volume.

76 A personal anecdote – this recalls for me my days in the Finance Department of Crown Zellerbach Canada, where I tried to devise some more realistic method of depreciating their assets than the straight-line method which they used. After coming up with a dreadful formula which was an integro-differential equation involving several different variables, the office manager discovered my work (which I was doing on my lunch hour, outside company time!). Even when I approximated it by a series of exponentials with different decay times, he rejected it as quite silly, because (a) no accountant could use it, and (b) he had no reason to believe it more realistic than the straight-line method.

He was, of course, quite right (although I was too young and green to see this at the time!).

77 See Notes 72 and 75.
78 C. Lyas (1984) 'Philosophers and accountants', *Philosophy*, 59: 99; M. Power (1986) 'Taking stock: philosophy and accounting', *Philosophy*, 61: 387; and see also both authors in this volume.
79 E. Stamp (1981) 'Why can accounting not become a science like physics?' *Abacus*, 17: 13.
80 Problems about action at a distance first became notorious during the Newton/Leibniz conflict, and prevented French scientists from accepting Newtonian ideas until Laplace (French attitudes were ridiculed by Voltaire at this time). Nevertheless the problem continues today in a more subtle form (in the problems of local quantum field theory, the existence of a universal frame of reference in cosmology and the applicability of Mach's Principle). Moreover it really began with Parmenides' rejection of empty space. Parmenides here was also reacting against the atomism of Democritus. The modern form of this debate is whether nature is simply 'wheels within wheels' in an endless elaboration of quantum field theory, or whether there are fundamental 'building blocks', like the quarks. In this form, these questions will always remain open.
81 See R. Sterling in Note 73 ('Towards a science of accounting').
82 For an interesting discussion of this by a physicist, see R. Savit, *J. Futures Markets*, 8: 271 (1988). For more general ideas about the application of physics ideas to economics (and vice versa), see *The Economy as an Evolving Complex System* (D. Pines (ed.), New York, Addison-Wesley 1988).
83 See Note 79.
84 A striking example of this is the report of Nicholas F. Brady (presently US Treasury Secretary) that 'Black Monday' was accidentally set off (and later stopped) by the decisions of a few Japanese fund managers in Tokyo. This idea is confirmed by R.T. Murphy (*Harvard Business Review*, March 1989) who claims further that the collapse of Continental Bank of Illinois was caused by Japanese money managers, acting on the basis of a mistranslated press report.
85 See ref. 46.
86 But not necessarily – in the formal system of 'noughts and crosses', for example, the maximum number of strings of nine members is 362,880, even before we 'interpret' the strings as 'wins' or 'draws' which leads us to throw away most strings in which the game is completed before the ninth move.
87 A good description of what is entailed by a formal system is given in Nagel and Newman (Note 32), or in R. Hofstadter, *Gödel, Escher and Bach: The Eternal Golden Braid* (Harvest 1977).
88 See Notes 51 and 52.
89 N. Chomsky, *Aspects of the Theory of Syntax* (MIT Press 1965).
90 For those unfamiliar with some of the terms of linguistics, it should be noted that they have slightly different meanings from those employed in normal parlance. In particular, 'semantics' refers to the study of meaning in language (of words, etc., and the relationship to the structure of phrases); 'syntax' refers to the structure of a language *without reference to its semantic content* (insofar as this is possible); 'grammar' refers to the

entire structure of a language, including the phonetic, syntactical, and semantic structure; and 'lexicon' refers to much more than the vocabulary of language – the lexicon contains not only the definitions of words and the connections between them (the latter sometimes being called the 'field structure'), but also the phonological features relevant to the description of individual lexical items (words, syllables, suffixes and prefixes, word endings denoting, for example, verbal tense, etc.). As Chomsky has put it (*Language and Mind*, Harcourt, Brace & Jovanovich, 1972, p. 141) 'the lexicon is concerned with all properties, idiosyncratic or redundant, of individual lexical items'. Further technical terms will be explained as we go along.

91 These 'flow diagrams' representing 'interacting structures' are very common in modern linguistics. For those who are suspicious of such simple representations of something as complex as language, who dislike 'systems' vocabulary, or who (having some understanding of non-linearity in mathematics) realize how misleading such diagrams can be, rest assured – we shall not be lulled into acquiescence by the theory. I am merely presenting the theory in its own terms – the criticisms come later!

92 See Note 90.

93 The 'tree' can be regarded as a pictorial 'interpretation' of the deep structure, which is otherwise representable as, for example, a string of brackets with symbols in between.

94 N. Chomsky, *Syntactic Structures* (Mouton 1957).

95 See Note 94, and also Notes 52 and 89 and N. Chomsky, *Rules and Representations* (Columbia University Press 1980).

96 See, for example, N. Chomsky, *Cartesian Linguistics* (Harper & Row 1966); the reader is cautioned that the version of history offered by Chomsky in this book has been strongly contested by historical linguists. See also Chomsky's *Language and Mind* (Harcourt, Brace & Jovanovich, 1972).

97 This point figures very large in twentieth-century analytic philosophy, but it is already evident in much of, for example, Socratic philosophy. It is preoccupation with issues like these, on the part of philosophers, that often seems to antagonize physicists. The writings of some linguists on the problem of logical vs. surface structure are discussed by Chomsky in *Cartesian Linguistics* (Harper & Row, 1966) (see, for example, pp. 42–77).

98 Many writers *have* however assumed the identity of deep structure and logical structure. Such an opinion would be strongly rejected by analytic philosophy – thus, for example, B. Russell often waged war on the subject/predicate relationship (inherent in the deep structure of most languages), considering it to have been the cause of more bad philosophy than anything else! Compare, for example, B. Russell, 'On denoting' (*Mind*, 14: 479 (1905)), or any of dozens of his books (for example, *An Inquiry into Meaning and Truth*, (Oxford University Press 1944)).

Index